Turning Mirrors
into
Windows

Angel and Big Joe
Photograph courtesy of Learning Corporation of America

Turning Mirrors into Windows

Teaching the Best Short Films

Marion Bue

1984
Libraries Unlimited, Inc.
Littleton, Colorado

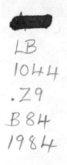

LIBRARIES UNLIMITED, INC.
P.O. Box 263
Littleton, Colorado 80160-0263

Library of Congress Cataloging in Publication Data

Bue, Marion, 1926-
    Turning mirrors into windows.

    Filmography: p. 227
    Includes index.
    1. Moving-pictures--Catalogs. 2. Moving-pictures in
education. 3. Moving-pictures--Reviews. I. Title.
LB1044.Z9B84 1984   011'.37   84-7182
ISBN 0-87287-397-8

Most people are mirrors, merely reflecting the mood and emotions of the times; few are windows bringing light to bear on the dark corners, where troubles fester; and the whole purpose of education is to turn mirrors into windows.

—Sydney J. Harris
Pieces of Silver

Table of Contents

5   ANNOTATED FILMOGRAPHY (cont'd)

Foreword

On the day that I decided to quit teaching, I was convinced not to quit by a woman I call a miracle worker. Her name is Marion Bue, and I am delighted to be writing the foreword to her book. If the truth be known, I requested the privilege and am honored that she granted it to me. The reasons are many. Aside from saving my teaching career, Ms. Bue introduced me to the world of film and to the joys of teaching through media. Nowhere in my professional training was I introduced to a more successful teaching tool. In one evening, she planted seeds that continue to grow.

Her idea is simple enough—good films taught by good teachers bring great results. Why is it that so few people know that? One reason is that few people have been shown the way. This manuscript fills this tremendous need. You will be introduced to the best films available to you and to the best methods to teach them, presented by the best teacher I have ever had.

Welcome to the magical thoughts of Marion Bue. May they make your life in education as rewarding as they have made mine.

—John Matoian
Director of Development
Scholastic Productions
New York, New York

Preface

The function of the language arts program of the secondary school is to develop and refine the skills of reading, writing, listening, and speaking. The school itself, however, has much larger tasks: to transmit the cultural heritage, to help students live in a world whose only constant is change, and to develop concerned citizens who will make informed and compassionate decisions.

Time is growing short. McLuhan's vision of the global village is here. The actions of one country affect everyone. Nuclear annihilation and terrorism threaten, human rights are nonexistent in many countries, millions of people are unemployed and homeless, while others die of starvation and unclean water. National economies falter, crime escalates, thousands drop out with drugs and alcohol, yet in the United States only 53.9 percent of the eligible voters voted in the last national election.

The problems are staggering, but they are not insoluble. There is an urgent need for understanding, for information, for skills in interpersonal and international relationships, and for the will to *act*. It is to teachers who care about these needs, as well as about literacy, that I direct this book because film can be their most important ally.

For many secondary students, high school is terminal. It is the last chance for education to challenge young minds. Film, the most powerful medium in the world, is awesome in its ability to change thinking and behavior. It has no peer in its power to impart concepts, ideas, and information quickly, interestingly, and, if it is well crafted, indelibly. The problem for the educator is: Of the thousands of films available, how can I find the ones that meet the needs of my class as I perceive them? How can I be sure that the information is accurate, that it is the best film available on the subject, and most of all, that it will help my students survive in the twenty-first century?

This book is organized to make that task as easy as possible. The first two chapters contain essential background information on the use of film in the classroom. Chapter 3, Using Specific Films, contains synopses of a number of films with suggestions for activities before and after viewing. The films were chosen because they most easily illustrate the variety of academic approaches and teaching techniques available to teachers who use film. This section also contains related materials in literature, poetry, and film. Reviews of more films appear in the next chapter, Film Reviews. The activities suggested in

Using Specific Films are easily adaptable to these films. In many cases, the suggested related materials are also appropriate. Since space does not permit indepth treatment of all the fine films available, an annotated filmography is also included. In some cases these films have a more limited use because of their content or their academic level.

Pertinent purchasing or rental information is given for all films: the film's running time; *c* or *b & w* for color or black and white; the sales price, followed immediately by the rental price; the distributor; and the film's production date. Some films, especially feature-length ones, are not available for purchase and can only be leased or rented. In a very few cases, purchase prices are only available upon application to the distributor. Although price information is as accurate as possible, film prices do fluctuate, depending upon the number of films purchased, film company promotions, and other variables.

Several appendixes follow the text. Appendix A provides descriptions of selected film producers and distributors. Appendix B lists additional film distributors and Appendix C gives addresses of the film rental departments of colleges and universities. Many companies offer fine services to teachers; information, announcements of recent acquisitions, study suggestions, and, in some cases, teaching demonstrations. Teachers should not hesitate to write or phone them for catalogues and other information.

I hope that this book will encourage teachers to find and use the best films for their classes. Only by directing the power of the school system toward developing a literate and just society can we ensure that everyone will ultimately have an equal opportunity for life, liberty, and the pursuit of happiness.

Acknowledgments

Synopses and critiques of the following have been excerpted from reviews written by the author for *Media & Methods* magazine.

An Acquired Taste
All Summer in a Day
Americas in Transition
Board and Care
Brooklyn Bridge
Can't It Be Anyone Else?
The Case of the Legless Veteran
Chillysmith Farm
Close Harmony
Coming of Age
The Cop and the Anthem
Crac
Crossbar
The Day after Trinity
David: A Portrait of a Retarded Youth
Directors at Work: The Director and
    the Image
The Electric Grandmother
Equality
Family of Strangers
Football in America
Forever Young
From Mao to Mozart: Isaac Stern in
    China
Front Line
Harlan County, U.S.A.
A Helping Hand
If You Love This Planet
In Our Water
Itzhak Perlman: In My Case Music
Josie
Last Stronghold of the Eagles

Let There Be Light
The Life and Times of Rosie the Riveter
Little Miseries
Marathon Woman: Miki Gorman
A Matter of Time
Myself, Yourself
No Maps on My Taps
No Place to Hide
Pardon Me for Living
Paul Robeson: Tribute to an Artist
Possum Living
Psychling
Public Enemy Number One
Quilts in Women's Lives
Remember Me
Rendezvous
Schoolboy Father
The Sky Is Gray
Soldier Girls
The Sorrows of Gin
Split Cherry Tree
Stages: Houseman Directs *Lear*
Stepping Out: The DeBolts Grow Up
The Sun Dagger
Survival Run
Travelling Hopefully
Vietnam Requiem
The Voyage of Odysseus
The Way of the Willow
The Weavers
The Willmar Eight
The Workplace Hustle

1 THE NEW FILMS

Suppose that education was to learn of an entirely new resource—one with high student interest, that crossed many disciplines, that taught many things faster than traditional methods, that could inculcate generally accepted values, that increased understanding of the racial and political diversity of the world, that offered much-needed intellectual discipline, and could even be used to teach basic skills. Imagine a resource that offered challenging and informative experiences to the students even as it beguiled them. Education would rush to learn to use such a resource with maximum effectiveness.

Incredibly, it hasn't happened. Although properly chosen films, with teachers trained in their use, can do all of the above, and more, film companies today have no more share of the educational dollar than they had twenty-five years ago when their product was far less effective. Colleges and universities offer no teacher training in the use of short films, few school systems offer any in-depth help to teachers, and professional organizations such as the National Council of Teachers of English still regard film only peripherally in the curriculum. School administrators, faced with budget cuts, emasculate or eliminate the most important resource they have other than teachers and books.

Why has this marvelous teaching tool been relegated to such unimportant status that today its existence seems threatened? To teachers who have seen firsthand the films' effectiveness, it is incomprehensible. The answer must be that the educational leadership—college professors, school superintendents, supervisors, and professional organizations—does not understand the potential of what can be called the *new* films as opposed to the *educational* or *curriculum* film with which everyone over twenty-five years old was indoctrinated.

What are the new films? What distinguishes them from the traditional educational film? How can we make the educational leadership aware of how it is depriving students by not making these superb films an important component of the instructional program?

The new films are made by filmmakers of creativity and integrity using the best techniques and production facilities available. Like good writers, these filmmakers pose questions, postulate answers, or speculate on the needs, values, and concerns of society. But unlike writers, filmmakers receive little exposure. Their films are not reviewed in newspapers, popular magazines, or on television. Critiques of their work, if written at all, appear in specialized periodicals read by other filmmakers, media specialists, and film librarians. Commercial theaters seldom, if ever, show short films. The millions of viewers watching the Academy Awards each year may know that awards are given for four short films, but they are indifferent because they have no opportunity to see them.

The result of this neglect is that these filmmakers have had no forum to display their work other than public libraries or schools. Although business and cable television have recently begun to use these films, education still lags far behind. The educational leadership must understand that films reach far beyond the basic tasks of the schools. No student is excluded from film because of reading deficiencies, or a lack of verbal skills. Every student can participate in film despite low self-esteem and feelings of alienation. Before film, each student is truly equal. Through film students encounter the world as it is, a world of anxiety and violence, but also of beauty.

Through film we see individuals struggling, usually successfully, with physical and mental handicaps that would demoralize many of us. Films explore our fears about the threat of nuclear destruction and global war, about our self-concepts, and about our relationships with others. They reflect our fears of aging and of being friendless and alone.

Films recall incidents in our national history with the implication and hope that those who understand history will not be condemned to repeat it. They sharpen our awareness of threatening environmental problems, of bureaucratic indifference, and of the urgent need to concern ourselves with each other.

Films also show women as resourceful members of society — loving homemakers, capable blue-collar workers and executives, and artists of vision. Children enchant us with their beauty and innocence, musicians and dancers make us proud to be human beings, and people exhibit such incomparable grace under extraordinary pressures that the spirit is strengthened. All of the films help us to understand who we are and our possibilities for the future.

This book is a plea for education to set aside its bias toward print and to admit superb filmmakers to an equally honored status with fine writers. It is a plea for education to understand that basic skills can be taught while, at the same time, we nurture beauty, justice, compassion, and courage.

MISCONCEPTIONS ABOUT FILM

Administrators and teachers often have misconceptions about the use of film in the curriculum. Some misconceptions may have a partial basis in fact, but they are not necessarily accurate and need not exist if the school attached enough importance to film to change the conditions that give rise to them. The reasoning is circuitous. The misconceptions are used to justify the failure to give film its proper place in the curriculum; the failure makes the misconceptions appear to be true, which means that ... and so it goes, with students and teachers the real losers. Fortunately there are districts that have enlightened teachers and audiovisual directors to prove the misconceptions wrong, but without administrative support, their work is difficult and time-consuming. Such forward-looking districts are rare because the misconceptions are unquestioned and considered immutable.

The most difficult one to refute is probably: *only lazy teachers use film.* Regardless of the energy and skill of the individual teacher, the old round lesson plan philosophy dies hard. It is probably true there are teachers who use film in a lazy way. They may even reinforce the round lesson plan thinking by saying, "I have an easy day today. I have a film." Or they may borrow films from other disciplines, or use films for which neither they nor their classes are prepared. They may turn on the film and then correct papers, not realizing how clearly they signal to the class the film's unimportance. A group of teachers showing a film may arrange long coffee breaks, do personal errands, or even leave school, something they would never do if the class work was more traditional. Of course they may truly be indolent, but they may also have never experienced the effectiveness of a properly chosen and supervised film presentation.

It has been my experience that most teachers are very interested in classroom materials that offer more effective instruction. Further, in nine years of teaching two classes a week for teachers in the use of short films, I learned that it was invariably the best teachers who were the first to see the potential of the new films in the classroom.

These secondary teachers developed imaginative lesson plans that students completed with enthusiasm and skill because the assignments were intrinsically interesting. These same teachers shared with their colleagues masterful student essays, short stories, poetry, film scripts, personal writing, and letters. Some reported that students were interested in reading about particular films.

Elementary teachers brought in stories, poems, and descriptive paragraphs, but they also brought songs, art work, and even fingerpainting. These were by no means lazy teachers. They were hardworking and creative people – quick to realize the potential of a film and willing to invest the time necessary for an effective presentation and follow-up.

Perhaps lazy teachers use film, but it is far more likely that these teachers do not understand the power of film because they have never been exposed to it, as a student or as a teacher. The problem is one of leadership. Because administrators have never seen the new films and do not understand their uses, they call such teachers lazy. This misconception can be used to cut or eliminate film budgets and to deny support personnel and in-service training to teachers. University teacher-training departments, themselves ignorant about short films, strengthen this misconception by failing to educate teachers about them.

The same lack of understanding of the instructional potential of film underlies another misconception: *film is a rainy day activity.* This is sometimes perpetuated by media specialists who know nothing of the new films. Some years ago I heard a media specialist who, after explaining the services of the media center to the faculty, said, "Oh, and by the way, if it's raining and you need something to do at the last minute, come down to the center. We have some good films that the local utilities company gave us."

The remark sounds innocuous, but it illustrates the dichotomy between educators who consider film a vital resource and those who relegate it to an inferior status. (That the films are propaganda for nuclear power was left unsaid.) To believe that a rainy day activity should be a film of undetermined value, of no curriculum relevance, and of dubious worth as an example of quality filmmaking is to imply that film is not an integral part of education. A superb film is a wonderful rainy day experience. But it should be prepared for in advance with educationally sound materials.

Film is too easy is a misconception echoed by students as well as teachers and administrators. Most students have been watching films and television since childhood. They attend commercial theaters with audiences that are frequently disruptive. They are familiar with the rainy day philosophy at school. None of this, in their frames of reference, has interfered with their understanding of film. On one level it hasn't, but they probably understood little or nothing of the film's psychological, sociological, and personal implications. They do not know that symbolism, metaphor, foreshadowing, and other literary devices exist also in film. Even aesthetic merit frequently has to be pointed out.

Only a few interested students are aware of filmmaking techniques. Common film terms such as long shot, rack focus, and superimposition are unknown. Even the few familiar with them have never heard of film graphics, the symbolism of costume, or screen imagery. Although few teachers will probably want to teach filmmaking techniques, those who do will find interested, even fascinated students.

Ironically, it is the most capable students academically who understand first that appreciating film on more than a superficial level is not always easy. If our expectations for secondary students are on an elementary level, then, of course, film is too easy. But much more is expected of them in humanities, literature, and creative writing classes, for example. Film equals these subjects in importance and is equally deserving of serious study and equally rewarding when understood.

A misconception that sounds accurate when left unexamined is: *film encourages passivity*. If the film and the teacher do not demand involvement, there is no misconception: the film *does* encourage passivity. An effective teacher, however, using a stimulating film and stirring student engagement with it, knows that film does not encourage inaction. Good films demand ardent attention. Discussions may get out of hand. There are tears, anger, laughter, but the students are not passive. The problem lies with inadequately trained teachers – a university and administrative responsibility.

Educators know they are teaching a media-directed generation, but they still are strongly biased toward print as the only legitimate way to learn. They make no distinction about subject matter, the maturity of the learners, the effort expended, or the enjoyment of learning. Print is mysteriously superior. This prejudice leads to another commonly accepted misconception: *the printed word is the only way to learn*. No one questions the value of reading. But reading and film are not antithetical: they support and enhance each other. Teachers and students who are receptive to film are often equally enthusiastic about reading. Education needs a balance between them.

To be valid a film must reinforce literature, a corollary to the preceding misconception, is one that English teachers sometimes perpetuate. Films that reinforce literature enrich the language arts program immeasureably, but this misconception ignores other important aspects of the language arts program.

Many fine authors of books about writing, such as James Moffett, stress the importance of the precomposition experiences, but inexplicably they are silent about film. It is here that film has no peer. Because of its emotional content, it triggers powerful student writing seldom obtainable in any other way. It offers the class a shared experience from which no student, regardless of his or her status in the class, is excluded. Supported by a knowledgeable and effective teacher, film demands critical listening. Film strengthens verbal skills and often generates interest in reading. The use of language is an important component of teaching with film. Teachers who limit their use of film to the enrichment of literature deprive their students of exciting experiences.

That *film is too expensive*, often cited by administrators to justify decreasing or eliminating film budgets, may or may not be a misconception. If the proper research were done, film might prove to be very cost-effective. There are so many variables in assessing a film's worth. How many students will benefit from using the films compared with those who use a similarly priced set of books? How many years will each be used? Are there district objectives that may be fulfilled better and faster with film? Which medium will teach a particular concept faster and be more cost-effective in teacher time? Which medium has a more lasting result in a certain area? Which increases student interest in learning? What is the impact of one superb film compared with numerous filmstrips? Until such questions are answered, no one can verify or disprove that films are too expensive.

Some schools unquestioningly accept the misconception that *only information-giving films justify the expenditure of public funds.* These are usually the same schools that perpetuate the myth that because their students score well in a test of grammar and usage — a test of information — the school is fulfilling its function effectively. Ironically, schools adopting this philosophy waste money because information-giving films often lack creativity, taste, or technical expertise. Television has accustomed today's generation to the best in techniques.

Since a high-quality film and a mediocre one are priced competitively, school districts locked into information-giving films not only deprive students of important experiences, they also waste public funds. If the film is not a superior one, a sound filmstrip is as effective and far less expensive; a good teacher is more interesting. Of course wonderful information-giving films exist; some of them are described in this book. Finding them, however, requires diligent searching. A balance should be maintained between such films and the high-quality films that embrace many disciplines or stress values.

This misconception is closely related to the one most pervasive in education: *any film is better than none at all.* Teachers cling to this belief for understandable reasons. Since few school districts train teachers in film, they have no way to know that better films exist. Since teachers are not exposed to the best films, they cannot evaluate one film against another. Teachers who do get a chance to compare films, quickly discard this misconception. Since they do not have the time to search for excellent films, someone else must look for them, then give teachers the opportunity to choose from among high-quality films. This point is crucial in upgrading film education.

Teachers eager to bring variety to their work sometimes consider a mediocre film better than none at all. Home economics teachers use films that show out-dated refrigerators. Social studies teachers show supposedly current films, but the cars are 1973 models. Dating films made in 1970 are viewed with contempt or amusement by students. One might think these extreme examples, but they are commonplace in many districts. Even worse is the new, but unimaginative, film in which the narrator replaces the classroom teacher as lecturer. Such films are boring and wasteful since a sound filmstrip is as useful.

Unfortunately, audiovisual directors and purchasing agents help to perpetuate the mediocre film library by buying films by the pound from inferior companies because they offer free duplication or television rights. The film companies with exemplary products have invested too much in production, promotion, and distribution to be able to give their films away.

Acquiring the best films from every company should be the goal of every audiovisual director. But again, it takes time to locate and bring such films to the attention of teachers. In some districts free promotional films are listed in the audiovisual catalogue without regard for quality or possible propagandizing to add depth to the collection. Old films with torn sprocket holes and missing frames, which should be withdrawn, remain in circulation. Teachers are frustrated by such practices, but without administrative action it is impossible to eliminate them. As school funding becomes more precarious, there is more need for excellent materials. In film, the choice should always be for excellence in quality, use, and maintenance, at the expense of quantity.

Film has no relationship to reading is probably the most widely used misconception to justify not using film, and the one with the most profound implications for education. Reading a book and reading a film require many of the same skills: organizing, interpreting, evaluating, and *comprehending*. Both media are involved with listening, speaking, and writing. Both stress attention to details for understanding. Film and reading share many common literary terms: symbolism, metaphor, style, theme, form, foreshadowing, plot, and characterization. Film uses both the story-telling devices of fiction and the organizational patterns of nonfiction. Most important of all, it shares the humanistic concerns of all great literature. Many short films explore the same themes that have always concerned our greatest writers. Film cannot help the student to decode the printed symbol, but it can strengthen all of the other skills involved in reading. This misconception has no basis in fact. A lack of understanding alone can account for it.

Film is a demanding taskmaster. Keeping up with the proliferation of high-quality films and acquiring an in-depth knowledge of existing ones is arduous. One must respect film to learn to use it effectively, but there are teachers who possess the necessary enthusiasm and interest and who love to share their knowledge with others.

If universities and colleges instituted teacher-training classes in the use of short films, taught by such people, and if school superintendents appointed them as media specialists, these misconceptions would largely, if not entirely, disappear.

FILM, AFFECTIVE EDUCATION, AND TEACHING VALUES

The new films are effective in education principally because they are inseparable from affective education and the inculcating of humanistic values. For some educators, however, affective education connotes an either-or situation, in which advocates supposedly teach "life-adjustment" courses and opponents "educate." Educators, as well as the public, tend to confuse education with permissiveness—a lack of discipline and of a dress code or a surfeit of student control of his or her education through an elective program. Perhaps there are a few advocates who in their zeal to promote affective education, neglected some of the important more traditional aspects.

None of this has anything to do with affective education, which has never been tried in an organized, large-scale way, although it is founded on sound psychological principles. Education is still obsessed with information-giving, standardized tests, basic skills, conformity, and order. The daily schedule of a 1983 tenth-grader differs very little from his 1933 counterpart: five or six periods of fifty minutes each, devoted to English II, biology, geometry, foreign language, physical education, and, with luck, an elective. Even when suggestions for improvement are made, the solution is always for more of the same: more reading labs, more math and science, a stricter dress code, more suspensions, more basic skills. No one addresses the problem of giving education meaning, except in vocational classes. The lack of meaning explains much of education's ineffectiveness.

The schools stress objectivity, although psychology demonstrates the importance of subjectivity to any learner. Recently on television a United States senator was asked about his strenuous efforts on behalf of a bill to aid parents seeking organ transplants for their seriously ill children. The senator's explanation? Since he had faced the same situation in his own family, the legislation was meaningful to him. People internalize whatever possesses the deepest meaning for them. And with internalization comes attitudinal or behavioral change.

The human brain constantly seeks to synthesize meaning from all it observes. The meaning created from this effort determines behavior. Students confronted with meaningless activities several hours a day react by dropping out, tuning out, or becoming a behavior problem. If the meaningless days become years, is it surprising that many students do not graduate? The new films help such students immediately because the gestalt of meaning does not depend upon the reading or verbal skills they have never acquired.

Emotion is involved in all learning, and the degree to which the emotions are involved determines the personal relevance and thus the retention of the learning for each student. Tears indicate that communication is taking place between the filmmaker and the viewer. Films such as *Peege* and *Night and Fog* are frequently met with stunned silence. The observant teacher knows that the learning is indelible.

The importance of self-concept in learning has been repeatedly demonstrated. The Pygmalion syndrome is at work in every classroom. If students feel they can meet a challenge successfully because the teacher expects them to, classroom performance is improved. Film can aid a sensitive teacher immeasureably in establishing such a classroom environment because participation in film is not dependent upon factors over which the teacher has little or no control. Every student can feel good about his or her performance and relationship with the class and the teacher.

Teaching values is in somewhat the same either-or position as affective education. Critics see it as interfering with the responsibilities of the home. Others confuse teaching values with the presentation of controversial issues. Surely there are values all can agree are desirable: integrity, justice, kindness, reliability, friendliness, cooperation, courage, helpfulness, perseverance, faith, humor, open-mindedness, beauty, creativity, excellence, and the meaningfulness of life. These values are explored by most of the short films described in this book.

Teachers who believe in affective education and teaching values are not do-gooders or zealots. They are teachers who want to take advantage of what is known about establishing a favorable learning environment. For such teachers film is their most important resource.

For many years I have had a plan for teaching values that I have hoped to see implemented in all schools. All interested educators and members of the community would meet to agree upon the values to which students should be exposed, without violating individual political or religious beliefs. Such a list might include kindness, integrity, justice, compassion, generosity, and cooperation. Many delightful films are available that teach these concepts at every grade level.

After the list is agreed upon, suitable films would be purchased for each grade level K-12. In a single school or small district, the films could be deposited directly with the teacher(s) of the particular grade who would work out their own procedure for sharing.

In larger schools films could be packaged in containers and rotated from school to school for a specified period where they would be available to any interested teacher. Handbooks containing study suggestions for the films for each grade level would be given to each teacher.

An effective implementation of this program for teaching values would have benefits ranging from the intangible to the openly spectacular. Teachers would have fresh film experiences for their students each year. Teachers would be working toward an agreed-upon goal using such fascinating materials that success is almost guaranteed. Schools using such a program for a period of time would see positive changes in behavior in both staff and students.

If such a plan could be effectively implemented in all the classrooms of America, many problems which now seem almost insoluble would be lessened. Kindness, justice, and cooperation would characterize our country. Such is the power of film and education.

2 TEACHING WITH FILM

I have found several ideas and techniques, developed through trial-and-error, rewarding in teaching film. Results are often immediate, teaching is more enjoyable, and instruction is more effective. These ideas include the following:

TEACHING TIPS

Use only those films that you personally respond to. If a film doesn't challenge, intrigue, or move you, don't use it. Don't listen to experts or critics or even to those whose opinions you usually respect if they try to persuade you that you should use a film for which you feel no enthusiasm. A teacher who is genuinely excited by a film can always transfer that sense to the class. The reverse is equally true; students are quick to read indifference. Be sure that the film reaches you; it means that you and the filmmaker have communicated. When that happens, the chances are very good the filmmaker's message will reach the class.

Don't create a threatening situation. We enjoy a challenging situation *if* we believe that we can cope with it. The teacher who, after showing a film, turns off the projector and says, "Well, what does it mean?" presents the class with a threatening situation. There is a frantic search for the right answer, but there isn't one, a new experience for many students, especially the "good" ones. "What do you think?" usually elicits a similar reaction for the same reason.

A much better start is the nonthreatening request: "Tell me what you saw." Anyone can respond to it and most students will. "Tell me what you saw" should be used until all students feel comfortable and nonthreatened by responding. If the teacher wishes, this can easily develop into an oral language lesson. For example:

A Day in the Life of Bonnie Consolo is about an armless woman who uses her feet in the way most of us use our hands. The film consists of examples of Ms. Consolo's amazing dexterity with her feet. An oral language lesson might proceed in this fashion:

Teacher: "What did you see?"

Student: "I saw a woman who could really use her feet."

Teacher: "What do we call that ability to use your hands or feet, or any part of your body, quickly and skillfully?"

Student: "Dexterity."

Teacher: "Good for you. We saw a woman who shows dexterity using her feet. Do you see that most of the film was about that? (They do.) Then that is our big topic. Now I want you to give me specific examples of how Bonnie Consolo used her feet. Any example."

Students: "Wrote a check." "Drove a car." "Put on mascara." "Baked bread." "Killed a fly." "Tied her son's shoes." "Cut his hair." "Sliced tomatoes." "Watered her plants."

The teacher could easily go on to develop the concept of the paragraph with a topic sentence and supporting details, but the point is that all students have participated in a nonthreatening way. Students are also trained to watch closely. By the time all have contributed what they saw, the entire class will recall the film better than any individual would have done before the discussion. If you are having difficulty getting a discussion started following a film, try the approach of "Tell me what you saw." Results are frequently amazing.

A variation of this technique is to ask, "What did you see *first*? And then what happened? ... What did you hear as he crossed the room?" These questions require the students to remember sequentially, which they easily learn to do if the right films are used.

Pyramid Film's three-minute film *Claude* is a charmingly animated film about a small, superintelligent boy, with an egg-shaped head, who lives in an opulent house with his materialistic, cliché-ridden parents. "Claude, can't you do anything right?" nags Mother. "You'll never amount to anything," echoes Father. Claude ignores the constant nagging, having better things to do with the small black box he has invented. Finally, in desperation he takes his revenge in a sardonic, but funny surprise ending. *Claude* is a comment on the way many adults deal with a creativity they don't understand. Sequential recalling for *Claude* would be similar to this example:

1. titles ... white background

2. Claude appears with black box ... white background

3. bumps wall ... Mother and color background appear: "Claude, can't you do anything right?"

4. horn honks, Father in fancy car appears in brightly colored background: "Claude, you'll never amount to anything."

5. Claude and box (white background) going down steps. Mother nagging Claude at the dinner table. Claude spills milk. Father nags. Mother nags again.

6. Claude and box (white background) walk in front of color background while Mother sits in a swing talking on the phone: "Claude, can't you do anything?"

7. Claude and box (white background) walk in front of Father's television set: "You'll never amount to anything."

8. white background. Claude sits down. Color background. Mother and Father walk into view: "Claude, can't you do anything?" "Claude, you'll never amount to anything."

9. Claude pulls lever. Parents disappear. Claude walks off color background into white background.

Sequential recall emphasizes careful watching, listening, and observing of details; all are essential to understand film. (*Claude* also offers the teacher an opportunity to explain the terms *literal* and *figurative*.)

Stress the skills common to film viewing and reading. The connection usually suggested between films and books is that a film may encourage students to read further about a subject. While this is true, it is far from the only relationship between the two. Except for subtitled silents and foreign films, film cannot possibly help the student to decode the printed symbols of reading. But reading is a complex subject involving much more than the process of decoding; it is dependent upon reader motivation and the opportunity to organize, interpret, and evaluate – all important comprehension skills. The student who practices these skills improves his or her ability to process language.

Film usually follows the organizational patterns of fiction, essays, and expository prose. Students who learn to recognize these patterns will be better readers and writers. Distinguishing the main idea and separating it from the supporting details is an important skill in both participating in a film and in reading. Both media share many common terms: symbolism, metaphor, tone, structure, style, characterization, plot, foreshadowing, climax, denouement, etc.

Film can be used to develop concepts important in reading: identifying, defining, locating, recalling, listing, and reporting. Interpretation, the next level, involves these skills: inferring, predicting, concluding, classifying, comparing, contrasting, analyzing, and imagining.

At a higher level, these acquired skills are applied to problem-solving and criticism. The final and most important level is *internalizing*. The will to act is crucial to society. For only internalization can bring about change. For example, almost fifty years ago John Steinbeck pointed out the plight of the poor and homeless in *The Grapes of Wrath*. Yet today millions are in this situation all over the world, many of them in America. Obviously, the many admiring people who read the book and saw the film did not translate their reaction into a need for change. Thousands of the students who have read *Lord of the Flies* still elect leaders whose slogans are power threats, and, if necessary, war. *To Kill a Mockingbird* and *Raisin in the Sun* have been widely used in schools for several years, but unemployment falls most heavily on blacks, and racist groups like the Ku Klux Klan continue to grow. Such examples could be multiplied many times, but the point is obvious. If we are to solve the problems of society, knowledge must be translated into behavior change.

In any good film program, countless opportunities exist to develop these common skills. The task of the teacher is to become aware of the connections and to reinforce them at every opportunity. One of film's greatest attractions is that teachers grow in ability and understanding along with the class. Do not be afraid to try even though you feel inexperienced. With a fine film presented in a good environment, student experience is positive even if the teacher is not yet aware of everything involved in the film. With good films, teachers become effective quickly.

Stress the underlying meaning of film. If untrained, students will continue to watch film superficially. Try to get them to place film in a larger context than may be immediately apparent to them. Ask questions about the filmmaker's intent: "What do you think the filmmaker wanted us to think about when he made this film?" "What do you think the filmmaker is commenting on?" "What do you think the filmmaker's intent was in making this film?" Experiment with questions until you find the one the class best understands. If the film is allegorical, ask for an explanation of the allegory. Conceptualizing is difficult for many students because they have seldom been asked to do it, especially in a context where there is no "right" answer. Start with one of the many films where success is guaranteed. For a more detailed explanation see *Joshua in a Box*.

Help students to understand that in film there are no "right" answers, any more than in other works of art. So much of education today involves the continuous search for the right answer. It is not necessarily even the right answer as the student perceives it, but the one calculated to produce the grade the student wants. One of a film's greatest strengths is that it cannot be reduced to a right answer. There is only the thoughtful appraisal of the film by each student. The teacher's task is to help the student shape those personal perceptions into an understanding of the filmmaker's intent (the theme of the film) as the student sees it.

In helping with conceptualization, the teacher can ask the student these questions: "Was there a major conflict in the film? Between whom? Were there secondary conflicts? What was the outcome of the major conflict? Has the central character changed at the end of the film? What has she or he learned?" If these and similar questions follow the inquiry, "What did you see?," students can formulate a statement of the filmmaker's intent or theme. Remind them that, although there are no wrong answers, a reasonable statement of the intent should be based on the following considerations:

- It must account for all the details in the film.

- It must exist within the film itself; one cannot go outside the film to find the filmmaker's intent.

- It must not be contradicted by other events, incidents, or points made in the film.

Ask the students frequently to state the intent of the filmmaker in one or two sentences. Then ask various ones to read their ideas aloud. Students are usually surprised and pleased that all answers can be worded individually and still be acceptable, a new experience for many.

Encourage students not to reject a film because they do not understand or like the subject matter. As with any art form, minds must occasionally be stretched or opened by new experiences. Students who say, "I don't like folk music," may love *The Weavers* and thereafter be more open to folk music. A common student reaction to *Bonnie Consolo*, the story of an armless woman is, "She's gross." When someone points out Ms. Consolo's refusal to feel self-pity, her amazing resilience, a student's attitude toward her changes, and she receives the respect she deserves. Some teenagers don't like films about the aged, but *Peege, Close Harmony*, and *Forever Young* change their minds.

Help students to be aware that irony gives film a more complex meaning. Since irony is another difficult concept for students, it is best to start with films where success is guaranteed. Learning Corporation of America's *Ransom of Red Chief* and *The Cop and the Anthem*, both O. Henry stories, are ideal because the irony is obvious, the films are funny, and the productions are excellent. In more difficult films these questions may be helpful:

- What is the difference between appearance and reality?

- What is the difference between expectations and fulfillment?

- What is the difference between what the character thinks and the viewer knows to be true?

For other films that teach irony, consult the Index of Themes. After this concept is taught, check to see if students are understanding less-obvious ironies in other films.

CHOOSING FILMS

Basic to all film selection is the constant search for the best-made, the most effective, the most involving film. Since film is generally priced by size rather than quality, no school needs to settle for less than the best. This search for quality, however, is a time-consuming, on-going process that no one with other full-time responsibilities can assume. The selection of a film specialist is as crucial as the selection of the film itself. The specialist must have a demonstrated, creative interest in film, and the ability to share the appreciation of excellent films with other teachers. The film specialist should be given these responsibilities:

To know the quality films that are available and present them to interested teachers for evaluation. Catalogues and recent production brochures from all reputable distributors should be read and made available to teachers in a central location. The film specialist should attend at least one (preferably more) of the major film festivals each year, such as the American Film Festival held in New York City in May or June of each year. Hundreds of the best short films, which have been prescreened by knowledgeable people, are shown. Further distinctions are made at the festival by the awarding of Blue and Red Ribbons (first and second choice) in each category of film. To pay for a film specialist to attend such a festival could save a district hundreds of dollars, but more importantly, could assure a positive film experience for the students.

Other festivals offer the specialist further opportunities for acquiring background in film. Distributors gladly send films to preview that are being considered for purchases. Many of them have preview facilities in their offices and are pleased to show their products to prospective buyers.

To arrange to show preselected films to teachers for their evaluations. Too often district selection is a hit-or-miss process that leaves the majority of teachers uninvolved and the film library imbalanced among the various disciplines and grade levels. An organized procedure is necessary to ensure that all interested teachers have an opportunity to participate. An effective one is the following:

a. Through contact with distributors, attendance at festivals, and the suggestions of teachers, the film specialist locates the best films available for every discipline and level.

b. On a given date(s), all of the films for a particular discipline are shown at a central location. Any interested teacher may attend, but only the teachers of the discipline may vote on recommendations for purchase.

c. After all of the films have been shown, the teachers should recommend purchase, taking care to provide fairly for the subdivisions that occur in some subject areas such as social studies.

This evaluation procedure ensures that all interested teachers, who are presumably the ones who use the films, make the selections. It has the further advantage of familiarizing teachers with films in advance of purchase, so they can plan ahead for them. Most importantly, it gives teachers control of the materials that affect their professional lives.

To develop lesson suggestions and background information about each film that would be available to any teacher. Since the college work of teachers and administrators seldom includes any training in film other than the operation of projectors, it is not surprising that teachers are hesitant about teaching with film. When the film specialist develops materials for them, it is a very cost-effective in-service training. Those who are confident of their abilities in film would also welcome such help as a time-saver. Assistance should include suggestions about establishing good classroom environment and general principles of teaching film.

To demonstrate effective teaching with film when requested by any classroom teacher or group of teachers. Teaching by example is the most effective method of in-service training, especially in an area where teachers have had little or no college training. It would strengthen the film program through contact by the film specialist with the classroom teacher, who may be wavering in commitment to film because of a lack of confidence.

To ensure that all disciplines and levels obtain a fair share of available film funds. Few districts make provisions for an equitable distribution among disciplines and levels, probably because it is difficult to do. The most demanding representatives often receive the lion's share. In some cases, teachers have lost interest in film for various reasons relating to quality, availability, condition, or distribution. The film specialist should interview teachers to determine the status of film in each discipline and level. After needs have been assessed, the film specialist and a representative committee of teachers (including interested teachers who are not assigned to the committee) should determine a fair allocation of funds to each group.

To ensure that needed films are added to the library each year. This responsibility is somewhat similar to the preceding one except that it requires the film specialist to be familiar with the existing library. This is especially important if the district has not previously had an organized procedure for equitable distribution. For example, a district may have several excellent films on Dr. Martin Luther King, Jr. Another fine one is offered to social studies teachers for evaluation. Teachers new to film or unfamiliar with the existing library might well recommend buying it; thereby using badly needed funds for an unnecessary purchase. At the same time, the science department, which in the past has never had its fair share of films, needs one about the brain. Someone who knew the resources of the film library could help to keep the situation in balance. Since every district is different, it is impossible to be specific in this area, but a film specialist could not only keep the library in balance but also recommend district-owned films to teachers.

To ensure that all disciplines and levels have films that are restricted to their areas, as many districts now do with books. Opponents of such restrictions offer persuasive arguments against them, but every teacher has experienced turning on the projector only to have the class moan, "I've seen that film three times." Spontaneity is lost, and it is difficult to regain the interest of the class. Again, without restrictions, films are sometimes used that are beyond the maturity level of a class. Since many wonderful films exist for all disciplines and levels, the opposition to restrictions is understandable only if film funds are severely limited or not distributed equitably.

A film specialist who fulfilled all of these responsibilities would strengthen the instructional program of any school district because a knowledge of the potential of film and an ability to communicate its excitement enriches education immeasureably.

INCORPORATING FILM INTO THE CURRICULUM

Many avenues are open to a school seeking to incorporate film into its curriculum in an organized manner. To have an effective program presupposes an emphasis on excellent films, in-service training of staff, a fair distribution of available funds for film among all disciplines and levels, an evaluation policy that involves all interested teachers, and a strong administrative policy for the maintenance of film and equipment and films distribution and return. Here are some suggested ways to begin incorporating film into the curriculum.

Incorporate film into every part of the curriculum. If all other conditions are met, this one has the potential to be the most satisfactory because it involves all students. However, in some schools it is not possible due to teacher resistance or to lack of funds. A strong in-service training program could help to overcome a teacher's reluctance, which is usually based on a lack of self-confidence. If this problem can be solved and adequate funds appropriated, this incorporation is the most effective because film can be integrated with all other classroom skills: language, writing, speaking, listening, art, music, physical education, and even mathematics.

Incorporate film into a core program. This is much easier to do now than it would have been a few years ago because of the proliferation of films that involve several disciplines. Superb films exist that explore many fields at once, especially in language arts, psychology, sociology, humanities, family living, contemporary problems, and special education. The study of history and government, even science, could be combined with the study of these other fields. Many people in education are not aware that many fine films have been produced that cut across diverse disciplines.

When students work in a core program, they experience the interrelatedness of education. However, if students in the core are in other classes that use the same films, the problem becomes financial because there must be an infusion of fresh films each year to avoid duplication. An ideal solution is to use films for the core that are available only through rental or long-term leases. These cannot be purchased at any price, even by a district that had the funds. With administrative and financial support, a core program is an exciting approach.

Incorporate film as a departmental activity. In districts with limited funds, this approach works well. Departments plan a series of films involving their classes. Major drawbacks can be the lack of a large enough room, inadequate preparation of some classes, and differing teacher attitudes. Teachers must work together to select and order films, prepare lesson plans, assign responsibility for room arrangement and projection, and agree in advance on teacher and student behaviors. If teachers view this as an opportunity to drink coffee or correct papers, it cannot be successful. If the teachers work together well, accepting responsibility for supervision, the plan has several advantages: teachers strengthen one another, students have a sense of community, and the classes can see brilliant films normally unobtainable.

In an interesting experiment in group teaching, five language arts teachers combined their classes to show the feature film *Walkabout*. In a film as rich as this one, a major problem is deciding the approach: sociological, aesthetic, anthropological, technical, or literary? The teachers agreed that each would accept responsibility for one aspect of the film. After working individually with their classes, the groups met together to exchange insights. Students were amazed that one film could be so rich in implications and visual techniques. This was a marvelous example of creative film teaching.

Incorporate film as a separate study. Popular in urban areas a few years ago, film study as a separate discipline is now almost nonexistent. Reasons are the failure of universities and colleges to grant to film study full academic credit toward admission; more stringent requirements for high school graduation; inadequately trained teachers; the present recession; a persistent, inaccurate belief on the part of many parents and administrators that film, reading, and writing are unrelated; and the failure of education to acknowledge that it faces a media-directed generation.

It is interesting to note that universities such as the University of California, which will not grant admission credit for high school film study, offer advanced degrees in the subject at their institutions. For example, UCLA's film school, is one of the largest and best-known in the world. Why does this institution not consider film a worthy subject for study at the high school level?

On April 13, 1983, Dr. Leroy Hay, a high school English teacher and the Teacher of the Year for 1983, was interviewed on ABC's "Good Morning America." When asked about the teaching of reading, Dr. Hay replied, after explaining his method of teaching, "We just can't say that students shouldn't look at television. We should teach them to read what's there." He succinctly stated the need to admit visual literacy to the curriculum. Education, however, continues to cling to the belief that print is all students need to know to survive in a new century. It is as though one must either abandon print *or* accept the visual media. Fortunately, this is far from the case. For confirmation, teachers need only be aware of the 2,000,000 paperback copies of *The Thornbirds* printed after ABC telecast its 1983 mini-series. This in addition to the millions of copies sold when the book first appeared in 1980. The schools do not have the power to change public acceptance of the visual media. Training students to understand and use them would be far more productive than to endlessly deplore the quality of television and film.

THE PHYSICAL ENVIRONMENT

No filmmaker, however talented, can communicate with a viewer who is constantly distracted by noise, light, and movement. Since much of what is learned in film is intuitive and emotional, it is extremely important to provide the best physical environment within the limits of a school setting or the teacher's control. Some guidelines to enforce a receptive environment are necessary. Students who understand the reasoning behind them, usually respond favorably. Once established, the rules are easy to maintain. Suggested rules include the following:

Do not allow the students to talk to each other or back to the screen, chew gum, unwrap candy or other food, move about unnecessarily, or put their heads down on their desks. All of these behaviors are common in commercial theaters, but students must understand why they are unacceptable in school. Explain that the filmmaker is trying to communicate with them and cannot do it when such behavior occurs. Most students accept this, and some come to dislike the disorder in commercial theaters.

Allow no interruptions. In a school setting this is usually not possible, but it should be the teacher's goal. Post a sign on the door or take your phone off the hook. If other adults enter the room, whisper. Do not talk during the film, move about unnecessarily, or interrupt with messages if it can be avoided. Be interested in the film even though you may have seen it several times. There is always something new in any fine film. Leave the room with visitors if talk is unavoidable. Consistent teacher behavior disfavoring interruptions reinforces to the class the importance the teacher places on the film.

Make the room as dark as possible. If you do not have darkening curtains, tape black construction paper to the windows, if the room is used only for film. If it is a regular classroom, make blinds of heavy black cardboard or tagboard that fit tightly into the window frame and can be inserted and removed quickly. If all else fails, paint the windows with black poster paint. Do whatever is necessary to admit as little light as possible because it distracts from the impact of film.

Seat each student so that she or he views the screen from the best position possible. Those who sit too far to the side are presented with a distorted picture. Students have apparently accepted this so often that they do not recognize the distortion until they move to a more favorable location. In some classrooms not much adjustment is possible, but if the room has portable chairs, proper seating can make a great difference in student acceptance and understanding of the film.

Project the best picture possible. Get the best projector and the biggest and best screen that the equipment allows. Remember that the further back the projector, the larger the picture, but at some point the picture may lose clarity.

Show respect for film as a learning resource by refusing to play games with it. Do not run the projector backwards (a frequent student request) or repeat a particular sequence without a legitimate objective.

Check the film before the class comes into the room. Have the projector threaded and adjusted before the lesson begins. Not only does this save instructional time, but it also assures the momentum of a successful introduction. Handle the film as minimally as possible because fingerprints show through it.

Be sure to return the film to the audiovisual department or to the film company on time. If loan privileges are abused, strong administrative action is needed.

3 USING SPECIFIC FILMS

These study suggestions are included primarily for teachers who may lack experience in teaching with film. The films are not necessarily the best of those mentioned in this book, but are included in this section because they most easily illustrate the following:

1. The process of constructing suggestions to bring out important concepts in the film. (This is always with the understanding that students may offer other concepts not noted by the teacher.)

2. The wide range of subject matter and academic levels available through film, from basic skills to college level assignments.

3. To illustrate the various approaches open to teachers who use film; aesthetic, sociological, literary, historical, scientific, anthropological, psychological, or technical.

Except by coincidence, no one unfamiliar with a particular class can offer study suggestions that are completely applicable because each class and each teacher is unique. Teachers can, of course, choose from these suggestions those which are appropriate. Occasionally teachers have been successful in using the guides exactly as written, but since good instructors vary greatly in style and interests, they should choose to do this only with those films and activities with which they are comfortable.

But teachers using this section of the book should not limit themselves to these films. The suggestions are intended for adaptation to the films in the longer reviews and the annotated filmography. Teachers should study all of the films, the suggested activities, and then choose those that best meet the needs of the class and the teacher.

Best of all, the teacher should originate his or her own ideas about teaching with film.

AMERICAN PARADE:
With All Deliberate Speed
(32 min, c, $580/81, BFA Films, 1976)

THEMES

Are "separate but equal" schools equal? The courage of men who tried to upgrade schools in the South before the *Brown vs. Topeka* decision. The right of all citizens to equal educational opportunity. The psychological damage caused by segregation.

CURRICULUM AREAS

Social studies, humanities, psychology, sociology, black studies

SYNOPSIS

Before the Supreme Court decision of 1954 ordering desegregation of schools, the lives of many Americans, both black and white, were affected by the growing opposition to the separate but equal doctrine then in force in the schools. In Clarendon County, South Carolina, the Rev. J. A. DeLaine, a black minister, and a white judge, J. Waites Waring, each suffered extreme persecution. Rev. DeLaine tried to upgrade the black schools, and Judge Waring tried to uphold the law. Actor Paul Winfield movingly portrays the minister, a man of will and powerful oratorical style.

Despite threats to his family and himself and the burning of his home, Rev. DeLaine persisted. When Judge Waring supported his efforts with his legal decisions, he, too, was threatened and ostracized. Finally Thurgood Marshall, then chief counsel for the NAACP intervened. He developed a case that joined the Clarendon case with others, resulting in the 1954 decision that ordered integration "with all deliberate speed."

The film is included here because many students are unaware of the struggle that occurred from the time that slavery ended until the civil rights achievements of the 1950s and 1960s. The particular case delineated in the film is representative of many that took place. The persecution of Rev. DeLaine and Judge Waring was typical of the accepted treatment of those men and women, black and white, who "didn't know their place."

The film has a magnificent performance by Paul Winfield and a balanced point of view. The white judge and black minister are equally admirable men. It is not a film in which all the whites are bad and all the blacks are good. Often those films generate only resentment. *With All Deliberate Speed* brings understanding. It is an important piece of American history.

BEFORE VIEWING

Ask the class if they have ever wanted to, thought they should, or *did* take a stand that they knew would be unpopular with their friends, teachers, or family. What happened when they did? How did they feel? If they didn't take a stand, do they wish they had? Would they do it again? What did it cost them? Was it worth it? Tell students they are going to see a film about two men who took unpopular stands.

AFTER VIEWING

Suggestions for discussions and compositions

a. How does the film make the students feel — angry, resentful, indifferent? Are they aware that such events occurred in this country within the lifetime of many people now living?

b. Ask students to explain the separate but equal doctrine established by the Supreme Court in the *Plessy vs. Ferguson* decision of 1896. Why did courageous people like Rev. DeLaine struggle to overturn the decision?

c. What did the Supreme Court mean when it used the phrase "with all deliberate speed"? Is the phrase a contradiction in terms? Have students examine the calendar of desegregation events on page 23. Has the country proceeded with all deliberate speed? Is the impatience of many blacks justified?

d. What is integration? Is attending the same school an integration even though the groups do not interact except when necessary? What is token integration?

e. Ask students if integration has been successful in their school. What is the situation? Total integration with interacting groups? Token integration? No integration? If their school is not integrated, why isn't it? Is it due to the racial composition of the total community, geography, economics, or facism?

f. Should busing be used to achieve integration?

g. Tell students they have been informed by the school board that they are being transferred to another school to achieve racial integration in the community. How do they respond? Would their family and friends support their decision if they resisted the school board's order?

h. Have the class write a letter to the editor of their local paper stating their views on education in their community for both blacks and whites.

i. Ask students what men in recent times have paid an even heavier penalty than Rev. DeLaine and Judge Waring for trying to act on their beliefs.

Suggestions for advanced assignments

a. Have students read Rev. Martin Luther King, Jr.'s famous speech, "I Have a Dream." Ask students how close they believe the country is to achieving Rev. King's dream. They will need to research statistics on employment, salary levels, educational attainment, and health care to answer the question accurately.

Suggestions for advanced assignments (cont'd)

b.   It has been said that it is arrogant of the Anglo society to assume that black students cannot learn unless they are side-by-side with Anglo students. Ask students if it is possible to agree with this statement and still favor school integration.

c.   Ask students to respond to the following excerpt from the *Brown vs. the Topeka Board of Education* decision:

> To separate Negro children from others of similar age and qualifications solely because of their race generates a feeling of inferiority as to their status in the community that may affect their hearts and minds in a way unlikely ever to be undone.... We conclude that in the field of public education the doctrine of "separate but equal" has no place. Separate educational facilities are inherently unequal.

d.   Have students research the status of school integration in the United States. Has there been progress? What is the status of integration in the students' state, community, and school?

e.   Frederick Douglass [1875(?)-1895], born to slavery, was one of the great men of American history. Escaping from slavery after seven years of servitude, he became one of the century's great orators, a splendid writer, philosopher, editor, and a militant leader in the fight to abolish slavery. His interests were by no means only racial. He was the only man to attend the first women's suffrage convention, and he became a close friend of early feminists Susan B. Anthony and Elizabeth Cady Stanton. His lifelong struggle for freedom for black people laid the groundwork for many subsequent achievements and changes, including those in education. The following is a famous excerpt from a speech Douglass made on the Fourth of July, 1852, before slavery was ended:

> What, to the American slave is your Fourth of July? I answer; a day that reveals to him, more than all the other days in the year, the gross injustice and cruelty to which he is a constant victim. To him, your celebration is a sham; your boasted liberty, an unholy license; your national greatness, swelling vanity; your sounds of rejoicing are empty and heartless; your denunciation of tyrants, brass fronted impudence; your shouts of liberty and equality, hollow mockery; your prayers and hymns, your sermons and thanksgivings, with all your religious parade and solemnity, are, to him, a mere bombast, fraud, deception, impiety, and hypocrisy — a thin veil to cover up crimes which would disgrace a nation of savages. There is not a nation on the earth guilty of practices more shocking and bloody than are the people of the United States at this very hour.
>
> — From a speech delivered to the
> Rochester Ladies Anti-Slavery Society, July 4, 1852

Tell students to imagine themselves as white Southerners in 1852. They are to compose a letter to the Charlotte, North Carolina, *Courier* responding to Douglass's speech.

Basic skills: supporting the topic sentence

Explain to students that the topic sentence is usually the first sentence in the paragraph. Everything else in the paragraph must be related to the topic sentence.

a. Ask them to use the following sentence for their topic sentence:

The schools for black students in the South were unequal to those for white students.

b. Have them write three sentences giving three examples of inequality from the film.

1. _____
2. _____
3. _____

c. Ask them to write a concluding sentence about inequality between the schools.

d. Ask them to develop a paragraph by using the topic sentence, the three supporting sentences, and their sentence of conclusion.

ADDITIONAL STUDY AIDS

A Calendar for School Desegregation

1896-*Plessy vs. Ferguson*
The Supreme Court held that "separate but equal" facilities did not violate the constitutional rights of the deprived students. This, in effect, upheld segregation.

May, 1954-*Brown vs. the Topeka Board of Education*
This landmark decision overturned the doctrine that separate facilities are equal. The Supreme Court ordered the school districts to proceed with desegregation "with all deliberate speed."

September, 1957
President Dwight D. Eisenhower ordered federal troops to Little Rock, Arkansas, to uphold a court order admitting black students to the previously all-white school.

September, 1958
The Supreme Court ordered the resumption of integration at the Little Rock, Arkansas, high school after it had been discontinued.

September, 1958
The Supreme Court, in a unanimous decision, rejected the claim of Governor Orval Faubus and the Alabama legislature that they were not bound by the 1954 *Brown vs. Topeka* decision.

ADDITIONAL STUDY AIDS (cont'd)

A Calendar for School Desegregation (cont'd)

April, 1960
> The *Southern School News* revealed that 94 percent of Southern black students still attended racially segregated schools.

May, 1963
> The Supreme Court stated that it "never contemplated that the concept of 'deliberate speed' would countenance indefinite delays in the elimination of racial barriers in schools."

July, 1964
> President Lyndon B. Johnson signed the Civil Rights Act. Title VI barred racial discrimination in any federally assisted activity.

March, 1967
> Alabama is placed under a single injunction to integrate all schools.

April, 1971-*Swann vs. Charlotte-Mecklenburg Board of Education*
> The Supreme Court upheld busing to achieve integration as constitutional. It also ruled that flexible quotas and other devices were legitimate tools for the elimination of *de jure* segregation.

March, 1982
> The United States Senate voted to adopt legislation that would virtually eliminate busing as a means of achieving racial integration.

RELATED RESOURCES

Films

Almos' a Man	*Remember Me?*
Equality	*Rosie Greer: The Courage to Be Me*
The Hangman	*Strange Fruit*
Only the Ball Was White	*The Sky Is Gray*
Paul Robeson: Tribute to an	*The Way of the Willow*
Artist	*Youth Terror: The View from*
The Phans of New Jersey	*behind the Gun*

Poetry

> Brooks, Gwendolyn. "*Chicago Defender* Sends a Man to Little Rock." *Poetry of Black America: Anthology of Twentieth Century Poetry.* Harper & Row, 1973

> Cullen, Countee. "Incident." *Norton Anthology of Poetry.* W. W. Norton & Company, rev. 1973

> Hayden, Robert. "Frederick Douglass." *A Geography of Poets.* Bantam Books, 1981

> Hughes, Langston. "Freedom." *Poetry of Black America: Anthology of the Twentieth Century.* Harper & Row, 1973

Lee, Don L. "With All Deliberate Speed." *Jump Bad: A New Chicago Anthology.* Broadside Press, 1971

Short story

Bradbury, Ray. "The Other Foot." *Social Problems through Science Fiction.* St. Martin's Press, 1975

Books for young adults

Douglass, Frederick. *My Bondage and My Freedom.* Dover Press, 1969

Oates, Stephen B. *Let the Trumpet Sound: The Life of Martin Luther King, Jr.* Harper & Row, 1982

Walter, Mildred Pitts. *The Girl on the Outside.* Lothrop, Lee, & Shepard, 1982

Books for adults

Clark, Kenneth. *Prejudice and Your Child.* Peter Smith, 1975

Kluger, Richard. *Simple Justice: The History of the Brown vs. Topeka Board of Education and Black America's Struggle for Equality.* Knopf, 1976

Olson, Otto, ed. *Thin Disguise: Turning Point in Negro History: Plessy vs. Ferguson, a Documentary Presentation.* Humanities Press, 1967

Peltason, J. W. *Fifty-Eight Lonely Men: Southern Federal Judges and School Desegregation.* University of Massachusetts, 1971

Porter, Judith D. *Black Child: White Child: The Development of Racial Attitudes.* Harvard University Press, 1971

AN AMERICAN TIME CAPSULE
(4 min, c, $110/35, Pyramid Films, 1975)

THEMES
American history

CURRICULUM AREAS
History, filmmaking, humanities

SYNOPSIS
An American Time Capsule interests students because of its technique. Using a kinestatic or flash frame technique, 1,300 visuals (paintings, still photographs, newspaper headlines, early newsreels, posters, political cartoons) flash before the viewer. Each image is photographed at rates ranging from one-twelfth to two-thirds of a second, all to the quick, involving rhythm of Sandy Nelson's drumbeat. The film is a chronological capsule building to a climax and made more intricate by the restrained use of pans, filters, and zooms. Beginning with the Revolutionary War, the images pour in a furious barrage, ending with President Ford.

When the film was originally presented on the "Smothers Brothers Comedy Hour" in 1968, audience response was overwhelming. The Smothers brothers commissioned Charles Braverman to make another, similar film. The result was the even more sophisticated *World of '68*, which detailed one year of American history. Students are fascinated by both of these films and are surprised by their own retention of the material presented in them.

Either film is ideal for filmmaking classes because the kinestatic technique is one that the amateur can easily adapt to a situation of little money or simple equipment. The results are generally splendid.

BEFORE VIEWING
Ask students to list, in jumbled chronological order, ten events or people from American history: the invention of the airplane, the Civil War, "Teddy" Roosevelt, Custer's last stand, the moon shot, the *Declaration of Independence*, the assassination of President Lincoln, World War II, the Gold Rush, and Dwight Eisenhower's election to the presidency.
Have the students try to place these events in chronological order.

AFTER VIEWING

Suggestions for discussions and compositions

a. Ask students to redo their lists and discuss accuracy and improvement.

b. Discuss what events the filmmaker considered important by the stress he placed on them.

c. Ask students if a person from outer space saw this film, what would his impression of America be?

d. Discuss with students if another filmmaker, using different events, could create another impression.

e. If the class is interested, discuss kinestasis with them. In that technique, a 16-mm sound film (the kind that most schools use) is projected at 24 frames per second. If an image is projected at one-twelfth of a second, it may be below the level of consciousness, and we are not aware that we have seen it. This often leads to a discussion of subliminal advertising, another very interesting topic for most students.

f. Ask students to imagine making a short film called *An American Time Capsule* that should include fifteen to twenty of the most important people, events, inventions, or dates in American history. What ones would they select? How would they present each one?

Time	Visual	Soundtrack

BOARD AND CARE
(27 min, c, $450/55, Pyramid Films, 1981)

THEMES
The emotional needs of the mentally handicapped. The role of the "normal" adult in determining how the handicapped should live. The rights of the mentally handicapped. The need for caring relationships.

CURRICULUM AREAS
Family living, psychology, sociology, special education, language arts, teacher training

SYNOPSIS
Like all of us, Ricky and Lila, the teenagers of Ron Ellis' Academy Award-winning film, are searching for closeness with another person. But they differ from most of us in an important way: both Ricky (Richard Goss) and Lila (Laura Ellis) are victims of Down's syndrome, or mongoloidism. This reality gives the film a power and poignancy impossible to achieve with professional actors. (*Board and Care* was filmed at Porterville State Hospital, Porterville, California.)

Ricky is the son of a Central Valley farmer; Lila is a student in an institution for the mentally retarded. They meet briefly at a picnic and enjoy being together. Later, Ricky, determined to see Lila again, leaves for the school, but officials have already decided to transfer her to another institution. Ricky arrives to see a tearful Lila being driven away.

It is a powerful, bittersweet story that with a less sensitive filmmaker might easily have slipped into sentimentality. At first the viewer may be disturbed by the "difference," but as one is caught up in the couple's longing for a special relationship, the difference magically disappears. This, of course, is the message for our students – we are all more alike than we are different.

BEFORE VIEWING
Since filmmaker Ron Ellis is very interested in having people understand the humanity of victims of Down's syndrome, an ideal introduction would be to have the parent of such a child talk to the class. This presumes a capable parent who intuits the needs of the class, and a mature, thoughtful class interested in understanding the humanity of the child. If this is not possible, prepare the class with facts about Down's syndrome, previously called mongoloidism. Emphasize that no one is responsible for such a disorder. It is not hereditary, nor is it the result of any factors over which the parents or the medical profession have control.

Discuss whether victims of Down's syndrome should control their lives? Should they have special relationships? Who should govern their futures?

Board and Care
Photograph courtesy of Pyramid Films

AFTER VIEWING

Suggestions for discussions and compositions

   a. Ask students if they felt the ending was satisfactory? Discuss the term *bittersweet*, often applied to an ending such as this one. Is it appropriate for this film?

   b. Have students write an epilogue to the story. What happens to Lila and Ricky? Are they changed by this experience?

   c. Ricky's father calls him "dummy." Ask students what effect would this have on Ricky. What does it tell them about the Father? (Since many students call handicapped students in their schools "dummy," this is an excellent opportunity to confront the problem without identifying individuals.)

   d. Have students had any contact with a victim of Down's syndrome? How did they feel? Embarrassed? Resentful? Patronizing? Sympathetic? Uncomfortable? How did they behave? Do they wish they had behaved differently? What would be the ideal attitude for them to adopt?

   e. Discuss whether social workers should determine behaviors and goals for people such as Lila and Ricky. Who should determine them?

   f. Explain to a student that he or she is a social worker on the staff of the institution that Lila attended. Her caseworker has asked for a meeting with the student and with three other staff members to discuss whether Lila should be sent to the new school. Hold the meeting with five students playing the staff members and the caseworker. Two favor the transfer, two oppose it. The caseworker is undecided. The student – the social worker – must reach a decision.

   g. Ask students to identify the common human bond that all people, handicapped or physically capable, share.

Suggestions for advanced assignments

   a. Invite a lawyer to the class to discuss the legal rights of young, mentally handicapped persons. If possible, ask the lawyer to view the film with the class.

   b. Ask a teacher of the mentally retarded to speak to the class about the educational opportunities available for them in their school or district. Ask students to look for needs that they believe are not being met.

   c. Have the class compose a Bill of Rights for handicapped students in their school, including the physically handicapped. Post it on the school bulletin board or in your classroom. Ask them to consult with handicapped students in preparing their poster.

   d. Explain to the class that filmmaker Ron Ellis is concerned that everyone understand that his sister Laura, and others like her, feel anger, love, pain, jealousy, loneliness, and all other human emotions. Ask them if Ellis's view is realistic or if he is romanticizing the mentally handicapped?

   e. Ask students to write a paper explaining the legal and emotional rights that you believe the mentally handicapped should have. If new laws are needed, suggest what they should be.

Basic skills: writing the informal letter

Students are to imagine that they are a brother or sister of Lila or Ricky. They are upset about what has happened. For release, they write a letter to a close friend explaining how they feel. They can mention how they think the action will affect Lila or Ricky.

Explain that in writing an informal letter, they must remember these three things about the form:

   1. **Commas**
      Separate the city from the state. *Chicago, Illinois*

      Separate the day from the year. *May 24, 1984*

      Place a comma after your friend's name in the salutation. *Dear Lisa,*

      Place a comma after the last word of your closing. *Your friend,*

   2. **Indentation**
      Indent the first sentence and the first sentence of each succeeding paragraph.

   3. **Capitalization**
      Capitalize the first letter of the closing. If there is more than one word in the closing, only the first word is capitalized. Show them examples of one-word and two-word closings, such as Sincerely, Yours, Yours truly, Always, Your friend, Best regards, Love, Love always, With love, Affectionately.

(Form appears on page 32.)

Familiarize the students with an example of the form:

> Chicago, Illinois
>
> May 24, 1984

Dear Lisa,

I'm just so upset that I had to write you. Since you're my closest friend I think I can say things to you that I wouldn't tell anyone else. You know my sister Laura. Things have always been hard for her. Sometimes I even feel guilty because they aren't hard for me. Today I feel really bad. I think the people that run the school that Laura goes to have really made a mistake....

Thank you, Lisa, for being such a good friend.

> Affectionately,
>
> Francine

ADDITIONAL STUDY AIDS

For further information about Down's syndrome, refer to *Encyclopaedia Britannica* under the heading Down's Syndrome or to *Encyclopedia Americana* under Mongolism.

RELATED RESOURCES

Films

Backtrack	*David: Portrait of a Retarded Youth*
Being Part of It All	*No Other Love*
Best Boy	*One of Our Own*

Short stories

Hood, Hugh. "Gone Three Days." *None Genuine without This Signature.* ECW Press, 1980

Keyes, Daniel. "Flowers for Algernon." *Introduction to Psychology through Science Fiction.* Random House, 1974

Lardner, Ring. "Haircut." *200 Years of Great American Short Stories.* Houghton, 1975

Porter, Katharine Anne. "He." *Twelve Short Story Writers.* Holt, 1975

Schor, Lynda. "Class Outing." *True Love and Real Romance.* Coward, McCann, & Geoghegan, 1979

Books for young adults

Brown, Christy. "From My Left Foot." *Ordinary Lives.* Apple-Wood Books, 1982

Keyes, Daniel. *Flowers for Algernon.* Harcourt, 1966

Ross, Bette M. *Our Special Child.* Walker, 1981

Spencer, Elizabeth. *The Light in the Piazza.* McGraw-Hill, 1960

Steinbeck, John. *Of Mice and Men.* Viking, 1937

Books for adults

Mitchell, Joyce Slayton. *Taking on the World: Empowering Strategies for Parents of Children with Disabilities.* HJB, 1982

Vine, Phyllis. *Families in Pain.* Pantheon, 1982

CLOSE HARMONY
(28 min, c, $450/40, Learning Corporation of America, 1981)

THEMES
The isolation between generations. One person *can* make a difference.
Stereotypes can be changed. Old age, loneliness, communication.

CURRICULUM AREAS
Psychology, sociology, gerontology, language arts, music, guidance

SYNOPSIS
The growth of affection and understanding between children and oldsters
is the theme of this joyous, energetic film featuring music teacher Arlene
Symons, the fourth and fifth graders of Friends School in Brooklyn, and
the adults of the Council Center for Senior Citizens.

While serving as a volunteer music instructor in various senior citizen
groups, Ms. Symons was struck by the homogeneity of performers and
audience at concert times. Where were the young and the middle-aged?
What could be done to encourage them to interact with their elders, either
actively or as observers?

Ms. Symons's solution? A joint concert featuring her fourth and fifth
graders and the adult group where she served as volunteer choir director.
Format for rehearsal and performance was simple. Each group rehearsed
separately but corresponded as pen pals. The final rehearsal together
brought excitement, recognition, and tentative touching. The second
brought lunch prepared by the children for the seniors. Judged as music,
the group's concert is not exceptional, but as an interpersonal project, it is
overwhelmingly successful.

In a time when old people are often shunted away in retirement centers
and interaction with younger people is difficult, Ms. Symons
demonstrates that one caring person can make a difference.

BEFORE VIEWING
Tell the class that the film is about an unusual kind of concert with unique
problems because the youngest member of the chorus was nine and the oldest
was ninety. What kind of problems might the director encounter in such a
group? Consider choice of music, vocal range, stamina of performers,
suitability of music, etc. Ask the class to think about the old people they know.
Do any of them sing in a group? Are any of them interested in music? Can they
imagine themselves singing in a group, perhaps a church choir, with them?

AFTER VIEWING
Suggestions for discussions and compositions
    a.   What do they think of this project as a whole? Why was it successful?

    b.   How many of them would like to take part in it? Why?

(Suggestions for discussions and compositions continues on page 36.)

Close Harmony
Photograph courtesy of Learning Corporation of America

Suggestions for discussions and compositions (cont'd)

    c.   Ask them how the concert affects the lives of the seniors and the children.

    d.   Discuss with the class some of the remarks that the children made:

Dylan: I go places sometimes, and like supermarkets, and these old people come around, and let's say I bump into them, and I say I'm sorry, and they go, ugh, ugh, ugh. Besides my mother says some of these old ladies don't like children at all, so at first I didn't want to write to a pen pal.

Jenny: Some old people just don't like to be with young people because they are scared.

Mary: When I am old, as old as fifty, maybe older, I'm not going to make people give up their seats for me. I think that if we give them respect they should give us back respect.

Lindsay: You could be a very young person when you are eighty, and old when you're forty, fifteen when you are five.

Jonathan: When you get old, people don't want to care for you anymore.

Philip: I always had an impression of old people, but when I started to write to my pen pal, I just didn't think that way anymore.

Rachel: I used to think that when they were young they didn't have as much fun as I do. When she wrote that she used to play all sorts of games, I thought that if maybe she had a lot of fun like she used to, maybe I'd still have fun when I was old.

    e.   Ask the class how many of them would be comfortable spending an hour alone with an old person. What would they talk about if they initiated the conversation?

    f.   Ask students if children and old people have anything in common? What do the participants in the concert share?

    g.   Help students to develop a pen-pal relationship with an older person in their area.

    h.   Ask the class to discuss the older people whom they admire. (Do not elicit names unless students want to volunteer them.) What are the person's skills, interests, activities, and philosophy? How are these individuals different from other older people?

Invite an interesting older person to speak to the class about her or his life. Ask students to inquire about the person's changing lifestyles and about evolving attitudes toward war, movies, value systems, the economic situation, etc. Record a short interview with an older person. With her or his permission, play it to the class and ask them to comment.

Suggestions for advanced assignments

a. Ask students to research the living conditions of people over sixty-five in the United States. How many live with relatives, in communal homes, alone, in retirement centers, in nursing homes? How do these statistics compare with those of other industrialized countries such as Sweden, England, France, Japan, etc.?

b. Organize a debate on the following topic: Resolved, that the structure of American society contributes to the generational gap.

c. Develop a generational project for the class. For examples, consult the next section.

ADDITIONAL STUDY AIDS

Examples of Intergenerational Projects

In San Diego, California, through a program known as SCOPE (Senior Citizen Opportunities in Public Education) older people are employed for five hours a week to provide scholastic and emotional support to youngsters in two elementary schools.

In Fitchburg, Massachusetts, 300 students joined with retired citizens in an energy conservation effort. The volunteers replaced air filters, sealed vents, cleaned refrigerator coils, and assisted in dozens of energy-saving activities for neighborhood residents.

Columbia University in New York City established SHE (Student Help for the Elderly), which is founded on the premise that students can provide relatively low-cost, high-quality services to older persons who cannot afford such services. Students are paid three dollars an hour to shop, cook, and provide companionship to older persons who are housebound.

For five weeks in 1979, twenty-five eighth-graders in Columbus, Ohio, spent two periods of their class day at a nearby retirement center. Students exchanged views, shared experiences, and offered assistance to the residents. The activity replaced their regular English and American history classes, but these subjects were learned through assignments such as daily journals, taped oral history, and reports of student observations of the elderly.

From these and similar projects, some guidelines have emerged that are critical to their success.

Provide for mutually beneficial exchanges. To reduce stereotypes and to promote mutual respect, all participants must give as well as receive.

ADDITIONAL STUDY AIDS (cont'd)

Involve both young and old in program planning. The most successful programs are those that respond to the needs and interests of the participants.

Start small. Small-scale intergenerational projects give participants a sense of achievement and allow time for program evaluation and possible modification before substantial commitment of time and resources.

Don't operate in a vacuum. In every community there are agencies that work with the elderly. Try to involve these groups since they can be very helpful in planning, identifying community resources, and recruiting capable older people for the project.

Encourage one-to-one exchange. Friendships are one of the most important results of intergenerational projects.

RELATED RESOURCES

Films

Chillysmith Farm	*Piece of Cake*
Forever Young	*Portrait of Grandpa Doc*
The Lost Phoebe	*The Shopping Bag Lady*
Never Give Up	*The Stringbean*
Peege	*Sunshine's On the Way*

Poetry

Jeffers, Robinson. "Age in Prospect." *Modern American and British Poetry.* Harcourt, 1950

Masefield, John. "On Growing Old." *Modern American and British Poetry.* Harcourt, 1950

Sassoon, Siegfried. "Everyone Sang." *Oxford Book of Twentieth Century Verse.* Oxford University Press, 1977

Short stories

Lardner, Ring. "The Golden Honeymoon." *The American Short Story.* Vol. II, Dell, 1980

Vonnegut, Kurt, Jr. "Tomorrow, Tomorrow, Tomorrow." *Looking Ahead.* Harcourt, 1975

Books for adults

Bluh, Bonnie. *The Old Speak Out.* Horizon Press, 1979

Kastenbaum, Robert. *Growing Old: Years of Fulfillment.* Harper & Row, 1979

Robbin, Alexandra. *Aging: A New Look.* American Guidance, 1982

Scott-Maxwell, Florida. *Measure of My Days.* Knopf, 1968

CLOSED MONDAYS
(8 min, c, $210/35, Pyramid Films, 1974)

THEMES

Reality versus illusion. What is the nature of art? The perception of new phenomena. Art as part of life.

CURRICULUM AREAS

Language arts, art, film study, humanities, filmmaking

SYNOPSIS

In the night a street wanderer stumbles through an open door into a museum. As he laughs scornfully, an abstract painting leaps into movement. A kinetic computer runs wild and destroys itself. A painting of the jungle comes alive.

At his touch the pop art computer undergoes a series of surrealistic changes. It becomes, in turn, an apple, the world, Albert Einstein, a TV set, an arm with many hands, and finally melts to an amorphous lump. The intruder is frightened when figures in a garden painted by Rousseau threaten. Finally, he is transfixed by the image of a scrub girl who complains that she is doomed to being eternally unhappy and to scrubbing the cold stone floor because the artist failed to see more of the beauty of life. The man is moved to tears by her plight. Confused, he turns to run from the museum, but is himself magically turned into a bronze statue.

A winner of the Academy Award for best animated short subject, the film is remarkable for its life-like illusion and movement. The intruder's face, at once humorous and poignant, reflects beautifully the effect of art on the mind and heart of the viewer, and communicates his deep feelings toward it. This is a fascinating and challenging film.

BEFORE VIEWING

Have a number of paintings or sculptures available. Ask the students if they understand the way the artist viewed the world from studying her or his art. They probably will not do this very successfully, but the question will introduce them to one of the major ideas in *Closed Mondays.*

Talk to the class about their visits, or lack of them, to art museums. Have them describe what they liked best. Can they name or describe a particular work of art? Was there a favorite? Do they know why? Were there paintings they didn't understand? If two students saw the same painting, try to get each to articulate her or his feelings about it. Do they agree? Would they like to go to a museum again? Try to discover how the students feel who have never been to an art museum. Would they like to go if they had an opportunity? Tell them they are going to see a film about a man who stumbled by accident into a museum at night—a man who didn't like art and would never have gone by design.

AFTER VIEWING

Suggestions for discussions and compositions

a. People often react with the bumbling defensiveness of the intruder when they are confronted with art that they don't understand. Discuss with students the reason for this reaction.

b. The intruder is scornful and skeptical from the time he enters the museum. Ask students if attitude affects the way one views art.

c. *Closed Mondays* explores the difference between illusion and reality. The canvasses seem to grow in size and depth. Ask students if they were really moving or if they were responding to the viewer's perceptions of them?

d. Pablo Picasso once said, "One should no more try to understand art than one should try to understand the song of a bird." Explore with the class Picasso's statement.

e. The mad computer is transformed into an apple, a globe with a face on it, Albert Einstein, a TV set, a pop art sculpture, and finally into a lump. Discuss with students what these changes symbolize. Nature, society, science, media, and art? What do they have in common? How do they relate to the film?

f. How does the artist's perception of life affect what he creates? Ask the class to ponder the scrub girl and her words.

g. Ask students to choose a work of art about which they have strong feelings. Ask them to write a dialogue between themselves and the characters or designs in the work.

h. What does it mean to experience a work of art statically? What does the film seem to suggest about static reactions?

i. Ask students to write a science fiction story in which a character metamorphoses.

j. The film suggests that art is not static, and that it need not be laid to rest in a museum. If this is true, ask students how they should interact with art? Where should they look for it? Why go to a museum? What is art for?

k. Explore with the class the intention of the filmmaker in turning the intruder into bronze at the end of the film. Some possibilities to consider are the following: art doesn't just imitate nature: it is nature in suspended animation; he has become an exhibit for the next day's museum visitors; he may have been imprisoned by his own resistance; the ability of art to make us sad, fearful, happy, depressed, or anxious may have transfixed and immobilized him permanently; it may be man's quest for significance in the world.

Suggestions for advanced assignments

a. Anthropologist Ruth Benedict has said, "We do not see the lens through which we look." Discuss with the class her meaning. If this statement is true, how does it affect us when we see new phenomena such as modern art?

b. Discuss with students what an artist does when he transforms his personal vision into a work of art.

c. In the end of the film, the skeptical viewer is himself changed into a work of art. Ask students to explain this enigma.

d. Ask students to examine any work of art — sculpture, painting, even a beautiful building such as the Parthenon, the Taj Mahal, the Doges' Palace, or the cathedral of Notre Dame. They are to write what they believe to be the artist's perception of the world from their study of his or her work.

e. Organize a field trip to an art museum for your class.

f. Ask the art teacher in your school to visit the class and give everyone an art lesson. Have the students write about their feelings during the lesson.

g. Ask students to write their responses to the following quotation: "Painting is only a bridge linking the painter's mind with that of the viewer." (Eugene Delacroix)

RELATED RESOURCES

Films

Apple Dolls
Brooklyn Bridge
The Incredible San Francisco Artists' Soapbox Derby
Never Give Up
Quilts in Women's Lives
Sentinels of Silence

Books

Berger, John. *Ways of Seeing*. Penguin Books, 1972

Nelson, George. *How to See*. Little, Brown & Company, 1981

THE DAY AFTER TRINITY
(90 min, c, $950/125, Pyramid Films, 1981)

THEMES
The beginning of the atomic age. The invention of the bomb at Los Alamos, New Mexico. The story of J. Robert Oppenheimer and the responsibility of scientists for their creations. The proliferation of the bomb.

CURRICULUM AREAS
Science (particularly physics), history, philosophy, humanities, language arts, sociology, government, psychology, values

SYNOPSIS
On July 16, 1945, the day known in history as "Trinity," the first atomic bomb was exploded near Alamogordo, New Mexico. Shortly afterwards American planes dropped the first A-bombs on Hiroshima and Nagasaki. The Atomic Age had begun, and life was never again to be the same for anything living.

This fascinating, frightening, and ultimately touching documentary examines the effects of the bomb on the world, on the Japanese at Hiroshima and Nagasaki, and most of all, on the scientists responsible for its creation, especially J. Robert Oppenheimer, the father of the bomb.

The film documents Oppenheimer's brilliant assemblage of scores of scientists who were lured to the secret Los Alamos laboratory by his tremendous status as a theoretical physicist. The 4,500 men and women whom he directed were responsible for designing, assembling, and testing the A-bomb, while maintaining complete secrecy.

Film clips, interviews with Oppenheimer's Los Alamos colleagues and their families, and stills are intercut with previously unseen footage of the bomb and its aftermath. Particularly chilling are the comments of the scientists at the Trinity site. The destruction of the atmosphere and the decimation of New Mexico are two of the possibilities they mention. The next scene is one of the most disturbing and memorable in the film. On a slender, inadequate-looking steel frame, the bomb, resembling a giant diver's helmet with wires and cords attached, is hoisted while a narrator reads from a 1945 memorandum about the potential danger of the device. With Oppenheimer's, "Ready?" and then, "Should we have a chaplain here?," this terrifying, unprecedented event seems so ordinary that it is only on reflection that we can absorb what we have witnessed.

Two months after Hiroshima and Nagasaki, Oppenheimer resigned his position with grave doubts about the use of nuclear power. According to his brother, Oppenheimer's first reaction at Los Alamos after Hiroshima was, "Thank God, it worked," followed almost immediately by "What have we done?" The attitudes of the scientists interviewed are a mixture of pride that they had beaten other nations to the bomb and sadness and uneasiness over its destructive capability. When Oppenheimer, after being appointed director of the Institute of Advanced Studies at Princeton, publicly argued for international control of atomic weapons, his security clearance was lifted by President Dwight D. Eisenhower, an episode that friends state helped to destroy him. The film closes with Oppenheimer, the physicist and poet quoting from the *Bhagavad Gita*, "Now I am become death, the destroyer of worlds."

The Day after Trinity is a superb film. Without moralizing or editorializing, it heightens our awareness of our age. Everyone should see it.

BEFORE VIEWING
Discuss this question with the class: Suppose you were asked to do something that you believed to be morally wrong that would result in death or injury to a great many people that were unknown to you. However, you will also be admired and praised for this effort by many people. Furthermore, if you don't agree to do it, someone else will, and this time it could result in death or injury to someone you care about. Would you agree to go ahead even though you believe it is morally very wrong? Would you decline to participate? How would you feel regardless of your decision?

AFTER VIEWING
As the distinguished scientists speak, their faces and voices betray their ambivalent feelings about their roles in history. Pride in accomplishment is mixed with regret and sorrow over the bomb's destructiveness. This is the central issue, and the corollary is: What do we do now that we are involved in an arms race and faced with the real possibility of destroying the earth? Ask the students if they would work as physicists in a defense project such as the Manhattan Project if the war were publicly sanctioned, such as World War II, or Korea. Would they work on such a project if there were no war, but to beat a political enemy to the newest missile, antimissile, satellite, etc.? Try to get the class to commit itself to a position.

Suggestions for discussions and compositions

a. Discuss with the class what force(s) has kept development of the bomb continuing even after the Hiroshima-Nagasaki bombings.

b. Ask students what have been the psychological effects on mankind of the development of the bomb? Did the scientists at Los Alamos anticipate these?

c. J. Robert Oppenheimer was one of the most complex men ever to play an important role in American history. Ask the class to write a detailed physical, psychological, and personal description of Oppenheimer. Have students note his stature among scientists, his interests outside of science, and the seeming paradox of his nature. Do they think he was aware of the contradiction between much of what he said and his work on the bomb?

Suggestions for discussions and compositions (cont'd)

d. The film closes with Oppenheimer, whose life was destroyed because of his advocacy of worldwide control of the bomb, remembering a line from the *Bhagavad Gita*: "Now I am become death, the destroyer of the world." Ask students to comment.

e. Do students think the same motives of hate and fear of a perceived evil that led to the development of the bomb are still operating today?

f. Have students investigate the positions of nuclear freeze advocates and opponents. Advocates believe that the United States has more than enough weapons; opponents argue that we must exceed the Soviet arsenal for us to be safe from attack. What position would they take?

g. Ask students to study the civil defense plans for their community. Are they adequate? Do they ensure their safety? Diagram on the board the plan of evacuation for your school. What is the reaction of the class? Can safety be assured by any plan?

Suggestions for advanced assignments

a. Ask students to select one of the following quotations and develop the most complete paper possible during a specific time allotment:

> "The unleashed power of the atom has changed everything save our modes of thinking, and we thus drift toward unparalleled catastrophes."
> — Albert Einstein

> "It would be madness to let the purposes or the methods of private enterprise set the habits of the age of atomic energy."
> — Harold Laski

> Shortly before his death in 1967, J. Robert Oppenheimer was asked about the proposed talks to ensure nuclear nonproliferation. He answered, "It's too late for that, it should have been done the day after Trinity."

> "Concern for man himself and his fate must always form the chief interest of all technical endeavors, concern for the great unsolved problems of the organization of labor and the distribution of goods—in order that the creations of our mind shall be a blessing and not a curse to mankind."
> — Albert Einstein

> "If we threaten to destroy future generations we harm ourselves.... If their existence is in doubt, our present becomes a sadly incomplete affair, like only one word of a poem, or one note of a song. Ultimately, it is sub-human."
> — Jonathan Schell

b. Discuss with the class H. G. Wells (1866-1946). Explain that he was a English novelist, historian, philosopher, scientific writer, and one of the most popular writers of his era. *War of the Worlds*, adapted by Orson Welles in his panic-inducing radio broadcast, *The Island of Dr. Moreau, Things to Come, The Time Machine,* and *The Invisible Man,* all made into popular films, are among his many writings. In *The World Set Free*, Wells made two predictions about the atomic bomb, which have become famous. Ask students to comment on one of them.

> Nothing could have been more obvious to the people of the early twentieth century than the rapidity with which war was becoming impossible. And as certainly they did not see it. They did not see it until the atomic bombs burst in their fumbling hands.

> The catastrophe of the atomic bombs which shook men out of cities and businesses and economic relations, shook them also out of their old-established habits of thought, and out of the lightly held beliefs and prejudices that came down to them from the past.

c. Organize a panel of students to discuss the future of atomic energy: military, energy, medical, and social.

d. Ask students to make a time line of the important dates in the development of the bomb and the efforts to control it. Ask them to project what they think will happen in 1999. Consult the calendar of the development of the bomb.

e. Oppenheimer chose the location for the secret laboratory at Los Alamos, New Mexico. Explore with students the relationship between the area and the task to the two very different sides of Oppenheimer's personality.

ADDITIONAL STUDY AIDS

A Calendar of the Development of the Atomic Bomb and Its Aftermath

1896

Frenchman Henri Becquerel planned to expose uranium salts to sunlight to see if they would become excited and fluoresce. However, the day was cloudy and he placed the salts in a drawer with a photographic plate. When he resumed his experiments, he developed the plate and found signs of radioactivity.

1934

Italian physicist Enrico Fermi bombarded uranium with neutrons and found indications he was changing the uranium into a heavier element. A

ADDITIONAL STUDY AIDS (cont'd)

A Calendar of the Development of the Atomic Bomb (cont'd)

strip of aluminum foil, three-thousandths of an inch thick, placed as a guard against radiation prevented him from seeing what he had actually done.

1936

Swiss researchers, who forgot to insert the foil when duplicating Fermi's experiments recorded the energy bursts.

1937

In France, Irene Joliet-Curie, daughter of Pierre and Marie Curie, saw elements about half the weight of uranium after neutron bombardment.

1937

Enrico Fermi, now living in the United States, duplicated the experiments in order to confirm them. The significance was clear. Someone would develop the bomb. The problem was who.

1939

European scientist, Leo Szilard went to Albert Einstein for help in determining how and when the bomb should be developed.

August, 1939

Albert Einstein wrote a letter to President Franklin D. Roosevelt that said in part:

> "In the course of the last few months it has been made probable through the work of Joliet in France, as well as Szilard and Fermi in America, that it may be possible to set up a nuclear chain reaction in a large mass of uranium by which vast amounts of power and large quantities of new radium-like elements would be generated....
>
> "This new phenomenon would also lead to the construction of bombs.... A single bomb of this type, carried by boat and exploded in a port, might very well destroy the whole port together with some of the surrounding territory."

He also warned that Germany had stopped the sale of uranium from Czechoslovakian mines — an ominous sign.

1939

President Roosevelt promised immediate action in his response to Dr. Einstein.

February, 1940

The first federal funds were appropriated so that Enrico Fermi could use graphite to moderate the reaction of the neutrons to make them more effective.

1940
> At the University of California, Glen Seaborg's team bombarded uranium 238 and made plutonium, bomb material.

1941
> British scientists learned to separate the fissionable U235 from the dampening effect of its companion U238 by gaseous diffusion. The refined product would be much more potent.

December 2, 1942
> American and European scientists started the first chain reaction in a pile of uranium and graphite bricks in a squash court on the University of Chicago campus. The first power surge was no greater than a kitchen match.

July 16, 1945
> The first atomic bomb was exploded at Alamogordo, New Mexico.

August 6, 1945
> The bomb was dropped by American planes at Hiroshima, Japan.

August 9, 1945
> The bomb was dropped by American planes at Nagasaki, Japan.

1982
> Over one million people gathered in New York's Central Park to protest, in orderly fashion, against the bomb.

August, 1982
> The House of Representatives defeated a nuclear freeze resolution by two votes.

November, 1982
> The nuclear freeze issue was on thirty-nine ballots, nine of them states. Almost all passed overwhelmingly.

January 1983
> The nuclear freeze movement has become international in scope with the United States, Germany, and Japan especially strong.

RELATED RESOURCES

Films

Hiroshima-Nagasaki, August 1945
If You Love This Planet
Lovejoy's Nuclear War
Nick Mazzucco: Biography of an Atomic Vet

No Place to Hide
Nuclear Watchdogs
Survivors: A Film about Japanese-American Atomic Bomb Victims
War without Winners II

Poetry

Burke, Kenneth. "If All the Thermonuclear Warheads." *Of Quarks, Quasars, and Other Quirks: Quizzical Poems for the Supersonic Age.* Thomas Y. Crowell, 1981

Jacobsen, Ethel. "Atomic Courtesy." *Of Quarks, Quasars, and Other Quirks: Quizzical Poems for the Supersonic Age.* Thomas Y. Crowell, 1981

Kunitz, Stanley. "The Last Picnic." *Norton Anthology of Modern Poetry.* W. W. Norton & Company, rev. 1982

Lewis, Cecil Day. "The Dead." *Modern Poets: An American and British Anthology.* McGraw-Hill, 1970

Marks, Shirley. "Early Warning." *Of Quarks, Quasars, and Other Quirks: Quizzical Poems for the Supersonic Age.* Thomas Y. Crowell, 1981

Short stories

Asimov, Isaac. "Hell-Fire." *The Far Ends of Time and Earth.* Doubleday, 1979

Lessing, Doris. "Report on a Threatened City." *Stories.* Knopf, 1981

Books for young adults

Nonfiction

Bender, David L. *The Arms Race.* Greenhaven Press, 1982

Briggs, Raymond. *When the Wind Blows.* Schocken Books, 1982

Ford, Daniel. *The Cult of the Atom: The Secret Papers of the Atomic Energy Commission.* Simon and Schuster, 1982

Kaku, Michio, and Jennifer Trainer, eds. *Nuclear Power: Both Sides.* W. W. Norton & Company, 1982

Kiefer, Irene. *Nuclear Energy at the Crossroads.* Atheneum, 1982

Nuclear War: What's in It for You? Pocket Books, 1982

Rubenstein, Robert E. *When Sirens Scream.* Dodd, Mead, 1981

Sampson, Fay. *The Watch on Patterick Fell.* Greenwillow, 1982

Schell, Jonathan. *The Fate of the Earth.* Knopf, 1982

Taylor, L. B. *The Nuclear Arms Race.* Impact Books, 1982

Weissman, Steve, and Herbert Krosney. *The Islamic Bomb.* Times Books, 1982

Fiction

Burdick, Eugene, and Harvey Wheeler. *Fail-Safe.* McGraw-Hill, 1962

Niven, Larry. *Ringworld.* Ballantine, 1970

O'Brien, Robert C. *Z Is for Zachariah.* Atheneum, 1974

Shute, Nevil. *On the Beach.* Morrow, 1975

Vonnegut, Kurt. *Cat's Cradle.* Delacorte, 1969

Wilhelm, Kate. *Where Late the Sweet Birds Sang.* Harper & Row, 1976

Books for adults

Calder, Nigel. *Nuclear Nightmares.* Penguin Books, 1981

Clayton, Bruce. *Life after Doomsday.* Deal Press, 1980

Dunn, Lewis A. *Controlling the Bomb: Nuclear Proliferation in the 1980's.* Yale University Press, 1982

Katz, Arthur M. *Life after Nuclear War: The Economic and Social Impacts of Nuclear Attacks on the United States.* Ballinger, 1982

Kennan, George F. *The Nuclear Delusion.* Pantheon Books, 1982

Oppenheimer, J. Robert. *Letters and Recollections.* Harvard University Press, 1982

Rosenberg, Howard A. *Atomic Soldiers: American Victims of Nuclear Experiments.* Beacon Press, 1981

Wasserman, Paul. *Killing Our Own: The Disaster of America's Experience with Atomic Radiation.* Dell, 1982

Zuckerman, Solly. *Nuclear Illusion and Reality.* Viking Press, 1982

THE ELECTRIC GRANDMOTHER

(Full version: 49 min, c, $625/50, LCA, 1982;
edited version: 32 min, c, $450/40, LCA, 1982)

THEMES

The nature of love and constancy. Loneliness, aging, the fear of loving. The place of machines in our lives.

CURRICULUM AREAS

Language arts, science fiction, short story, psychology, guidance, family living

SYNOPSIS

Tony Award-winning actress Maureen Stapleton, supported by actor Edward Herrmann, stars in this stunning adaptation of Ray Bradbury's science fiction story, *I Sing the Body Electric*.

The story concerns young Agatha and her two older brothers, who, following the death of their mother, visit the Fantocinni robot factory to order a grandmother to their exact specifications. The grandmother – who is whimsically delivered to them by helicopter in an ornate sarcophagus – soon becomes a loved member of the family, accepted by all except the antagonistic Agatha. Since the Fantocinni agreement guaranteed success in thirty days and the grandmother had failed to win Agatha's love, she is to be returned to the factory. On the day of the scheduled return, she saves Agatha's life, but is herself struck by the car that could have killed her granddaughter. Although feared dead by the family, the grandmother explains that she cannot die, that she will always be there when they need her. Agatha bursts into tears of relief; the antagonism caused by her fear that the grandmother, like her mother, would leave her has dissipated.

In a beautiful visual sequence, the children undergo various stages of growth until, as adults, they no longer need the grandmother, and she returns to the Fantocinni factory. Time passes, and the children, now old, again seek her help. Lovingly she responds, "I will always be there when you need me," and she returns to them again in the family home. *The Electric Grandmother* is a beautiful visual and emotional experience, which has received the acclaim of national television critics.

BEFORE VIEWING

Ask the class what it considers the ideal grandmother. List on the board their suggestions. Challenge their imaginations by asking them what an electric grandmother might be. Offer a hint by telling them the film was made from a Ray Bradbury story.

AFTER VIEWING

Suggestions for discussions and compositions

    a. Compare the electric grandmother with the list that the class has made which is on the board.

b. Ask students to discuss what the grandmother brought to the family that was missing in their lives.

c. Discuss whether it is safer to love a machine than a human being.

d. Ask students what the family gives to the grandmother that she cannot get at the Fantocinni factory.

e. Share with the students the lyrics to the music, which are included on page 52. Ask them what feelings they arouse in them. Have them compose a stanza of their own.

f. Discuss with the class the similarities between the needs of children and very old people.

g. Most human beings want to have someone who will always be there. Explore with students the possibility of having such a person.

h. *The Electric Grandmother* makes students aware that life is change. Discuss with them the changes the family underwent. Should they fear change? How can they prepare for it?

i. Ask students to try and identify with Agatha's fear of losing her grandmother. Was hers a normal reaction? Ask them if they ever feared losing something they valued. What did they do about it?

j. In the first stories about robots, they were often portrayed as machines who wanted to destroy people, conquer the world, etc. In *Star Wars*, director George Lucas's robots, R2D2 and C3PO, contribute enormously to the success of the film because they are so likable. Ask students what qualities they have that make audiences enjoy them so much.

k. Ask students if they could have any kind of robot to serve them, what kind would they choose? What would they have it do for them? Why?

Suggestions for advanced assignments

Ray Bradbury took the title of the story from a poem by Walt Whitman. Here is the opening stanza from "I Sing the Body Electric":

> I sing the Body Electric,
> The armies of those I love engirth me and I engirth them,
> They will not let me off till I go with them, respond to them,
> And discorrupt them, and charge them full with the charge
> of the soul.

a. Ask students to develop a paper explaining the relationship between the stanza from Whitman's poem and *The Electric Grandmother*.

Suggestions for advanced assignments (cont'd)

b. In *2001: A Space Odyssey*, director Stanley Kubrick offers another view. Hal, the robot computer, sings and cries while the two spacemen remain cold and calm even when one of them drifts into space to his death. Discuss with students Kubrick's view of the future of technology. What is his view of the future for humanity?

Basic skills: writing the topic sentence

Ask students to write a paragraph using either of these topic sentences. If they do not have a grandparent, have them choose an older person they are fond of. Be sure that they support their topic sentence by giving details about why they love the person they have chosen. Explain that these are called supporting sentences.

a. I love my grandmother because_____.

b. I love my grandfather because_____.

ADDITIONAL STUDY AIDS

Lyrics from *The Electric Grandmother*

Timothy, Timothy, never you fear
Trouble won't trouble you now that I'm here
I know the secret that grandmothers know
Trust me to love you and help you to grow.

Grandmothers know how to keep away harm
Go off to sleep with your head on my arm.
Dreams will bring happiness all the night through
I'll be here waiting to help them come true.

Turn about, round about, sharing our days
Teaching each other in so many ways.
Tell me the best that you dreamed you could be
I'll be the sunlight that helps you to see.

RELATED RESOURCES

Films

A Family of Strangers   *Portrait of Grandpa Doc*
A Matter of Time   *Things in Their Season*
Peege   *This One's for Dad*

Short stories

Asimov, Isaac. "Robbie the Robot." *The Complete Robot*. Doubleday, 1982

Bradbury, Ray. "I Sing the Body Electric." *The Stories of Ray Bradbury*. Alfred A. Knopf, 1978

Books for young adults

Heinlein, Robert A. *Friday*. Holt, 1982

Kornhaber, Arthur, and Kenneth L. Woodward. *Grandparents/Grandchildren: The Vital Connection*. Anchor Press, 1981

Krasnoff, Barbara. *Robots: Reel to Real*. Arco Publishing, 1982

Rutland, Jon. *Exploring the World of Robots*. Warwick Press, 1979

EQUALITY
(60 min, c, $696/65 two days, Best Films, 1979)

THEMES
The demand for equality among all racial, sexual, political, age, and economic groups in the United States. Defining equality. Can we achieve equality?

CURRICULUM AREAS
History, psychology, sociology, contemporary problems, humanities, language arts, ethnic studies, values

SYNOPSIS
Most Americans take the concept of equality for granted. After all, it was established as a national goal in the Declaration of Independence. We seldom define, however, what we mean by equality. Do we really have equality of race, lifestyle, age, and economic opportunity? *Equality* is almost overwhelming in its ability to stimulate composition and discussion. Without editorializing, it examines these controversial issues. Interviews are intercut with animation and with scenes of such diverse activities as a KKK meeting, a commune in southern Missouri, the National Socialist Peoples' Party, and a debate between Gloria Steinem and Marabel Morgan. National figures and lesser-known citizens speak for the aged, the poor, blacks, American Indians, Japanese-Americans, Jews, gays, women, and children. The viewer is struck by the enormity of the problem the country faces in trying to reconcile these sometimes conflicting, often strident, demands for equality.

The film demands that one think. In the process, values are developed and ideas clarified. In the present atmosphere of narcissism, the final words of the narrator are significant: "As we search for equality, we discover that part of the solution lies within each of us."

BEFORE VIEWING
Read this excerpt from the Declaration of Independence aloud to the class:

> ....We hold these truths to be self-evident, that all men are created equal, that they are endowed by their Creator with certain inalienable Rights, that among these are Life, Liberty, and the pursuit of Happiness.
> —Congress, July 4, 1776

Discuss with the class equality from the perspective of the Declaration of Independence. Do we all have an equal opportunity for life? Liberty? The pursuit of happiness? Raise some questions with the class that will make them ponder these ideas. Infant mortality among babies born on Indian reservations is seven times higher than for the Anglo population of the United States, for example. Have they had an equal opportunity? Is there equal justice among people threatened with the loss of liberty? Do people receive the same sentence throughout the United States when accused of the same crime? Is there an equal chance for happiness? Do we discriminate because of age? Sex? Race? Appearance? Economic background? The class will realize that even defining *equality* is difficult, perhaps impossible. The confusion of the class is mirrored by the bewildering array of demands and opposing statements by the groups in the film. It should help to reinforce the idea that there are no easy solutions to the problem of equality.

AFTER VIEWING

Suggestions for discussions and compositions

a. Discuss with students the view that equality would mean the destruction of our society. Is this view contradictory to the Preamble? What do people who hold this view mean? Do they agree with them?

b. Do students think people are always going to be in conflict? Can they ever learn to work together for their mutual benefit?

c. Foster a dialogue with students about Marabel Morgan's statement: "Your husband was born to be a conqueror, to make decisions, and if you [women] do it you are robbing him of his very nature." Do they agree that men are *born* to be conquerors or is this a culturally induced belief of some people?

d. Explain to students that feminists believe that strip-teasing is degrading to the person because it makes the individual a sex object rather than a human being. Strip-teasers defend their right to perform in that role if they wish. Do they agree?

e. Former senator Fred Harris of Oklahoma has said, "If we can get the rich off welfare by stopping the tax subsidies, we can get this country back to work." Ask the class what this means. They will have to research the statistics regarding tax subsidies, the so-called tax loopholes.

f. Pauline London says that, "The U.S. government owes the black people a living whether anybody agrees or not." This statement angers many people. Challenge students to look at it from her perspective, even though they may not agree with her. Ask them to remember that blacks were the only people brought here against their will.

g. Do students believe that everyone should be forced to retire at age 65?

h. It has not been very long since students were children. Do they think that they were deprived of any rights because they were children?

i. The narrator says that, "At least part of the solution lies within each of us." Discuss with the class his meaning. Do students agree with

Suggestions for discussions and compositions (cont'd)

> him? Can people change their attitudes? Do students know of anyone who has?

j. For one person's definition of equality read Sydney J. Harris's fine essay, "Identity Is Not Equality." Do students agree with him?

Suggestions for advanced assignments

Require students to choose one of the following quotations and develop a response in writing that explains the statement. They can agree or disagree with it, but must support their ideas.

> Democracy, which is a charming form of government, full of variety and disorder, and dispensing a sort of equality to equals and unequals alike.
>
> — Plato (428-348 B.C.)

> Equality and justice, the two great distinguishing characteristics of democracy, follow inevitably from the conception of men, all men, as rational and spiritual beings.
>
> — Robert M. Hutchins
> Former president, University of Chicago

> Together, blacks and whites, can move our country beyond racism and create for the benefit of all of us an open society, one that assures freedom, justice, and full equality for all.
>
> — Whitney Young
> Former director, Urban League

ADDITIONAL STUDY AIDS

People appearing in the film include the following:

Gloria Steinem, feminist and publisher of *Ms.* magazine

Marabel Morgan, author of *The Total Woman*, opponent of feminism

Commander Matt Koehl, National Socialist White Peoples' Party

The Rev. Jesse Jackson, minister and civil rights spokesman

Jeremy Rifkin, Peoples' Bicentennial Committee

Fred Harris, former United States senator from Oklahoma

Sol Davidson, businessman

Pauline London, Welfare Rights Organization

Herbert J. Gans, author of *More Equality*

Michael Novak, Executive Director, Ethnic Millions, Polish Action Committee

Maggie Kuhn, founder of the Gray Panthers (a senior citizens group)

Lisa Richette, Judge, advocate of childrens' rights

Kathleen Kinkade, East Wind Commune, Missouri

RELATED RESOURCES

Short story

Parker, Dorothy. "The Standard of Living." *Tell Me a Story*. McGraw-Hill, 1957

Books

Broom, Leonard. *The Inheritance of Inequality*. Routledge and Kagan Paul, Limited, 1980

Dalphin, John R. *The Persistence of Social Inequality in America*. Schenkman Publishing Company, 1982

Gans, Herbert. *More Equality*. Random House, 1974

Katz, Nick, and Mary L. Katz. *A Passion for Equality: George Wiley and the Movement*. W. W. Norton & Company, 1977

Lewis, Michael. *The Culture of Inequality*. University of Massachusetts Press, 1978

Wattenberg, William. *All Men Are Created Equal*. Wayne State University, 1966

FAMILY OF STRANGERS

(Full version: 46 min, c, $625/50, Learning Corporation of America, 1980; edited version: 31 min, c, $450/40, Learning Corporation of America, 1980)

THEMES

Learning to become a family. The importance of communication.

CURRICULUM AREAS

Sociology, family living, psychology, language arts, guidance, values

SYNOPSIS

The marriage of two previously married adults can be enormously complicated when either or both bring children into the new relationship. Jealousies, slights, and criticisms that might go unnoticed under other circumstances assume major importance when strangers are faced with intimate family living. The marriage of Dominic Ginetti (Danny Aiello), widowed father of Ginger and Roseanne, to Marie Mills (Maria Tucci), divorced mother of Carrie, creates just such a strained situation.

Petty incidents among the girls escalate rapidly into major ones, accompanied by arguments, name-calling, tears, and even a physical battle between Carrie and Ginger. When Ginger breaks Carrie's beloved treasure box, the family is truly divided. Shocked by the first real argument between the parents, the girls draw closer together, but the truce is broken for Carrie when Dominic announces plans to adopt her. In fury and desperation, she slaps him. The next day she is too ill to go to school.

Dominic, who has stayed at home to be with her, produces the treasure box expertly repaired. Later, following lunch and an outing at the park, he tells Carrie that he respects her wish not to be adopted. At home a happy and reassured Carrie teaches Dominic to dance. The strangers have begun to be a family.

Divorce and its ramifications are of major concern to many students. The film is useful in psychology, sociology, family living, language arts, guidance, and values. It can serve as reading enrichment for younger students because it is based on Betty Bates's popular book, *Bugs in Your Ears.*

BEFORE VIEWING

Invite the class to discuss their ideas about what constitutes a family. What is a stranger? Write the title of the film on the board. Is it possible for strangers to be a family? What do they think the film is about?

AFTER VIEWING

Do the Ginettis fit their definitions of a family? Do they think they ever will? What was really keeping them apart? Was it just that they were strangers?

Suggestions for discussions and compositions

a. Communicate to the class that sometimes our less-than-perfect behaviors are not caused by incidents or situations that seem to have brought them on. The real cause may be hidden from us in our subconscious. What may have been the covert reasons for the conduct of the Ginettis and Carrie? Discuss each person individually.

b. Ask students how some of these hidden feelings might have been resolved if the family members had been able to talk openly with each other. Would this have lessened the conflict?

c. Do all families have similar conflicts even though there may be no divorce in the family? Ask the class if there are strangers in their families.

d. Some of the students may have been in situations similar to that of the Ginettis. Are there any positive experiences they can share with the class?

e. Ask students to write a paragraph that begins with these words:

   From my parents I have learned_____

f. Carrie worries about her real father and refuses to accept that he is an alcoholic or that he will not return to her mother and her. Have students pretend that they are Carrie and write a letter to the father expressing their feelings.

g. If students were psychologists with a family counseling practice, what advice would they offer to the Ginettis and Carrie? Ask them to discuss their recommendations for each person as an individual and for the family as a unit.

h. As *Dear Abby* you receive the following letters. Respond to them making sure that you answer all parts of the question.*

   Dear Abby,

   My name is Carrie Mills. My mother just got married for the second time. She married a monster named Dominic. He wants to adopt me, but I don't like him or his two daughters. In fact, I don't want to live with them. Should I run away? Should I try to find my real father and live with him? Should I go to court and try to keep Dominic from adopting me?

   Angry About Being Adopted

---

*Dear Abby assignments by John Matoian, Scholastic Productions.

Suggestions for discussions and compositions (cont'd)

Dear Abby,

My name is Marie Mills Ginetti. Ginetti is my new married name. I am happy as a lark but I have a problem. My husband's two daughters resent me. They simply refuse to accept me. Do you have any insight into why they dislike me so much? Do you have any suggestions as to what I can do to help them?

A New Mama

Dear Abby,

My name is Dominic Ginetti and I am the proud papa of three daughters. The trouble is the three girls don't get along. You see, two of them are mine; the third is a lovely girl I want to adopt. How can I get them to stop fighting? How can I get them to accept one another? Should I go ahead and pursue this adoption? Will this solve my problem and theirs?

A Puzzled Pop

i. Have students ask their mothers or fathers to write a paragraph about what they are really like. They should then bring it to school and write their reactions to them.

j. Ask students to be a perfect son or daughter or brother or sister from Monday through Thursday. They should be polite, obedient, helpful, and agreeable. On Friday they should share their experiences with the class or present them in writing.

k. From magazines or other materials, students can assemble a collage that demonstrates their conceptions of *family.*

Basic skills: using comparison and contrast, compound sentences, semicolons, and coordinate conjunctions

a. Discuss the film with emphasis on comparison and contrast.

b. Explain the use of the semicolon and of the conjunctions *and* and *but* in joining independent clauses. Emphasize that the clauses must be related.

c. Duplicate and distribute the next exercise:

A Family of Strangers

Directions: Study the following situations that occur in the film. Write two independent clauses that together describe the situation. Combine the two clauses with a semicolon, followed by *and* or *but*. Use each conjunction at least twice. Capitalize the first word of the first clause and put a period at the conclusion of the second clause to form a complete sentence.

Examples:

1. What Carrie told her mother about Marie's appearance as she dressed for her wedding. What Marie answered.

    Carrie told her mother she looked beautiful ; Marie didn't think so.

2. What Carrie wanted to do with her plants Ginger's attitude about the plants

    _____

3. Carrie's opinion of her father What her father was really like

    _____

4. Carrie is Marie's daughter Whose daughters are Ginger and Rose?

    _____

5. Marie's offer when Carrie was sick Dominic's action at the same time

    _____

6. Dominic wanted to adopt Carrie How she felt about it

    _____

7. Carrie got the drumstick at dinner What Rose did

    _____

8. Dominic offered to repair the treasure box What Carrie thought of the idea

    _____

9. Dominic returned the repaired treasure box to Carrie How she felt about it

    _____

10. Marie asked the girls to do the dishes How they responded

    _____

RELATED RESOURCES

Books for young adults

Nonfiction

Angell, Judie. *What's Best for You.* Bradbury Press, 1981

Bradley, Buff. *Where Do I Belong?* Addison-Wesley Publishing Company, 1982

Gardner, Richard, M.D. *The Boys' and Girls' Book of Divorce.* Bantam Books, 1982

Gardner, Richard, M.D. *The Parent's Book of Divorce.* Bantam Books, 1982

Jackson, Michael, and Jessica Jackson. *Your Father's Not Coming Home Anymore.* Ace Books, 1982

Rofes, Eric, ed. *The Kids' Book of Divorce.* Vintage Books, 1982

St. George, Judith. *Do You See What I See?* Putnam, 1982

Fiction

Donovan, John. *I'll Get There, It Better Be Worth the Trip.* Harper & Row, 1969

Godden, Rumer. *The Battle of Villa Fiorita.* Viking, 1963

Holland, Isabelle. *Of Love and Death and Other Journeys.* Lippincott, 1975

Peck, Richard. *Father Figure.* Viking, 1978

Wells, Rosemary. *None of the Above.* Avon Books, 1974

FOREVER YOUNG

(58 min, c, $750/60, Learning Corporation of America, 1981)

THEMES

Aging. The importance of a positive outlook and of having interests as one grows older. Thoughts of the old on illness, sex, and death.

CURRICULUM AREAS

Language arts, psychology, sociology, gerontology, values

SYNOPSIS

In this youth-worshipping culture, most of us share a common fear of aging. To examine this phobia, an Academy Award-winning filmmaker went directly to a group of people who are experts on the subject of aging—all are over the age of 66. The group includes the late Roger Baldwin, 93, founder of the American Civil Liberties Union; Fred Ennis, 82, sky diver; Norma Stoop, 71, film critic; Abe Lass, 72, author and musician; Eddie Allen, 83, balloonist; Frank Keyser, 71, sculptor; Max Lerner, 76, columnist, and 19 other equally engaging oldsters. All of them speak candidly about their enjoyment of life, health, happiness, and sex, as well as about their perspectives on aging and death.

Although they admit there are problems connected with aging, they do not brood about them or let them interfere with their delight in life. These remarks are typical: "I made up my mind that I'm not going to sit in a chair rocking back and forth and listening to the sound of my arteries hardening." "My friends sometimes say, 'You've never grown up. You're still a child.' I think that's a compliment." "Age is a relative thing. I'm unwilling to concede that a given date can determine whether one is young or old." Probably the most significant remark of all is, "I don't feel I'm doing well for someone my age. I don't want anyone to think of me as a 69-year-old who is doing well. I want them to think of me as a person who is doing well."

The film is an engaging presentation of people and ideas. Although each person is different, all demonstrate the same positive qualities—looking forward, being interested in their own lives and the lives of others, and taking a straightforward approach to life. The contribution of each individual is skillfully woven into the main and secondary themes of the film and each has sharp dramatic impact.

The fear of aging is such a common phenomenon that the film can be of enormous help to people of all ages. As the well-known film critic Judith Crist wrote in her *Los Angeles Times* review, "*Forever Young* is a paen to growing old, sung by those who know all about it. Invigorating is the word for this film. It's a vacation—or a sort of adrenalin—in itself. In our society, wherein face-cream ads console one about aged skin at age thirty—it's a high just to spend 58 minutes with people who feel that life begins at sixty—and gets better thereafter."

Forever Young
Photograph courtesy of Learning Corporation of America

The film is stimulating and reassuring for all classes, particularly gerontology, humanities, psychology, language arts, family living, sociology, guidance, and values.

BEFORE VIEWING

Ask the class this question, "What does it mean to be old?" Try to get the students to define the term *old*. Ask the students what old people are like. Don't challenge their ideas but write them on the blackboard. Common misconceptions include:

You can't teach them anything new.

They complain a lot.

They always talk about the past.

They are weak physically and can't do much.

They are sick a lot.

They don't like young people, particularly teenagers.

They are afraid of new ideas or activities.

They don't know what to do with their time.

They are usually crankier than younger people.

They're always lonely.

The class will probably have other suggestions to add to the list. Before you leave the subject, ask for a show of hands in response to, "How many of you ever think about getting old?" If the response is open, ask if any will volunteer how they feel when they think about growing old. Common responses include "I'm afraid," "I don't want to," and "I put it out of my mind because it scares me." Reassure them that these are common responses, and tell them that they are going to see a film about a group of older people who are happy with their lives.

AFTER VIEWING

Suggestions for discussions and compositions

a. Ask the class to compare the people in the film to the list of misconceptions on the board. Do they seem to fit the stereotypes? How are they different?

b. Which person in the film did they enjoy most? What qualities does that person possess that makes her or him interesting?

c. Ask students what advice these people emphasized in dealing with the problems of growing older. It works for them. Would it work for every older person?

d. Inquire about which person was a surprise to the students. Why?

Suggestions for discussions and compositions (cont'd)

e. Discuss with them if they have learned anything from observing and listening to these people.

f. Norma Stoop, the film critic, expresses her thoughts about the unimportance of other people's opinions. Do students agree or disagree with her?

g. What do students think is the best way to deal with the problems of aging?

h. Henry W. Longfellow once said, "For age is an opportunity no less than youth itself." Explore with the class Longfellow's meaning. Do they agree with him?

i. Ask students to describe the kind of older person they think they will be.

j. Inquire why it is important to prepare when one is younger for the years when one will be old.

k. Discuss with the class if the film changed their attitudes about growing older.

Suggestions for advanced assignments

a. Here are some statements made by the people in the film. (Ashley Montague's fine book, *Growing Young*, substantiates both physiologically and psychologically, the ideas expressed by the oldsters in the film.) Ask students to choose one and comment on it in as much depth as possible.

> "The society is so youth-oriented that there's a stigma about growing old."

> "You solve the problems of retirement, not in retirement. You solve the problems before you retire, and the life that you live prepares you for that retirement."

> "Age is a relative thing. I'm unwilling to concede that a given date can determine whether one is young or old."

> "My friends sometimes say, 'You've never grown up. You're still a child.' I think that's a compliment."

> "I look on the idea of dying as one more big adventure because none of us really knows what's going to happen, and, boy, it might be something ... it might be something fantastic."

"Without love there really is no life ... no life that's of any consequence."

    b.   Reproduce "Myths and Facts about Aging" on page 68, prepared by the National Council on Aging. Let the students take a test on their misconceptions before they see the facts. Discuss the facts as opposed to the misconceptions.

Basic skills: using adjectives

Explain that adjectives are words that describe. Ask students to list five adjectives for each of these older people:

Norma Stoop, 71, film critic (she dances in the disco)
1. _____ 2. _____ 3. _____ 4. _____ 5. _____

Eddie Allen, 83, balloonist
1. _____ 2. _____ 3. _____ 4. _____ 5. _____

Sari Dienes, 81 (she has on a headband)
1. _____ 2. _____ 3. _____ 4. _____ 5. _____

Fred Ennis, 82, skydiver
1. _____ 2. _____ 3. _____ 4. _____ 5. _____

List five adjectives that describe all of these people:
1. _____ 2. _____ 3. _____ 4. _____ 5. _____

ADDITIONAL STUDY AIDS

Myths and Facts about Aging

Myth: Older people experience a loss in learning ability.
Fact: Learning ability does not decline significantly with age. In fact, vocabulary and conceptual skills often grow after age sixty.

Myth: Most older citizens are set in their ways.
Fact: Being "old" means that one has survived and it is impossible to survive without adaptation. Today's older persons have lived through more technological and social change than any group in history.

Myth: Workers find it increasingly harder to perform their jobs as they grow older.
Fact: Studies show that older workers have less absenteeism, fewer on-the-job accidents, are more satisfied with their jobs, and are no less efficient.

Myth: A lot of older persons live in institutions.
Fact: Most older persons live in family settings. Four of five men and three of five women live with their spouse or another person.

Myth: Most older women are married and most older men are widowers.
Fact: Exactly the opposite. Only 39 percent of older women are married, while nearly 79 percent of older men are.

Myth: A loss of sexual vigor inevitably occurs after age sixty-five.
Fact: There is no physiological basis for the loss of interest in sex after one ages. Sexual vigor can be maintained until death unless there are health reasons for loss.

Myth: Most older people are confined physically or require some type of unusual care.
Fact: Only 10 percent of the people over sixty-five are confined in any serious way. Despite health problems that do develop in older age, most older people do not consider themselves seriously handicapped in pursuing their daily activities.

Myth: There are more old women than there are old men.
Fact: The current proportion is sixty-nine males to one-hundred females over sixty-five years of age.

Myth: The proportion of older citizens in the low-income group is no different than in the society at large.
Fact: The elderly can generally be described as a low-income group. The proportion of the poor that are elderly is greater than the proportion of the poor in the general population.

Myth: Senility is the cause of most of the loss of mental ability that occurs in old age.
Fact: What is called "senility" may actually be the by-product of anemia, malnutrition, or infection. Most elderly diagnosed as having functional disturbances can be helped.

The above information was obtained from the National Council on Aging.

RELATED RESOURCES

Films

Chillysmith Farm	*Portrait of Grandpa Doc*
Close Harmony	*A Private Life*
The Lost Phoebe	*The Shopping Bag Lady*
Peege	*Sunshine's on the Way*
Piece of Cake	

Short story

Parker, Dorothy. "Wonderful Old Gentlemen." *Collected Stories of Dorothy Parker*. Modern Library, 1945

Books

Kumin, Maxine. *Our Time Here Will Be Brief*. Viking Press, 1981

Mandel, Evelyn. *The Art of Aging*. Winston Press, 1981

Montague, Ashley. *Growing Young*. McGraw-Hill, 1981

Pritchett, V. S. *The Turn of the Years*. Random House, 1982

Robey, Harriet. *There's a Dance in the Old Dame Yet*. G. K. Hall, 1982

GYM PERIOD
(14 min, c, $300/20, Teleketics, 1975)

THEMES
Self-determination. Sports as American myth. America as a competitive society. Motivation.

CURRICULUM AREAS
Language arts, psychology, physical education, sociology, values

SYNOPSIS
Although as a film *Gym Period* is somewhat studied and pretentious, as a psychological study of motivation, self-affirmation, competition, and failure, it is richly involving. Almost all students can identify with it because the situations and ideas are familiar.

"After three years some of you still haven't made it to the top yet," the crew-cut, overweight coach tells his high school gym class as he points to the ropes dangling from the gym rafters. As names are called, boys scramble toward the top, are timed, and pass or fail. For Jerome, miserably aware that the coach was referring to him, it means another humiliating display of his inability to keep up with the others. Again he struggles toward the rafters, fails, and descends to the jeers of the other boys and the disappointment of the coach.

Given a choice of other activities, the boys turn gleefully to "murder ball," a game that involves standing inside a circle while others throw the ball at you as hard as possible. Filmed during an actual game, several of the boys who are struck hold their heads in pain. Jerome doesn't participate in the throwing, but stands uneasily inside the circle until the game ends.

Meanwhile, a white-suited gymnast, older and very poised, enters the gym to practice on the parallel bars. He is superb — perfection. As the class leaves, Jerome continues to watch the gymnast. Alone in the gym except for the swinging white figure, Jerome struggles painfully up the rope again. A few feet from the top he gasps, groans, and falls. The gymnast continues practicing.

BEFORE VIEWING
a.   Ask the class to make a list of words, phrases, or sentences that describe themselves. (The list is not to be seen by anyone else.)

b.   Ask them to make another list describing the way others expect them to be, for example, to be smarter, more aggressive, better at football, neater in appearance or roomkeeping, or seeking a career goal that the student may not want, etc.

c.   Ask them to make a third list of the qualities they would like to have that they think they do not have at present. They should put aside the three lists.

AFTER VIEWING

Suggestions for discussions and compositions

a. Explore with students what they think really happened at the end. What does the gymnast symbolize? Why does he continue to practice?

b. The coach is not a cruel or a sadistic man. Ask students why he insists that Jerome keep trying. Is it really important that Jerome climb the rope in x minutes?

c. Ask students if repeated failure causes a person to believe that he or she is a failure. Did the coach help or damage Jerome emotionally?

d. Should rope climbing be competitive? Are there any areas of accomplishment that should not be competitive?

e. Should one accept competition without question?

f. Ask students to write a composition about what their lives would be like if there were no competition. How would they change? What changes would be most noticeable?

g. What do students think of competition with oneself? If Jerome had merely improved, would that have been an accomplishment that should be recognized?

h. America is a country that supposedly values individuality. Ask students if Jerome was being allowed to be an individual? Should he have been? Are there times when individuality is not needed or wanted? Was this such a time?

i. What instincts of human beings does murder ball emphasize? Why did the filmmaker include this sequence? How does it relate to the rest of the film?

j. Discuss if young people should be held accountable for cruelty toward others even though they excuse their behaviors as only jokes. Was the jeering of the students when Jerome failed the climb cruel?

k. How does the filmmaker project the emotions of pride, jealousy, humility, contempt, and satisfaction without dialogue?

l. Ask students to write a paper about a time that someone else set goals for them. Did they reach them? If not, how did they react to failure? What did they learn from the experience?

m. Did Jerome have a superior talent or skill in another area? What do the class think it might be?

n. Have students laughed at others in their gym class who are not as successful? Did they think about how others may feel? How did they feel? Have others laughed at them? How did they feel? Do they look forward to a class where they do not do as well as most of the other students? How do they handle it?

Suggestions for discussions and compositions (cont'd)

    o.   What is the difference between a dream and a realistic goal? Are they living someone else's dream for them?

    p.   Ask the class to write a paragraph beginning with this sentence:

        "The trouble with being a teenager is...."

    q.   Ask students if Jerome made a mistake in trying to copy the gymnast's accomplishments? Would it have been better if he had tried to copy the gymnast's attitude? Do they emulate the attitudes of the people they admire?

    r.   Some time ago, sports philosophy was, "It's not whether you win or lose. It's how you play the game." Now the accepted maxim seems to be, "Winning isn't everything. It's the only thing." Discuss with the class if this change in attitude is an improvement. Are more people participating in sports because of it? Are sports themselves better? More interesting? More rewarding to participate in? To watch?

    s.   Have the students privately compare the three lists they made before the film. Draw heavy circles around the important areas of guilt, frustration, and failure. Have each student decide which goals are not in tune with his or her own feelings and desires. Draw heavy lines through these.

    t.   List on the board the heroes of the class. (See the *World Almanac* poll on the next page.) Have the group discuss why they consider these people heroes.

    u.   What does the class know about these people as persons? (The purpose of this exercise is to help the class understand how much fantasy contributes to the making of heroes.) What do they know about them except for their good looks or talent? What important qualities do they know nothing about? Ask the class to compare these people to the third list that each student made. Are there similarities and disparities?

Basic skills: writing a paragraph

    a.   Ask the class to state what they think the intent of the filmmaker is in *Gym Period*. What important idea does he want them to contemplate? Be sure a student doesn't say, "I think the intent is...." They should say, for example, "When we are forced to meet goals that someone else has established for us, our personal development may be impeded."

    b.   Have students list three scenes that they believe support their statements about the filmmaker's intent.

        1. _____

        2. _____

        3. _____

c. Ask them to use the statement of intent as their topic sentence, then develop a paragraph that uses the three scenes they have chosen as their supporting sentences. Then ask them to add a sentence of conclusion.

ADDITIONAL STUDY AIDS

Heroes of Young America: Third Annual Poll*

Top hero

Alan Alda, TV and film actor, best known for his role as "Hawkeye" Pierce on the TV series, *MASH*; won an Emmy as best actor in 1982.

Others

Clint Eastwood, actor, recently starred in *Every Which Way But Loose, Firefox,* and *Honky-Tonk Man.*

Bo Derek, star of *10* and *Tarzan and the Ape Man.*

Tom Selleck, star of the series *Magnum*, first runner-up.

Stephanie Powers, star of the series, *Hart to Hart.*

Rick Springfield, rock star, appears on the soap opera, *General Hospital.*

Pat Benatar, cabaret singer turned rock singer, highest vote-getter among the women.

Carol Burnett, TV and film actress.

Sugar Ray Leonard, welter-weight boxing champion.

Tracy Austin, tennis player.

Walter Cronkite, TV journalist and former anchorman, CBS "Evening News."

Barbara Walters, TV journalist.

Jim Davis, cartoonist, creator of the lasagna-loving cat, "Garfield."

Judy Blume, author, primarily of young adult novels.

Neil Armstrong, former astronaut.

Sandra Day O'Connor, first woman on the Supreme Court.

---

*From *World Almanac and Book of Facts* (New York: Newspaper Enterprise Association, 1983).

RELATED RESOURCES

Films

An Acquired Taste
Beauty Knows No Pain
Crossbar
The Flashettes
Horse Latitudes
Men's Lives

Psychling
Sign of Victory
Survival Run
This One's for Dad
Women in Sports

Short stories

Cain, James M. "Queen of Love and Beauty." *The Baby in the Icebox and Other Short Fiction*. Holt, Rinehart, 1981

Fitzgerald, F. Scott. "The Third Casket." *The Price Was High: The Last Uncollected Stories of F. Scott Fitzgerald*. Harcourt Brace Jovanovich, 1981

O'Rourke, Frank. "The Heady World Series." *Baseball 3000*. Elsevier/Nelson Books, 1979

THE HANGMAN
(12 min, c, $215/22, CRM/McGraw-Hill Films, 1963)

THEMES
The responsibility to protest injustice. The interdependency of all humanity: the protection of the rights of one is the protection of the rights of all. Tyranny establishes itself when citizens are fearful, prejudiced, or apathetic.

CURRICULUM AREAS
Sociology, history, psychology, humanities, language arts, guidance, values, filmmaking

SYNOPSIS
Using Maurice Ogden's gripping poem, this brilliantly animated film, narrated by actor Herschel Bernardi, tells in ballad form about a gaunt, ominous creature known as the Hangman who comes to a small town in rural America. When he first plants his small gallows tree in the town square, the citizens are unconcerned because he assures them that the intended victim is "not one of us." Sure that the executioner will leave when he has claimed the life of the alien, the townspeople are surprised to find him still in the town square in the morning. Laughing, he assures them that the previous day's hanging was just to "stretch the rope."

When a citizen cries, "Murderer," the Hangman seizes him while the others shrink in fear. His third victim is a Jew, the fourth a black. Each time he claims a victim, the survivors, pleased that they are unharmed, fail to act on the growing list of injustices, secure in their belief that the Hangman will leave when he has found the victim he seeks.

As the scaffold grows larger and the number of victims increases, all questions and objections cease. At last there is no one left in the town but the Hangman and the narrator of the story. When the Hangman calls his name, he goes to the town square confidently because he has always given the executioner complete obedience and loyalty. But as the Hangman stretches the rope once more, the man cries, "You have tricked me, Hangman. The scaffold was built for *other* men." "No," says the Hangman, "First the alien, then the Jew. I did no more than you let me do."

As the Hangman places the rope around his neck, the man listens desperately for someone to cry, "Stay." No sound is heard in the silent, empty square.

The film is frightening, but its emotional power is undeniable. We readily see that we are the citizens, too frightened, apathetic, or unaware to speak out against the respectable abuses that we see everywhere, whether political, social, economic, or attitudinal. The film shocks us into a new awareness of the interdependency of all human beings.

The Hangman is one of the most brilliantly animated short films ever made.

The Hangman
Photograph courtesy of CRM/McGraw-Hill Films

BEFORE VIEWING

Talk to the class about the responsibility of the individual to the group and vice versa. What do each of them owe the group, if anything? What does the group owe the individual? If possible, personalize the discussion by using the hypothetical example of a student who has been treated unjustly. What should the group do? Would it, in fact, do anything?

If this discussion goes well, talk to the group about Adolph Hitler and his persecution of the Jews. How was one man able to imprison and murder six to nine million Jews? Why did many Germans ignore these atrocities?

AFTER VIEWING

Suggestions for discussions and compositions

a. Ask students what fears and prejudices of the townspeople the Hangman used to manipulate them?

b. The Hangman knew that most people believe that terrible things happen only to other people, not to them. Discuss with the class how he used this common feeling to his advantage. Can they think of other examples where people believed *it* would happen only to someone else?

c. Another human reaction is to want to avoid confrontation or violence if possible. Explore appeasement with the class. Ask them how the Hangman used this principle to carry out his deadly plans?

d. Can students point out any examples of suffering in this country because people are too uncaring or apathetic to try to correct them?

e. The Bible says that we are our brother's keeper. Discuss with students how they can reconcile this with the admonition mind your own business. Which maxim do they follow?

f. How far should one person go to protect the rights and freedoms of another?

g. Have students study Maurice Ogden's poem, "The Hangman." Tell them to use the same town, the same ballad style, the Hangman, the townspeople, and the first person narrator to create their own poems, but reverse the outcome of the story. What would they do to defeat the Hangman?

h. Can they apply the theme of this film to school, politics, business, civil rights, and ecology?

Suggestions for advanced assignments

a. Throughout history the theme that we are responsible for each other has been a subject for novelists, playwrights, essayists, and poets. Here, from *Hamlet* is one of William Shakespeare's musings on the subject:

> Thus conscience does make cowards of us all;
> And thus the native hue of resolution
> Is sicklied o'er with the pale cast of thought,
> And enterprises of great pitch and moment,
> With this regard, their currents turn awry
> And lose the name of action.

b. The following quotation is attributed to Martin Niemoller, a clergyman who became a hero when he was sent to Dachau by the Nazis:

> In Germany they came first for the Communists and I didn't speak up because I wasn't a Communist. Then they came for the Jews and I didn't speak up because I wasn't a Jew.
>
> Then they came for the trade unionists and I didn't speak up because I wasn't a trade unionist.
>
> Then they came for the Catholics and I didn't speak up because I was a Protestant.
>
> Then they came for me and by that time there was no one left to speak for me.

c. Ask students to research this theme of responsibility in literature. They should locate works that appeal to them and share them with the class.

ADDITIONAL STUDY AIDS

The Hangman

1.

Into our town the Hangman came,
Smelling of gold and blood and flame,-
And he paced our bricks with a diffident air
And built his frame on the courthouse square.

The scaffold stood by the courthouse side,
Only as wide as the door was wide;
A frame as tall, or little more,
Than the capping sill of the courthouse door.

And we wondered whenever we had the time,
Who the criminal, what the crime,
The Hangman judged with the yellow twist
Of knotted hemp in his busy fist.

And innocent though we were, with dread
We passed those eyes of buckshot lead;
Till one cried: "Handman, who is he
For whom you raise the gallows-tree?"

Then a twinkle grew in the buckshot eye,
And he gave us a riddle instead of reply:
"He who serves me best," said he,
"Shall earn the rope on the gallows-tree."

And he stepped down, and laid his hand
On a man who came from another land-
And we breathed again, for another's grief
At the Hangman's hand was our relief.

And the gallows-frame on the courthouse lawn
By tomorrow's sun would be struck and gone.
So we gave him way, and no one spoke
Out of respect for his hangman's cloak.

2.

The next day's sun looked mildly down
On roof and street in our quiet town
And, stark and black in the morning air,
The gallows-tree on the courthouse square.

And the Hangman stood at his usual stand
With the yellow hemp in his busy hand;
With his buckshot eye and his jaw like a pike
And his air so knowing and businesslike.

And we cried: "Hangman, have you not done,
Yesterday with the alien one?"
Then we fell silent and stood amazed:
"Oh, not for him was the gallows raised...."

He laughed a laugh as he looked at us:
"... Did you think I'd gone to all this fuss
To hang one man? That's a thing I do
To stretch the rope when the rope is new."

Then one cried, "Murderer!" One cried, "Shame!"
And into our midst the Hangman came
To that man's place. "Do you hold," said he,
"With him that was meat for the gallows-tree?"

And he laid his hand on that man's arm,
And we shrank back in quick alarm,
And we gave him way, and no one spoke
Out of the fear of his hangman's cloak.

That night we saw with dread surprise
The Hangman's scaffold had grown in size.
Fed by the blood beneath the chute
The gallows-tree had taken root;

Now as wide, or a little more
Than the steps that led to the courthouse door,
As tall as the writing, or nearly as tall,
Halfway up the courthouse wall.

3.

The third he took — we had all heard tell —
Was a usurer and infidel,
And: "What," said the Hangman, "have you to do
With the gallows-bound, and he a Jew?"

And we cried out: "Is this one he
Who has served you well and faithfully?"
The Hangman smiled: "It's a clever scheme
To try the strength of the gallows-beam."

The fourth man's dark, accusing song
Had scratched our comfort hard and long;
And, "What concern," he gave us back,
"Have you for the doomed — the doomed and black?"

The fifth. The sixth. And we cried again:
"Hangman, Hangman, is this the man?"
"It's a trick," he said, "that we hangmen know
For easing the trap when the trap springs slow."

And so we ceased, and asked no more
As the Hangman tallied his bloody score,
And sun by sun, and night by night,
The gallows grew to monstrous height.

(Poem continues on page 80.)

The wings of the scaffold opened wide
Till they covered the square from side to side;
And the monster cross-beam looking down,
Cast its shadow across the town.

Then through the town the Hangman came
And called in the empty streets my name-
And I looked at the gallows soaring tall
And I thought: "There's no one left at all

For hanging, and so he calls to me
To help pull down the gallows tree."
And I went out with right good hope
To the Hangman's tree and the Hangman's rope.

He smiled at me as I came down
To the courthouse square through the empty town,
And supple and stretched in his busy hand
Was the yellow twist of the hempen strand.

And he whistled his tune as he tried the trap
And it sprang down with a ready snap-
And then with a smile of awful command
He laid his hand upon my hand.

"You tricked me, Hangman!" I shouted then,
"That your scaffold was built for other men ...
And I no henchman of yours," I cried,
"You lied to me, Hangman, foully lied!"

Then a twinkle grew in the bloodshot eye:
"Lied to you? Tricked you?" he said, "Not I.
For I answered straight and I told you true:
The scaffold was raised for none but you."

"For who has served me more faithfully
Than you with your coward's hope?" said he,
"And where are the others that might have stood
Side by side in the common good?"

"Dead," I whispered; and amiably
"Murdered," the Hangman corrected me:
"First the alien, then the Jew ...
I did no more than you let me do."

Beneath the beam that blocked the sky,
None had stood so alone as I-
And the Hangman strapped me, and no voice there
Cried "Stay" for me in the empty square.

—Maurice Ogden

Reprinted by permission of the author.

RELATED RESOURCES

Films

American Parade: With All
Deliberate Speed
Joseph Schultz

Paul Robeson: Tribute to an Artist
Strange Fruit
Travelling Hopefully

HARLAN COUNTY, U.S.A.

(103 min, c, $1350, long-term lease, $150, Cinema 5, 1976)

THEMES

The struggle of deprived people for basic human rights. Relationships among individuals and families in times of stress. Human portraits of people considered expendable in the American industrial system.

CURRICULUM AREAS

Sociology, psychology, economics, labor relations, contemporary problems, language arts, history, filmmaking, women's studies

SYNOPSIS

For many people, unions have now become establishment institutions, fat with pension funds, highly paid leaders, and a suggestion of Mafia connections. Union membership is declining nationally, and people assume that America is largely middle-class with enough largesse for everyone. Some even consider unions passé. *Harlan County* is a stirring reminder that in 1973 many Americans were still struggling for the basic human rights that most of us take for granted: decent housing, adequate health protection and care, and a living wage.

Portraying a classic twentieth-century confrontation between labor and management, the film documents the efforts of 180 coal-mining families to win a United Mine Workers contract at the Brookside mine in Harlan County, Kentucky. The strike began in 1974 after the miners voted to join the UMW, but the Duke Power Company, parent company of the Brookside mine, refused to sign a standard UMW contract. This was the first major labor confrontation in Harlan County since the bloody struggles of the 1930s when five men were killed.

Secure in its size, power, and money, Duke Power used both threats and the law to fight the strikers, and we see both used in the film.

The real beauty of *Harlan County* is that it allows us to know intimately the strikers and their families. Filmmaker Barbara Kopple is overtly on their side, and we see that though the mining families are an abused people, they are eloquent, courageous, and quick of mind and body. Individual portraits are memorable: a tall, gaunt woman who says, "I'm not after a man. I'm after a contract"; the old miner who remembers working ten-hour days for six cents an hour; an emaciated woman with the classically sad face of the chronically deprived, whose voice breaks when she speaks of the losses in her life; a miner with black lung, who is matter-of-fact in accepting his impending death.

It is the women—wives, mothers, daughters, sisters, sweethearts of the miners—who dominate the film. They march, picket, and get jailed, although they want to be tender and attractive, but life has contravened their desires.

Harlan County won the Academy Award as best documentary, the *Emily* as the best of the hundreds of films submitted at the prestigious American Film Festival in 1977, and then won the John Grierson Award for best documentary at the same event. It is a superb achievement.

BEFORE VIEWING

Discuss the topic of strikes with the class. Should people have the right to strike? What groups, if any, should? What actions should be taken before a strike? What if the group believes it has no alternative? What if a group believes its health and safety are threatened? Should people strike for more money?

AFTER VIEWING

Discuss the most memorable people or scenes in the film. This is called image-skimming. Do not comment upon the value of the chosen images because some students find this threatening. If everyone contributes, most of the outstanding scenes will be covered. It is especially important to review a long film such as *Harlan County* because it makes the subsequent assignments easier.

Suggestions for discussions and compositions

a. Ask students to imagine that they are reporters for the *Harlan County Herald* and have been assigned to cover the strike against Duke Power. They are to write a story that presents both sides objectively. They must remember to identify people, places, and things and tell who, when, where, what, and why.

b. Ask the class to write a short sketch giving their impressions of each of these groups: the mine management; the miners; the women; and the local police.

c. Have students write a paragraph describing the person in *Harlan County* that they liked most and reasons for their choice.

d. Have students contribute a eulogy to be read at the funeral of Lawrence Jones, the miner who was killed during the strike.

e. Assign writing a poem. Students should express their feelings about miners. They may write about a Harlan County miner(s) or about coal miners in general.

f. Students should imagine that they are reporters for the *Harlan County Herald* sent to interview one of the miner's wives. They are to list ten questions that they would ask her.

g. Ask students to research the history of coal. What is its importance in our lives? How would our lives be different without it? What alternatives to coal do we have?

h. What are the students' feelings about the mining families of Harlan County? Are they admirable? Lovable? Intelligent? Industrious? Humorous? Do they see their struggle for what they consider basic rights as worthwhile?

Suggestions for discussions and compositions (cont'd)

i. Many national film critics have called the film "a celebration of the human spirit." Discuss with students what the critics mean. Do students agree?

j. Norman Yarborough, head of Eastover mine, said, in observing the women of the striking families, "I would not like to see my wife reverting to this type of behavior." Ask students if there is irony in his remark? Sexism?

k. Even though the strike is settled, filmmaker Barbara Kopple does not end the film at that point. Discuss with students her implication in showing the miners continuing to struggle for other rights.

l. Do students think the film is objective? Is it intended to be? Why?

m. After the sheriff has been reprimanded by striker Lois Scott (whom he has known all of his life), the camera remains on him as he walks across the road to confer with law enforcement. What do students learn about him by watching his walk?

n. Ask students to study the statistics on recorded coal mine disasters in the United States. Although more than 32,596 miners have been killed, significant progress was made after the Kellogg, Idaho, accident in 1972 in which 91 miners were killed. This was attributed to better enforcement of safety regulations. Now the government has moved to decrease the safety requirements as an impediment to industry. Do students think safety requirements should be lowered for this reason?

o. Assign research on important coal mine disasters in the United States or abroad. Ask the class to write a poem or a ballad about one, or a group, of the miners involved.

Suggestions for advanced assignments

a. Black lung, the so-called miner's disease, is a continuing subject of controversy between the miners and the federal government. More than 4,000 miners each year die of black lung. The government pays $824 million a year in benefits to the victims. The present administration is trying to reduce that figure by tightening benefit requirements. In March of 1981, 170,000 members of the UMW walked off their jobs to protest the proposed restrictions and 5,000 miners marched on Washington, D.C. Ask students to research this controversy and report their findings to the class.

b. What should government and corporate liability be for black lung? Is there a pattern of response to worker disability from these organizations? Ask the class to research this controversy and report their findings.

c. In 1976, Joseph Yablonski, who was contesting W. A. (Tony) Boyle for the presidency of the UMW, was murdered, along with his wife and daughter. Boyle was convicted of the murder and is now serving time in prison. This event profoundly affected the Harlan County strike. Assign research about this event and its repercussions in Harlan County and in the nation.

d. Divide the class into groups representing management, miners, miner's families, and the local police. Have each group draw up a list of grievances to be presented at a town meeting.

e. Plan a field trip to a coal mine. If this is not possible, locate someone in the community who is familiar with mines or mining to speak to the class about the problems and hazards of being a miner.

f. Talk to the students about whether they have changed their minds about strikes since the original discussion before the showing of *Harlan County*.

g. Arrange to show the feature film *The Stars Look Down* (1939), which is available from the Museum of Modern Art (see the address in the Appendix) or from Budget Films, 4590 Santa Monica Boulevard, Los Angeles, California 90029. This is a relatively little-known British film similar to *How Green Was My Valley*, but less romanticized. It demonstrates the relationship between government, industry, and labor. *The Stars Look Down* is from a novel by A. J. Cronin, directed by Carol Reed, and stars Sir Michael Redgrave, Margaret Lockwood, and Emlyn Williams.

ADDITIONAL STUDY AIDS

Barbara Kopple

Barbara Kopple, a young New York filmmaker, went to Harlan County, Kentucky, in 1972 with a $9,000 loan and a commitment to make a film about the Miners for Democracy campaign for control of the United Mine Workers. But Kopple became involved with the miners and their families. Four years and $350,000 later she produced this remarkable film, a film as passionate and partisan as it is informative.

As the strike progressed, Kopple made many trips back to New York seeking additional funds for the film. Contributors were various foundations, the United Church of Christ, the United Methodist Church, and dozens of individuals.

What they supported is a film that details the history and present life of the Harlan County mining families, their heritage of unionism, the commitment of the families to the mines, their hopes and dreams. Above all, it captures the people of Harlan County as individuals, with an unusual emphasis on women.

ADDITIONAL STUDY AIDS (cont'd)

Information about Black Lung

Black lung is a disease caused by the accumulation of coal-mine dust in the lungs. At least two forms, simple and complicated, have been identified. The diagnosis of the simple form is made on the basis of Xrays of the patient's lungs and a history of exposure to coal dust. The simple form of black lung is not disabling, does not affect life expectancy, and will not worsen in the absence of further exposure to coal dust, unlike the complicated form which often leads to shortness of breath because of decreased lung function and to premature death.

—Derived from "Black Lung" in
The Encyclopedia Americana vol. 4
(Danbury, CT: Grolier Incorporated, 1981), p. 34

Principal U.S. Mine Disasters*
(From Bureau of Mines, U.S. Department of the Interior)

Note: Prior to 1968, only disasters with losses of 50 or more lives are listed; since 1968, all disasters in which 5 or more were killed are listed. Only those in which 100 or more miners lost their lives are included here.

September 6, 1869	110	Plymouth, Pennsylvania
March 13, 1884	112	Pocahontas, Virginia
January 27, 1891	109	Mount Pleasant, Pennsylvania
January 7, 1892	100	Krebs, Oklahoma
January 1, 1900	200	Scofield, Utah
May 19, 1902	184	Coal Creek, Tennessee
July 10, 1902	112	Johnstown, Pennsylvania
June 30, 1903	169	Hanna, Wyoming
January 25, 1904	179	Cheswick, Pennsylvania
December 6, 1907	361	Monogah, West Virginia
December 19, 1907	239	Jacob's Creek, Pennsylvania
November 28, 1908	154	Marianna, Pennsylvania
November 13, 1909	259	Cherry, Illinois
April 8, 1911	128	Littleton, Alabama
October 22, 1913	263	Dawson, New Mexico

*The last mine disaster in the United States in which more than 40 lives were lost occurred in Kellogg, Idaho, in 1972. There have been 45 other mine disasters judged as major by the United States Bureau of Mines other than those listed here.

April 28, 1914	181	Eccles, West Virginia
March 2, 1915	112	Layland, West Virginia
April 27, 1917	121	Hastings, Colorado
June 8, 1917	162	Butte, Montana
March 25, 1947	111	Centralia, Illinois
December 21, 1951	119	West Frankfort, Illinois

RELATED RESOURCES

Poetry

MacLeod, Norman. "Coal Strikes." *Social Poetry of the 1930's.* Burt Franklin and Company, 1978

Patchen, Kenneth. "May I Ask You a Question, Mr. Youngstown?" *Contemporary Poetry in America.* Random House, 1973

Phillips, Louis. "78 Miners in Mannington, West Virginia." *Traveling America with Today's Poets.* Macmillan, 1977

Short stories

Ball, Bo. "Sideburns." *Editor's Choice: Literature and Graphics from the United States Small Press.* The Spirit That Moves Us Press, 1980

Cain, J. M. "Coal Black." *The Baby in the Icebox and Other Short Fiction.* Holt, Rinehart, 1981

Conroy, Jack. "Down in Happy Hollow." *The Jack Conroy Reader.* Burt Franklin and Company, 1979

Hubbard, L. Ron. "Mine Inspector." *Lives You Wished to Lead But Never Dared: A Series of Stories.* Theta Books, Inc., 1979

Lewis, Richard O. "Black Disaster." *Alfred Hitchcock's Tales to Make Your Teeth Chatter.* Dial Press, 1980

Still, James. "I Love My Rooster." *The Run for the Elbertas.* University Press of Kentucky, 1981

Books for young adults

Bornstein, Jerry. *Unions in Transition.* Messner, 1982

Books for adults

Dreiser, Theodore, et al. *Harlan Miners Speak: Report on Terrorism in the Kentucky Coal Fields.* Da Capo, 1970

RELATED RESOURCES (cont'd)

Books for adults (cont'd)

Husband, Joseph. *A Year in a Coal Mine.* Arno Press, 1977

Lloyd, A. A. *Come All Ye Bold Miners: Ballads and Songs of the Coalfields.* Humanities, 1978

Witt, Matt. *In Our Blood: Four Coal Mining Families.* Highlander, 1979

HIROSHIMA-NAGASAKI, AUGUST 1945
(16 min, b & w, $300/35, Museum of Modern Art, 1945)

THEMES
The destruction of Hiroshima and Nagasaki. The suffering of the victims who did not die. The destructiveness of the bomb. America's moral dilemma.

CURRICULUM AREAS
History, sociology, psychology, humanities, science, guidance

SYNOPSIS
On August 6, 1945, the United States dropped the first bomb on Hiroshima, Japan. Three days later another bomb fell on Nagasaki. Shortly afterward Japanese cameramen recorded the unparalleled horror and devastation in both cities. When the Japanese government surrendered, the film was confiscated by the United States and sent to Washington, D.C., where it was labeled TOP SECRET.

Twenty-five years later the film was declassified and returned to Japan by the Library of Congress. From this footage, filmmakers Eric Barnouw and Paul Ronder created this film, an authentic account of the immediate aftermath of the holocaust, the only nuclear bombing of human beings.

Since this eyewitness account of what occurs during a bombing is the only one in existence, it is crucial that everyone has an opportunity to see it. We hear of limited nuclear war, of surviving nuclear war — the film makes it clear that the ones who died in the blast were the lucky ones. Surviving would not be an option many would choose were it offered.

The United States, Japan, and much of the Western world are currently engaged in a struggle between those in each country who favor an even stronger nuclear defense and those who favor a freeze on all further nuclear weapons and disarmament of the existing ones. Since the deployment of the Pershing II and cruise missiles in Europe in December 1983, disarmament talks between the United States and the Soviet Union have been terminated.

BEFORE VIEWING
Although difficult for many to watch, the Hiroshima-Nagasaki film is very important. It is factual, nonpropaganda material that shows the physical, psychological, and scientific damage done by the bomb.
Since the objectives of the individual teacher vary, no specific suggestions are made for introducing the film. One should describe the nature of the film and use discretion about who should view it. Older students should be encouraged to watch, but offered an alternative assignment if they do not wish to.

AFTER VIEWING
Frequently students are too moved by this film to initiate discussion. The following discussion/composition suggestions can be used immediately following the film if students do not have questions.

Suggestions for discussions and compositions

a. President Harry S. Truman made the decision to drop the bomb on Hiroshima and Nagasaki. He has been widely praised for his courage and denounced for his inhumanity. Have the class research President Truman's reasons for his decision. Do they agree or disagree?

b. Discuss with the class if there was an alternative course of action that President Truman might have followed that would have shortened the war without the enormous loss of life and the suffering of the Japanese people at Hiroshima and Nagasaki.

c. Ask students to read Sydney J. Harris's excellent essay, "Who Will Speak for Mankind?" Does it relate to the film? How? Could anyone have spoken for the people of Hiroshima? For the Jews in Germany? The massacred victims in Lebanon?

d. Ask students to write a story about what their city would be like after a nuclear attack.

e. Have students imagine that they were young people far from the epicenter of the Nagasaki bomb. They were injured, but not nearly as severely as the people that they encountered. Ask them to describe their lives for the first few hours after the blast. What do they see, hear, smell, touch? How do they feel?

f. Many Americans were horrified by the bombing of Hiroshima. Can students suggest other activities in which Americans are required to participate (perhaps unknowingly) that some citizens believe are immoral or unjust?

g. There is strong pressure throughout the Western world and Japan for a nuclear freeze, but government officials are pressing for an even larger defense budget. Much of this would be spent for more nuclear missiles. Ask the class where citizens can obtain objective information. Is it possible to be objective about this terrible controversy?

Suggested assignments for advanced students

a. Ask students to study this famous excerpt from "Meditation XVII" by John Donne (1572-1631). They should try to relate the quotation to the film they have seen.

> No man is an island, entire of itself; every man is a piece of the continent, a part of the main. If a clod be washed away by the sea, Europe is the less, as well as if a promontory were, as well as if a manor of thy friend's or of thine own were: any man's death diminishes me, because I am involved in mankind, and therefore never send to know for whom the bell tolls; it tolls for thee.

b. Hermann Hagedorn has also written about the responsibility of all of us for our fellow man. Have the class respond in writing to the thoughts Hagedorn presents in a portion of *The Bomb That Fell on America*.

> The bomb that fell on Hiroshima fell on America too.
> It fell on no city, no munition plants, no docks.
> It crased no church, vaporized no public buildings,
>   reduced no man to his atomic elements.
> But it fell, it fell.
> It burst. It shook the land.
> God have mercy on our children.
> God have mercy on America.

RELATED RESOURCES

Films

The Day after Trinity
If You Love This Planet
Lovejoy's Nuclear War
Nick Mazzucco: Biography of an Atomic Vet

No Place to Hide
Nuclear War: A Guide to Armageddon
Survivors: A Film about Japanese-American Atomic Bomb Victims
War without Winners II

Other films that could be ordered

Atomic Cafe (88 min, c, rental: apply, New Yorker Films, 1982)
The unintentionally often-hilarious advice given by the government for civil defense against atomic attack. Although often amusing, the film indirectly points out that there is no defense.

Bombs Will Make the Rainbow Break (18 min, c, $390/45, Films, Inc., 1982)
In their art and letters to President Reagan, young students explain how the bomb is affecting their lives.

Dark Circle (80 min, b & w and c, rental: apply, New Yorker Films, 1983)
A contemporary portrait of the nuclear age, told through the eyes of those most directly concerned. It includes a tour through the secret world in which the hydrogen bomb is made.

Ten Seconds That Shook the World (50 min, b & w, $700/65, Films, Inc., 1963)
The documentary relates the story of a discovery that has changed the world forever—the dropping of the bomb on Hiroshima from the B-29 bomber, the *Enola Gay*.

To Die, to Live: The Survivors of Hiroshima (63 min, c, $850/90, Films, Inc.)
The film presents the thoughts and feelings of the Hiroshima survivors.

RELATED RESOURCES (cont'd)

Other films that could be ordered (cont'd)

Truman and the Atomic Bomb (15 min, c, $160/25, Learning Corporation of America, 1969)
    The film explores Truman's decision to drop the bomb and his moral and political reasons behind it.

Poetry

    Bantock, Gavin. "Hiroshima." *Twenty-Three Modern British Poets.* The Swallow Press, 1971

    Brain, Lord Russell. "Hiroshima." *Poems from the Medical World.* MTP Press, Ltd., 1980

    Enright, D. J. "Monuments of Hiroshima." *Here and Human: An Anthology of Contemporary Verse.* Transatlantic Arts, 1980

    Hikmet, Nazim. "I Come and Stand at Every Door." *Folksingers Workbook.* Oak Publications, 1973

Short stories

    Bryant, Edward. "The Hibakusda Gallery." *Particle Theory.* Pocket Books, 1981

    Mrazek, Slawomir. "The Pastor." *Faith and Fiction.* Eerdmans, 1979

Books for young adults

    Children of Hiroshima. Publishing Committee for "Children of Hiroshima," Oelgeschlager, Gunn, and Hain, Inc., 1983

Books for adults

    Akisuki, Tatsuichiro. *Nagasaki 1945, The First Full-Length Eye Witness Account of the Atomic Bomb Attack on Nagasaki.* Charles River Books, 1982

    Hiroshima and Nagasaki: The Physical, Medical, and Social Effects of the Bombing. Committee for the Compilation of Materials on Damage Caused by the Atomic Bombs in Hiroshima and Nagasaki. Harper & Row, 1981

    Maruki, Toshi. *Hiroshima, No Pike.* Lothrop, Lee, and Shepard, 1982

For other books related to the atomic bomb, see the study suggestions for *The Day after Trinity.*

IN OUR WATER
(58 min, c, $840/100, New Day Film Co-op, Inc., 1982)

THEMES

The pollution of our water. The indifference of federal, state, and local officials. The dilemma of citizens with no legal recourse. The radicalizing of citizens because of government inaction.

CURRICULUM AREAS

Social studies, ecology, sociology, psychology, biology

SYNOPSIS

The indifference of local, county, and state health officials, and even U.S. senators, is frightening and infuriating in this stunning documentary concerning chemical pollution in local drinking water. Some officials were outwardly receptive, some were patronizing, some hostile, but ultimately none acted to help a citizen seriously concerned about his family, his neighbors, and his community.

The problem began in 1973 when Frank Kaler, a house painter in South Brunswick, New Jersey, who lives with his family in a house adjacent to the Jones Industrial Service landfill, noticed that his water had the same noxious odor as the huge sunken tubs filled with toxic wastes at the disposal site.

Vegetables cooked in the water turned black, pasta disintegrated, and Kaler's family developed skin lesions when they bathed. Unwilling to accept the situation, Kaler requested testing of the water by county and state health officials. Although their tests showed the water safe to drink, tests by an independent agency revealed it to be seriously contaminated by inorganic chemicals.

When the state office of the Environmental Protection Agency (EPA) declined to verify the results of local agencies, Kaler turned to the EPA itself, which found dangerous levels of contamination by both organic and inorganic chemicals. Still no official acted. Kaler appeared before the U.S. Senate committee investigating contamination. Although he was praised for his public-spiritedness no action was taken.

Concerned now about radioactivity, he pressed the State of New Jersey to test. Four-and-a-half years later the state reported that the radioactivity level exceeded government standards for safety. The citizens of New Jersey who used the contaminated wells were never officially notified that the water was a serious health hazard.

Six years after Frank Kaler began his struggle, the landfill was closed. Currently, the Jones Industrial Service is seeking court approval to reopen. Conservative Frank Kaler is now politically aware and eloquent. "I used to tell my kids," he says, "when we went to the parades, 'Take off your hat.... This is your flag, your country.' Today I teach my kids that

SYNOPSIS (cont'd)

they can buy their share of American justice if they have enough money. That the laws are made by the rich and the powerful, and the richest and most powerful are the industrialists. They run the country."

The most serious consequence of Frank Kaler's story may be the erosion of his belief in this country's system of justice. This feeling, which is shared by many, must somehow be reversed. *In Our Water* should be required viewing in every school and community.

BEFORE VIEWING

Discuss with students the importance of water in their lives. What if they had to search each day for clean water as people do in other parts of the world? The world's water supply is rapidly dwindling; some experts predict that a shortage of water will be the world's next great crisis. What will happen in America if there is not enough water? How will people behave? What will the government do?

After the importance of water is discussed, narrow the discussion to the student's community water supply. How adequate is it? What about the quality? What chemicals are used for purification? Are there chemicals in the water, not added at the purification plant, that were not in the water a few years ago? Tell the class it is going to see a film about a man who discovered that the water in his home had been poisoned and what happened to him when he sought help from public agencies charged with his protection.

AFTER VIEWING

Ask the class to express its first reactions to the film. Interest? Surprise? Anger? Indifference? Concern? What is the students' view of Frank Kaler? A hero? Troublemaker? Foolish? Stubborn? If the students are encouraged to talk without evaluation of their attitudes, the teacher should understand their present views of the problem of water and of citizen participation in seeking redress from government agencies.

Suggestions for discussions and compositions

a. What was the responsibility of the local health officials that Frank Kaler first contacted? Ask students what they should have done. Why did they fail to act?

b. Frank Kaler's long struggle to obtain safe drinking water turned him from a politically conservative house painter into a political activist. What incidents do students think were most significant in his metamorphosis?

c. Some people who have viewed the film ask, "Why didn't Frank Kaler just move?" Discuss with students if moving would have been a satisfactory solution to his problem.

d. Nurseryman Teddy Kordus faced a serious moral problem in trying to sell his property. If he told the truth about water conditions, the nursery would never sell. If he concealed damaging information, he would be behaving unethically. Ask the class what Kordus should have done.

e. Ask students to imagine that they are officials of the South Brunswick health department. They are to write Frank Kaler letters and explain why they cannot help him.

f. Discuss with the class why many of the other citizens of South Brunswick (whose water had not yet been affected) did not help Frank Kaler.

g. Water is essential to maintain life but it also brings us many pleasures. Ask students how our lives would be different if there were only enough water for drinking purposes.

h. Filmmaker Meg Switzgable produced *In Our Water* because her father had cancer, which he believed was environmentally induced since his neighbors had cancer in statistically significant numbers. Discuss with students what recourse such victims should have, if any, against governmental agencies that do not act.

Suggestions for advanced assignments

a. Invite the superintendent of your local water processing plant to speak to the class about the purification of local water. Ask students to research the environmental effects of the chemicals used for the process and of any that are already present in the water.

b. Assign students to research the history of the EPA since 1980. They should note particularly the former occupations of the top officials of the agency. What changes have occurred, if any?

c. Invite a member of the Sierra Club or National Wildlife Federation to speak to the class about water quality and availability.

d. Ask students to research the extent of water pollution in rivers and lakes of the United States. How does this affect the health of the American public? How does it affect the fishing industry? Recreational fishing? Wildlife?

e. The Conservation Foundation is a nonprofit research and communications organization dedicated to improving the quality of the environment and to improving wise use of the earth's resources. Ask students to write to it for information on the present and future availability of water. Have them share their findings with the class. The foundation's address is: The Conservation Foundation
1717 Massachusetts Avenue, N.W.
Washington, D.C. 20036

f. Ask students to write to their congressmen or senators for information concerning the safety of water in their state and community.

g. Invite a representative of a federal, state, county, or local water agency or environmental agency to appear before the class to discuss the availability of clean water or projected shortages.

Suggestions for advanced assignments (cont'd)

h.   Plan a trip to the local water-processing plant. Ask the class to take notes of the chemicals used and research them for possible toxicity.

i.   Ask students to prepare a map of the United States that shows the most dangerous areas of water pollution. Does underground seepage pose a threat to your community?

j.   Students can collect samples of warning labels on household products. They should bring them to school and make a collage to post in the classroom.

k.   Organize the class into a town meeting, with students representing Frank Kaler, Teddy Kordus, and health officials. Students should present their concerns to their fellow citizens.

l.   According to the EPA, on April 7, 1983, there were 14,000 toxic waste dumps considered very dangerous to human beings in the United States. Many of these are still unknown, even to local citizens near one of the dumps. Ask students to research their areas by writing to the EPA for information. They should share their findings with the class.

RELATED RESOURCES

Books for young adults

Powledge, Fred. *Water: The Nature, Uses, and Future of Our Most Precious and Abused Resource.* Farrar, Straus and Giroux, 1982

Pringle, Laurence. *Water: The Next Great Resource Battle.* Macmillan, 1982

Regenstein, Lewis. *American the Poisoned.* Acropolis, 1982

Wasserman, Harvey, and Norma Solomon. *Killing Our Own.* Delacorte, 1982

Books for adults

Eckholm, Erick P. *Down to Earth: Environment and Human Needs.* International Institute for Environmental Development, 1982

Lake, Elizabeth. *Who Pays for Clean Water?* Westview Press, 1979

Ricciuti, Edward. *Killers of the Seas.* Macmillan, 1975

Thomas, Bill. *American Rivers: A Natural History.* W. W. Norton & Company, 1978

Water Foundation. *Water: Will There Be Enough?* 1979

JOSEPH SCHULTZ
(13 min, c, $220/20, Wombat Productions, Inc., 1972)

THEMES
Moral responsibility. War.

CURRICULUM AREAS
Language arts, social studies, humanities, values

SYNOPSIS
The film is based upon an incident that occurred in the Yugoslavian village of Orahovica during World War II. Schultz is one of a group of German soldiers who have just captured the town and are ordered to execute some villagers who have been lined up against a haystack and blindfolded. When he is ordered to fire, Schultz, without explanation, refuses. Given the choice of firing on the doomed men or joining them, he chooses the latter. In a starkly simple, but moving sequence, he carefully removes his helmet, decorations, and gun and lays them on the ground before joining hands with the villagers. His comrades purposefully miss him in the first fusillade, but during the second their bullets find the mark, and Joseph Schultz's body falls on the pile of bleeding victims.

Throughout the film a military photographer records the events. With enormous impact the black and white stills taken on that July day in 1941 appear intercut with the action, adding a chilling realism to the scene. We are struck by the integrity with which the filmmaker has duplicated the original events.

The film is short, direct, and simple. There is no narration, little dialogue, and no condescension. We are left to contemplate the dilemmas of duty, obedience, and authority when juxtaposed against our own morality.

BEFORE VIEWING
Discuss with the class the idea of following an unjust order. Start with an example of behavior with which they are familiar: the unjust treatment (following orders) of a fellow student, a sibling, or a stranger. Progress to the concept of citizens following an unjust law, or to the military following orders even though they may be against the person's personal moral beliefs. Tell the class it is going to see a film of a soldier who was faced with such a dilemma.

(Text continues on page 99.)

Joseph Schultz
Photograph courtesy of Wombat Productions, Inc.

AFTER VIEWING

Suggestions for discussions and compositions

a. Discuss with students why Joseph Schultz thought it was necessary to give up his own life for what he believed. Would it not have been just as effective if he had shot over the villagers' heads so that his commanding officer would never have known about it?

b. Ask students how morally responsible they think we are for our own actions. Is the fact that we have been ordered to do something sufficient justification?

c. Have students think of famous individuals who have gone against the group, the nation, or laws that they considered unjust in order to maintain their own integrity. (Socrates, Martin Luther King, Martin Luther, Henry Thoreau, General "Billy" Mitchell are examples.)

d. Ask students to imagine being Joseph Schultz. You have asked for, and received, permission to write a letter to your loved ones explaining the events of the day. Write such a letter.

e. Students should imagine themselves as one of Joseph Schultz's buddies who was a member of the firing squad and has been ordered to write a letter to Schultz's family explaining the circumstances of his death and his feelings about participating in it.

Suggestions for advanced assignments

a. Ask students to write a story or an essay about Joseph Schultz's life that might have caused him to make such a decision. They should mention the training, incidents, and forces that might have shaped his ultimate moral decision, answering the captain's question, "Why?"

b. Explain to students that in the Nuremberg trials following World War II, when the Nazis were being tried for atrocities against the Jewish people, the German defense was that they were "following orders." Allied judges held that this was not sufficient justification and the Nazis were executed or imprisoned. Discuss with students what implications this has for the firing squad. For United States soldiers at My Lai during the Vietnam War? For the September, 1982, massacre of Palestinian refugees in Lebanon by the Christian Falangists? For the murder of four American nuns and Archbishop Oscar Romero of El Salvador by the army of that country? Has the principle gained acceptance?

c. Explain to the class that an elegy is a formal, sustained poem written as a tribute to one who is dead. (Read "To an Athlete Dying Young" by A. E. Housman.) Request students to write elegies for Joseph Schultz.

d. Arrange to show the feature film *Paths of Glory*, which is available from United Artists, or *Breaker Morant*, which can be obtained from Films, Inc. These fine films deal with the execution of soldiers who were following orders.

RELATED RESOURCES

Films

American Parade: With All Deliberate Speed	*Paul Robeson: Tribute to an Artist*
The Case of the Legless Veteran	*Strange Fruit*
The Hangman	*Travelling Hopefully*

Books for young adults

Becker, Stephen. *When the War Is Over*. Random House, 1969

Boll, Heinrich. *The Lost Honor of Katharina Blum*. McGraw-Hill, 1975

Bolt, Robert. *A Man for All Seasons*. Random House, 1966

Faber, Doris, and Howard Faber. *The Assassination of Martin Luther King, Jr.* Watts, 1979

Cormier, Robert. *The Chocolate War*. Pantheon, 1974

Dreiser, Theodore. *An American Tragedy*. World, 1948

Kerr, M. E. *Gentlehands*. Harper & Row, 1978

Montgomery, Elizabeth R. *Gandhi: Peaceful Fighter*. Garrard, 1970

Oates, Stephen B. *Let the Trumpet Sound: The Life of Martin Luther King, Jr.* Harper & Row, 1982

Plato. *The Trial and Death of Socrates*. Hackett Publications, 1980

Rashke, Richard. *The Killing of Karen Silkwood*. Penguin Books, 1982

JOSHUA IN A BOX
(5 min, c, $135/40, Churchill Films, 1970)

THEMES
What are our limitations? Do we impose limitations on ourselves? What is freedom? Do we really want freedom? How do we cope with frustration?

CURRICULUM AREAS
Language arts, psychology

Joshua

SYNOPSIS
Confined in a box, Joshua, a small, strange-looking figure struggles energetically to gain his freedom. With each attempt to liberate himself, his struggles become more violent. At last he is free outside the box, triumphant and defiant, so defiant that he gives the box the raspberry. But as he looks at the box, his feelings change, and he begins to cry. In an intriguing metamorphosis, Joshua becomes another box, with himself again inside.

Because it has many possible interpretations, *Joshua in a Box* is a superb film with which to teach careful observation, a skill that students must develop if they are to understand allegorical, nonverbal films. If students watch carefully, they will be able to develop at least one reasonable interpretation of the film.

BEFORE VIEWING
a. Make sure that all students have pen and paper.

b. Tell the students that *Joshua* is an animated, nonverbal film that has an allegorical meaning. (Explain this concept if the students do not understand it.) They must watch carefully so that they can list *in*

BEFORE VIEWING (cont'd)

> *detail* what happened. What does he do? How does he look? What sounds does he make? What happens to him?

AFTER VIEWING

Suggestions for discussions and compositions

    a. Ask the students to list what they have observed, without discussion with other students. (Emphasize that there are no grades.) They might list these items, for example:

> He is inside the box.
>
> He tries hard to get out several times, hitting his head, falling down, etc.
>
> He finally gets out. He looks happy and gives the box the raspberry.
>
> He looks at the box and begins to cry.
>
> He changes into a box himself. (Some students believe this is a new Joshua, and perhaps it is.)

    b. Collect these papers so that you can check whether they are beginning to observe carefully.

    c. Discuss with the class what the box represents. What does Joshua represent? His change in behavior? The metamorphosis? The new box? Emphasize that there are no right answers.

    d. Ask the class to write what they believe to be the most reasonable assumption about the message of the filmmaker. Again, emphasize that there are no right answers, but that they are to write in terms of *ideas.* They should not say "the box means this" or "Joshua's tears mean that," but should tell what these symbolize. This is very difficult for many students, and they need many opportunities to express themselves in this manner. Again, emphasize that there are no right answers, but their writing must be consistent with what happened in the film. The following are ideas that have been suggested by secondary students:

> When we are young our parents place many restrictions on us. As we grow up, we rebel more and more until we finally gain independence. We think we are happy, but once we are free of our parents, we may feel bad that we no longer have them to depend on as much. Then we grow up and become the restrictive parent we have tried to escape.

> Most of us want very much to be free. We fight against any restrictions that are placed on us. But when we finally get free, we realize that we needed those boundaries around us so we put ourselves back into the same place or one like it. In other words, we really can't handle too much freedom.

Some of us don't like being forced to go to school so we try in every way to get out. We treat the teachers with disrespect and give them the raspberry when we do get out. We cause as much trouble as we can. But once we are out, we find out that it wasn't so bad there. So we try to put ourselves back, and if we can't, we go some place similar like continuation high school.

LEO BEUREMAN

(13 min, c, $247, rental, inquire Centron (Coronet) Films, 1970)

THEMES

Making the most of life. The indomitability of the human spirit. Seeking to help others, though grievously handicapped oneself.

CURRICULUM AREAS

Language arts, special education, psychology, filmmaking, guidance, values

SYNOPSIS

Leo Beureman has become a contemporary short film classic, which richly deserves the innumerable awards it has won, including an Academy Award nomination. In 1980 it was chosen as one of the twenty best films of the preceding decade because many people believe that it is still the most inspiring film ever made about courage in the face of seemingly insurmountable physical handicaps.

Both with severe physical handicaps, Leo, who is also deaf, is a prisoner in his own horribly twisted and deformed body. Despite these grievous burdens, he refuses to allow himself to feel fear, defeat, or self-pity. He is determined to live his life as fully as possible, conceding nothing.

Each day he drives a tractor to his corner (his by silent assent of all the town's citizens), where, using specially constructed pulleys and chains, he slowly and painfully lowers himself and his cart to the sidewalk. Then he becomes an independent businessman, selling pencils and similar supplies and insisting on giving full value for money received. An independent merchant has no need for charity. He says that he manages to "enjoy life fairly well."

When asked for what he wished, he replied, "One of my greatest wishes is that I could get into some very profitable business and help the poor."

As compelling as Leo himself is, the film has many other strengths. It offers a beautiful script, read with skill and artistry by actor Alexander Scourby, an original soundtrack, scored and performed in Vienna, and tasteful direction. The effect is one of quiet serenity and courage, devoid of sentimentality. In its category, *Leo Beureman* is unequalled.

BEFORE VIEWING

Ask the class what physically handicapped people are really like. Group discussion may reveal stereotyped thinking, assumptions, and misconceptions that affect how we behave toward the handicapped. You may wish to bring out that Leo Beureman is cruelly handicapped, perhaps more so than anyone the students have ever seen, but he refuses to accept his condition if it means that he must become totally dependent on others.

AFTER VIEWING

Since *Leo Beureman* is such a moving film, ask the class to respond to it in writing. Be sure they are prepared with pen and paper so that no discussion will be necessary when the film ends.

Suggestions for discussions and compositions

a. Ask students what scene from the film is most memorable to them. They should be specific in their descriptions.

b. What scene made students the most uncomfortable? (If this is used as a part of a writing assignment, ask the students to try to explain why.) What scene(s) made students the happiest or the most comfortable? Can they explain why?

c. How does Leo's need for independence show in the film?

d. How do students feel as they watch Leo deal with his terrible handicaps?

e. Ask the class what loneliness is. Is it the same as being alone? Do they think Leo is lonely? When?

f. Discuss with students what important areas in life that most of us take for granted were forever denied to Leo despite his best efforts to live a normal life.

g. Leo was not famous; he was not a public servant, artist, or statesman. Yet when he died the people of Lawrence, Kansas, erected a memorial to him on his corner. Why do students think the townspeople were so affected by him?

h. Inform the class that the film is a remarkable example of filmmaking. For example, in the opening sequences we do not see Leo. Only his wheelchair is visible as narrator Alexander Scourby talks about Leo's early life and his near-death from failing to hear a train whistle. Ask students to describe the psychological effect on the audience when the filmmaker shows Leo gradually.

i. Tell the students to imagine that they are Leo sitting in a wheelchair on a street corner in Lawrence. Business is slow so there is time to write in a diary. What does Leo think and feel (emotionally and physically) as he watches the life around him?

Suggestions for advanced assignments

a. Ralph Waldo Emerson wrote: "Discontent is the want of self-reliance: it is infirmity of will." Ask the class to write a paper that relates the quotation to the life of Leo Beureman.

b. The following prayer from German theologian Reinhold Niebuhr is a familiar one: "O God, give us serenity to accept what cannot be changed, courage to change what should be changed, and wisdom to distinguish the one from the other." The problem for most of us is to know the point at which struggle must change to acceptance. Discuss

Suggestions for advanced assignments (cont'd)

with students how this quotation relates to the lives of people such as Leo Beureman, as well as to those who have handicaps or conditions in their lives that seem to others much less debilitating.

c.   Have a volunteer seated in a wheelchair. Other volunteers try to show the difference between empathy and sympathy. Discuss the differences in the attitudes and how the recipient feels in each case. Ask other volunteers to show friendliness without being patronizing.

d.   Ask volunteers to approach the volunteer in the wheelchair as though they are seeing him for the first time. What are their reactions? Discuss them and how the person in the wheelchair may feel.

For other assignments to use with *Leo Beureman*, refer to *Who Are the DeBolts and Where Did They Get 19 Kids?*

ADDITIONAL STUDY AIDS

Students often want to know about Leo's life after they have seen the film. The following information has been supplied by Centron Films:

Shortly after the release of the film, Leo became blind. He spent the last years of his life in a rest home, as unwilling as ever to admit to helplessness. Although his mail now had to be "read" to him by the tedious method of drawing the shape of each letter individually on his back, he continued to correspond with the film's producer, using a ruler to guide his pencil across the page:

"You remember me. I starred in the movie. You know I was hit by disagreeable blindness. And to be hard of hearing (stone deaf) makes it much, much worse. But I have received a number of letters from many parts of America and Canada, saying how they enjoy and are helped, as I showed what courage can do. Well, I expect you are tired of reading this scribbled letter, so will close. I mainly wanted to thank you for all your nice treatment...."

Leo Beureman died November 7, 1974. Yet his story continues. In March following his funeral some of his friends sought permission from the City Commission to install a bronze plaque in his memory, asking to imbed it in the sidewalk at the location which had become known simply as *his* place. A controversy erupted, not over whether there should be such a memorial (everyone seemed in favor of that) but on what the appropriate wording for the tribute should be. Pro's and con's were discussed on television and in the press, being picked up eventually by a national wire service. Reading the story, Leo's friends from coast to coast spoke out for him. The plaque, just as Leo's admirers had designed it, can now be seen in downtown Lawrence, Kansas. Few men have, or deserve, such recognition.

RELATED RESOURCES

Films

Crossbar
A Day in the Life of Bonnie
  Consolo
Get It Together
Gravity Is My Enemy
I'll Find a Way
Moira: A Vision of Blindness

See What I Say
Sign of Victory
Stepping Out: The DeBolts Grow
  Up
Survival Run
Who Are the DeBolts and Where
  Did They Get 19 Kids?

Poetry

Owen, Wilfred. "Disabled." *Oxford Book of Twentieth Century English Verse.* Oxford University Press, 1973

Books for young adults

Bigger, Jama Kehoe. *Then Came a Miracle.* Revell, 1982

Blank, Joseph P. *Nineteen Steps Up the Mountain.* Harper & Row, 1976

Clark, Brian. *Whose Life Is It Anyway?* Avon, 1981

Keller, Helen. *The Story of My Life.* Pendulum Press, 1974

Kellogg, Marjorie. *Tell Me That You Love Me, Junie Moon.* Farrar, Straus and Giroux, 1968

Killilea, Marie. *Karen.* Dell, 1980

Konigsberg, E. L. *Father Arcane's Daughter.* Atheneum, 1976

Lash, Joseph P. *Helen and Teacher.* Delta, 1981

Mathis, Sharon Bell. *Listen for the Fig Tree.* Viking Press, 1974

Medeff, Marl. *Children of a Lesser God.* J. T. White, 1980

Pomerance, Bernard. *The Elephant Man.* Grove Press, 1979

Trumbo, Dalton. *Johnny Got His Gun.* Lippincott, 1939

Uhlman, Fred. *Reunion.* Farrar, Straus and Giroux, 1977

Valens, Evans G. *The Other Side of the Mountain.* Warner Books, 1979

Books for adults

Brickner, Richard. *My Second Twenty Years*. Basic Books, 1976

Eisenberg, Myron G., ed. *Disabled People as Second-Class Citizens*. Springer, 1982

Loomer, Alice. *Famous Flaws*. Macmillan, 1976

NIGHT AND FOG
(32 min, b & w, c, $525/55, Films, Inc., 1955)

THEMES
The Holocaust. Man's inhumanity to man. Prejudice.

CURRICULUM AREAS
World history, humanities, language arts, psychology, ethnic studies

SYNOPSIS
The unspeakable events of the Holocaust have been relived in newsreels, films, and television specials. We have followed the trial of Adolph Eichmann, the Nazi deathmaster. Some may remember the Nuremberg Trials. As an evocation of the horror and despair of that ghastly time, French filmmaker Alain Resnais's *Night and Fog* is without peer.

Told in French, with English subtitles, the whole nightmare is experienced again—the disease, pain, despair, and death. Photographs confiscated from the Germans show human beings subjected to inhumane medical experimentation. Empty-eyed deportees watch as their friends are buried; emaciated bodies shuffle toward the crematoriums. Most horrifying to watch is a bulldozer that shovels up the carnage for a mass burial.

Resnais's format for this haunting, semidocumentary film is simple. A poet, visiting the death camp some years later, speaks to us in the present tense, his tone urgent but hypnotic. As he speaks, the images alternate between the black and white German photographs and the color film of the present remains of the horror. What he sees is so ghastly that the narrator is beyond emotion—he is almost matter-of-fact in his choice of words. The effect is unforgettable.

Night and Fog is neither nationalistic nor political. It is elegy of remorse that man carries within himself such capacity for evil. Because it is emotionally overwhelming, this film should only be used with careful preparation and as a part of a unit on the period. Otherwise the film becomes exploitive.

BEFORE VIEWING
The assignment assumes that the class is studying the Nazi period and the Holocaust so that they will understand the film without further elaboration. Students are frequently unable to talk about it, but this is an effective time for a writing assignment. Tell students that when the film is over they are to respond in writing in any way they choose, but without further interaction with the teacher or students. (Be sure they have pen and paper ready.)

AFTER VIEWING
Allow the class to start writing immediately. Students should respond with their feelings, whatever they may be. If more time is needed, allow for it at the next session of the class. Because of the assumption that other work on the Holocaust has been structured, it is impossible to offer

AFTER VIEWING (cont'd)

discussion/composition suggestions. Instead, additional materials are suggested to build the unit specifically on the Holocaust in language arts, humanities, or as a supplement to social studies materials.

RELATED RESOURCES

Films

Feature films

The Diary of Anne Frank (170 min, c, Films, Inc., 1959)
    As young Anne Frank and her family hid in an attic during the Nazi persecution, she kept a diary of their daily life. Just before the war ended, Anne and her family were taken to a concentration camp where Anne died. The film was nominated for Academy Awards as best picture, director, music, and for Ed Wynn's performance. Shelley Winters and the cinematographer won Academy Awards.

Judgement at Nuremberg (186 min, c, United Artists, 1961)
    A fictionalized version of the 1948 trials in which Nazi leaders were tried for crimes against humanity. The film is very long with little action, but it places the issues in focus clearly and interestingly. It received an Academy Award nomination as best film of 1961. Academy Awards went to screenwriter Abby Mann and to actor Maximilian Schell.

We Were German Jews (58 min, c, Blackwood Productions, 251 W. 57th Street, New York, N.Y., 1982)
    In the fall of 1942, two young German Jews, Herbert and Lotte Strauss, escaped from Germany to avoid deportation to concentration camps. Later they emigrated to the United States where they have lived ever since. Recently they returned to Germany to confront their past. While it is not recommended for general use, it would be a poignant addition to a study of the Holocaust, particularly when Herbert discusses the loss of his family who all perished in the camps.

Short films

Kitty—A Return to Auschwitz (see Annotated Filmography, page 241).

The Legacy-Children of Holocaust Survivors (23 min, c, Films, Inc., 1980)
    Five adults whose parents survived the Holocaust and the terrors of the camps discuss the effects of their parents' experiences on their own lives. They speak of a conspiracy of silence and a generally overprotective attitude of parents eager to protect their children from the horrors they have known.

The Music of Auschwitz (see Annotated Filmography, page 245).

Poetry

Many heartrending poems about the Holocaust are collected in *Voices within the Ark: The Modern Jewish Poets*, edited by Howard Schwartz and Anthony Rudolf and published by Avon Books in 1980. A study of these poems would help students understand the pain and suffering, not only of the victims of the Holocaust, but also of their survivors, and of their brothers and sisters in spirit. Some of the most beautiful poems are these:

Ruth Becker (Israeli), "Don't Show Me"

Marvin Bell (American), "Getting Lost in Nazi Germany"

Stephen Berg (American), "Desnos Reading the Palms of Men on Their Way to the Gas Chambers"

Edith Bruck (Italian), "Sister Zahava" and "Why Would I Have Survived?"

Irving Feldman (American), "The Pripet Marshes"

Alfred Grünewald (German), "The Lamp Now Flickers"

Henryk Grynberg (Polish), "Poplars"

Anthony Hecht (American), "More Light! More Light!"

Alfred Kittner (German), "Old Jewish Cemetery in Worms"

Naum Korzhavin (Russian), "Children of Auschwitz"

Primo Levi (Italian), "For Adolph Eichmann" and "Shema"

William Pillen (American), "A Poem for Anton Schmidt"

Anne Ranasinghe (Sri Lankan), "Auschwitz from Colombo" and "Holocaust 1944"

Nelly Sachs (German), "O Night of the Crying Children" and "O the Chimneys"

Hans Sahl (German), "Memo"

Thomas Sessler (German), "You Move Forward"

Boris Slutsky (Russian), "How They Killed My Grandmother"

Daniel Weissbort (English), "Murder of a Community"

Also see in the following books of poems:

Brinnin, John Malcolm. "Dachau." *A Geography of Poets: An Anthology of the New Poets.* Bantam Books, 1980

Hayen, William. "Riddle: From Belsen a Crate of Gold Teeth." *A Geography of Poets: An Anthology of the New Poets.* Bantam Books, 1980

Books for young adults

Bor, Josef. *The Terezin Requiem*. Knopf, 1963

Eisenberg, Azriel. *The Lost Generation: Children of the Holocaust*. Pilgrim Press, 1982

Epstein, Leslie. *King of the Jews*. Coward, 1979

Frank, Anne. *The Diary of Anne Frank*. Modern Library, 1952

Friedman, Ina R. *Escape or Die: True Stories of Young People Who Escaped the Holocaust*. Addison-Wesley, 1982

Gross, Leonard. *The Last Jews in Berlin*. Simon and Schuster, 1982

Haas, Gerda S. *These I Do Remember: Fragments from the Holocaust*. Cumberland Press, 1982

Hart, Kitty. *Return to Auschwitz*. Atheneum, 1982

Hersey, John. *The Wall*. Knopf, 1960

Infield, Glenn B. *The Secrets of the S.S.* Stein and Day, 1982

Jacot, Michel. *The Last Butterfly*. Bobbs-Merrill, 1974

Mann, Peggy, and Gizelle Hersh. *Gizelle, Save the Children*. Everest House, 1982

Meier, Lily. *Auschwitz Album*. Random House, 1982

Moscovitz, Sarah. *Love Despite Hate: Child Survivors of the Holocaust and Their Adult Lives*. Schocken Books, 1982

Ruby, Lois. *Two Truths in My Pocket*. Viking Press, 1982

Sanders, Leonard. *Act of War*. Simon and Schuster, 1982

Schaeffer, Susan Fromberg. *Anya*. Macmillan, 1974

Schwartz-Bart, Andre. *The Last of the Just*. Atheneum, 1960

Stachow, Hasso C. *If This Be Glory*. Doubleday, 1982

Staden, Wendelgard, von. *Darkness over the Valley*. Ticknor and Fields, 1981

Tec, Nechama. *Dry Tears*. Everest House, 1982

Uhlman, Fred. *Reunion.* Farrar, Straus and Giroux, 1977

Wallant, Edward L. *The Pawnbroker.* Harcourt Brace Jovanovich, 1961

Wiesel, Elie. *Dawn.* Hill and Wang, 1961

Books for adults

Cargas, Harry James, ed. *When God and Man Failed: Non-Jewish Views of the Holocaust.* Macmillan, 1981

Dinnerstein, Leonard. *America and the Survivors of the Holocaust.* Columbia University Press, 1982

Feig, Konnilyn G. *Hitler's Death Camps: The Sanity of Madness.* Holmes and Meier, 1981

Rossil, Seymour. *The Holocaust.* Watts, 1981

Weisenthal, Simon. *Max and Helen.* Morrow, 1982

AN OCCURRENCE AT OWL CREEK BRIDGE
(27 min, c, $455/50, Films, Inc., 1961)

THEMES

Man's inhumanity to man. The value of life. Class status even in death. Nature's beauty is usually unobserved.

CURRICULUM AREAS

Language arts, psychology, history, filmmaking

SYNOPSIS

Although set in the Civil War period, this riveting, Academy Award-winning film, based on the short story by Ambrose Bierce, first published in 1891, is very contemporary. The twenty-two years that have elapsed since its production have not lessened its impact or the relevance of its subject matter.

Trapped in his own area while trying to sabotage a Union train, Payton Farquhar, Southern aristocrat, is being readied for hanging. It is dawn; an ominous silence is broken only by the sounds of nature and the shuffling of the Union soldiers preparing for the execution. Slowly the camera focuses in on the doomed man who stands on a bridge in a beautiful wooded gorge. The stillness is disturbed by the terse dialogue of executioners.

The defendant with a rope around his neck, stands on a plank. It will serve as a makeshift trapdoor, the bridge as a makeshift gallows. Suddenly he is catapulted into the river below. As he struggles to free himself from the rope, the viewer's hopes are roused. Is it possible that he will escape? Yes, he is free of the ropes. Smiling, the prisoner surfaces for air and starts to swim downstream toward his home. The music becomes "I'm a Living Man."

As he swims the prisoner stares in amazement at every flower, at each beautiful tree, and at a spider crawling across a shiny leaf.

In the background an officer cries, "Fire!" This voice sounds cruel and distorted. His hands are bleeding, but Farquhar joyously heads for shore where he pulls himself up, exhausted but elated. On the soundtrack we hear again, "I'm a Living Man," as the Southerner races toward his home.

In a riveting, slow-motion sequence, he runs between rows of stately elms bordering the driveway of his plantation, holding out his arms to his wife who runs toward him. As he reaches her, the wife throws out her arms, and the camera cuts to Farquhar's body hanging from the bridge. Love and death are juxtaposed in a stunning, ironic ending.

An Occurrence at Owl Creek Bridge is part of a trilogy by French filmmaker Robert Enrico, an American Civil War aficionado. The other two films, both in black and white, are *Chickamauga* and *Mockingbird*. Both are civil war stories by Ambrose Bierce. The films are distributed by CRM/McGraw-Hill Films.

BEFORE VIEWING

The film is a superb blending of descriptive and narrative detail. It is an excellent tool with which to teach students careful watching and listening. Encourage them not only to remember details but sequences. Symbolism is also easily taught by using this film.

AFTER VIEWING

Suggestions for discussions and compositions

a. Were students surprised by the ending of the film?

b. The ending is *ironic*. Discuss with students what contrasts form the irony of the ending.

c. Discuss with the class what the film (and Ambrose Bierce) is defining as important to a man that he may only realize at the moment of death.

d. Why do the voices of the Union soldiers sound cruel and distorted to Farquhar as he is trying to escape? Ask students to comment.

e. Encourage dialogue about whether Ambrose Bierce is arguing against capital punishment in his film.

f. Ask students if one group of men should have the right to summarily execute a fellow human being.

g. Have students define the theme of the film in one sentence.

h. Ask students to comment on the manner in which Robert Enrico (the filmmaker) arouse sympathy for Payton Farquhar.

Assignments for advanced students

a. Tell students the film could be said to be a struggle between man's dreams and hopes and his natural instinct toward violence. Have them explain this statement in as much detail as possible.

b. If the identification of man with nature is life's meaning, what is life's curse? Ask the class to explain by using the film to support ideas.

c. At the moment of his death, Farquhar knew what his fundamental joys were. Ask students how the filmmaker manipulates us so that they identify with the hanged man.

d. Read aloud the beginning of *An Occurrence at Owl Creek Bridge*:

> A man stood upon a railroad bridge in Northern Alabama, looking down into the swift waters twenty feet below. The man's hands were behind his back, the wrists bound with a cord. A rope loosely encircled his neck. It was attached to a stout cross-timber above his head, and the slack fell to the level of his knees. Some loose boards laid upon the sleepers supporting the metals of the railway supplied a footing for him and his executioners—two

Assignments for advanced students (cont'd)

private soldiers of the Federal army, directed by a sergeant, who in civil life may have been a deputy sheriff. At a short remove upon the same temporary platform was an officer in the uniform of his rank, armed. He was a captain. A sentinel at each end of the bridge stood with his rifle in the position known as "support," that is to say, vertical in front of the left shoulder, the hammer resting on the forearm thrown straight across the chest—a formal and unnatural position, enforcing an erect carriage of the body. It did not appear to be the duty of these two men to know what was occurring at the center of the bridge; they merely blockaded the two ends of the foot plank which traversed it.

Beyond one of the sentinels nobody was in sight; the railroad ran straight away into a forest for a hundred yards, then, curving, was lost to view. Doubtless there was an outpost further along. The other bank of the stream was open ground—a gentle acclivity crowned with a stockade of vertical tree trunks, loopholed for rifles, with a single embrasure through which protruded the muzzle of a brass cannon commanding the bridge. Midway of the slope between bridge and fort were the spectators—a single company of infantry in line, at "parade rest," the butts of the rifles on the ground, the barrels inclining slightly backward against the right shoulder, the hands crossed upon the stock. A lieutenant stood at the right of the line, the point of his sword upon the ground, his left hand resting upon his right. Excepting the group of four at the center of the bridge not a man moved. The company faced the bridge, staring stonily, motionless. The sentinels, facing the banks of the stream, might have been statues to adorn the bridge. The captain stood with folded arms, silent, observing the work of his subordinates but making no sign. Death is a dignitary who, when he comes announced, is to be received with formal manifestations of respect, even by those most familiar with him. In the code of military etiquette silence and fixity are forms of deference.

The man who was engaged in being hanged was apparently about thirty-five years of age. He was a civilian, if one might judge from his dress, which was that of a planter. His features were good—a straight nose, firm mouth, broad forehead, from which his long, dark hair was combed straight back, falling behind his ears to the collar of his well-fitting frock coat. He wore a moustache and pointed beard, but no whiskers; his eyes were large and dark grey and had a kindly expression which one would hardly have expected in one whose neck was in the hemp. Evidently this was no vulgar assassin. The liberal military code makes provision for hanging many kinds of people, and gentlemen are not excluded.

The preparation being complete, the two private soldiers stepped aside and each drew away the plank upon which he had been standing. The sergeant turned to the captain, saluted and placed himself immediately behind that officer, who in turn moved apart one pace. These movements left the condemned man and the sergeant standing on the two ends of the same plank, which spanned three of the cross-ties of the bridge. The end upon which the civilian stood almost, but not quite, reached a fourth. This plank had been held in place by the weight of the captain; it was now held by that of the sergeant. At a signal from the former, the latter would step aside, the plank would tilt and the condemned man go down between two ties....

1. Ask the students how they would film this opening.

2. Discuss their ideas for filming.

3. Ask each student to write a script for the opening, including the action, the soundtrack, the type of shot, and dialogue, if any. It should look something like this:

Shots		Sound	Dialogue
Shot 1.	Long shot showing man on bridge staring into water	Birds, water, insects	None
Shot 2.	Close-up of condemned man's face	Same	None
Shot 3.	Shot of captain, etc.		
Shot 4.	Etc.		

4. This procedure forces students to think in terms of trying to tell a story with pictures. They usually find it difficult, but interesting.

5. Have members of the class read their scripts aloud and draw inferences from their shot descriptions.

6. Show the film.

7. Lastly, ask students to discuss their ideas for filming compared with Robert Enrico's actual film (for which he won an Academy Award).

Basic skills: teaching symbolism

a. Ask students what death symbols are present when they first see the doomed man (charred tree stump, smoke, ominous-sounding birdcalls, etc.).

b. Students should comment on what is symbolized by the sunrise just before the execution.

c. Discuss why the filmmaker shows Farquhar scrutinizing a leaf, tree, and spider as he escapes downstream.

d. Ask the class what is symbolized by the distortion of the Union soldier's voices as their commander orders them to fire at the fleeing man.

e. What is symbolized by the spider spinning its web that Farquhar sees as he swims downstream?

f. Discuss with students what is symbolized when the camera cuts directly from the wife's outstretched arms to the man hanging from the bridge.

RELATED RESOURCES

Films

Joseph Schultz
Night and Fog
Strange Fruit

Books

Becker, Stephen. *When the War Is Over*. Random House, 1969

PAUL ROBESON:
Tribute to an Artist
(29 min, c, $450/50, Films, Inc., 1981)

THEMES

A magnificent human being. Unjust treatment of an individual by society. Unfair persecution because of political beliefs. The McCarthy era in American history.

CURRICULUM AREAS

Social studies, black studies, language arts, drama, music, human relations

SYNOPSIS

Paul Robeson is a renowned actor, internationally famous concert singer, film star, university graduate in English literature, lawyer, political activist, and All-American athlete. Yet generations of Americans have never heard of him. Narrated by actor Sidney Poitier, this film is a long-overdue tribute to a true Renaissance man.

Paul Robeson set many records in his lifetime. He was an All-American football player at Rutgers; the star of *Othello*, the longest-running Shakespearean play in Broadway history; the first black actor to appear in a leading role with an all-white company; and the actor selected by his colleagues to read the funeral oration for President Franklin D. Roosevelt.

When Robeson, angered by the unjust treatment of black people, began to speak out politically, however, the anxieties and insecurities of the United States in the 1950s destroyed his career. Following a concert in Peekskill, New York, on December 4, 1949, in which 140 concertgoers were injured by groups protesting Robeson's appearance, the sale of his records was prohibited, his passport was cancelled, and concert offers were withdrawn. In a final indignity, he became the only player in the history of the All-American College Hall of Fame to have his name erased from the record. The team of 1917-1918 has only ten players.

Blacklisted in America and unable to travel abroad, Robeson was finished. After ten years of litigation, the Supreme Court held that no citizen may be denied a passport because of his political beliefs or associations. Robeson had helped to establish a valuable principle in American jurisprudence, but it cost him ten years of the most potentially productive years of his life. For him, vindication came too late.

Paul Robeson was one of America's most courageous and accomplished citizens. This film is a splendid opportunity to set the record straight.

BEFORE VIEWING

Ask the class to write its gut response to the following phrases:

a. a black man who is All-American in football

b. a black man who is All-American in football and a Phi Beta Kappa

c. a black man who is All-American in football, a Phi Beta Kappa, and valedictorian of his university graduating class

d. a black man who is All-American in football, a Phi Beta Kappa, valedictorian of his class, and a lawyer

e. a black man who is All-American in football, a Phi Beta Kappa, valedictorian of his class, a lawyer, and a leading concert singer

f. a black man who is All-American in football, a Phi Beta Kappa, valedictorian of his class, a lawyer, a leading concert singer, and a renowned stage and screen star

g. a black man who had accomplished all this and risked it to become a political activist for the civil rights of black people; this was before the civil rights movement of the 1960s.

AFTER VIEWING

The accomplishments of Paul Robeson are particularly significant since they occurred during a period when racism was generally accepted in the United States. Discuss with the class how his accomplishments are related to the thoughts expressed in the previewing activities. (Much of the success of this assignment depends upon the willingness of students to be open about their own preconceived stereotypes.) What was in Robeson's background that set him apart from others? What were his outstanding personal qualities, other than his vocal, athletic, and acting abilities?

Suggestions for discussions and compositions

a. Racial prejudice is often based on unfounded stereotypes that people of different backgrounds and ethnic origins have about each other. Because of films, radio, books, and, to a limited extent, television, the stereotype of a black person was Jack Benny's amiable, wise-cracking valet, Rochester; the hand-wringing, screeching servant, Butterfly McQueen of *Gone with the Wind*; the none-too-bright but funny, Amos and Andy (who were actually two white men) of radio fame; and the rolling-eyed, shuffling, superstitious film comedian, Stepin Fetchit. Although racial attitudes in the North were not as overtly rigid as they were in the South, blacks were supposed to know their place. Ask students why Robeson was threatening to many Americans brought up in such a society.

b. On the basis of his accomplishments Paul Robeson was surely a remarkable man. Discuss with the class what, other than his failure to conform to the stereotype, explained his persecution by a large segment of the public. What does the United States Constitution say about freedom of speech?

c. Have students write obituaries for a newspaper about the death of Paul Robeson. They should include facts about his birthplace, parents, education, career, and death.

d. Paul Robeson's dream was of equality for black people in the United States. Do students have dreams they would be willing to fight for? Or have fought for?

e. Have students read the excerpt (see page 122) from Paul Robeson's valedictory speech at Rutgers University. If they knew nothing else about him, what would they learn about him from this address?

f. Ask students about the McCarthy era blacklist. Who determined who would be on it? How did it affect artists whose names were on the list?

g. Ask students if Paul Robeson's name should have been removed from the All-American football team at the Hall of Fame.

h. Read aloud to the class Pulitzer Prize-winning poet Gwendolyn Brooks's famous poem about Paul Robeson. Ask them to explain in one sentence the point she is making about him.

Suggestions for advanced assignments

a. Have students research the McCarthy era in American history. What other artists (writers, actors, musicians, painters) had their careers destroyed during this period? Report to the class those that are especially interesting.

b. Ask students to research other people in American history who have equalled or surpassed Paul Robeson's varied record of accomplishment in many fields. How many did they find?

c. Ask students to lunch with a person from an entirely different group than they usually would. How did they feel? Was it successful? Would they do it again?

d. Have students conduct a poll on a controversial subject. They should note particularly the reaction of students and staff who oppose the subject of their polls.

e. Ask students to carry around a controversial book. They should be aware of the reactions of people who read its title.

ADDITIONAL STUDY AIDS

Amendment I of the
Constitution of the United States

Congress shall make no law respecting an establishment of religion or prohibiting the free exercise thereof; or abridging the freedom of speech, or of the press; or of the right of the people peaceably to assemble and to petition the Government for a redress of grievances.

ADDITIONAL STUDY AIDS (cont'd)

Paul Robeson

Paul Robeson was born in Princeton, New Jersey, in 1898. He graduated Phi Beta Kappa from Rutgers University in June, 1919, where he was valedictorian of his class. Following his graduation from Rutgers in English literature, he obtained his law degree from Columbia University in New York City.

He made his New York stage debut with Margaret Wycherly in 1922 in *Taboo*. Later he played the same role in England with Mrs. Patrick Campbell. His other Broadway roles included leads in *All God's Chillun Got Wings, The Emperor Jones, Black Boy, Porgy, The Hairy Ape, Showboat*, and the title role in *Othello*. He was the first black actor to play a title role in a Shakespeare play.

Following this, he made his debut as a concert singer and was an immediate success both here and abroad.

His films include: *Sanders of the River, Jericho, King Solomon's Mines, Proud Valley, Emperor Jones,* and *Showboat*. He died on January 23, 1976, in Philadelphia.

Excerpt from Robeson's Valedictory Address, Rutgers University, June, 1919

We of the younger generation especially must feel a sacred call to that which lies before us. I go out to do my little part in helping my untutored brother. We of this less-favored race realized that our future lies chiefly in our own hands. On ourselves alone will depend the preservation of our liberties and the transmission of them in their integrity to those who will come after us. And we are struggling on, attempting to show that knowledge can be obtained under difficulties; that poverty may give place to affluence; that obscurity is not an absolute bar to distinction and that a way is open to welfare and happiness to all who will follow the way with resolution and wisdom; that neither the old-time slavery, nor continued prejudice need extinguish self-respect, crush manly ambition, or paralyze effort; that no power outside of himself can prevent man from sustaining an honorable character and a useful relation to his day and generation. We know that neither institutions nor friends can make a race stand unless it has strength in its own foundation; that races like individuals must stand or fall by their own merit; that to fully succeed they must practice the virtues of self-reliance, self-respect, industry, perseverance, and economy.*

---

*From "The Whole World in His Hands: A Pictorial Biography of Paul Robeson." Copyright © 1981 by Susan Robeson. Published by arrangement with Lyle Stuart.

Robeson's Testimony before the
House Un-American Activities Committee, 1956

Mr. Robeson: I stand here struggling for the rights of my people to be full citizens in this country and they are not. They are not in Mississippi and they are not ... in Washington.... You want to shut up every Negro who has the courage to stand up and fight for the rights of his people.... That is why I am here today....

Mr. Scherer: Why do you not stay in Russia?

Mr. Robeson: Because my father was a slave, and my people died to build this country and I am going to stay here and have a part of it just like you. And no fascist-minded people will drive me from it. Is that clear?*

Found among Robeson's Collection
after His Death

The weakest things in the world can overmatch
　　the strongest things in the world.
Nothing in the world can be compared to water
　　for its weak and yielding nature; yet in attacking the hard and
　　the strong nothing proves better than it. For there is no
　　alternative to it.
The weak can overcome the strong, and the yielding can overcome
　　the hard:
This all the world knows but does not practice.
Therefore, the Sage says:
He who sustains all the reproaches of the country can be the master
　　of the land;
He who sustains all the calamities of the country can be the king of
　　the world.
These are words of truth,
Though they seem paradoxical.*

Lao-tzu, *Tao Tê Ching*

ADDITIONAL STUDY AIDS (cont'd)

Gwendolyn Brooks

Born in Topeka, Kansas, on July 7, 1919, Gwendolyn Brooks became the first black woman to win the prestigious Pulitzer Prize for poetry. In 1968 she became poet laureate of Illinois succeeding Carl Sandburg. In 1976 her career was capped by her election to the National Institute of Arts and Letters. Ms. Brooks is still in demand as a lecturer and reader of her poetry on college campuses.

RELATED RESOURCES

Films

Almos' a Man	*Only the Ball Was White*
American Parade: With All	*Strange Fruit*
Deliberate Speed	*Travelling Hopefully*
California Reich	*Youth Terror: The View from*
Equality	*behind the Gun*

Poetry

Paul Robeson*

That time
we all heard it,
cool and clear,
cutting across the hot grit of the day.
The major Voice
The adult Voice
forgoing Rolling River
forgoing tearful tale of bale and barge
and other symptoms of the old despond.
Warning, in music — words
devout and large,
that we are each other's
harvest:
we are each other's
business:
we are each other's
magnitude and bond.

—Gwendolyn Brooks

*Reprinted by permission of the author.

Short story

Wright, Richard. "Almos' a Man." *The American Short Story. Vol. I.* Dell, 1977

Books for young adults

Douglass, Frederick. *Narrative of the Life of Frederick Douglass.* Harvard University Press, 1960

King, Martin Luther, Jr. *Why We Can't Wait.* Harper & Row, 1964

Lee, Harper. *To Kill a Mockingbird.* Popular Library, 1977

Robeson, Susan. *The Whole World in His Hands: A Pictorial Biography of Paul Robeson.* Citadel Press, 1981

PEEGE
(26 min, c, $465/40, Phoenix Films, 1974)

THEMES
Communication between generations. Old age and death. The problem of aging parents.

CURRICULUM AREAS
Language arts, psychology, sociology, drama, humanities, gerontology, family living, guidance, values

SYNOPSIS
Peege, a 1974 release, is a classic among short films because of its emotional power. Students and adults alike are frequently moved to tears by the film, and praise it to those who have yet to see it. The story is one that is played out in thousands of American homes.

The parents (Barbara Rush and William Schallert) and their three sons are paying a last visit at Christmas to their dying grandmother, Peege. They approach the visit with the usual trepidations, "What shall we talk about? Will she know us? How much longer will she live?"

Whether Peege does know them is not clear. Strapped in her chair, tubes in her veins, saliva running from the corner of her mouth, she answers their well-meaning, desperate questions dully and mechanically. Christmas presents are accepted silently, without recognition. Finally the Mother, overcome by Peege's condition and the meaningless conversation, dissolves in tears. Awkwardly the Father makes the usual pseudo-hearty excuses for leaving, "It's time for Peege to have her Christmas dinner," etc. All of the family, except the oldest grandson (Bruce Davison), kiss Peege goodbye for what they know is the last time.

The grandson, Greg, begins to reminisce with Peege. In a series of flashbacks, we learn that Peege was once a warm, earthy woman with a special relationship with her adored grandson. Patiently, softly he reminds her of the incidents he remembers most lovingly, but again there is no response from Peege. Near tears, Greg whispers despairingly, "I know that somewhere inside there is the grandmother I remember. I want you to know that I love you."

Still there is no response from Peege. Greg, weeping, stumbles out to the car where his family is waiting. Everyone is upset, but as the camera cuts back to Peege we see that she is smiling for the first time.

Peege is about communication—about looking for connections between people who love each other. Few of us can confront the old and the dying without being aware of our own mortality. Young people know they will ultimately become old. *Peege* suggests, in unforgettable terms, a way in which we can confront our fears.

Peege
Photograph courtesy of Phoenix Films

BEFORE VIEWING

Ask students to respond in writing immediately after they have seen the film. Tell the class that it is about a dying grandmother, a situation most must confront at some point. Explain the importance of writing without interacting with anyone else so that the thoughts are one's own, uninfluenced by anyone else. Be sure they have paper and pen ready.

AFTER VIEWING

Allow the students to respond in writing. Be sure they check their papers for correct spelling and punctuation when they have finished.

Suggestions for discussions and compositions

a.   Ask students what Greg would have learned about communication if he had seen his grandmother's smile after his conversation with her. Have they learned anything about communication from seeing *Peege*?

b.   Have the class write an account of a good time they shared with a grandparent. If they do not have grandparents or they have not lived near them, write about any older person with whom they have shared a rewarding experience.

c.   Students should choose a grandparent (or a great grandparent) and describe what they think she or he may have been like as a young person.

d.   Can students imagine themselves as old? Ask them to write a description of what they think they will be like as an old person. Is it the kind of old person they would like to be? What determines what kind of person we will be when we are old? Some psychologists say that we should begin preparing for old age when we are very young. Ask students what they mean.

e.   In the course of living, each of us loses people that we care about. Explain that many people write a sympathy note to someone who has lost a loved one. Ask students to pretend that Greg is a close friend. They are to write a sympathy card to him about the death of his grandmother.

f.   Inform the class that many schools offer classes in thanatology. If such a class were offered, would they take it?

g.   Tell students that in many societies, such as China's, the old are revered and their advice is sought. If American society were like that, do they think people would fear growing old as much as they do now?

h.   How do students feel about being young with their lives ahead of them after seeing a film such as *Peege*? Does it make them even more appreciative of their lives? If they think about it from *their* point of view is *Peege* a depressing film?

Suggestions for advanced assignments

a.   In his play, *I Never Sang for My Father,* Robert Anderson wrote: "Death ends a life but it does not end a relationship, which struggles on in the survivor's mind toward some resolution which it may never reach." Discuss the meaning of the quotation in as much depth as possible. Ask students if it applies to Greg. To his father (Peege's son)? To Greg's brothers?

b.   Discuss with students that instead of emphasizing death, which is a normal part of all life, perhaps we should emphasize life. Can they write a celebration of life that also includes events such as in *Peege*?

c.   Ask students to draw a picture of themselves with a grandparent. What are they doing? They should share with the class if they can.

d.   Ask the class to role-play four older people, who are seventy or eighty years of age. Each must decide in advance what kind of older person he or she will be. Which person would the class most like to be like?

RELATED RESOURCES

Films

Close Harmony	*Piece of Cake*
Forever Young	*Portrait of Grandpa Doc*
The Lost Phoebe	*The Shopping Bag Lady*
Never Give Up	*The Stringbean*

Poetry

Bahe, Liz Sohappy. "Grandmother Sleeps." *Carriers of the Dream Wheel: Contemporary Native American Poetry.* Harper & Row, 1975

Berry, Wendell. "The Grandmother." *A Geography of Poets: An Anthology of the New Poetry.* Bantam Books, 1981

Hart, Joanne. "When Your Parents Grow Old." *Anthology of Magazine Verse and Yearbook of American Poetry.* Monitor Book Company, 1980

Lowell, Robert. "Grandparents." *The Poet in America: 1650 to the Present.* University of Texas Press, 1972

Merwin, W. S. "Grandmother and Grandson." *New Poets of England and America.* World, 1967

Sarton, May. "Halfway to Silence." *Norton Anthology of Poetry.* W. W. Norton & Company, rev., 1973

Sarton, May. "Old Lovers at the Ballet." *Norton Anthology of Poetry.* W. W. Norton & Company, rev., 1973

Poetry (cont'd)

Sassoon, Siegfried. "Two Old Ladies." *Oxford Book of Twentieth Century English Verse.* Oxford University Press, 1977

Shapiro, Karl. "My Grandmother." *The Voice That Is Great within Us: American Poetry of the Twentieth Century.* Bantam Books, 1970

Willard, Nancy. "Foxfire." *I Hear My Sisters Saying.* Thomas Y. Crowell, 1976

Short stories

Bradbury, Ray. "The Leave-taking." *The Stories of Ray Bradbury.* Knopf, 1980

Olsen, Tillie. "Tell Me a Riddle." *Fifty Years of the Short Story.* Doubleday, 1970

Porter, Katharine Anne. "The Jilting of Granny Weatherall." *The American Short Story, Vol. II.* Dell, 1980

Books for young adults

Branfield, John. *The Fox in Winter.* Atheneum, 1982

Hammer, Richard. *Mr. Jacobsen's War.* Harcourt Brace Jovanovich, 1981

Krementz, Jill. *How It Feels When a Parent Dies.* Random House, 1982

Levoy, Myron. *A Shadow like a Leopard.* Harper & Row, 1982

O'Neal, Zibby. *A Formal Feeling.* Viking Press, 1982

Books for adults

Rubin, Diane. *Caring: A Daughter's Story.* Holt, Rinehart, 1982

Sarton, May. *As We Are Now.* W. W. Norton & Company, 1973

RENDEZVOUS
(9 min, c, $225/35, Pyramid Films, 1970)

THEMES
A fast ride through the streets of Paris seen from the point of view of an unseen driver.

CURRICULUM AREAS
Language arts, France, filmmaking

SYNOPSIS
This deceptively simple little film offers rich rewards because it teaches sensory awareness, point of view, observation of details, and even poetry.

With his camera mounted on the hood of a Ferrari, the famed French filmmaker Claude Lelouch takes a nine-minute ride through the streets of Paris toward his rendezvous. The resulting film, shot in one take, with no photographic tricks or changes in camera speed, is of great interest to students because of their interest in sports cars.

Tension builds as the viewer becomes the driver. The screeching of tires, the whining of the engine as it accelerates, the unknown destination, the sights and sounds of the streets, the imagined feelings of the driver stimulate even the most reluctant student to write. Paragraphs, essays, and poetry result.

The car whizzes past the Eiffel Tower, the Louvre, the Arch of Triumph, and the Place de Concorde, making the film useful in French classes interested in the cultural environment. And Lelouch, of course, belongs in filmmaking classes. Exhilarating, stimulating, and fun, as well as practical, *Rendezvous* is a bargain.

BEFORE VIEWING
Tell the class it is going to take a fast ride through the streets of Paris in a sports car. (Many of the students enjoy recognizing that the car is a Ferrari.) As they watch, they are to imagine that they are the driver. They are to notice what he sees, what he hears, and to imagine what he feels (emotionally and physically). They should imagine even what he smells. Emphasize observing and listening. Then show the film for enjoyment. This assignment works especially well with remedial students who have difficulty writing.

AFTER VIEWING
Suggestions for discussions and compositions
Ask the class to have paper and pencil ready. You are going to show the film again and this time you want them to write as fast as they can. No one is to stop writing. Write words and phrases *only*, no sentences because there won't be time. Tell them that you want them to write down everything that the driver *sees*, everything he *hears*, everything he *does*, what they imagine he *feels, smells,* and *thinks*. Emphasize that they must write quickly and that they

AFTER VIEWING (cont'd)

will be given time when the film is over to add any details they have not had time to list.

A student might list the following words:

He sees: buildings, other cars, the road stretched out before him, traffic signals, bicycles, trees, shrubs, sidewalks, the Arch of Triumph, the Eiffel Tower, pedestrians, trucks, obstructing traffic, hills, ambulances

He hears: tires screeching, signals clanging, motor roaring, horns honking, engines accelerating, gears shifting, people shouting, traffic moving, sirens screaming, fire bells clanging

He feels: foot pressing the accelerator, his hand on the gear shift, eyes squinting, body pressed against the car as he turns a corner, tension of his body from concentration

He does: grips the wheel, swerves to avoid obstacles, speeds up and slows down, shifts gears, stops abruptly, glides to a stop when he reaches his destination, approaches a beautiful woman, etc.

He smells: the burning of rubber, the exhausts of other traffic, the interior of his car, the morning air.

Writing a poem

The class should have many descriptive words and phrases. Give them an opportunity to add any words they have not had time to list. Ask them to look through their lists and circle ten key words or phrases. These key words are to be repeated several times to give their poem unity. Choosing freely from their words and phrases, they are to arrange them into any poetic form. You might remind them that the first word of each line of poetry is often capitalized and that key words may be emphasized by placing them at the beginning or ending of a line. Remind them that present-tense verbs are more exciting. Indicate any misspelled words and ask the students to look them up in the dictionary. Have the students copy their poems in ink on another piece of paper. If you have a copy machine, it is satisfying to copy these poems for the class because for many students it is their first opportunity to see their work reproduced.

SCHOOLBOY FATHER
(30 min, c, $450/40, Learning Corporation of America, 1981)

THEMES
A teenage father who wants to take responsibility for his child. The difficulties of teenage parenting. The pain of unwanted pregnancy.

CURRICULUM AREAS
Family living, sex education, sociology, language arts, guidance

SYNOPSIS
Each year hundreds of thousands of teenagers are caught up in the painful dilemma of an unwanted pregnancy. Adopting, aborting, rearing the child in a one-parent house, marrying prematurely—all options can bring their share of unhappiness.

Schoolboy Father, based on Jeanette Eyerly's popular novel, *He's My Baby Now*, introduces us to one of these young people, sixteen-year-old Charles Elderbury. Blessed with an appealing personality and good looks, he gets good grades, is popular with his peers, and maintains a job that will soon buy him a long-awaited car.

Charles's pleasant life is shattered when he learns that he is the father of a child, born after a short affair with a girl he had met at summer camp. Realizing the void in his own life because he had never known his father, he wants desperately to be a good father to his son.

Hurt and angry when he discovers that the child's mother, whom he has not seen in many months, has agreed to allow the infant to be adopted, Charles refuses to sign the necessary papers. He is convinced that with his mother's help, he can care for his son. Reluctantly, his mother agrees, but Charles soon learns that good parenting involves much more than he can handle. Finally forced to face the reality of the situation, he signs the release form and tearfully gives over the baby for adoption. The grief he experiences is a high price to pay for the lessons he has learned about life and himself.

With an effective performance by young Bob Rowe as Charles and a powerful, unsentimental script, the poignancy of *Schoolboy Father* makes it memorable in the classroom.

BEFORE VIEWING

Ask students to complete the following opinion survey*

A. Premarital intercourse is:
1___Totally unacceptable; sex should only occur in marriage.
2___Acceptable only if the couple is engaged.
3___Acceptable if the two people have expressed love/commitment.
4___Acceptable under any situation where both people agree.
5___Acceptable if birth control measures are used.
6___Acceptable under any circumstances.
7___Other _____

B. Birth control is
1___Never acceptable.
2___Acceptable if the couple is married and cannot afford children.
3___Necessary for anyone who is sexually active, unless pregnancy is desired.
4___A responsibility for the female partner.

C. In an unwanted pregnancy
1___The couple should marry under all circumstances.
2___The girl should have an abortion.
3___The girl should have the baby and raise it.
4___The boy should be responsible for the financial burden.
5___The boy should have the option to take the child and raise it.
6___The parents of one of the people involved should be responsible.
7___The baby should be put up for adoption.

D. Sex education is
1___The responsibility of the parents only.
2___The responsibility of the parents and the school.
3___The responsibility of the school only.
4___Something that should be left to the individual child.
5___Other _____

AFTER VIEWING

Suggestions for discussions and compositions

a. Ask students to review their responses to the opinion survey completed before the film. Have their opinions changed?

b. Discuss with the class the relationship of freedom, responsibility, and independence. Who was carrying much of the load for Charles?

c. How do students feel about Charles for trying to keep his baby? Was he being impractical? Should he have asked for his mother's help? Is it fair to a parent who has already raised a family to ask them to assume the responsibility for another child?

_____

*Reprinted by permission of Learning Corporation of America, New York, N.Y., from the leader's guide accompanying the film *Schoolboy Father*. All rights reserved.

d. What are students' goals for themselves in ten years? Where do they hope to be? Would an unwanted pregnancy now interfere with those goals?

e. Ask the class whose responsibility it is to provide sex information to teenagers? Parents? School? Church? Friends? What if the parents don't or can't provide it?

f. Discuss with students proposed federal law that would require any federally funded clinic giving birth control or abortion information to anyone under eighteen years old to notify the parents of the action. Will this help pregnant teenagers or make it more difficult for them?

g. Ask students what parents should do if the sexual behavior of their children affects their lives? To what extent are parents responsible?

h. Is there something students want as much as Charles wanted to keep his child? What are they willing to do to get it or keep it?

i. Ask students how their school handles pregnant mothers? Are they allowed to remain in school? In the regular classroom? Are they offered help with their problems? Should they be?

Suggestions for advanced assignments

a. Encourage discussion about the ramifications for society – social, economic, and psychological – if the epidemic nature of teenage pregnancy is not reversed.

b. Do students think Mrs. Elderbury is a good mother? Was her behavior favorable to Charles's growth toward independence?

c. Discuss if society's standards have changed since students' parents were teenagers. Which change, if any, has been positive? Negative? Neither, just different?

d. Ask students to write a paper on their definition of *love.* They should interview a ten-year-old, a teenager, a young adult (25-35 years old), a middle-aged person, and an old person (70-80 years old). They should find out how each would define love. Are the definitions different from theirs? What happens to the views of love as one grows older?

e. Discuss if children and teenagers should be protected from sexual propaganda on television and in the movies.

f. Students should pretend that they are Mrs. Elderbury, Charles's mother. She is confiding in her friend, Mary Fields, about the situation: what happened, how she feels about helping with the baby, what she thinks will happen if she tries. Ms. Fields is sympathetic, but offers no advice.

g. Have students be Daisy Dallinger and Charles meeting several months after Charles gives up the child. What do they say to each other? What are their attitudes? Angry? Forgiving? Indifferent? Embarrassed? Caring? Hostile?

RELATED RESOURCES

Films

Am I Normal?	*Taking Chances*
Dear Diary	*Teen Mother: A Story of Coping*
Mother, May I?	*Teenage Father*
Sweet Sixteen and Pregnant	

Books for young adults

Nonfiction

Foster, Sallie. *The One Girl in Ten: A Self-Portrait of the Teenage Mother*. Arbor, 1981

Fromm, Erich. *The Art of Loving*. Harper & Row, 1956

Gordon, Sol. *Facts about Sex for Today's Youth*. Ed-U-Press, 1979

Pomeroy, Wardell. *Boys and Sex, Girls and Sex*. Delacorte Press, 1981

Walworth, Nancy. *Coping with Teenage Motherhood*. Rosen and Richards, 1979

Fiction

Bawden, Nina. *The Birds on the Trees*. Harper & Row, 1970

Blume, Judy. *Forever*. Bradbury Press, 1975

Dreiser, Theodore. *An American Tragedy*. Signal Classics, 1973

Elfman, Blossom. *A House for Jennie O*. Houghton Mifflin, 1976

Hansen, Caryl. *I Think I'm Having a Baby*. Avon/Flare, 1981

Mohr, Nicholasa. *Nilda*. Harper & Row, 1973

Price, Reynolds. *A Long and Happy Life*. Atheneum, 1962

Ray, Karen. *The Proposal*. Delacorte, 1981

Windsor, Patricia. *Diving for Roses*. Harper & Row, 1976

Witt, Rene L., and Jeanine Michael. *Mom, I'm Pregnant*. Stein and Day, 1982

Books for adults

Howard, Marion. *Only Human: Teenage Pregnancy and Parenthood.* Continuum, 1975

Oettinger, Katharine. *Not My Daughter: Facing Up to Teenage Pregnancy.* Prentice-Hall, 1981

THE SHOPPING BAG LADY

(11 min, c, $400/35, Learning Corporation of America, 1975)

THEMES

Intergenerational understanding. The discovery that old people were once young. Kindness to others. Stereotyping the old. Our common human bonds.

CURRICULUM AREAS

Language arts, psychology, humanities, gerontology, family living, values, guidance

SYNOPSIS

Many teenagers find it impossible to imagine growing old. Conversely, they find it difficult to imagine that old people were once teenagers like themselves. At some point an incident may occur which brings understanding.

Such an experience is the theme of this poignant story of teenage Emily's encounter with a "shopping bag lady," one of the thousands of homeless women who live in Manhattan's subways, parks, and vacant buildings, and carry all their possessions in a shopping bag.

Emily, who is having difficulty sharing a room with her grandmother, and her friends thoughtlessly tease the old woman (superbly played by Mildred Dunnock). As they are leaving for home, Emily accidentally drops a puppet she has made. Childlike, the old woman seizes it eagerly, and in her loneliness, talks to it and caresses it as though it were a child.

Later in Central Park, Emily's friend accuses the old woman of trying to kidnap her young brother, a patently trumped-up charge that Emily verifies to the police, who take the shopping bag lady to the hospital. As Emily goes through the meagre possessions that the woman has inadvertently left behind, she discovers the photograph of a young, beautiful actress, Annie Lewis, the aged woman in her youth.

Shocked by her discovery, Emily stares at her fourteen-year-old face and then rushes to the hospital to apologize. Having given the woman the puppet, Emily leaves as the shopping bag lady croons to her child.

At home, Emily views her grandmother with new understanding and patience. Her grandmother was once young and beautiful also. It is a moving story about our common bonds, our need for love and understanding from each other.

The Shopping Bag Lady
Photograph courtesy of Learning Corporation of America

BEFORE VIEWING

Discuss the title with the class. What is a shopping bag lady? Do they think such women exist? Where? If students know they live in Manhattan, ask why that area might produce such a group of women. Ask for a volunteer to research the question and to report to the class. Tell students they are going to see a film about a high school girl and a shopping bag lady.

AFTER VIEWING

Suggestions for discussions and compositions

a.   Have students ever had an experience similar to Emily's that made them realize that someone close to them had once been young? Can they share it with the class? Have they had the opposite experience of realizing that they would someday be old? How did they feel? How can we handle fears about growing old?

b.   Emily and her friends were very thoughtless in their initial treatment of the woman. Can students explain their behavior? Should young people be held responsible for being rude and for lying, as in Emily's verification of the kidnap story? Is age an excuse for moral defects? Is anything an excuse?

c.   Discuss with the class how Emily's discovery of Annie Lewis helped her relationship with her grandmother.

d.   Ask students what is symbolized by the puppet's importance to the old woman?

e.   The old woman had saved items from her past. If someone in 2035 were to find a scrapbook of the students' lives up to now, what kind of person would she or he judge them to be?

f.   Ask the class to write their impressions of their grandparents' youth. Were those times fun? Strange? Exciting? Frightening? Were they very different from theirs? How?

g.   Ask students to write a paragraph describing what they think their grandmother or grandfather was like as a teenager. If they can, take it home and ask her or him how accurate they are.

h.   If students could return to any point in time (or go ahead into the future) what period would they choose? Why? If they would remain in the present, they should explain why they are not interested in changing.

i.   If students had to put their most valued possessions into two shopping bags, what would they choose?

j.   Ask students to describe the dress, hairstyles, music, manners, speech, and entertainment of their peers. Imagine that they are seventy years old. How will they view what they have just described?

k.   It is the knowledge that we must die that gives life meaning. If they were to discover the date of their own death, would they want to know?

1. What would they most like to know or understand better before they die?

Suggestions for advanced assignments

a. Students should ask a grandparent if he or she has a photograph of themself that they may take to school. Ask them to show it to the class and talk for a few minutes about some of the most interesting aspects of their lives.

b. Ask students to fill out the following form:

    What kind of future do you envision for yourself?
    Ten years from now: _____
    Twenty-five years from now: _____
    Fifty years from now: _____

Basic skills: developing questions

a. Students should interview and write a biography of a grandparent.

b. Give the class time to prepare a list of questions to be used in the interview. Remind them that starting with, "She was born...." and following her life in chronological order is not very interesting. Each student should develop twenty-five to thirty-five questions.

c. Allow the class a reasonable period to gather the answers. Have them bring them to school and organize the material into paragraphs.

RELATED RESOURCES

Films

Chillysmith Farm	*The Lost Phoebe*
Close Harmony	*Peege*
Dr. Heidegger's Experiment	*Piece of Cake*
Forever Young	*Portrait of Grandpa Doc*
The Jilting of Granny	*A Private Life*
Weatherall	*The Stringbean*

Poetry

Crane, Hart. "My Grandmother's Love Letters." *Norton Anthology of Modern Poetry.* W. W. Norton & Company, rev., 1973

Meynell, Alice. "Letter from a Girl to Her Own Old Age." *Salt and Bitter and Good: Three Centuries of English and American Women Poets.* Paddington Press, 1975

Rosen, Michael. "Going through the Old Photos." *First Poetry Book.* Oxford University Press, 1979

Books for young adults

Campbell, R. W. *Where Pigeons Go to Die*. Rawson, 1978

Farber, Norma. *How Does It Feel to Be Old?* Creative Arts Book Company, 1981

Laurence, Margaret. *The Olden Day's Coat*. Knopf, 1980

Rousseau, Ann Marie. *Shopping Bag Ladies*. Pilgrim Press, 1981

Schulman, L. M. *Autumn Light*. Thomas Y. Crowell, 1978

Books for adults

Cohen, Stephen Z., and Bruce Michael Gans. *The Other Generation Gap*. Follett Publishing Company, 1978

Cowley, Malcolm. *The View from 80*. Penguin Books, 1980

Stegner, Wallace. *The Spectator Bird*. Doubleday, 1976

SOLO
(16 min, c, $325/50, Pyramid Films, 1972)

THEMES

Man against nature. The exhilaration of physical effort. The joy of achievement. Man's potential for higher consciousness. The satisfaction of solitary effort.

CURRICULUM AREAS

Physical education, language arts, psychology, humanities, filmmaking, guidance, values

SYNOPSIS

Silhouetted against a predawn sky, a lone climber begins his ascent to the snowy peak of a mountain. Slowly, painstakingly, he inches his way up its sheer rock face. Gently he extricates a little frog from a crevice, tucks it in his pocket, and resumes his climb.

From then on, he seems to risk his life in every frame of the film until he reaches the summit. Along the way he swings joyously at the end of a rope at dizzying heights. A misplaced piton and he falls abruptly, saved only by a rope tied to more secure pitons. He finds tenuous toeholds in the rock. Finally he edges up a crevass, feels for a handhold on the edge of an overhanging rock, and pulls himself to the summit. As he stands upright on the peak he waves exultantly.

On his descent he playfully rolls down a snowfield, until once again he is in an Alpine meadow where he tenderly releases his companion, the frog.

The strengths of the film are many. Mike Hoover, the climber, is marvelous; the photography is superb; and the film develops carefully the conflict between man and nature. Although it is filmed as one climb, *Solo* was actually filmed on several mountains over a period of months.

The feeling of the climber's solitude and his challenge to the mountain are strengthened by the musical score and the natural sounds. Nominated for an Academy Award in 1972, this stunning, nonverbal tour de force conveys the beauty and excitement of a sport that few dare try.

BEFORE VIEWING

Let the class ponder this question: When was the last time they felt really alive? Winning or trying their best at an athletic event? Being awarded an unexpected honor? Finishing a difficult test and knowing they had done really well? Working hard at a job and having the boss recognize it with a promotion or a raise in pay? Driving home for the first time in their car? Sailing a boat successfully on a sunny day? Tell the class it will see a film about a young man who finds fulfillment in climbing mountains by himself.

Solo
Photograph courtesy of Pyramid Films

AFTER VIEWING

Suggestions for discussions and compositions

a. Have students ever had to make a great physical effort to reach a goal? How did they feel? Do they understand the climber being willing to risk his life to accomplish his goal? What is his reward? Is it worth the physical effort involved?

b. Discuss with the class the relationship of the climber to nature. Is it ecological or emotional or both? Have the students ever felt the same feeling when they have been alone in a place of natural grandeur?

c. Ask students if it is true that the more difficult the struggle to reach a goal the greater one's sense of satisfaction when it is reached?

d. Discuss with students why winning or accomplishing a goal brings such a sense of satisfaction. Does this help to explain why spectator sports are so popular in the United States? Would they go to watch their favorite athletic event if they knew beforehand their team would lose?

e. If students knew they couldn't win in a particular circumstance, what would they do? Would they quit?

f. How does the title *Solo* influence their concept of the film before they see it?

g. As the climber works his way up a long, vertical crevass, the camera focuses on him from several different perspectives. How many of these can students describe? Why does the filmmaker present different views of the climber in the same sequence?

h. What does the lack of dialogue contribute to the film? Is silence to them an effective sound?

i. As the climber walks across a snow field, the camera pulls back to reveal the entire mountain and the climber. Ask students what effect this produces. Why would the filmmaker want this effect?

j. *Solo* is an excellent example of fine editing. Although the film was actually made during twenty-one climbs and at several different sites, it appears as though it were made at one time. Ask students how the editor has produced this effect. Why does he want this effect?

k. Give students the form that follows (see page 146). Ask them to write the story of their fall from a mountain.

It's a Bird, it's a Plane?

SCHWARTZ HIGH JUNIOR FALLS FROM MOUNTAIN: LIVES TO TELL THE STORY TO STUDENT ASSEMBLY!

Suggestions for advanced assignments

a.   Discuss with the class the view that every human being is existentially and theistically alone. Whether one faces nothingness or God, each person is ultimately alone, and must face life alone as the climber does in *Solo*. What support do the forces of nature give him? What support do most of us have?

b.   King Sisyphus was a mythological Greek figure who was condemned to roll a stone uphill forever. As the stone reached the top of the hill, it rolled backward so Sisyphus could never cease trying to push it uphill. The myth says that mankind is forever sentenced to the same fate; that the reward of life is in the struggle, not in the accomplishment. Do students agree?

c.   Are there things in life that can only be done alone? Ask students the difference between being lonely and being alone. Was the climber in *Solo* really alone?

RELATED RESOURCES

Films

Fall Line   *Horse Latitudes*
Flight of the Gossamer Condor   *Psychling*

Poetry

Stafford, William. "A Story." *Poets' Tales: A New Book of Story Poems.* World Publishing Company, 1971

Thomas, R. S. "Alpine." *Literature of Sports.* Heath, 1980

Young, Andrew. "Climbing in Glencoe." *Literature of Sports.* Heath, 1980

Short stories

Helprin, Mark. "The Schrenderspitze." *Prize Stories of the Seventies: From the O. Henry Awards.* Doubleday, 1981

Hubbard, Ron L. "Mountaineer." *Lives You Wished to Lead But Never Dared: A Series of Stories.* Theta Books, Inc., 1979

London, Jack. "Up the Slide." *The Unabridged Jack London.* Running Press, 1981

Maupassant, Guy de. "The Inn." *The Dracula Book of Great Horror Stories.* Citadel Press, 1981

Short stories (cont'd)

Paton, Alan. "The Quarry." *Short Story International*. Cultural Exchange, 1979

Scott, J. M. "A Winter Night's Story." *Short Story International*. Cultural Exchange, 1981

Books for young adults

Healey, Larry. *The Hoard of the Himalayas*. Dodd Meade, 1982

Roth, Arthur J. *Eiger: Wall of Death*. W. W. Norton & Company, 1982

SPLIT CHERRY TREE

(28 min, c, $550/50, Learning Corporation of America, 1982)

THEMES

The father-son relationship. Family loyalty. The importance of education and of openness to change.

CURRICULUM AREAS

Literature and composition, psychology, family living

SYNOPSIS

A film based on a work of recognized literary merit and made with taste and integrity is a find. If it also says something valuable to students, it is a treasure. Such a film is this striking adaptation of Jesse Stuart's autobiographical tale of growing up in the hills of Kentucky.

The story is a familiar one to teachers. Young David Sexton arrives home too late to help his hard-working, uncommunicative father with the chores because he has been kept after school by his teacher, Professor Herbert. The father goes to school seeking revenge against the teacher. Instead, he becomes interested in the teacher's explanation, his philosophy, and his teaching methods and begins to understand what he has missed. When Professor Herbert shows him how to use a microscope, the father's, "I see," is metaphorical as well as actual.

Initially embarrassed by the rough, unsophisticated appearance of his father at the school, David observes his father's reactions, and he, too, changes. He realizes that his father is honest and well-meaning. Ultimately, he defends his father against the ridicule of some of his classmates. Together father and son leave for home, each with a new understanding of the other, and closer than they have ever been before.

The film catches the ambiance of Stuart's story. The exterior photography is spare and beautiful, reflecting the quality of life in the mountains of Kentucky. Actress Colleen Dewhurst and actor Roy K. Stevens are physically and emotionally believable in their roles

BEFORE VIEWING

Discuss with the class the people who have been influential in their lives. What qualities did these people have? Was there conflict? Misunderstanding? A difference in goals? Was an understanding brought about by a learning experience? Ask the class to name the person who has been most influential: father, mother, teacher, minister, sibling, other. Collect the papers and divide the class into small groups of four or six according to the person that each has named.

    a.   Give each of the students a paper with a circle and the spokes of a wheel. Tell them to add more spokes if they need them. In the center of the circle, they should write the person who has been the most influential in their lives (see page 150).

BEFORE VIEWING (cont'd)

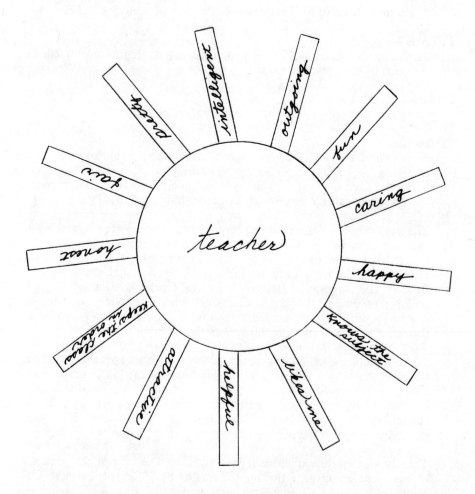

b.   The group is to discuss the qualities of the person that has made him or her influential in their lives. Everyone writes down everything that is mentioned.

c.   The students return to their desks and select the spokes that apply to the person they have selected.

d.   They then develop a topic sentence from the center of the circle and supporting details of the paragraph from the spokes.

e.   They are to develop a paragraph using the topic sentence and the supporting details.

f.   They should then add a sentence of conclusion.

AFTER VIEWING

Suggestions for discussions and compositions

a. Ask students why the Father is hostile to the school? Why does he change after talking to the teacher? What is the purpose of education?

b. Part of the conflict between the teacher and Luster was their differing philosophies of education. Ask students what Luster learned about education that helped him to change his mind. Is the ability to change one's thinking a sign of weakness or growth?

c. Discuss with the class how dialogue is used to create characterization in the story. Explain that there are three forms of English spoken in the film — formal, informal, and dialectical.

d. David grew in maturity and understanding because of the conflict between his father and the teacher and because of his own conflict with his classmates. What do students believe that David learned that caused him to change?

e. Ask students to write an epilogue to the story. What happens to David? The teacher? Luster?

f. Ask the class to write an account of the conversation between David and his father on the way home from school.

g. Students should read Jesse Stuart's story. Does the tone of the story seem to them the same as the tone of the film? What do they prefer?

h. Ask students to describe the best teacher they have ever had. What were the qualities that made him or her memorable to them? Is this person also the teacher from whom they learned the most?

i. Have students ever changed their minds because they understood something better, such as another's position on an issue or on a personal or political situation?

j. In a recent nationwide poll, teenagers chose Suzanne Somers and Burt Reynolds as their ideal parents. Can students explain this vote? Do they really know anything about Burt Reynolds as a person? Do they agree with the results of the poll?

k. Ask students to describe their ideal parent.

l. It has been said that discipline is not punishment. It is proof that adults care about the young people in their charge. Do students agree or disagree?

m. Will students bring up their children the same way they have been raised? What changes would they make? What if social standards change (as they have in their parents' lifetime)? Will they be adaptable or is it difficult for them to change?

Suggestions for discussions and compositions (cont'd)

    n. Do students judge people by the way they look, dress, or speak? What does this tell them about themselves?

    o. Ask students to think about themselves. Are there many things about their parents they don't understand? Can they share any of them with the class?

    p. Have they ever felt ashamed or embarrassed because of any member of their family? Ask them to think about what they did. Would they handle it differently today? What did they learn from the experience? Did they grow as David did? (Explain that this assignment is for their eyes only.)

Suggestions for advanced assignments

    a. Ask the class to attend a function they have never before attended, such as a play, a ballet, an opera, a football game, a church service. Ask them to be prepared to write an account of their experience.

    b. Ask students to attend a meeting of a civic group: a planning commission, school committee, environmental protection group, etc. They should write up the dynamics, or interaction, between individuals or subgroups within the group.

RELATED RESOURCES

Books for young adults

Chambers, Aidan. *Breakstone.* Harper & Row, 1978

Ellis, Mel. *An Eagle in the Wind.* Holt, Rinehart and Winston, 1978

Gaines, Ernest J. *In My Father's House.* Knopf, 1978

Lenz, S. *The German Lesson.* Hill and Wang, 1972

Peck, Richard. *Father Figure.* Viking Press, 1978

THE WAY OF THE WILLOW
(29 min, c, $440/45, Beacon Films, 1982)

THEMES
Adapting to a new culture. Forgetting a tragic past to start anew. The problems of refugees. Music as communication. "Am I my brother's keeper?"

CURRICULUM AREAS
Language arts, humanities, world history, psychology, sociology, guidance, values, immigrant education

SYNOPSIS
One of the most effective uses of film is to help students understand people of other cultures, whom American students might never encounter. This Blue Ribbon winner at the American Film Festival introduces the Tran family, Vietnamese boat people, whose sufferings are incomprehensible to more fortunate people.

The film dramatizes the problems faced by Tran Ngoc Hung, his pretty but seriously depressed wife, Ahn, and their small son, Huy. As the film opens, the Trans are resettling in Montreal, Canada. In addition to leaving their homeland, being attacked by Thai pirates, and losing their other son to a shark, the Trans are now experiencing the bureaucracy of a Canadian military reception center.

Their home becomes a small, sparsely furnished apartment selected by their Canadian sponsors, the Renshaws. In the apartment, Ahn's only remembrance of her homeland is the tiny Buddhist shrine she arranges in the living room. Depressed to the point of irrationality, Ahn paints a wall with scenes of Vietnam. When the landlord's angry complaints drive her deeper into despair, the patient, loving Hung tells her softly, "We must bend like a willow," but he realizes he cannot reach her.

Huy's accidental poisoning is the last straw for Ahn. Although the child will recover, Ahn runs barefoot from the hospital into the freezing Canadian winter. Finally she breaks into tears, the first she has shed.

When we next see the Trans, they are guests in the Renshaw home where we learn that Ahn had been a piano teacher in Vietnam. Encouraged by Hung and her hosts, Ahn easily plays the same Chopin nocturne that Nancy Renshaw struggled with earlier in the film. Ahn's depression lifts as she realizes that she can communicate and that she can contribute to those who have helped her through her music.

BEFORE VIEWING
Ask the class if there are members of their families who came to this country as immigrants. If so, are there experiences these family members had that can be shared with the class? How were they received in this country? Were there difficulties in language, employment, education,

BEFORE VIEWING (cont'd)

housing? Was there social discrimination? Were they homesick for their own country? (Give the students an opportunity to talk this over at home before the film is shown.) It would also be interesting to have a recent immigrant share experiences.

AFTER VIEWING

Discuss the feelings of the Trans as recent immigrants. What might have been done to make it easier for them on entry? Did the Trans immediate past experiences make it more difficult for them in Canada? The feelings of the Renshaws should also be considered. They live in a conservative Canadian community. What are their probable feelings, expressed and otherwise? What was the commitment of the Renshaws to the Trans? What should be the commitment of anyone toward those less fortunate? Are we really our brother's keeper?

Suggestions for discussions and compositions

a. Ask students if the Trans settled in their community, would they try to help them. Do they know of institutions, groups, or individuals who would?

b. Discuss with the class how the film emphasizes the importance of communication in personal relationships.

c. Ask students to imagine being Nancy Renshaw. They have observed the Trans during their first day in Canada, including their time at the reception center. They should write a diary entry explaining what the day has been like for the Trans.

d. Ask students to be Ahn or Hung. They are to write a letter to a relative in Vietnam after living in Canada for a few weeks explaining how they feel about their new country and about leaving Vietnam.

e. Students should describe a time when they were alone and isolated in an unfamiliar cultural, ethnic, or linguistic setting. How did they handle their feelings? Would they repeat the experience voluntarily?

f. It has been said that everyone is a prisoner of his own experiences — that no one can eliminate prejudice, one can only try to be aware of it. Ask students if this is true. Can they write down prejudices that they have become aware of? They should not share this confession with the class.

g. Ask students how one can show respect for cultural differences in language, food, dress, customs, religion.

h. Have the class write a composition about the people, places, and things they would most miss if they moved to a strange country, particularly a non-Western one.

i. The issue of bilingual education is very controversial in this country at present. Proponents believe that new immigrants should be taught in their native language. Opponents believe that new immigrants should be taught in English because, even though it may be more difficult initially, learning will eventually be easier. Do students think schools should offer bilingual education or should new immigrants sink or swim because it will ultimately be better for them?

j. The bilingual ballot is another controversial subject in this country. Opponents believe that anyone who votes here should be able to read English. Proponents believe that the requirement to speak English deprives some citizens of their right to vote. Where do students stand on this issue?

k. Ask students to write a composition on the topic, "Am I My Brother's Keeper?" Which of the Renshaws was more committed to the principle that we are our brother's keeper?

Suggestions for advanced assignments

a. Assign several members of the class in groups to research the history of recent immigrants to this country: the Vietnamese, the Cubans, the Hmong, etc. What has been the impact on the schools, the economic situation, social problems, health, welfare, and employment? What have the problems been for the immigrants? Are most of them being assimilated into the larger society? What positive contributions have been made? Students should make possible recommendations to the class about future regulations for the group that they have studied.

b. Discuss with the class some of the statements made in the film:

Commentary:	"Canada is the largest freedom-loving country in the world."
Ahn:	"Are we free?"
Hung:	"I don't know."
Landlord:	"If you intend staying here, show a little respect."
Nancy Renshaw:	"There's more to this than paying rent and fixing teeth."

c. Ask students to compose a questionnaire to test the attitudes of people toward admitting large groups of immigrants, such as the Cubans, to this country.

d. Organize a debate on the topic: Resolved, I am my brother's keeper.

e. Ask students to compare the immigration experience of the Vietnamese to another large group, the Cubans, for example.

Suggestions for advanced assignments (cont'd)

Are there similarities in their reasons for emigrating, their reception in their new country, language problems, schooling, and employment? How can they explain the differences if they exist?

f. Ask a visitor who speaks an unfamiliar language to come to the class and spend the period teaching the class a few words and phrases in the language. Ask the person to give simple directions and explanations to the class. Students should be prepared to write a paper about how they felt during the lesson. Did they change their opinions about bilingual education? Would they repeat the experience until they did understand the language? (This question can bring important insight about the nature of learning.)

g. Invite a Jewish rabbi or cantor to speak to the class about the expulsion of the Israelites in Old Testament times or about the expulsion of the Jews from Nazi Germany.

h. Invite a Buddhist priest to explain the Buddhist religion to the class.

i. Invite a recent immigrant to speak to the class about his or her experiences in this country. Ask students to be prepared with questions for the speaker.

j. Ask students to smile and say hello to five students or staff members that they do not know. They should note their reactions and be prepared to share them with the class.

k. Role-play a group of immigrants and officers of the relocation center. The officers are cold and unfriendly, although not actually rude. Have the immigrants talk to the class about their feelings during their reception. The officers can ask for name, passport, reasons for entering the country, and set health examinations, eye examinations, and assign them to sponsors — all without explanation. If the officers are individuals who speak another language, the assignment is more interesting and effective.

Basic skills: teaching sentence combining

Ask students to combine each of the three sentences into one sentence. They may add or subtract words whenever necessary.

Example:
a. Ahn is a Vietnamese woman.

b. She is the wife of Hung.

c. She is the mother of Huy.

Ahn, a Vietnamese woman, is the wife of Hung and the mother of Huy.

1.
a. The Trans were refugees from Vietnam.

b. They were called Boat People.

c. They were terrorized by pirates.

2.
a. The Trans had two sons.

b. Both sons were on the boat.

c. One son was killed by a shark.

3.
a. Nancy and George Renshaw were their sponsors.

b. The Renshaws were from a church group.

c. The church is in Montreal, Canada.

4.
a. Ahn is lonely for Vietnam.

b. She sets up a small Buddhist shrine in their apartment.

c. She paints pictures of Vietnam on the walls of their apartment.

5.
a. The landlord is very angry about the painting.

b. His anger depresses Ahn.

c. Hung tells her, "We must bend like a willow."

6.
a. Huy played behind the refrigerator.

b. He found some poison and ate it.

c. He was rushed to the hospital.

7.
a. Huy recovers from the accident.

b. The crisis was too much for Ahn.

c. She runs out barefoot into the snow.

8.
a. Hung runs after Ahn in the snow.

b. He overtakes her and tries to comfort her.

c. Ahn breaks down and cries for the first time.

(Outline continues on page 158.)

Basic skills: teaching sentence combining (cont'd)

9.

a.   Ahn plays the piano at the Renshaw home.

b.   She plays Chopin's "E Flat Nocturne."

c.   The Renshaws learn for the first time that Ahn had been a piano teacher in Vietnam.

10.

a.   Ahn had discovered a way to communicate with people through her music.

b.   She had discovered a way to make friends with people.

c.   She had discovered a way to repay those who helped her.

RELATED RESOURCES

Films

The Phans of New Jersey

Short stories

Silko, Leslie. "Lullaby." *Southwest Fiction*. Bantam Books, 1980

Strete, Craig. "When They Find You." *If All Else Fails*. Doubleday and Co., 1980

Theroux, Paul. "Clapham Junction." *World's End and Other Stories*. Houghton Mifflin, 1980

Theroux, Paul. "Yard Sale." *World's End and Other Stories*. Houghton Mifflin, 1980

Books

Kerr, Judith. *The Other Way Round*. Coward, 1975

Kessner, Thomas, and B. B. Caroli. *Today's Immigrants: Their Stories*. Oxford University Press, 1981

Loescher, Gil, and Ann Dull. *The World's Refugees: A Test of Humanity*. Harcourt Brace Jovanovich, 1982

Richlin, Nahid. *Foreigner*. W. W. Norton & Company, 1978

Richter, Conrad. *Country of Strangers*. Knopf, 1966

Richter, Conrad. *The Light in the Forest*. Knopf, 1953

Said, Kurban. *Ali and Nino*. Random House, 1976

WHO ARE THE DeBOLTS AND
WHERE DID THEY GET 19 KIDS?
(72 min, c, $950/125, Pyramid Films, 1977)

THEMES
The treatment of the handicapped. The importance of love in child development. Becoming a whole person. Sharing with others. Assuming responsibility. Finding one's identity. The concept of family.

CURRICULUM AREAS
Special education, language arts, psychology, sociology, family living, guidance

SYNOPSIS
In addition to their own six children, Bob and Dorothy DeBolt of Piedmont, California, adopted twelve others, six of whom are severely physically handicapped.

Told with affection and understanding by master filmmaker John Korty, the documentary shows how the couple and their children became a family of fulfilled individuals despite seemingly insuperable odds. Korty spent almost two years with them, shooting over 80,000 feet of film. The result is this inspiring story of the DeBolts for which Korty won an Academy Award.

Although the family life of the DeBolts is extremely interesting, the individual children are most memorable. There is small, black Karen, born without legs and arms, romping in glee with her father or playing football with the rest of the family. There are Tuck and Ahn, paralyzed Vietnamese teenagers, proudly throwing the paper on a route rejected by normal boys as too difficult. Twe, a blind girl from Vietnam, hopes to see again after surgery, but she doesn't regain her sight. Ly, paralyzed by polio, was further injured when the American plane airlifting her from Saigon crashed. But most poignant of all is J.R., blind and paralyzed, struggling slowly and painfully each day as he tries to reach the top of the stairs. It is a film of such impact that many viewers are unable to talk about it.

Of all of the films available to schools, this film may be the most useful. It is surely one of the most beautiful.

BEFORE VIEWING
Recent polls have shown that two-thirds of us have negative feelings toward the handicapped. Discuss with the class their feelings toward the physically handicapped. Do they feel uncomfortable? Guilty? Helpless to do anything? Resentful? (They somehow deserve it?) Fearful? Alienated? Curious? Indifferent? You may want to discuss *Dibs in Search of Self* by Virginia Axline (Ballentine Books, 1964), a beautiful book about a child who is handicapped emotionally.

Who Are the DeBolts and Where Did They Get 19 Kids?
Photograph courtesy of Pyramid Films

AFTER VIEWING

Suggestions for discussions and compositions

a. Have the students changed their attitudes in any way after seeing the film?

b. Which of the DeBolt children would they most like to have for a friend?

c. What do they think is the best way to behave with a handicapped person? Why?

d. Discuss with the students why Dorothy DeBolt says that the most important thing in the family is the relationship between her and Bob?

e. When J.R. arrives and introductions are being made, Dorothy says to him, "You can always tell Karen by her hooks." Later Bob says, "You've got the best blindfold in the house, J.R." What do students think of such comments to such severely afflicted children? Are they cruel? Bob and Dorothy are obviously not cruel people. Why would they make such remarks?

f. Who is really handicapped? Ask students if it is those who can't see or those who can't love.

g. What facilities have students seen in their community that are provided especially for the handicapped? Have they noticed places where a person in a wheelchair would have a difficult time? In school? Public buildings? Churches? The bus or train?

h. Explain to students that when a handicapped child attends regular classes it is called mainstreaming. Should all students, regardless of handicap, be mainstreamed?

i. Discuss the advantages to society and to the handicapped of mainstreaming.

j. If students were employers, which of the DeBolt children would they be most interested in hiring? They should give reasons for their choices.

Suggestions for advanced assignments

a. Bernard Baruch said, "The greatest freedom we have is the freedom of self-discipline." Ask students how this film illuminates the quotation. Would Baruch have approved of Bob and Dorothy DeBolt?

b. The major search of each of us is to find our own identity. Ask students how Bob and Dorothy DeBolt help their children search for self-identity.

c. Filmmaker John Korty said, "I wanted to show—not what it is like to be handicapped—but what it is like to be fully alive." Does the class believe he has succeeded?

d. Psychologist Erik Eriksen has said, "The worst father of all is the good but intangible father." Ask students how this quotation relates to Bob DeBolt.

e. Bob DeBolt says, "Nurturing does not mean coddling." How do students distinguish between them?

f. Ask students about the Pygmalion syndrome (see page 163). How does it affect the DeBolt children?

g. It has been demonstrated that trained handicapped persons are a great asset to the companies they work for. Ask students how their employment possibilities could be increased.

h. Ask students what could they do as a class to help integrate handicapped students into the school.

Basic skills: writing dialogue

a. Ask the students to write a conversation between themselves and any one of the DeBolt children.

Example:

Why do you try so hard to climb those stairs, J.R.?

Because all the others can and I want to do it too.

b. Show how quotation marks must be placed around the speaker's exact words.

"Why do you try so hard to climb those stairs, J.R.?"

"Because all the others can and I want to do it too."

c. Show students how to set off the speaker from what he has said with commas, question marks, or exclamation marks.

"Why do you try so hard to climb those stairs, J.R.?" I asked.

"Because all the others can and I want to do it too," J. R. replied.

d. Teach them how to add descriptive words or phrases.

"Why do you try so hard to climb those stairs?" I asked quietly.

"Because all the others can and I want to do it too," J.R. replied with a smile.

e. Ask students to add more to the conversation. Show them that the speaker may be added to the beginning of the conversation.

f. Ask students to recopy the conversations and to read a few out loud.

ADDITIONAL STUDY AIDS

The Pygmalion Syndrome

The Pygmalion syndrome, or the Pygmalion effect derives its name from an ancient Greek myth about a sculptor whose name was Pygmalion. He carved a statue of a girl he called Galatea. She was so beautiful that he fell in love with her and prayed that she might come alive. His wish was granted. Pygmalion and Galatea were married and lived happily ever after.

George Bernard Shaw employed the myth as the basis for his hit play, *Pygmalion*, which was later made into a famous Broadway musical, *My Fair Lady*, and then into an Academy Award-winning film, also called *My Fair Lady*. The film starred Rex Harrison as a linguistics and speech teacher who bet a friend that he could take the most ignorant, unkempt, Cockney flower girl and in three months pass her off in London society as a duchess. He passed her off not just as a duchess but as a princess. The flower girl expresses the essence of the Pygmalion syndrome when she says in the fifth act of the play, "The real difference between a lady and a flower girl is not how she behaves, but how she is treated."

When one has positive expectations of oneself, they are likely to be fulfilled. The same is true when one has positive expectations of others and they are aware of them.

Information about the DeBolt Children

Biological children:
Mike, born 1948, flyer in Hawaii
Mimi, born 1949, AASK coordinator
Stephanie, born 1951, Outward Bound counselor
Noel, born 1952, special education student
Mary Donelle, born 1960, student
Melanie, born 1960, student

Adopted children:
Marty, Korean-Caucasian, born 1954
Kim, Korean-Caucasian, born 1953, law student
Tuck, Vietnamese, born 1954, paraplegic, premedical student, volunteer teacher
Ahn, Vietnamese, born 1955, war-wounded paraplegic, pre-engineering student
Sunee, Korean-Caucasian, born 1967, paralyzed
Dat, Vietnamese, born 1957, construction technologist
Trang, Vietnamese, born 1959, engineer
Karen, American black, born 1966, quadruple amputee, student
Wendy, Korean, born 1968, battered child, once blind, one eye, student
Phong, Vietnamese, born 1966
J.R. (John), American Caucasian, born 1964, blinded because he was not given treatment for the disorder that caused his paralysis
Ly, Vietnamese, born 1960, paralyzed by polio, further injured in crash of American airlift plane
Twe, Vietnamese, born 1961, blind

RELATED RESOURCES

Films

Crossbar

A Day in the Life of Bonnie Consolo

Get It Together

Gravity Is My Enemy

I'll Find a Way

Leo Beureman

Moira: A Vision of Blindness

See What I Say

Sign of Victory

Stepping Out: The DeBolts Grow Up

Survival Run

Poetry

Blades, Leslie. "Out of Blindness." *The Now Voices: The Poetry of the Present.* Scribner's, 1971

Cannon, Melissa. "Crippled Child at the Window." *Anthology of Magazine Verse and Yearbook of American Poetry, 1980.* Monitor, 1980

Noyes, Alfred. "Spring and the Blind Children." *Oxford Book of Twentieth Century English Verse.* Oxford University Press, 1973

Owen, Wilfred. "Disabled." *Oxford Book of Twentieth Century English Verse.* Oxford University Press, 1973

Silkin, Jon. "Death of a Son." *Norton Anthology of Modern Poetry.* W. W. Norton & Company, 1973

Wright, James. "Mutterings over the Crib of a Deaf Child." *Contemporary Poetry in America.* Random House, 1973

Short stories

McIntyre, Vonda M. "Only at Night." *Fireflood and Other Stories.* Houghton Mifflin, 1979

Thomas, Piri. "Mighty Miguel." *Stories from El Bario.* Knopf, 1978

Books for young adults

Allen, Anne. *Sports for the Handicapped.* Walker, 1981

Blank, Joseph P. *Nineteen Steps up the Mountain.* Harper & Row, 1976 (about the DeBolts)

Hayden, Torey L. *Murphy's Boy.* Putnam, 1983

Keller, Helen. *The Story of My Life.* Pendulum Press, 1974

Books for young adults (cont'd)

Killilca, Marie. *Karen.* Dell, 1980

Lash, Joseph P. *Helen and Teacher.* Delta, 1981

Lund, Doris. *Patchwork Clan: How the Sweeney Family Grew.* Little, Brown & Company, 1982

Valens, Evans G. *The Other Side of the Mountain.* Warner Books, 1978

Books for adults

Glasser, William. *The Identity Society.* Harper & Row, rev., 1976

Reid, Robert. *My Children, My Children.* Harcourt Brace Jovanovich, 1977

THE WILLMAR EIGHT
(50 min, c, $850/90, California Newsreel, 1981)

THEMES

The economic oppression of women. The changing roles of women. Management-labor relations. Career education for women.

CURRICULUM AREAS

Language arts, economics, contemporary problems, sociology, women's studies, psychology

SYNOPSIS

In 1977, Willmar was a small, conservative community of 18,000 in the center of Minnesota. The terms feminist, political activist, and radical were unknown, and traditional values seemed secure. Yet eight women struggled through snow in subzero weather picketing Willmar's Citizens National Bank.

Gifted actress-producer Mary Beth Yarrow, a Willmar native, and director Lee Grant tell the story of the strike in this incisive and engrossing documentary.

In 1977, eight women, full-time employees of the bank, began questioning the personnel practices of their employer. Pay was so low that the women were eligible for government food stamps, although no male employee was. Pay was so low that none of the women were eligible for a loan from their own bank. There was no access to promotions because they had to train men for higher-paying positions. The final explosion came when the women were asked to train a young man for a management position for which the women were not considered. They filed charges of sex discrimination and unfair labor practices with the National Labor Relations Board (NLRB) and went on strike.

Although director Grant tried to present both sides of the story, she was met with an impenetrable wall of silence from the townspeople. We learn that in Willmar, friendship is more important than justice. Few people wanted to risk a social rift.

In March, when the strike ended, the town was bitterly divided. The bank was sold because of declining profits. The NLRB had ruled against the women. The lesson is clear, however: sex discrimination hurts everyone.

Although the women lost the strike, they gained a sense of themselves and of their power to control their lives. They also cemented a bond among them — a sense of community and friendship hitherto unknown in their lives.

The issues suggested by the film are varied. It is probably the best film available for developing an understanding of the economic discrimination against women, the changing role of women, and the need for equitable personnel practices.

SYNOPSIS (cont'd)

California Newsreel, the distributor of *The Willmar Eight*, has a fine teaching manual available for use with the film. Besides increasing viewers' understanding of the outcome of sex discrimination in the workplace, the manual's purpose is to recenter viewers' attention on their own goals and expectations for their careers, to help them air their grievances, reevaluate traditional job roles, and reconsider the part they play in social change. The manual suggests activities that provide exercise for viewers in investigating possible sex bias at places of employment in their community, and in publicizing their findings.

BEFORE VIEWING

Discuss the issue of economic opportunity for women. Ask students if women should be paid the same for equal work. Should women have an equal opportunity for advancement? Are women entitled to equal respect in the workplace, without personal or sexual harassment? Should women strike when personnel practices are unfair? Try to get the class to commit itself without arguing the merits of either position.

Then tell the class the film is about eight apolitical women in a small, conservative community in Minnesota. The women went on strike against the bank where they worked, charging unfair labor practices and sexual discrimination.

AFTER VIEWING

Write the defeated proposed Equal Rights Amendment (ERA) on the board: "Equality of rights under the law shall not be denied or abridged by the United States or by any state on account of sex." Discuss whether the suit could have failed if the ERA had been the law of the land. Do women need more protection than is currently granted them under the law? The Reagan administration believes they do not. On what basis could the NLRB have ruled against the women?

Suggestions for discussions and compositions

a. Ask students what the women learned about themselves even though their strike was unsuccessful. How do they think they were changed from the women they had been before the strike?

b. On March 18, 1869, Susan B. Anthony, a noted feminist, said "Join the union, girls, and together say, 'Equal pay for equal work.' " Over a hundred years have elapsed since that speech, yet women are still struggling for economic equality. How can students explain this?

c. Discuss with students why many of the townspeople in Willmar, both men and women, disapprove of the strikers.

d. Before the strike the eight women described themselves as "apolitical." Ask the class what it means to be apolitical. In the 1980 national election only 53.9 percent of the eligible voters in the United States voted. Is apoliticism the cause? If so, what do students see as the implications for the country?

e. How would students describe the results of the strike in terms of the community as a whole? Which were positive? Negative? Was the strike worthwhile?

f. Students should imagine that they are the television anchorman Dan Rather and write a news segment for the evening program about the Willmar strike, which is in progress. They should include who, when, where, why, and identify people, places, and things completely.

Suggestions for advanced assignments

a. According to the American Banker's Association, women hold 85 percent of the clerical positions (the lowest-paid positions) in the nation's banks. Approximately 15 percent of the banks are unionized. Great numbers of women are locked into ill-paid, dead-end jobs without the benefits and protections that organized labor has enjoyed for years. Ask students to comment.

b. Invite a member of the National Organization for Women (NOW) to view the film with the class and comment on it from the feminist point of view. The class should be prepared with questions to ask her.

c. Ask students to read the salary comparisons for men and women in the federal civil service (see pages 169-70). They should note the categories in which women's salaries equal or surpass those of men.

d. Elizabeth Cady Stanton, an early feminist, suggested this change to the Preamble to the *Declaration of Independence*: "We hold these truths to be self-evident, that all men and women are created equal." Ask the class to comment.

ADDITIONAL STUDY AIDS

"Women 1982: The Year That Time Ran Out"*

1982 was the year that time ran out for the proposed equal rights amendment. Eleanor Smeal, president of the National Organization for Women, the group that headed the intense, 10-year struggle for the ERA, conceded defeat on June 24. Only 24 words in all, the ERA read simply: "Equality of rights under the law shall not be denied or abridged by the United States or by any state on account of sex." Two major opinion polls had reported just weeks before the ERA's defeat that a majority of Americans continued to favor the amendment.

The effort to achieve an equal rights amendment dated from 1923, when legislation was first introduced in Congress. By 1972,

---

*The World Almanac & Book of Facts, 1983 edition, copyright © Newspaper Enterprise Association, Inc., 1982 New York, NY 10166.

ADDITIONAL STUDY AIDS (cont'd)

"Women 1982: The Year That Time Ran Out" (cont'd)

the proposed amendment passed the House and Senate by wide margins. The bill stipulated a period of 5 years during which three-fourths of the state legislatures had to ratify the amendment in order for it to become part of the Constitution. Two hours after clearing Congress, the ERA was ratified by Hawaii. A year later it had been ratified by 30 states.

However, between 1973 and 1977, only 5 more states ratified, while 5 rescinded ratification. As the deadline approached, the amendment was 3 states short of the necessary 38. In the fall of 1978, Congress granted a 3-year, 3-month extension to June 30, 1982. But not one state passed the amendment after 1977. In mid-June 1982, the ERA went down to certain defeat with its rejection by the legislatures of Illinois and Florida—the 2 states in which supporters believed it had the best last chance.

NOW's Smeal said the blame for the defeat could not be placed solely on state legislators who voted against the proposed amendment. The real opposition, she said, was special corporate interests that profit from sex discrimination by paying lower wages to women and charging higher insurance rates. Smeal maintained that major corporate interests made large contributions to the ERA opposition.

A Comparison of Salaries of Full-Time Federal Employees
Source: U.S. Office of Personnel Management

White collar:	Average salary Men	Average salary Women
Accountant	$31,261	$24,593
Architect	32,775	28,588
Attorney	40,092	34,578
Chaplain	31,948	16,789
Chemist	33,684	27,310
Clerk/typist	11,703	11,593
Dental assistant	13,653	13,560
Editor/writer	29,000	23,418
Editor, technical	28,278	24,038
Engineer, civil	33,197	24,417
Engineer, electrical	33,084	26,482
Engineer, mechanical	33,121	25,082
Law clerk	23,164	23,187
Librarian	30,728	27,473
Messenger	10,277	10,906
Nurse	21,498	22,840
Paralegal	30,042	23,501
Personnel management	33,306	26,868

	Average salary Men	Average salary Women
White collar:		
Pharmacist	$27,286	$24,960
Public relations	33,531	26,654
Purchasing agent	17,022	15,723
Secretary	14,825	15,836
Social work	28,675	27,164
Statistician	33,817	28,770
Technician, medical	17,011	15,819
Therapist, occupational	23,274	21,943
Therapist, physical	23,842	21,748
Blue collar:		
Baker	$18,514	$18,580
Barber	18,381	-0-
Beautician	-0-	20,034
Boiler operator	21,355	17,326
Carpenter	20,869	18,194
Cook	20,258	18,001
Electrician	21,600	17,956
Elevator operator	13,472	13,926
Forklift operator	18,461	16,864
Janitor	14,630	14,446
Laborer	14,344	14,125
Locksmith	19,852	18,859
Locomotive engineer	21,354	-0-
Machinist	22,207	18,029
Mechanic, A/C	21,329	16,451
Mechanic, aircraft	22,289	19,109
Mechanic, general	20,322	17,179
Painter	20,231	17,648
Pipefitter	22,626	18,573
Plumber	20,190	17,153
Pressman	21,341	19,327
Sheetmetal	21,203	18,695
Storeworker	16,753	12,859
Tractor operator	17,349	16,569
Vehicle operator	18,461	17,105
Warehouseman	17,715	16,500
Welder	20,946	17,741

RELATED RESOURCES

Films

Does Anybody Need Me Any More?	*The Life and Times of Rosie the Riveter*
The Fable of He and She	*Snowbound*
A Family Affair	*Soldier Girls*
A Jury of Her Peers	*Women in Sports*
Make It Happen	*The Workplace Hustle*
Moving Mountains	

Short stories

Asch, Sholem. "The Triangle Fire." *Women Working*. The Feminist Press, 1979

Graham, R. B. C. "Faith." *The Best Short Stories of R. B. C. Graham*. Ticknor and Fields, 1980

Jewett, Sarah Orne. "Tom's Husband." *Women Working*. The Feminist Press, 1979

Monney, Michael. "Women." *Squid Soup*. Story Press, 1980

Trow, George W. "Mrs. Armand Reef Likes to Entertain." *Bullies: Stories*. Little, Brown & Company, 1980

Weldon, Fay. "Alopecia." *Watching Me, Watching You*. Summit Books, 1981

Yezierska, Anzia. "America and I." *Women Working*. The Feminist Press, 1979

Books for young adults

Nonfiction

Peavy, Linda, and Ursula Smith. *Women Who Changed Things*. Scribner's, 1982

Ricci, Larry J. *High-Paying Blue Collar Jobs for Women*. Ballantine, 1981

Fiction

Amado, Jorge. *Gabriela, Clove, and Cinnamon*. Knopf, 1962

Chute, Beatrice Joy. *Katie: An Impertinent Fairy Tale*. Dutton, 1978

Cummings, Betty Sue. *Hew against the Grain.* Atheneum, 1977

Le Guin, Ursula. *The Dispossessed.* Harper & Row, 1974

Rachlin, Nahid. *Foreigner.* W. W. Norton & Company, 1973

Sargent, Pamela, ed. *Women of Wonder: Science Fiction Stories by Women about Women.* Random House, 1975

Spinner, Stephanie. *Motherlove.* Dell, 1978

Walker, Alice. *In Love and Trouble.* Harcourt Brace Jovanovich, 1973

Books for adults

Chafe, William. *The American Woman: Her Changing Social, Economic, and Political Roles.* Oxford University Press, 1972

Frank, Miriam et al. *The Life and Times of Rosie the Riveter.* Clarity Productions, 1982

Kanowitz, Leo. *Equal Rights: The Male Stake.* University of New Mexico Press, 1981

Kessler-Harris, Alice. *Out at Work: A History of Wage-Earning Women in the United States.* Oxford University Press, 1982

4 FILM REVIEWS

The films included in the study guides are films of broad application that most easily illustrated the various approaches and activities open to teachers who use film.

Although they are excellent films, there are many others of equal quality that lend themselves as easily to such activities. Since successful film teaching depends largely on the enthusiasm of the teacher, the films described in this section are included to give the instructor more choice. Any suggestions from the study guides are easily adaptable for these films.

AN ACQUIRED TASTE
(25 min, c, $575/55, New Day Film Co-op, Inc., 1981)

In this delightfully witty look at competition in America, filmmaker Ralph Arlyck takes us back through his high school and college years to recall his own moments of victory and defeat on his way to the top. Yearbooks, talk shows, home movies, conversations with family and friends, chats with junior high cheer leaders, class reunions, awards ceremonies whirl in a fast-moving, absorbing commentary on the drive to make it in American society, the society which the self-aware Arlyck mocks even as he takes part in it.

The forty-year-old filmmaker identifies with the youngsters he encounters on his return to his alma mater. Nothing much, he seems to say, has changed. Bored, angry, pressured, but largely good-natured and even idealistic, students are still competing for reasons no longer articulated. Achievement in sports, personal and professional, is still valued most of all in the climb to the top.

There is an old saying that if one wishes to know about water, one should not ask a fish. Perhaps students won't be able to see the irony and intelligence of Arlyck's filmed essay, but they will realize their affinity with him. It's a look into their own future.

A marvelously valuable and entertaining film for language arts, sociology, psychology, and filmmaking, *An Acquired Taste* was a Blue Ribbon winner at the 1982 American Film Festival.

AFTER THE FIRST
(14 min, c, $300/20, Teleketics, 1975)

Beautifully photographed on location in Indiana, this brief film is simple but disturbing. A boy is given a rifle as a birthday present. Over the objections of his mother, who recognizes the boy's emotional sensitivity, he is taken on a rabbit-hunting trip by his well-meaning, but relatively insensitive father, who views the hunting outing as the boy's initiation into the activities of manhood.

Excited by the power of his new gun, the boy enters into the trip enthusiastically, but when he wounds a rabbit his father explains he must kill it for humane reasons. Drawing near, he looks at the face of the fatally wounded rabbit and, for the first time, realizes the cruelty and finality of death. Recognizing his son's dismay, the father says reassuringly, "It's easier after the first." The boy is torn between his admiration for his father and his own feelings about the death of the rabbit.

At first glance, the film appears to be about the pros and cons of hunting, and students will want to discuss this. A stronger theme is the conflict of values between generations, a problem many secondary students face in their own lives. Another theme is effective parenting. Which parent actually prepared the boy best for the world he will encounter?

After the First is a lovely film that leaves many important questions unanswered. It is superb for writing and discussion assignments.

ALL SUMMER IN A DAY
(25 min, c, $550/50, Learning Corporation of America, 1982)

With a different ending added to the film, Ray Bradbury's well-known story of the cruelty of children on an unnamed planet becomes instead a tale of growth and forgiveness, without losing its original intensity or its intriguing premise: What is it like to live on a planet where it rains constantly and the sun shines but once every nine years?

As the film opens, the teacher and her class are making excited preparations because the sun will shine today. Young Margot, a former earthling from Willard, Ohio, is the only one who remembers the beauty of the sun, flowers, and butterflies. As she describes the sun, her classmates are interested, but one, William, is jealous. As a joke, he locks Margot in a small room so that she will miss the great event.

At last the rain stops. The children stare wonderingly as the sun appears. Smiling and shouting, they run joyously through the fields gathering armloads of flowers. Some lie back listening to the hum of bees and admiring the butterflies.

No one remembers the imprisoned Margot, whose cell admits only a small ray of light. The sun soon disappears. The flowers vanish. As the rain begins to fall again, the children return to their classroom with their flowers. Conscience-stricken, they release Margot, who stands in the rain and cries, refusing the sorrowful William's proffered bouquet. Gently the other children offer their flowers to Margot who accepts them. Then slowly she walks toward the tearful William, accepts his bouquet, and with her arm around his shoulders, walks away with him. The rain continues to fall.

All Summer in a Day raises questions about jealousy, cruelty, and forgiveness, as well as about the importance of the sun in our lives.

ALMOS' A MAN
(39 min, c, $716, rental, inquire Perspective Films, 1977)

Richard Wright's most consistent theme is that the search for personal freedom is the only means of finding one's identity. The film is the poignant, disturbing story of Dave, an uneducated young black farmworker of the 1920s, who longs for self-respect and manhood. He confuses having a gun with being treated like a man, with having the respect of others, and being free to make his own decisions. As he pushes a plow for a neighboring white farmer, Jim Hawkins, he dreams of going hunting as his employer does.

Dave badgers his mother about the gun, but she will not yield in her opposition. Finally, he secretly buys a second-hand gun for two dollars. While he is secretly target practicing, he accidentally kills Hawkins's mule, Jenny.

Terrified, Dave tries to conceal his pathetic blunder, but Hawkins knows the truth, and offers to let Dave work for twenty-five months for two dollars a month to pay for the dead mule. Dave's father gratefully accepts the offer, meanwhile assuring Dave that he is going to beat him unmercifully when they get home. Dave retrieves his gun, which he had buried in his panic. We last see

(Annotation continues on page 177.)

All Summer in a Day

Photograph courtesy of Learning Corporation of America

him lying on a boxcar, with no money in his pockets, clutching an unloaded gun and heading out of town to "freedom." His naiveté is moving and exasperating.

With so many young men equating force with manhood, the story of Dave and his gun becomes an important one. The focus of the film is the impotence and futility of his solution. *Almos' a Man* is a powerful resource for humanities, language arts, and psychology.

AMERICAS IN TRANSITION
(29 min, c, $495/50, Icarus Films, 1982)

Although Latin America is often in the news these days, Americans do not know much about the actual situation there. Media reports, especially from El Salvador and Guatemala, are contradictory. Even as the United States offers aid to the governments of Latin America, congressmen, high church officials, and prominent citizens speak about the widespread suffering of the citizens at the hands of these same governments. Imprisonment, torture, and murder are common according to these sources. Where does the truth lie? Is the United States unwittingly aiding a cruel and repressive government? Yes, says this 1981 Academy Award nominee and Blue Ribbon-winning documentary that examines the roots of military dictatorships in Latin America, their attempts at democracy, and the role of the United States in the region's development.

Narrated by actor Ed Asner, the film traces the history of United States involvement in Nicaragua with its support of the dictator Somoza; the intervention by twenty thousand marines in the Dominican Republic in 1965; the overthrow and assassination of President Allende of Chile in 1973; and the present military assistance to El Salvador.

Interviews with Carlos Fuentes, the prominent Mexican author and diplomat, Lyman Kirkpatrick, former director of the CIA, and Sister Peggy Healey, a Catholic missionary, are intercut with film footage from eleven filmmakers, the U.S. Army, the Canadian Broadcasting Company, the United Nations, and NBC News. The result is a brilliant, sobering documentary. It should be required viewing for everyone.

It is a superb introduction to the study of the relations between the United States and Latin America for history or government classes. It is equally useful for humanities or sociology. Students fortunate enough to be born in a country such as the United States, are frequently impatient or contemptuous of people of other cultures, particularly of the Third World. *Americas in Transition* helps such students to understand that, in many countries, people are victims of political circumstances beyond their control.

ANGEL DEATH
(33 min, c, $425/50, Media Five, 1979)

Paul Newman and Joanne Woodward narrate this harrowing documentary illuminating the tragic facts behind the fastest-rising street drug in the United States, PCP.

Using actual case histories, the film forces the viewer to watch the effects of the drug on its victims. The first victim is a young man who is under the influence of PCP as he is interviewed. As he stares vacantly at the camera, his mumbling speech and incoherent answers betray his lack of comprehension. Although not expressed directly, his low self-esteem and loneliness are painfully apparent. Another victim, totally out of control, is forcefully subdued by Los Angeles police. Another addict tells the horrifying story of the murder of a good friend. The film is informative as well as frightening. It is sobering to watch for those who may see themselves as addicts, as well as for those who may see themselves as the addicts' victims.

Some dismiss *Angel Death* as "just another attempt to scare kids." It isn't. Among students who never use drugs the reaction was very positive, "I'll never start on that." "I'm glad I don't." One student, referring to the addict who was interviewed while under the influence of the drug, said frankly, "I had no idea I looked so stupid." The class laughed, but the student looked thoughtful. Students flirting with the idea of using PCP or any other such dangerous drug may reconsider after seeing *Angel Death*. It is an effective film for drug education, sociology, psychology, and family living.

THE ANIMALS ARE CRYING
(Full version: 28 min, c, $425/40, Learning Corporation of America, 1973; edited version: 16 min, c, $280/30, Learning Corporation of America, 1973)

What are we to do about the millions of unwanted cats and dogs that must be destroyed each year in the United States? Produced for the American Humane Society, this poignant, hard-hitting film documents the needless suffering of these animals, and emphasizes the importance of controlling animal reproduction.

In the opening sequence, a sack of kittens is abandoned to certain death because the owner did not take them to an animal shelter and failed to find a home for them.

A scene at the shelter shows long lines of owners eager to sacrifice their pets, even animals they have had for a long time. Reasons seem superficial: "I'm redecorating my apartment." "My place is too small." "I'm going on vacation." Few of the excuses are valid for an owner interested in the pet's welfare.

The humane society workers are forced to put the animals to death. The scene is distressing to the workers and the animals. Young viewers should have the option not to watch this sequence. They should, however, be encouraged to watch because the emotional impact can make a lasting impression that could lead to at least a partial solution to the problem in the future.

The final scene is hopeful. A family plans for the spaying of its pet. *The Animals Are Crying* is a strong film for sociology, family living, language arts, and values.

BACKTRACK
(14 min, c, $265/25, BFΛ, or Phoenix Films, 1977)

Backtrack is an earlier effort of filmmaker Ron Ellis who won the 1981 Academy Award for his *Board and Care*, a story about two young victims of Down's syndrome, one of whom is Ellis's sister, Laura. She appears in this film also, playing the daughter of actor Alex Courtenay, a lonely drifter who is unaware of her existence.

Returning to his home town for the first time in many years because of his mother's death, Courtenay learns that he has a daughter. Unaware of the child's handicap, he pleads with her mother to be allowed to see her. Reluctantly, she agrees to the visit. Because he has become aware of the futility of his life, the child is particularly important to Courtenay. Perhaps he will have someone to love.

He waits nervously for his daughter, alone in the living room of her home. As the door opens, he looks up eagerly to see her standing uncertainly in the doorway.

The film raises important questions about responsibility, especially to those who are handicapped. It also raises issues about the quality of the lives of Alex, his daughter, and her mother. Ask students to finish the story. Many of them have strong feelings about Alex and his daughter.

BEAUTY KNOWS NO PAIN
(25 min, c, $475/50, $100 wk., Benchmark Films, 1977)

Filmmaker Elliott Erwitt has accomplished the impossible in this chronicle of the selection and training of the Kilgore College Rangerettes, the nationally known women's drill team that performs at football half-times. Although he disparages the Rangerettes, many viewers react to them with delight. Female students ask the way to Kilgore, Texas, and high school principals urge their band leaders to adopt Rangerette techniques on the local playing field.

To some observers, the drill team and the Marine Corps have much in common. Both undergo tortuous training, both emphasize teamwork and patriotism, and both forbid individuality. Both groups believe they are superior to the rest of humanity. Gussie Nell Davis, Rangerette director, is as tough and demanding as any marine sergeant, although she can ooze charm and motherliness. Her motto is, "Smile, smile, smile, because beauty knows no pain."

To make the team, the women must survive a rigorous and, to some, demeaning selection process. After learning the group's routines, the jittery aspirants perform before a selection committee of Rangerettes who are frequently none too kind in their comments. A few seem influential in the selection, with the majority following their leads.

When the finalists' names are posted, hysteria reigns. There are tears, screams, and sobs of joy as winners and losers embrace to console or congratulate each other. A few losers slip quietly away, struggling to control their tears.

In a grand finale, the Rangerettes, with their newest recruits, proudly perform a patriotic routine manipulating huge American flags. Because some viewers see the team as the embodiment of the American dream, and others as a monstrous perversion of it, the film is wonderful for writing/composition assignments. Interesting questions are raised: Are the Rangerettes merely sex objects? Is subordinating one's individuality desirable? Is the selection process inhuman? What motivates a young woman to submit to such an ordeal? Are they really the American ideal as Gussie Nell Davis believes? *Beauty Knows No Pain* offers no answers.

The film is superb for womens' studies, psychology, humanities, language arts, and values.

BEST BOY

(104 min, c, $150, classroom, Documentary Films, 1980)

The words of filmmaker Ira Wohl serve as the best introduction to this 1980 Academy Award-winning documentary: "My name is Ira Wohl and this is my cousin Philly. Philly is fifty-two years old, and he's been mentally-retarded since birth. In 1938 when he was twelve, he started to become self-destructive. His parents, not knowing how else to deal with it, sent him to live in an institution. They hoped he would learn discipline there and he did, but it was an unhappy experience for all of them, so after two years they brought him home and that's where he's been ever since.

I suppose I'm as guilty as everyone else in the family of always having taken Philly for granted: I remember them saying that his mind had stopped growing when he was five and I guess I always accepted that. But three years ago, at a family gathering, I began to wonder what would happen to Philly after his parents were gone, so I spoke with them and his sister Frances about it. I told them I thought he needed to become more independent, and although the idea was very difficult for them to deal with, they realized that for Philly's sake as well as their own peace of mind, something needed to be done. This film is a record of what they did, and how it changed Philly's life."

There are wonderful incidents in Philly's growth toward more independence. With Ira and a woman friend, he excitedly visits a zoo for the first time. He attends a school for retarded adults and meets with a little success. He runs his first solo errand to a Greenwich Village deli for an ice-cream cone. His happiest visit is backstage at *Fiddler on the Roof* where he encounters the late zany genius, Zero Mostel. "How old are you?" asks Mostel. "Sixteen," Philly replies without hesitation. "Me, too," says Zero, and together they burst into "If I Were a Rich Man."

But *Best Boy* is really the story of a family: Max and Pearl, his aged parents whose lives have been so altered by Philly's condition, his sister, and peripherally, filmmaker Ira Wohl. Max Wohl died during the film's production, but small, determined Pearl lived to see it before her recent death.

Philly eventually moved happily into a residential community for retarded adults where he will probably remain until his death.

Best Boy is excellent for classes in sociology, psychology, special education, adult education, humanities, family living, and language arts.

BOLERO
(27 min, c, $425/50, Pyramid Films, 1975)

Bolero succeeds where many music films do not: it humanizes the performing artists. The first half of this Academy Award-winning film explores the meaning of music to members of the Los Angeles Philharmonic Orchestra and to their then conductor, Zubin Mehta. In programming, for example, Mehta says, "What? 'Bolero' again? After tonight I never want to look at 'Bolero' again ... ever again." A horn player tells us, "I've left the house a little irritated at my wife, shall we say, and come to the symphony, and after the first few chords, it just seems to go away." A bassoonist speaks of the difficulty of playing his demanding solo, "It's easy in your own bathroom or bedroom, but when you get in front of all your colleagues, in front of the audience, and then in front of the tape machine and hear people say, 'One time and that will be it,' you get nervous."

The first part of the film also explains why the musicians chose their careers, their problems in playing "Bolero," and the way the performers relate to each other. The second half is a riveting performance of Ravel's exciting work. Many students who think they dislike classical music enjoy "Bolero" as played and photographed in this film. A single theme rises in volume with each repetition. As the excitement increases, viewer tension and camera activity also increase. At the final crashing chord a great white light follows a shot of Mehta singing and smiling, his hair flying, and his whole body swaying with the music. The viewer hears, sees, and feels the pulsating music. *Bolero* is fimmaking at its best.

BROOKLYN BRIDGE
(58 min, c, $895/100, Direct Cinema, Limited, 1982)

Begun in 1869 and completed twenty-four years later, the Brooklyn Bridge was an unparalleled technical achievement for its time. It cost the lives of at least twenty men, including its designer, John A. Roebling, and disabled many more. Although paralyzed by Caisson's disease (now known as the bends) and in severe pain, Roebling's son, Washington, directed the completion of the bridge from his Brooklyn Heights home, where he observed its progress from his window.

The film traces the evolution of the bridge from an awesome engineering feat to a symbol of American determination and technology.

Narrated by Julie Harris, Arthur Miller, Kurt Vonnegut and others, the film combines rare archival material with modern photography, art work, interviews, and clips of films that featured the bridge. Performers include Jimmy Stewart, Frank Sinatra, Laurel and Hardy, George Raft, and even Bugs Bunny.

Social studies, composition, humanities, and art classes will find *Brooklyn Bridge* stimulating. As history, sociology, visual art, and myth, it is superb. As a record of man's perseverance in the face of great odds, it is unsurpassed. The film was a Blue Ribbon winner at the American Film Festival.

CALIFORNIA REICH
(60 min, c, $185, rental, Films, Inc., 1975)

Young filmmakers Walter Parkes, 24, and Keith Crutchlow, 30, spent many months winning the trust of members of the California Nazi Party to make this stunning Academy Award nominee for 1977. The result is a documentary in the style of Frederick Wiseman. There is no voiceover, no one to intimate these people are freaks and no one to give us permission to ridicule them. It is just an organization of "decent, law-abiding folks, like you," filmed as they go about their ordinary activities. This very banality gives the film its horror.

Sociology rather than politics is its special focus. The emphasis is always on individuals, especially on Allen Vincent, the party's forty-year-old, ex-con leader in San Francisco. Having spent twenty years in prison, Allen found salvation and community in the American Nazi Party. He is surrounded by equally bizarre types: a small arms expert, impatient to "racify" football; a housewife who decorates a cake with a swastika on a flag of licorice; party members who decorate a Christmas tree with swastikas, a grandmother who proudly makes armbands for the family; a twelve-year-old who wants to show off his Nazi uniform at school.

Most ghastly are the parents who smile proudly as five-year-olds shout, "Niggers! Jews!" in answer to the question, "Who is it we don't like?" and then join in an allegiance to Adolph Hitler ("the immortal leader of my race, to the vision for which he stands, the hope and future of Aryan man").

Since the party claims only two thousand members nationwide, no real threat to the country is implied in the film. But it stunningly documents the educational malaise, the economic imparities, and the social frustrations that trap people into lives of bigotry and hatred.

CAN'T IT BE ANYONE ELSE?
(Full version: 50 min, c, $750/74, Pyramid Films, 1980;
edited version: 32 min, c, $450/55, Pyramid Films, 1980)

This stunning film by master filmmaker John Korty follows three remarkable children as they cope with life-threatening leukemia. Twelve-year-old Diana, whose cheerful defense is over-involvement in school activities, breaks only when confronted with a terrifying but necessary medical test. Ten-year-old Jim smilingly wears a "Bald is beautiful" T-shirt after chemotherapy has cost him his hair.

Sensitive medical personnel and concerned parents offer support. The film's most remarkable scene may be Jim's question-and-answer session with his classmates. Their direct, rather stark questions are answered with equal candor. The viewer is almost awed by the maturity of the children and the dedication of parents who daily face the challenge of living with a child whose death is imminent. One becomes aware that hope is the stuff of life.

Important themes are treated with honesty and without evasion: the medical procedure and prognosis for the victims, the therapy for the children and their families, and the need for emotional support in life-threatening situations. It is a beautiful film for classes in family living, sociology, psychology, health, science, guidance, and values.

THE CASE OF THE LEGLESS VETERAN:
James Kutcher
(60 min, b & w, $750/80, New Front Films, 1982)

In 1948 James Kutcher, a soft-spoken, unassuming file clerk for the Veterans Administration (VA) was fired from his $39-a-week job because of his membership in the Socialist Workers Party. Although he was an unlikely candidate for an opponent of the federal government, he decided, on principle, to fight the Federal Loyalty Program's decision.

Drafted in 1941, Kutcher fought in Africa and in Italy where he lost both legs in combat. After two-and-a-half years of rehabilitation, and with artificial legs, he secured employment as a VA file clerk. He was fired when the Socialist Workers Party was placed on Attorney General Tom Clark's subversive list. In 1953 the government tried to evict Kutcher and his aged parents from their housing. The public was shocked at this action, but was more outraged when the government tried to take away his disability pension in 1955. When the meetings of the Loyalty Board meetings were opened to TV cameras, its blatant disregard for constitutional rights was apparent to all citizens.

Blending extensive archival footage and interviews with famous literary and political figures with significant events such as the Rosenberg trials, the Smith Act trials, and other infringements of civil liberties, the film places the McCarthy era in appalling perspective.

Students are often unaware that such chilling events happened and can happen again, unless citizens are vigilant and concerned. There are those who say such films "put America down." On the contrary, they help to assure that by preserving the civil liberties of all, America remains the symbol of hope and freedom.

A Blue Ribbon winner at the American Film Festival, the film is valuable for any class interested in the McCarthy era and in the preservation of civil liberties.

CHILLYSMITH FARM

(55 min, c, $750/75, Filmakers Library, 1981)

For ten years Mark and Dan Jury filmed the lives of four generations of their close-knit, loving family. Sometimes these are the pleasant, ordinary activities of most families — picnicking, walking together, playing with the children. Their camera, however, also looks unflinchingly at the cruel situations families sometimes must confront. The patriarch of the family, Gramp, once proud and vigorous, becomes senile, losing control of his mind and body. Refusing to have him institutionalized, the family members perform the physically demanding, often unpleasant tasks necessary to care for him.

Gramp's wife, Nan, survives him and remains a loving and loved member of the family. When death comes, she meets it peacefully surrounded by her entire family, including her great-grandchildren. Dee and Mark Jury's third child is ushered into the world near his parents, his aunt and uncle, his brother and sister, and an unmarried aunt. Awe and love are almost palpable in the birthing room.

Chillysmith Farm will not suit those who want only pleasant events. The birth scene is explicit, and watching the deterioration and care of Gramp is difficult, but the film offers rewards to those willing to accept reality. Gramp's poignant death at home, the concern of the younger adults for children and oldsters, and most of all, the love and support the family gives each other makes us understand what being human is.

The film raises the important issue of individual responsibility in caring for the aged and emphasizes the value of family support. It is a valuable film for family living, psychology, gerontology, language arts, and sociology. It well deserved the Blue Ribbon it received at the American Film Festival.

COMING OF AGE

(60 min, or two 30 min reels, c, $695/70, New Day Film Co-Op, Inc., 1982)

Adults interested in developing an open dialogue among a group of teenagers concerning male-female relationships, racial identity, and family dynamics should see Josh Hanig's (*Mens' Lives*) newest effort, *Coming of Age*.

The film captures the experiences of a large group of racially and socially mixed Southern California high school students at a week-long camp where they are attended by teachers and counselors.

Rules at camp are simple: no sex, no drugs, no drinking. Candor, kindness, and responsive listening are encouraged. There is no ridiculing of unconventional or emotional responses.

The frankness of the students is provocative. Teenage women, apparently for the first time, tell young men how the male macho attitude makes them feel degraded. The men reveal how their attitudes are conditioned by what they are supposed to do, rather than by their actual feelings.

Young Asian-American, Hispanic, and black students interact with Anglo students in a no-holds-barred discussion of the racial attitudes that serve as barriers to friendship. The encounters are intimate and sometimes explosive. There are many tears and hugs, which are especially poignant when exchanged between the men because they have been conditioned against such behavior.

One might speculate how much the presence of the camera has influenced the student responses, but it is irrelevant; viewers are seeing openness and honest communication.

The young people demonstrate a mature awareness of society's influence on their behavior, as they discuss the difficulties of retaining their newly found insight when they return to their customary environment. Surely, for some of them this will be the first step in internalizing change.

Coming of Age is superb as a discussion starter for students, teachers, and counselors, and any group interested in furthering understanding among teenagers.

THE COP AND THE ANTHEM
(22 min, c, $550/50, Learning Corporation of America, 1982)

Actor Robert Morse is a splendid choice for Soapy, the leading character in this film of O. Henry's familiar story of irony and pathos. His engaging face and relaxed manner make the film entertaining and believable.

As winter approaches, Soapy, a friendly, down-at-the-heels type, is finding it hard to make it in turn-of-the-century New York City, and he thinks longingly of Blackwell's Island, the jail that has been in the past his winter home. Dreaming of good food and a warm bed, Soapy tries various infractions of the law to get himself arrested. He breaks a window, has a wonderful meal in a restaurant for which he cannot pay, steals an umbrella from a passerby only to find that the man had stolen it himself, makes advances to a woman who is pleased at the attention, and begs from theatergoers. Soapy cannot get himself arrested. As he walks by a church, he hears a hymn that reminds him of his mother and of his lost opportunities. He will reform, get a job, have a family. As Soapy ponders his future, a cop arrests him for planning to steal the collection box from the church. His destination is Blackwell's Island.

The Cop and the Anthem is a faithful adaptation of O. Henry's story and is helpful in teaching literature, particularly the use of irony. This is often a difficult concept for students, but this film should make it more understandable.

CRAC
(15 min, c, $325/45, Pyramid Films, 1981)

An old-fashioned rocking chair links the past with the present in this brilliantly animated, Academy Award-winning film from Canada.

From the time the chair is lovingly crafted from a tall tree until it is discarded, it plays a significant part in the saga of a Quebec family. Broken, repaired, repainted, and then broken again, the chair is finally tossed on a snowbank where it is rescued by citizens looking for a seat for the guard of the town's new museum.

During the day the chair is a utilitarian part of the museum's decor, but when night falls, it comes alive to relive the past with the shouts and laughter of children, engaging French-Canadian folk music, and a foot-tapping reel. It gives us a fascinating look at the old and the new, with an emphasis on the rapid change in lifestyle.

There are many uses for *Crac*. Students who enjoy challenge especially like the film because there are subtleties to explore beyond the story itself, which can be understood even by children. A teacher explaining literary terms would find it easy to illustrate *unifying device* by showing *Crac*. Students of film animation recognize the quality of planning and execution in the film. It is an affectionate visit for everyone to a happy, gentle time now gone.

CROSSBAR
(30 min, c, $450/40, Learning Corporation of America, 1981)

The lack of self-esteem of many students is a serious problem for the teacher. Even though students may not articulate their feelings, many are convinced they are failures, or at least, limited in ability. *Crossbar* helps motivate such students by presenting them with a young person who, in spite of seemingly insuperable odds, just will not say, "I can't do it."

Aaron Kornylo, an Olympic-class jumper, looses a leg in a farm accident, and with it, his hopes of a Gold Medal. Undeterred by his loss, he slowly struggles back to contention, only to find that the Olympic Committee has barred him from competition. Threatened with a boycott by other athletes, the committee reverses its stand. Although Aaron qualifies in the preliminaries, he stops short of further competition, having proved that he could reach his goal.

Crossbar helps students to examine their own goals and abilities. It also increases student awareness of the rights of the handicapped and the power of encouragement from family and friends. Questions are also raised about winning.

The performances of the four leading actors, John Ireland, Kate Reid, Brent Carver, and Kim Acttrall bring depth to the film. This is an unusually effective film for any class where motivation is important.

DAVID:
A Portrait of a Retarded Youth
(28 min, c, $450/50, Filmakers Library, 1980)

To most people mongoloidism suggests a person with severe mental, physical, and emotional handicaps. It does not suggest a teenager who has happily prepared for the lead in a play about the subject; one who has memorized his part, enjoyed the difficult performance schedule, and even won a major acting award for his efforts. These are the accomplishments of seventeen-year-old David MacFarlane, the subject of this film.

Surrounded and supported by his loving family, who refuse to allow him to think of himself as handicapped, David speaks easily of Down's syndrome and the way it has affected his life. The importance of a supportive family and friends, as well as the crucial part the public school system plays in the adjustment of a mongoloid child, are explored. The film is upbeat without implying that there are no problems. Seeing David overcoming his handicap and meeting with some successes will inspire others, both victims of Down's syndrome and people who love and work with them.

A DAY IN THE LIFE OF BONNIE CONSOLO
(16½ min, c, $385, rental, inquire Barr Films, 1975)

To write of the triumph of the spirit is to risk a cliché, but nothing else seems appropriate to describe the rich philosophy of Bonnie Consolo. Born without arms, she refuses to recognize herself as handicapped. "I look handicapped," she says, "and I guess I do things that make me look that way, but I don't feel I'm any different than anyone else."

"There is nothing around my house I can't do," she says, and filmmaker Barry Spinello's deceptively simple film bears her out. As his camera follows her around her home, we see her applying mascara, putting on jewelry, watering plants, baking San Francisco sourdough bread, gardening, and caring for her two young sons. Incredibly, she ties their shoe laces, cuts their hair, and helps the younger one as he eats his dinner. All this is done swiftly and easily with her feet. When her son says that he wishes she had hands, she answers matter-of-factly, "Well, so do I, but what can I do?"

She drives herself to the supermarket, shops as anyone else would, writes a check, tears it easily from her checkbook and gives it to the cashier. Staring, particularly by children, is handled with humor or a shrug. Her courage seems unquenchable. "I'm very proud of my kids and I can't even think of anything that's second best." Bonnie Consolo has it all.

It is a marvelous film for special education, guidance, psychology, language arts, and humanities — and for everyone.

David: A Portrait of a Retarded Youth
Photograph courtesy of Filmakers Library

A Day in the Life of Bonnie Consolo
Photograph courtesy of Barr Films

DIRECTORS AT WORK:
The Director and the Image
(28 min, c, $150/25, Museum of Modern Art, 1982)

Films that explain the techniques of film are frequently too difficult for secondary students. An exception is this fine film produced by David Shepard for the Directors Guild of America, which explores the way various directors plan and construct screen imagery. The directors interviewed are articulate, and the film clips that illustrate their ideas are entertaining and informative. Even a novice film student will be interested in an analysis of the famous shower scene from *Psycho* or in Alan Pakula's explanation of his attempt to inject suspense into Robert Redford's telephone call in *All the President's Men*. Other clips are from King Vidor's *The Crowd, Way Down East, Dirty Harry,* and *The Deer Hunter.*

The film is a companion piece to the equally enjoyable film, *Directors at Work: The Director and the Actor*, which is also produced by David Shepard and distributed by the Museum of Modern Art. Together they are a valuable film resource for any school district interested in teaching students to understand better this important medium. Since the film is a nonprofit effort on the part of the Directors Guild, schools should note the exceptionally low price. The films are a real bargain.

DOUBLETALK
(9 min, c, $195/30, Learning Corporation of America, 1976)

Much of our daily conversation consists of meaningless but pleasant remarks that allow society to function at an expected level: "Please," "Thank you," "How are you?" "Lovely day, isn't it?" "How are the children?" Such conversation is accepted, even welcomed because it gives us security in our behavior with strangers and casual acquaintances. Some people believe that society is carrying this too far. Too many people conceal their interests, their thoughts, even themselves, out of fear of offending someone who doesn't agree. *Doubletalk* makes the point that we do not really communicate with each other, but it does it with such great fun that it is easy to miss.

The plot concerns David who has made a date with Karen, whom he had met in a department store that afternoon. As he drives up to her imposing home in his beat-up Volkswagen Bug, he realizes uncomfortably that her family must be wealthy. When Karen's tennis-clad mother opens the door to usher David into a luxuriously furnished living room, the fun begins. From then on we hear not only the conversation of the actors, but also their thoughts. By the time Karen and her father enter the room, conversation and thoughts come so fast that the viewer can't catch them all in one showing of the film. The film is such a delight that everyone wants to see it again.

Doubletalk is marvelous for teaching the punctuation of direct quotations because students like to write their own conversations (and actual thoughts), but if we stop at that we have missed the point that so much of our conversation has nothing to do with who or what we are. The film should lead to discussion/composition about openness and honesty. Where do we draw the line? Where should we draw the line? Can we be honest with people? Why or why not?

END OF INNOCENCE

(28 min, c, long-term lease, $50, rental, inquire First Run Features, 1983)

End of Innocence touches on a theme rarely seen in short films—the influence that contemporary international events sometimes have on the personal lives of individuals, especially children.

Because his mother and her friends are among the thousands of Americans and others who demonstrate against the couple's death sentences, a young Jewish boy becomes aware of the scheduled execution of convicted atom spies Julius and Ethel Rosenberg. Tensions grow as the protests seem futile, and President Eisenhower rejects final pleas for clemency.

As the execution date nears, the child's dreams are confused and terrifying. His mother becomes Ethel Rosenberg in the death chamber. Another time he himself is in the electric chair. He cannot reconcile the images with his own secure life.

As the radio announces the death of the Rosenbergs, the boy's first thoughts are of the couple's two young sons. "Who will take care of them?" he asks his mother. The mother assures him that someone will take care of the Rosenberg's children, but the boy knows that they can be taken care of only physically. Their psychological horror cannot be cared for. The boy has learned about the quality of justice and mercy, bitterness, fear, and death. One is reminded of Golding's *Lord of the Flies.*

The child is appealing and the situation believable. It may be an autobiographical effort from filmmaker Stephen Stept. It is a moving film for work in psychology, humanities, language arts, and parenting.

A FAMILY AFFAIR

(28 min, c, $450/60, Visucom Productions, 1982)

Much of the impact of this film arises from the middle-class family that it follows, from the first violent interaction of the parents to the husband's appearance in court. Even though the husband assaults his wife, he supports his family financially, acts concerned and contrite after each incident, and appears a normal husband and father to outsiders. His wife accepts the traditional female role, loves her husband, and hopes to hold the family together.

However, with each battering incident, family tension increases. Attempts at reconciliation fail, and the father finally appears in court on charges brought by his wife, who then seeks a divorce. This familiar story line is not the most important aspect of this film. Its real strength is the detailed, extremely interesting guide that accompanies it. The first half of the guide answers common questions about wife abuse by relating them to specific incidents in the film. The second half contains information about the criminal justice system as it relates to spouse abuse, which would be helpful to anyone seeking assistance.

A Blue Ribbon winner at the 1982 American Film Festival, *Family Affair* is somewhat clinical in its approach, but the viewer gains enormously in understanding this very complex subject. If current statistics are correct, many students have this problem in their homes. The film could be an indirect, but effective means of encouraging them to seek help. It makes it clear that because something occurs behind the closed doors of the family home, the behavior is not exempt from moral and legal codes. It is a superior film for psychology, women's studies, sociology, family living, and guidance classes.

THE FEMININE MISTAKE
(24 min, c, $425/55, Pyramid Films, 1977)

The rise of the incidence of lung cancer in women so closely parallels the rise in the number of women who smoke that no one any longer doubts the correlation. Yet many high school girls still start to smoke each year. What can be done to stop this or to help those girls who may be wavering in their resolve to quit smoking? Not a scare film per se, *The Feminine Mistake* combines facts with demonstrations, the results of which are frightening.

It shows the depressing effects of one cigarette on a high school girl's respiration rate, the effects on the fetal heartbeat, and the prematurely wrinkled skins of older women who have smoked several packs of cigarettes a day during their adult lives.

Perhaps the most telling sequence is that of a happy-looking woman of 43 sitting on the beach at Waikiki, followed by photographs of the same woman (still 43), but now emaciated beyond recognition. She is a victim of throat cancer. She has no hair and speaks almost inaudibly. Painfully, she says, "I started smoking in high school because they said it was sexy, but this isn't very sexy, is it?" as she looks at her wasted body. Students grow thoughtful as she offers another observation, "They told me it would take some years off my life. So, I thought, I would die at 70 instead of 75. But nobody told me it would be in the middle of my life." Six days later, this brave woman died, but she performed a great service in allowing herself to be interviewed. For most students it is their first contact with anyone in such a desperate condition.

Another sequence that affects students is that of a lovely mature woman who speaks using an artificial voicebox because her cancerous larynx has been removed. Since her doctors have attributed her problem to smoking, she urges viewers not to start.

The author had the rewarding experience of having six students in one semester quit smoking after seeing *The Feminine Mistake*.

This film transcends categorization. Because its message is so important, it should be shown to all students who would not otherwise see it.

FOOTBALL IN AMERICA
(27 min, c, $425/75, Pyramid Films, 1983)

Since 1980 more than twenty million dollars has been awarded to football players paralyzed as a result of game injuries. School districts, administrators, teachers, and coaches have been held responsible. Originally a body contact sport, football has become a game of violence, attended by a win-at-any-cost philosophy. Many concerned educators and parents demand changes if football is to remain a part of the experience of young boys and youths.

The film notes that as the level of play rises, injuries escalate. In a Minnesota high school study, 78 out of every 100 players reported injuries. Nineteen players showed symptoms of cerebral concussion. An estimated 30,000-50,000 knee surgeries are reported each year. The best figures available confirm 122 deaths and 193 permanent paralyses related to American football.

As professional football becomes a more questionable role model, the psychological costs to younger players also need to be assessed. Harry Edwards, a sports sociologist, states that the "win-at-any-cost" ethic has caused many coaches and players to encourage violence and aggression at the expense of the more positive aspects of the sport. Many think we should not encourage violence in American life.

Most of the injuries are caused by improper or illegal playing techniques and faulty equipment. The National Football League agrees that young players should understand football's risks. After viewing *Football in America*, they issued the following statement: "Professionals play football for a living. They know the risks because almost to a man they have been through the agony of injury. The NFL Players Association believes, however, that young players in grade school or high school need to be aware of the risks. This film provides a graphic and effective message enabling them to make intelligent decisions about careers in football."

If the film stirs a healthy debate among parents, coaches, school administrators, and other interested adults about a safe future for football, it could help to eliminate risks to young people. It is highly recommended for classes in physical education, psychology, sociology, parenting, and adult education.

FROM MAO TO MOZART:
Isaac Stern in China
(84 min, c, $250 rental only, United Artists, 1980)

The Emily award is given each year at the prestigious American Film Festival to the highest-ranked film of the hundreds submitted. The 1982 Emily went to this charming, informative documentary about the 1979 visit of violinist Isaac Stern and his accompanist, David Golub, to the People's Republic of China. (The film had previously won the even more prestigious Academy Award as the best documentary of 1981.)

(Annotation continues on page 194.)

Football in America
Photograph courtesy of Pyramid Films

Since all Western music was banned in China during the Cultural Revolution, Stern and Golub were greeted with wild enthusiasm by thousands of Chinese who filled the rehearsal and concert halls. Invited to China as a master teacher, Stern occasionally employed a translator, but most often taught by using only his instrument and body language. As Stern demonstrates to young Chinese musicians the proper playing of Western music, they eagerly play back to him what they have learned. Music is a joyous bond between cultures.

As Stern and Golub travel freely about China, the viewer is offered unusual glimpses of Chinese art and culture, including many children who play their instruments with skill and musicianship. We also hear of the torture and imprisonment during the Cultural Revolution. Ten of the instructors at the National Music Conservatory were driven to suicide.

For many schools the rental price is high, but the film is well worth it. It has marvelous possibilities for music classes, and also opens up a world that many of us know little about.

FRONT LINE

(55 min, c, $750/75, Filmakers Library, 1981)

This powerful Vietnam War documentary is seen from the perspective of Neil Davis, a daring young Australian photographer who spent eleven years in the combat zone, much of the time with Vietnamese troops. His gentle manner and vivid personal recollections, combined with his stunning close-up footage of combat, produce an unforgettable testimony to the insanity and inhumanity of war.

Because of his close personal ties with the Vietnamese, Davis was allowed to cross enemy lines and film both sides in the conflict. His film thus becomes a record of events little-known here—the suffering of Asians at the hands of other Asians. One cannot help but be affected by the immediacy and sometimes horrifying intimacy of the scenes he has photographed.

Front Line was originally shown on PBS with great impact. Since then it has received many other awards, including a 1981 Academy Award nomination and the prestigious John Grierson Award at the American Film Festival.

There are educators who say, "But why should we go over the Vietnam War again? After all, it's over with. Let's put it behind us." While the wish is understandable, war as a topic is not behind us. It is frighteningly before us. Seeing films like *Front Line* could strengthen the determination of every citizen to seek peaceful solutions to international problems before we again become involved in a quagmire such as Vietnam—one that this country entered with the best of intentions.

Social studies, history, psychology, humanities, and language arts classes will find the film useful. Mature students who are interested in the important issues facing the United States today will particularly benefit from it.

GENTLEMAN TRAMP

(74 min, c, $115 rental, other inquire Films, Inc., 1974)

Screen immortal Charlie Chaplin is the subject of this moving tribute that follows the comedian from his birth in 1890 in the slums of London, until shortly before his death at age 88 in his home in Vevey, Switzerland.

Using film clips, home movies, stills, newsreels, radio broadcasts, and interviews, the film presents Chaplin's sorrows and triumphs in surprising depth for a film of this length. Walter Matthau and Lord Laurence Olivier, and his friends and admirers narrate the Academy Award-winning documentary.

The film covers Chaplin's deprived childhood, with an alcoholic father and a mentally disturbed mother, his early short comedies, and his feature successes: *The Kid, The Gold Rush, Modern Times, Limelight, City Lights, The Great Dictator*, and the less successful film, *A King in New York*.

Chaplin then suffered a series of disappointments and injustices, resulting in his voluntary exile in Europe where he finally found happiness with his young wife, Oona O'Neill, daughter of Eugene O'Neill. Scenes from their idyllic life with their eight children in a mansion in Vevey are among the most affecting in the film. The film reaches its climax with Charlie's return to America after a thirty-five-year absence to receive a special Academy Award and a standing ovation for his contributions to motion pictures.

The film moves many viewers to tears, but they are tears of gladness that this much-misunderstood genius who brought so much pleasure to millions of people around the world finally found the personal happiness that had so long eluded him. It is a beautiful film about an artist whom today's students scarcely know.

GET IT TOGETHER

(20 min, c, $375/50, Pyramid Films, 1977)

An automobile accident left Jeff Minnebraker a paraplegic, paralyzed from the waist down and confined to a wheelchair. This film tells us much about courage as Jeff, after his initial reaction of rage and self-pity, fought his way back to a satisfying personal life, a fulfilling career, and a role in society that brings him rewards few people achieve.

The accident occurred at the crucial postadolescent time when one struggles to find an identity. According to Jeff's own words he was floundering, "I was just a little kid, surfing, partying." If the accident had not forced him to examine himself, he believes his personal life would have deteriorated further. From this grim situation, a remarkably mature young man emerged.

Following his accident, he enrolled in college, married, and found employment as a recreational therapist in the same hospital in which he had been a patient. Audrey, his wife, speaks frankly of the problems the handicap causes in the marriage, both emotional and physical. She is especially critical of the attitude of many outsiders, quoting her cousin when he heard of the marriage, "Well, now we have a freak in the family."

The richest part of the film is watching Jeff as a physical therapist, as he swims, exercises, and plays tennis. The tennis scene is especially impressive to students, but it is Jeff's determination and love that give this film its wide appeal. Everyone responds to it. Jeff's inspiring message is, "You have to be creative, adaptive, and never say die."

A HELPING HAND

(21 min, c, $395/50, Kinetic Films, 1982)

The technical marvel of this film is the fitting of the myoelectric limb to preschoolers, children who were once thought too young for such help. The human marvel of it is the number of scientists, psychologists, and medical personnel who have devoted much skill and effort in helping these cruelly handicapped children to live life more fully.

Children who have lost an arm below the elbow form the largest group with missing or truncated arms and have been the most successful in using the new prosthesis. They must be patiently trained to use the correct muscles to control the electromyographic signal. The dedication shown by the personnel of the Ontario Crippled Childrens' Centre is inspiring.

As the film focuses on the training of two beautiful children, one exults inwardly when the children are able to use the limbs successfully and to appear normal.

Students are interested in the psychological and scientific aspects of the film, but they also understand that there are people whose satisfactions in life are derived from helping others.

A Helping Hand is useful for language arts, parenting, physiology, and science classes.

I'M A FOOL

(38 min, c, $681 rental, inquire Perspective Films, 1977)

Television star Ron Howard's somewhat naive manner, as well as his superb acting ability, make him the perfect choice for Andy, the insecure adolescent hero of Sherwood Anderson's funny-sad tale of ego-identification in a rural America that has long disappeared.

Andy works as an assistant to Burt, a black horseman, and together they travel the country racing horses. One day, as a spectator in the grandstand, Andy meets innocent, pretty young Lucy Wessen, the girl of his dreams.

Eager to impress her, Andy introduces himself as Walter Mathers, wealthy racehorse owner. Emboldened by the interest of Lucy and her two companions, he offers them advice about betting. When the horse Andy recommends wins, and Lucy obviously returns his interest, he realizes that he is now trapped in his own lies.

Helpless to extricate himself from his net of deceit, he gives Lucy a false address, realizing that he will never see her again. The beautiful relationship he has dreamed about is over before it has really begun, and Andy can blame no one but himself. As he rides out of town the vulnerable Andy berates himself, "I'm a fool."

Since most of us, at some point have lied and then could not extricate ourselves from the situation, identification with the hapless Andy is immediate. It is a lovely film to use with a class with whom the teacher has a trusting relationship so that students are not afraid to reveal themselves, for the strength of the film lies in how much we can recognize ourselves in it. Language arts, psychology, and values classes will find *I'm a Fool* intriguing and rewarding.

I'LL FIND A WAY
(26 min, c, $465/45, The Media Guild, 1982)

Born with spina bifida, a crippling malformation of the spine, nine-year-old Nadia De Franco wears a brace, cannot walk without crutches, and has undergone extensive physiotherapy all of her life. Incredibly, she is a fulfilled child who confidently looks forward to the future.

Nadia narrates this film with engaging matter-of-factness. As she describes her classmates, many of whom are more severely handicapped than she, she insists that they all want to be considered ordinary people who do not feel sorry for themselves or others. As we watch these young people play basketball, take field trips, sing in the choir, and attend classes, we see that Nadia has described their attitude accurately.

"My friends never feel sorry for me," Nadia says with such candor and warmth that viewers, especially young ones, are left with a permanently altered perspective on the meaning of disability. Disability isn't the end; it can be the beginning of a life as hopeful as one wishes to make it. The handicapped viewer will be inspired to emulate Nadia's upbeat attitude; nonhandicapped viewers may see their problems in more perspective. She is never more impressive than when asked what she would do if others stared at her braces or made remarks about her disability. "I don't know how I'll deal with it," she says with a smile, "But I'll find a way."

The film, which won the Academy Award, is outstanding for developing awareness of the importance of a positive attitude in facing life as a handicapped person. It is very valuable for special education, psychology, language arts, and values.

IF YOU LOVE THIS PLANET
(26 min, c, $495/45, Direct Cinema, Limited, 1982)

Dr. Helen Caldicott, National President of the Physicians for Social Responsibility, is a passionate and outspoken advocate of nuclear disarmament. This disturbing but informative documentary records her appearance before students in Plattsburg, New York, in 1981.

Following a review of the early development of the bomb by newscaster Ed Herlihy using early newsreels, Dr. Caldicott compares it to the apocalyptic weapons of today. Citing medical and scientific journals as her source, she describes the long-range medical and environmental effects of a single detonation of the 20,000 megaton bomb.

Her words destroy the myths that limited nuclear war and survival are possible. The students are transfixed as she describes the aftermath of a nuclear explosion — radiation contamination everywhere, disease for which there is no treatment, pain for which there is no relief, and few survivors.

In many parts of the United States, teachers are banding together to form the Educators for Social Responsibility and planning how best to teach about these awesome weapons without damaging the students psychologically. Dr. Caldicott's lecture would be extremely valuable in such a presentation. Time *is* running out. Dr. Caldicott's message is clear, "If we love this planet, disarmament cannot be postponed."

THE INCREDIBLE SAN FRANCISCO ARTISTS' SOAPBOX DERBY
(24 min, c, $395/35, Phoenix Films, 1979)

Originally started as a fund-raising event for the San Francisco Museum of Modern Art, the soapbox derby soon proved to be much more than that for both participants and spectators. The artists became more aware of engineering and racing; the spectators learned of the pleasure of looking at the world through the eyes of an artist.

The idea was simple; 104 of the Bay Area's best artists were given $200 to design a work of art that is also a car capable of rolling down a hill in true soapbox fashion. The artists' creations and their tongue-in-cheek comments when interviewed about them are hilarious. One car is actually a loaf of bread. "I wanted a two-tone car so I baked pumpernickel and white," confides the artist. The spectators are eating it as the driver crosses the finish line. One artist changed the entire $200 into pennies and a "mound" of pennies floats leisurely (and incredibly) down the hill. There is a banana. "Why, it's the fastest fruit," the artist says innocently. There is a television, which accidentally explodes with outrageous results, and a sleek, magnificently designed plexiglass tube in which the artist lies full-length.

... one of the finest art films I've seen ... imaginatively conceived, well-paced ... it will entertain and inform an unusually wide audience, from artists and designers to the same sort of everyday folks who lined that hill in San Francisco to enjoy that delightful outrageous event. Most art films cannot claim such broad appeal. This one can.

> —Peter Bermingham,
> Curator of Education
> National Collection of Fine Arts
> Smithsonian Institution

ITZHAK PERLMAN:
In My Case Music
(11 min, c, $325/50, De Nonno Pix, 1982)

This charming, Blue Ribbon-winning film displays the warm personality and philosophy of superstar violinist, Itzhak Perlman, at home, in concert, and in an appearance before a group of handicapped youngsters. Although physically handicapped himself, Perlman has not let it interfere with his role as husband, father, musician, or concerned human being.

He speaks of his boyhood in Tel Aviv and of willingly practicing three hours a day as a child. His love for his wife and two young children is obvious. Unlike many musicians who schedule their concerts where they will do the most to advance their careers, Mr. Perlman's criterion is, "Can my family go with me?"

Most touching of all, he plays his violin (including "Pop Goes the Weasel") for a group of delighted handicapped children. The portrait that emerges is of a man living life to the hilt and finding fulfillment in every activity.

It is, of course, a superb film for special education classes, but language arts, music, and guidance classes will profit from it also. It is a small film in size and price but it is big in ideas; be a good husband and father, do your best at whatever you choose to do as a career, and care about others. Itzhak Perlman is much admired for his music: in this film he comes through as an equally admirable human being.

JOHN BAKER'S LAST RACE
(35 min, c, $455/16, Brigham Young University, 1976)

The film is weak in production values, editing, and direction, but its subject matter is so compelling and John Baker such a remarkable young man, that any deficiencies should be overlooked.

It is the true story of a young Albuquerque athlete, John Baker, University of New Mexico track star and Olympic possibility. Learning at twenty-one that he had terminal cancer, his first thoughts were of suicide, but on reflection he decided to devote what remained of his life to helping children. The film is a record of his devotion and success.

Having accepted a position at Albuquerque's Aspen Elementary School, he devoted himself for the next eighteen months to his students, especially the "Duke City Dashers," a girls' track team. He didn't just work with the talented, but encouraged everyone. One of his greatest successes was Stephanie, an osteomyelitis victim, who later set sixteen records. Though often in severe pain, he willed himself to continue coaching until the Duke City Dashers were accepted in the national AAU championships in St. Louis, Missouri.

On Thanksgiving Day, two days before the Dashers won the national championship, John Baker died, but he had set an example of courage, love, and grace under pressure that the Albuquerque community still honors. The film's narration ends with these words: "When the community was asked if the name of Aspen School should be changed to the John Baker Elementary School, there was not one dissenting vote."

John Baker's Last Race is superb for classes in physical education, special education, language arts, psychology, family living, guidance, and values.

JOSIE

(25 min, c, $375/25 wk., Paulist Productions, 1981)

"Socies," "jocks," "do-nothings," "greasers," and "stoners"—these and crueler labels are pinned on high school students who may carry the scars for a lifetime. What can we do, within the curriculum, to help students see each other as human beings?

Josie obviously sees herself as one of the bottom group. Disliking herself and insecure about others, she compensates by wearing too much makeup and provocative clothes. In her desperation to belong, she encourages intimacies with boys for whom she feels nothing.

Actress Elizabeth Daly projects perfectly the sullen, slightly damaged-looking but vulnerable Josie in whom one student, Luke (James Van Patten), sees an inward beauty. Although he limps, he enters a running marathon, the price for a date with her. Fearful of real intimacy, Josie strikes out at Luke by acquiescing when a friend suggests slashing his running shoes. At the end of the race, Josie is forced to confront the reality of Luke's feeling for her and to see herself through his eyes.

There are flaws in the film (James Van Patten is not totally believable as an insecure teenager), but they are unimportant. There are hundreds of Josies in our classrooms and thousands of students who label and reject them.

Paulist Productions specializes in attractive, evocative films to help teenagers at critical points in their lives. *Josie* is one of their best.

A JURY OF HER PEERS
(30 min, c, $500/60, Texture Films, 1981)

This spare, beautifully paced and acted film opens in the dark stillness of a Southern farmhouse in the 1900s. As the camera eerily explores the rooms, we learn that farmer John Burke has been found strangled in his bed: his wife accused of his murder.

Outside, the sheriff, the prosecuting attorney, and a neighbor search for clues, while inside their wives gather a few personal items for the accused woman who is in jail. As the women go about their task, they uncover crucial details about the life of the couple, who have remained alienated from the community. Gradually they begin to understand the loneliness and oppression that Mrs. Burke has suffered. The final clue they find provides a strong motive for murder in one who has reached the limit of endurance. Unknown to the men, the women serve as a jury of her peers. They find the accused woman innocent, and conceal the evidence that would prove her guilt.

Susan Glaspell's Pulitzer Prize-winning story was difficult to film because it is largely psychological, but it is so well written and directed that understanding grows with each sequence. It reveals in a heartrending way the difference between a man's world and a woman's sensibility; one weeps for Mrs. Burke's lonely, wasted life. A 1981 Academy Award winner, *A Jury of Her Peers* is a masterpiece, unsurpassed for classes in language arts, psychology, and humanities.

KIDS FOR SALE
(22 min, c, $300/30, Mass Media Ministries, 1981)

Anyone who cares about children, as a parent or professional, will be interested in this documentary about the effects of television on children.

The innocent, trusting faces of the children are juxtaposed against a graphic depiction of the way television shapes their thoughts, values, and manners. Shots of actual programs illustrate the scope of the problem: racial, ageist, and sexual stereotyping; the physical and mental abuse of children, adults, and animals; violent crime, distorted male-female relationships, and cupidity. The manipulative techniques used to sell expensive toys and sugary products to children are examined, and strategies to combat them are suggested.

Interviews with children and parents are chilling as the youngsters innocently reveal their responses to television's stimuli. The parents vent their frustrations in trying to cope and their fears that they are not.

Kids for Sale, commissioned by the Action for Children's Television (ACT) organization, is part of a television-awareness series that includes *The Anonymous Teacher* and *The Thirty-Second Dream*. A national, nonprofit consumer organization, ACT works to improve broadcasting practices related to children. Through legal action, education, and research, ACT tries to encourage diversity and to eliminate commercial abuses in children's television. For information or membership write to Action for Children's Television, 46 Austin Street, Newtonville, MA 02160. Together, or separately, the films stimulate discussion in teacher-training, consumer-education, family living, parenting, psychology, sociology, and language arts classes.

LAST STRONGHOLD OF THE EAGLES
(30 min, c, $450/40, Learning Corporation of America, 1981)

In 1782 the United States adopted the bald eagle as our national symbol of freedom, grace, and power. But now, except in a few pockets, development has threatened this magnificent bird with extinction.

In southeast Alaska, however, the bald eagle has been relatively unaffected until recently. Three thousand pairs of nesting birds are estimated to be in that region because of its open space and adequate food supply. But development is coming quickly and alarmingly to southeast Alaska also. Ending in the spectacular winter gathering of thousands of eagles, the beautifully photographed film explores the life cycle of the bird and raises disturbing questions about its future.

Much controversy is currently being generated between government officials and environmentalists concerning ecological issues. Although *Last Stronghold of the Eagles* doesn't moralize, it does focus attention on the question: Are we now to repeat in southeast Alaska the same near destruction of the bald eagle that has occurred in other parts of the country?

LET THERE BE LIGHT
(58 min, b & w, $226.25/35, National Audiovisual Center;
produced 1946, released 1981)

Famed director John Huston filmed this eloquent documentary about the emotional casualities of World War II for the Army in 1946. Lost in the intervening years, the film, through the cooperation of the Defense Department, is now available to general audiences at a very reasonable cost.

Using black and white film, Huston turned his cameras on a wide range of emotional disabilities among the returning veterans at Mason General Hospital, Long Island, New York. There are men who can't talk, can't walk, can't remember their own names or those of family members—men who cannot function because of the combat horrors they have experienced.

With intelligence and grace the camera records the suffering on the face of each man as he moves through the painful process of psychological healing. In the end we realize that the disabilities we are witnessing are not abnormalities, but normal responses to the unendurable.

Although psychiatric techniques have undoubtedly improved since 1946, *Let There Be Light* is John Huston at his best. The film is in his words, "the most hopeful and optimistic, and even joyous thing I have ever had a hand in."

Even though there are no battle scenes, as a documentary about the psychological effects of war, the film is unparalleled. Secondary students are frequently unaware that a man's mind may be a battle casualty. The film is very useful for language arts, history, and psychology.

THE LIFE AND TIMES OF ROSIE THE RIVETER
(65 min, c, $795/100, Clarity Educational Productions, 1982)

The entry of the United States into World War II created an unprecedented demand for new workers. Since the men were needed in the military, women were subjected to propaganda calling upon them to "Do the Job He Left Behind." Rosie the Riveter, symbol of all the thousands of women who responded, was born. Filled with a new sense of accomplishment, Rosie wanted to stay when the war was over, but neither the economy nor the dominant view of women's place in the society sustained such hopes. The propaganda shifted to "woman's place is in the home," "don't take a job that a returning veteran needs," and "be feminine for him."

Five Rosies of this ousted group movingly recall their experiences in Los Angeles, New York, Detroit, and San Francisco. The concerns expressed in 1940 are surprisingly relevant to the issues today: racism, equal pay and opportunity for advancement, health and safety hazards, and the proper care of children.

The film is a stunning achievement. Propaganda images of working women are intercut with actual experiences. The complex relationship of ideology, propaganda, and social reality are explored. Rare archival films, posters, stills, ads, and music from the period are interwoven into the film. It is easy to understand how the media, which successfully brought the women into the war effort, turned against them when they were no longer needed and forced them from their meaningful jobs. Since the sex-role stereotyping of women is still prevalent today, the film does more than show us the past.

Rosie the Riveter is marvelous for American history, ethnic studies, women's studies, psychology, sociology, and language arts.

LITTLE MISERIES
(27 min, c, $395/25 wk., Paulist Productions, 1982)

John Ritter and Audra Lindley from the hit TV show, "Three's Company," star in this comedy-drama about a manipulative aunt who schemes and twists the truth as she tries to keep her only nephew near her.

Having decided that pretty Stephanie Faracy would be the ideal wife for him, the aunt arranges a blind date for the couple. To ensure her nephew's sympathetic cooperation, she tells him that Stephanie has leukemia.

As the couple's relationship deepens, an engagement is announced, and the lie revealed. Having reached the limit of his patience with his aunt, the nephew turns on her scornfully and threatens to leave forever. In a surprisingly poignant ending, the aunt reveals her true motivation.

Veteran character actor Edward Andrews adds to the comedy as the woebegone, but equally scheming uncle whose chief weapon is guilt. The theme that love must be freely given and not manipulated is made clear in the resolution.

The film is somewhat simplistic, causing high-achieving students to reject it, but other students like it very much. For many it is their first exposure to the concept of manipulative behavior. Paulist films are generally effective in raising the consciousness of teenagers about their problems, and *Little Miseries* is no exception.

THE LOST PHOEBE
(30 min, c, $519, rental, inquire Perspective Films, 1978)

Theodore Dreiser's poignant short story about a senile old man's search for his dead wife has been beautifully produced by the American Film Institute.

Alone in his house, old Henry entreats the dead Phoebe to answer him. Frantically he calls her name as he rushes from the house to search for her. Realizing that Henry is senile, kindly neighbors are concerned but reluctant to tell him flatly that Phoebe is dead. Awkwardly, they try to compensate by offering him food and advice.

Finally, as Henry searches through a grove of trees, he sees Phoebe, young and graceful, ahead of him. Smilingly she beckons, and he follows crying, "Phoebe! Phoebe!" At last, high on a hill above the river he nears his beloved. As he rushes to touch her, he, too, is claimed by death. As Henry lies dead at the edge of the river, his outstretched hand clutches a flower. As his hand slowly relaxes, the blossom drifts gently away. Henry, free of his fear and confusion, has been happily reunited with his wife.

The tenderness of Dreiser's widely anthologized story appeals to many students. They understand the concept of seeing what one desperately wants to see, and do not necessarily agree that old Henry is senile. The film sounds depressing, but its theme of age and love and need touches the viewer in a positive way. *The Lost Phoebe* is superb for a short story class and would be useful in psychology, humanities, and gerontology.

LOVEJOY'S NUCLEAR WAR
(60 min, c, $725/45, Green Mountain Post Films, 1975)

At his trial in Montague, Massachusetts, in 1974, local farmer Samuel Lovejoy said, "The environment must be protected, and life must be protected, and somehow we've got to be able to confront this all-pervading technology, that's beginning to drown us, with some counterbalance."

On trial for toppling a 500-foot steel tower erected by the local utility company as a part of its projected multibillion dollar nuclear (power) plant, Lovejoy had turned himself into the police with a four-page written statement of his reasons for his act of civil disobedience. His action forced the citizens of Montague to take sides.

In the nine years that have elapsed since Lovejoy's civil disobedience, most communities have not been so fortunate. Nuclear power plants are being built, the near-disaster at Three-Mile Island has occurred, rivers are being poisoned, and underground water and food sources are being polluted. The citizens of most American communities are just beginning to realize what technological advances have cost them. But communities such as Harrisburg, Pennsylvania, Times Beach, Missouri, and Love Canal understand because they have suffered.

Lovejoy's Nuclear War is a catalyst for discussion not only about the destruction of the environment, but also about the nature of civil disobedience. Americans are beginning to understand that they can no longer rely on large governmental agencies to protect them. Somehow they must take control of their lives. Is civil disobedience an unpatriotic act or is it the highest expression of citizenship since one has to be willing to accept the penalty? *Lovejoy's Nuclear War* is stimulating for classes in social studies, humanities, language arts, sociology, and science.

MAKEBELIEVE MARRIAGE

(Full version: 50 min, c, $625/50, Learning Corporation of America, 1979; edited version: 33 min, c, $450/40, Learning Corporation of America, 1979)

Secondary students find it fun to identify with this humorous, but informative, film about marriage in a high school family living class. The subject of marriage is absorbing, the two teenage film leads are engaging, and the setting well-known, if not always well-loved.

Trouble begins when Mr. Webster, teacher of the class, assigns couples to be marital partners. They are to budget, find housing, shop, have children, and encounter all the familiar domestic problems — unemployment, accidents, illnesses, and even divorce.

To his obvious dismay, Gary, the big-man-on-campus, is paired with Gail, the class intellectual. Unable to see each other because of their stereotyped thinking, which is complicated by Gary's jealous girl friend, the couple's relationship outwardly deteriorates. Even though each is secretly attracted to the other, they are unable to express their feelings openly.

When the situation seems impossible, Gail and Gary opt for divorce as the only solution. Although he reluctantly grants it, the teacher uses the opportunity to discuss his personal marital troubles as a failure in communications. Listening intently, Gail and Gary seem unimpressed, but later, in the empty stadium bleachers, they meet and decide to give their marriage another chance. As they leave happily together, we know that the couple has learned about communication and openness and about seeing beyond the stereotypes to the actual person. *Makebelieve Marriage* is a simple film, but a warm, enjoyable, and rewarding one. It's sure to please and inform.

MARATHON WOMAN:
Miki Gorman
(28 min, c, $450/50, Filmakers Library, 1981)

Sports films seldom feature women, but a ninety-pound Japanese-born woman runner, Miki Gorman, proves to be an extraordinarily worthy and exciting subject.

Having grown up in Japan and China and endured difficult wartime conditions, Gorman took the unusual step of emigrating to America in search of a better life. Here she found both a satisfying marriage and running, which she took up in an effort to "gain some weight." Amazingly, by the age of thirty-seven she had twice won the New York City and the Boston marathons.

After her first win in the marathon, she discovered that she was pregnant, but continued running until one week before the birth of her child. Candidly she tells us that her running accomplishments were easy compared to the twenty-two hours of labor she endured in childbirth. According to her, she has been late with all the important events of her life: marriage, motherhood, and marathons, but she has never used her age as an excuse for not trying.

The unusual discipline and determination demonstrated by her athletic accomplishments are very admirable, but she never seems more praiseworthy than after her loss in the 1978 New York City marathon when she accepts that her winning days are over. A champion in both victory and defeat, Ms. Gorman is a role model for all to emulate.

Marathon Woman is superb for physical education, language arts, health, guidance, values, and women's studies.

A MATTER OF TIME
(30 min, c, $450/40, Learning Corporation of America, 1981)

Lisl Gilbert's mother, once full of life and energy, is dying of cancer. It is only a matter of time, and Lisl is forced to confront her mother's death and her own feelings of loss and anger. Based on Roni Schotter's novel, this Emmy Award-winning film chronicles Lisl's struggles and her resulting growth.

Aired as an ABC Afterschool Special and named Outstanding Childrens' Program, *A Matter of Time* starts with a view of talented, confident Mrs. Jean Gilbert, artist, college professor, and respected civic leader. To sixteen-year-old Lisl her mother is a tower of strength, the epitome of success.

When investigative surgery reveals Mrs. Gilbert's terminal illness, Lisl's world starts to disintegrate. With her father and sister emotionally unable to cope and her friends uneasy around her, Lisl finds release through writing. Encouraged by the social worker assigned to the case, she tries to work through her fear and sorrow.

Through painful, honest communication with her mother, Lisl begins to understand that, despite her accomplishments, her mother is often as lonely and insecure as she herself is. Perhaps, then, Lisl reasons, she may someday become a special person too. As the film ends, she has discovered the strength to carry on with her own life.

Because of its sensitive subject matter, *A Matter of Time* should be used carefully. It could be most helpful to students who have been or who may be involved in the same situation. The film is excellent for language arts, family living, and guidance classes.

MEN'S LIVES
(43 min, c, $600/48, New Day Film Co-op, Inc., 1974)

Only recently has men's liberation begun to be seen as the other side of the historic oppression of women. The restrictions that imprisoned women placed a heavy burden of responsibility on men in trying to live up to society's definition of masculinity. *Men's Lives* is one of the few excellent films to document the problems of growing up male in America.

Two young filmmakers, Will Roberts and Josh Hanig, set out to document their own passage to masculinity, hoping then to relate it to the larger picture of the lives of all men. To do this, they interviewed teachers, coaches, students, children, even a few women. What they found is very revealing about the shaping of a man's life.

Small boys on the school playground readily point out which of the other boys are "sissies." A young girl volunteers that she would like to be a boy because boys get to do more, such as climb trees. Their female teacher accepts that boys must have higher economic goals since they will be breadwinners.

As they interview adolescents, the emphasis shifts to cars and football. A black teenager wants a "blue Cadillac"; a white boy's custom car helps him to feel "more like a man." An embarrassed teenage boy admits to liking ballet, while a football player explains he loves football because it's "kill them before they kill you."

Scoring with the opposite sex is the concern of the college-age group shown at a fraternity party. All accept that approaches to women cannot be done with any insecurity showing; total confidence is all.

There are poignant interviews with a school administrator who states that he is "not an emotional person," while the camera focuses on his nervously twisting hands. An articulate barber says that "men open up and tell me as a barber many things they wouldn't tell their father confessor." Another interviewee says, "Most men in this society see themselves as failures, and the reason is that there's always someone around the corner who has a nicer car or an extra room on the house. They strive to be that person, only to find out that there's someone with two cars, and both cars are nicer than theirs."

MOUNTAIN MUSIC
(9 min, c, $210/35, Pyramid Films, 1978)

Will Vinton, creator of the Academy Award-winning *Closed Mondays*, scores again with this clay animation of an ecological tale of the pollution and ultimate destruction of the environment by people, traffic, and noise.

Using clay for the background, as well as for the people and objects, the film opens on a scene of simple beauty and serenity in a mountain forest. A trio of musicians arrives and begins to play. At first the music is lovely, but soon the mood changes. More and more instruments, amplifiers, and percussion instruments are added. The music grows louder and more urgent.

As the music crescendos, people gather, animals wail as if in pain, the instruments become a sea of electronic devices. The music roars deafeningly. Suddenly the mountain erupts in a spectacular volcanic cataclysm, destroying everything in nature and carrying all before it.

Many students respond to *Mountain Music* because of their love and ecological concern for the environment. They know that the present administration is proposing to drill and mine in the areas immediately adjacent to our national parks, and that the National Park Service reports extensive vandalism and damage in parks such as Yellowstone, Yosemite, Grand Canyon, and General Grant.

Mountain Music encourages discussion about the destruction of the environment. It is excellent for classes in science, ecology, humanities, and language arts, and because of its superb clay techniques, it is effective in filmmaking classes.

MYSELF, YOURSELF
(30 min, c, $475/50, Mobius International, 1981)

Myself, Yourself is about the development of identity through the perceptions of others as three adults and two teenagers reveal how society's attitudes have influenced their feelings about themselves.

Children's librarian Lucille Cuevas recalls a particularly humiliating childhood incident when a well-meaning, but insensitive teacher read aloud a story about a black prince who wanted to be white, a passage taken from *The Story of Dr. Doolittle*.

A young Chinese-Canadian wonders how the Chinese culture can ever fit into the Canadian culture since he sees no evidence around him that, as a Chinese, he exists.

Toronto lawyer Roberta Jamieson, an Indian who has chosen to live on the reservation with her family, explains how the stereotyping of Indians as "savages" and "redskins" was counteracted for her by a teacher who presented her with the facts about her Indian heritage.

Two secondary students of East Indian descent believe that schools not only ignore their culture, but also the cultures of fifty other minority groups that attend their high school.

Although not especially creative in format, viewers respond to the film's straightforward plea to everyone who teaches to remember Roberta Jamieson's words at the end of the film, "Teach them that they are valuable, that every unique thing they bring is of value, and to act in harmony with one another. Not better, not worse, but together."

NANOOK OF THE NORTH
(64 min, b & w, $825/100, Films, Inc., 1921)

Made in 1921, Robert Flaherty's classic study of an Eskimo family trying to survive in the savage and inhospitable Arctic is often referred to as the first documentary. After more than sixty years, it is still a great human document that appeals in spite of its crude filmmaking techniques and inferior black and white photography.

Flaherty pictures the difficult Eskimo life, with Nanook at its center as Man, involved in the basic activities of survival. Each day he and his family struggle as they hunt for food and build igloos for shelter. Each day death is a possibility. But as Flaherty's camera follows the family in its daily activities, the interaction is warm and loving. Nyla, Nanook's wife, chews his heavy sealskin boots in the morning to soften them. Nanook watches his son play with a puppy or teaches him to use a bow and arrow. Nyla blows on the baby to warm him.

Flaherty also displays a wonderful sense of humor. In the opening scene, one at a time Nanook and his family of five crawl out of a kayak that seems scarcely large enough for one. In another, Eskimos stare in amazement as their friends busily crank the first phonograph they have ever seen. Students especially enjoy the scene in which Nanook has caught a huge seal that he cannot see beneath the ice. Slipping and sliding in Laurel and Hardy fashion, he beckons frantically to his family for help as the seal pulls him around aimlessly.

There is drama too, as Nanook finds food just in time, builds a shelter when they are caught in a killing storm, or placates the half-starved dogs. *Nanook of the North* is a film which should be seen by everyone; it is man involved in his most basic struggles, but maintaining his humanity.

NO MAPS ON MY TAPS
(58 min, c, $800/100, Direct Cinema, Limited, 1981)

Quick! Name the greatest tap dancer of all time. No, Fred Astaire and Gene Kelly do not qualify. In fact, they may not be among the top five. Undoubtedly you are saying, "Greatest according to whom?"

Maybe according to *No Maps on My Taps*. Although the film makes no comparisons, it introduces us to the work of five great black tap dancers, but only one, Bill (Bojangles) Robinson is familiar to general audiences. Exciting, exhilarating, spine-tingling—all such adjectives apply to these marvelous, sensual dancers—possibly the last of a dying genre. For the record, the other four dancers are John Bubbles, Chuck Green, Bunny Briggs, and Sandman Sims. Although John Bubbles is now too old to dance, he is seen in some rare early footage that shows he richly deserves the praise the others give him. As Church Green says, "When John Bubbles danced, Bill Robinson left the room."

The film provides intimate portraits of Green, Briggs, and Sims as they reminisce, jive on the streets, and warm up for the challenge on stage at a performance hosted by orchestra leader Lionel Hampton. Raised on the street during the Depression, the men learned to dance by challenging each other to be the best. Together they tell the story of tap as an expression of black culture, one which is now endangered.

Everyone enjoys the film enormously, but black students find it a source of special pride and satisfaction. Many students were unaware that tap dancing originated with American blacks. Everyone is impressed by the dazzling skill and electric energy of the dancers, as well as by their total devotion to dance. As one student said admiringly of Chuck Green, "Did you hear him say that Fred Astaire came to him for help?" A film for everyone that values joy, skill, and dedication to excellence.

STAGES:
Houseman Directs Lear
(54 min, c, $785/95, Texture Films, 1982)

Most teachers have had the experience of working through one of Shakespeare's plays with a resistant, baffled, and perhaps bored class, only to emerge at the end of it with many of the students saying, "I liked it," "It was pretty interesting," or even "Great." The problem is always the same—how to make the necessary explication understandable and interesting without losing student interest.

Using his own Acting Company, director John Houseman, a figure familiar to most students because of his television appearances, explains the text of *King Lear* to his actors until, in the words of Sheila Benson, film critic of the *Los Angeles Times*, "the bones of its meaning glow nakedly for everyone to understand." In the process, we understand the director's responsibility for every aspect of the play: acting, costuming, deciding on makeup, and setting. The principal players, intelligent, articulate, and often humorous, explain their approaches to their roles and clarify what they hope to project to the audience.

Lear is a disturbing and complex play, one not often used in secondary schools. But for teachers of English literature who value the insight into Shakespeare provided by a director of Houseman's calibre, the film is an invaluable opportunity. For drama students, the film is a unique view of a master director at work and of actors who approach their craft seriously.

NO PLACE TO HIDE
(29 min, c, $485 (6-year life-of-print license)/45,
Direct Cinema, Limited, 1982)

In the 1940s and 1950s, in the aftermath of Hiroshima and Nagasaki, officials sought to allay public uneasiness and fear by recommending procedures to assure Americans that they could survive a nuclear war. Today, that advice seems inaccurate at best and perhaps deliberately deceitful. Some of it is even funny. "The bomb is deadly. It's like a woman," says an officer to recruits in a military training film. "Wearing white will be helpful," says another. Bomb shelters were built and stocked, young schoolchildren were advised to hide under their desks, and older ones were advised to line up against the gym wall.

As the weapons grew more powerful, public awareness also grew: there's no place to hide. Demands for a nuclear freeze are now worldwide as people realize that reasonable plans for survival must start with this realization.

Actor Martin Sheen narrates this powerful documentary that incorporates many of the vintage film clips, cartoons, newsreels, and television programs that attempted to sell Americans on the idea that survival was possible. He urges us to think realistically about alternatives. It is a part of PBS's "Matters of Life and Death." If anyone doubts that it is a matter of life and death, this frightening, provocative film will spur thought. Another splendid documentary on the same subject is available, *Atomic Cafe*, but it has no narration. Student understanding cannot be taken for granted. *No Place to Hide* must be seen by all classes.

PARDON ME FOR LIVING
(30 min, c, $550/50, Learning Corporation of America, 1982)

Based on Jean Stafford's popular short story, *The Scarlet Letter*, this delightful film stars the inimitable Margaret Hamilton (the witch of *The Wizard of Oz*) as Miss Holderness, a sixth-grade teacher. Unpopular Emily Vanderpool and troublemaker Virgil Meade, two loners in her class, are drawn together when Virgil writes "sealed with a kiss" on the valentine he sends Emily. Although the message of the valentine is not particularly sentimental, the smitten Emily believes it is the start of a friendship.

After sharing a sandwich and conversation with Virgil, Emily is receptive when Virgil makes several unusual suggestions: she is to organize a petition against geography homework (Virgil's particular dislike), sew her school letter on her sock instead of her sweater, and present the petition to Miss Holderness while wearing a Civil War sword.

(Annotation continues on page 213.)

No Place to Hide
Photograph courtesy of Direct Cinema, Limited

Reluctantly, Emily agrees, only to learn that Virgil has tricked her. When she presents the petition to Miss Holderness, Virgil is unaccountably absent. Moreover, he is one of the few students not to sign the petition, thereby becoming one of the teacher's heroes. Emily becomes the school pariah, while Virgil basks in admiration.

When Virgil accidentally reveals that he was the mastermind behind the incidents, the tables are turned. Now Emily is the heroine; Virgil the outcast. When lonely Virgil begs for her friendship, she delivers an impassioned lecture on the subject. In the climactic scene, Virgil reveals that he has learned a valuable lesson about being a true friend.

Pardon Me for Living is ideal for classes in language arts, short stories, guidance and values. It is recommended for younger students.

PORTRAIT OF GRANDPA DOC
(28 min, c, $450/45, Phoenix Films, 1977)

Portrait of Grandpa Doc is a stunning companion piece to the classic short film, *Peege*. Barbara Rush and Bruce Davison reprise their roles as mother and son in the earlier film. Peege was Davison's paternal grandmother; in this film the late Melvyn Douglas is his maternal grandfather. Director Randal Kleiser again sensitively explores the relationship of the young to the old and the special grief that death brings.

A promising young artist, Davison is preparing for an exhibition of his paintings in a California gallery. As he struggles to complete a portrait of his grandfather who had died several years earlier, he remembers his own happy childhood. Loving scenes of the family gathered at their beach house with a smiling Grandpa Doc surrounded by laughing children. He remembers an exciting trip to a nearby amusement arcade and his grandfather's encouragement of his art by commissioning a medical design. All images flow into his mind until at last he has captured his grandfather.

His mother, unaware of the painting, arrives from California for the exhibition. Davison escorts her to the gallery, but leaves her alone to view his work. Eagerly scanning the gallery's walls, his mother is moved to tears by the tenderness, love, and power with which her talented son has evoked her beloved father. Later, mother and son share their feelings openly for the first time.

Some students find *Portrait of Grandpa Doc* more moving than the emotional *Peege*. Tears and then praise are the usual reactions. It is highly recommended for classes in humanities, language arts, psychology, gerontology, family living, guidance, and values.

POSSUM LIVING

(29 min, c, $460/55, New Day Film Co-op, Inc., 1982)

Frank Freed was an aerospace engineer with what seemed like a bright, assured future. When cutbacks forced Frank's dismissal and government assistance was unacceptable, Frank and his twenty-year-old daughter Dolly decided to try to maintain their middle-class lifestyle on less than $2,000 a year.

Their resulting search for the good life with no money is told by Dolly in this delightful film about an alternative way of living. Their experiences also led to Dolly's engaging book, *Possum Living*.

Dolly is an outspoken, down-to-earth, confident young woman with strong feelings about enjoying one's life. Whether shopping for food, prowling in the thrift stores, or working in her garden, her philosophy of conserving contrasts sharply with the materialistic concerns of her mother, brother, and stepfather. Interesting and sometimes intense family feelings surface throughout the film. Rivalry between mother and daughter is apparent in remarks such as the mother's, "You'll never be the cook your mother is."

But Dolly is at her funniest and most captivating when she appears on the "Merv Griffin Show" to promote her book. The bland affability and affluence of the host are hilarious when contrasted with Dolly's decidedly unconventional views and her emphasis on simplicity and self-reliance.

For initiating a discussion about consumerism, alternate lifestyles, and conservation, *Possum Living* is a delight.

PSYCHLING

(25 min, c, $495/50, CRM/McGraw-Hill Films, 1981)

Most of us know that a sense of accomplishment brings us personal satisfaction and a feeling that life is worthwhile. The achievement can be as small as losing ten pounds or it can be success in our chosen career. Anything where we have established a goal and met it successfully. Why, then, do so many of us fail to find this satisfaction? In this inspiring film, a 31-year-old athlete, John Marino, shows us that the difference is a positive mental attitude.

His goal? To ride a bicycle across the United States in record time, a feat which he accomplished in twelve days, three hours, and forty-one minutes. *Psychling* is a chronicle of his attempt to better his own world record set in 1978. Doctors at UCLA Medical Center have compared his ride to running 43 consecutive marathons, swimming the English Channel 18 times, or doing 1,000,000 consecutive pushups.

The film follows Marino and his crew through California's broiling Mojave desert, the plains of the Midwest, and the grueling challenge of the mountains of Pennsylvania. We see the changes that his body undergoes and his pain and near despair as the crisis approaches, 750 miles from his goal.

Throughout the film he discusses the philosophy that has made his incredible journey possible: having realistic expectations, being aware of the benefits, building toward the goal in small blocks, not viewing failure as negative, and understanding that sacrifices are necessary. Marino's advice is practical, yet inspirational and believable because we see him implementing it.

A superb film for classes in physical education, psychology, special education, language arts, and guidance.

PUBLIC ENEMY NUMBER ONE
(55 min, c, $750/75, Filmakers Library, 1981)

It is difficult not to admire Australian Wilfred Burchett, maverick war reporter and the first Western journalist to view the destruction at Hiroshima. One respects his resistance to extraordinary pressures, his stubborn determination to find the truth regardless of the consequences, and his persistence in the face of personal hardship. This admiration gives the film its final impact when Burchett must face the very real possibility that, after all, he has been wrong. This unexpected twist may also force the viewer to reexamine old, and perhaps rigid, attitudes of what constitutes right and wrong.

World War II was the last war in which Burchett was on the Australian side, as he firmly opposed the intervention of the West in Korea and Vietnam. Due to his friendship with Ho Chi Minh, he was able to live among the Viet Cong while he covered the Vietnam war, so the film contains footage rarely seen in the West. His reports outraged his compatriots and brought cries of "communist" and "traitor." Although Burchett maintained he was only working toward journalistic integrity, his government considered him a danger and denied him a passport for seventeen years.

A startling scene in the film occurs when filmmaker David Bradbury and Burchett are ambushed by Cambodian guerillas. Although both men escape death, Burchett cannot escape the recognition that the Pol Pot regime, which he has championed, has brought Cambodia to the brink of annihilation. Was he, after all, wrong?

The film raises many important questions for a democracy. Can we tolerate opinions considered subversive? Can we allow freedom of the press? Is a man a traitor who cannot support the war policies of his government?

Public Enemy Number One is for mature students of humanities, journalism, and social studies. The film was a Blue Ribbon winner at the American Film Festival.

QUILTS IN WOMEN'S LIVES
(28 min, c, $450/50, New Day Film Co-op, 1981)

Learning the joy of creative activity in daily life is an important lesson, one that interests many young people. Increasingly, they are turning to the past for inspiration and guidance. This desire must explain the enthusiastic response of many teenagers to a film about the unfamiliar topic of quilts.

Students respond not only to the intricacy and beauty of the quilts, but also to the sincerity of the seven quiltmakers who are interviewed in this intriguing film. Among them are a black woman from Mississippi, a California Mennonite, and a Bulgarian immigrant. Each woman tells her story simply, sometimes humorously, and each woman possesses a strong sense of self-worth. One says, "It's just like praying." Whether showing the creations of their grandmothers or their own intricate works made for their grandchildren, the women explain what making them has meant in their lives.

Quilts in Women's Lives is a lovely film for classes in history, art, women's studies, and language arts. It is a Blue Ribbon winner.

REMEMBER ME
(15 min, c, $310/35, Pyramid Films, 1980)

Dick Cavett narrates this Academy Award-nominated film about children in various parts of the world who live under conditions of poverty and/or violence. In a series of vignettes, the beauty of the children is contrasted with the squalor of their surroundings and the wasted potential of their lives.

An American boy, a victim of child abuse, is shown enroute to the hospital. In the Middle East, a young garbage sorter predicts her own future; a wife at twelve and mother at thirteen. Children in Asia are shown doing backbreaking and degrading tasks: carrying heavy loads, gathering cow dung by hand and shaping it into balls for fuel, and walking long distances to find clean water.

A twelve-year-old boy who wants to become a teacher becomes a beast of burden, dragging a heavy boat along a river. Another, the best in his class, must quit school to work twelve hours a day in a rug factory. Hospital scenes show the damaging effects of malnutrition. The film ends with children in a refugee camp, the victims of political chaos.

As these beautiful children tell their own stories in their own languages, without emotion or self-pity, the effect is unforgettable.

This is a much-needed film to increase the understanding of many relatively priviliged students who sometimes thoughtlessly blame disadvantaged children for the poverty and apparent hopelessness of their lives. It triggers many interesting assignments. Language arts, sociology, contemporary problems, family living, ecology, and parenting classes profit from seeing it.

SENTINELS OF SILENCE
(19 min, c, $285/16, Britannica Films, 1974)

The eloquent voice of Orson Welles blends perfectly with the images of huge, crumbling stone palaces and deserted temples in this film, shot entirely from a helicopter as it hovered over seven archeological sites of ancient Mexico. Like stucco ghosts, the ruins of the Mayans bake in the sun or are shrouded by fog. The images seem as lost in the mist, as the ancient peoples who once inhabited these buildings are lost to us. Who were they? What happened to them? Why did they leave these magnificent structures with their elaborate carvings, pyramid mounds, and steps leading, — where?

This stunning, Academy Award-winning film captures the air of mystery and magic that surrounds the ruins of Tulim, Chichen Itza, and Uxmal. Images, soundtrack, and narrator are melded into an unparalleled spiritual and aesthetic evocation of an ancient civilization.

It is an excellent film for classes in humanities and world history. It also, more importantly, instills pride in Hispanic students because many learn about the artistic accomplishments of the Mayans for the first time in this film. There is a Spanish version, *Centinelas del Silencio*, narrated by Ricardo Montalban and distributed by the same company.

THE SKY IS GRAY

(46½ min, c, $835, rental, inquire Perspective Films, 1981)

Black writer Ernest J. Gaines's short story about growing up in rural Louisiana has been affectionately transferred to the screen. It is the story of a boy's love for his stern, proud mother and of the experiences that determine his personal and social awareness. In themselves, the incidents are not of major importance, but they emphasize the independence and pride that the author believes are necessary for survival and growth.

The plot centers around the boy's much-feared trip to the dentist. While there, he hears the moans of unanesthetized patients, sees a minister strike a young man who says there is no God, and anxiously waits his turn for hours, only to be told that the dentist has left for lunch. In this casual treatment of pain, fear, and even of someone's time, much is revealed about the experiences of blacks.

As mother and son go to lunch to await the dentist's return, she refuses free food, refuses to accept a larger portion of salt pork than their money will buy, defends herself against a man's unwanted advances, and says, as she turns down the boy's coat collar, "You're not a bum. You're a man."

The film is aesthetically and emotionally rich, with all of the ambiance of the original story. Students who have read it can compare it to the film. For those students who have not, or cannot, read it, seeing *The Sky Is Gray* helps them understand how someone growing up in poverty and rejection by the larger society can acquire dignity and self-worth.

SOLDIER GIRLS

(87 min, c, $1250/150, Churchill Films, 1982)

This engrossing documentary follows three women recruits, Privates Johnson, Alves, and Hall, as they undergo basic training in the Army. Each reacts differently to their shared experiences: physically demanding marches, demeaning routine inspections and drills, the lack of privacy, and verbal abuse by male sergeants.

(Annotation continues on page 219.)

Soldier Girls
Photograph courtesy of Churchill Films

Private Johnson is severely and consistently disciplined for smiling, a habit she never really loses. Private Alves dislikes the Army and responds with ineptness, malingering, and a final furious outburst that results in her dismissal. Determined to do well, Private Hall quickly adopts the tough style and speech of the men in charge of her squadron.

Interesting questions are raised by the film: What is the motivation for a woman to subject herself to such treatment? What about the dehumanization of the noncommissioned officers? Are the attitudes displayed in the film necessary for the Army to function effectively? Is the supposed "softer" attitude of women merely a matter of cultural conditioning?

The film, which is the first serious look at women in the Army, amply documents the depersonalization necessary to turn a recruit into a good soldier. Near the end of the film, a male officer, Sergeant Abing, who had taunted and humiliated the women unmercifully, talks about the personal cost of his own military experiences. As a man who is full of rage, he says, "A large part of your humanity, a large part of your soul or whatever the hell you call it – it's never going to be there again. It's gone. And you don't know until it's over. And then, long afterward, as you grow older, you start to wonder."

A disturbing and provocative film, *Soldier Girls* is superb for career education, women's studies, psychology, sociology, social studies, and for any woman who might contemplate the military as a career.

THE SORROWS OF GIN
(60 min, c, $770/95, Films, Inc., 1979)

A splendid cast is featured in this engrossing dramatization of one of John Cheever's best-known short stories, *The Sorrows of Gin*, about the emotional isolation and loneliness in an affluent Connecticut suburb.

Edward Herrmann and Sigourney Weaver portray the parents of Amy Lawton (played by Mara Hobel of "Annie" fame), an eight-year-old girl who is searching for a sense of family. Caught up in their detached, sophisticated world, the parents are vaguely aware of their own alienation, but cannot articulate it. Their maid Rosemary (Eileen Heckart) speaks candidly of the loneliness of being in service. Later, the babysitter (Rachel Roberts), reacting to an unfair accusation of dishonesty, reveals her bitterness, frustration, and loneliness. Drinking gin is a release; it is the focus of unexpressed anguish.

The child's efforts to find a solution, which are both tragic and comic, lead finally to her attempt to run away. Alerted by the stationmaster, the father hurries to intercept her. As the film ends father and daughter are seated on a bench in the station pondering their mutual despair.

Although the theme of the failed American dream is not new, the film seems to have a special relevance for students in the current social and economic crisis. It may sound depressing, but student reaction is very positive. Students were interested in it, disturbed by it, wanted to talk about it. One can only surmise that *The Sorrows of Gin* strikes very close to home for many.

STEPPING OUT:
The DeBolts Grow Up
(52 min, c, $750/75, Pyramid Films, 1981)

Of all the films available to teachers, the most useful may be Pyramid's 1977 Academy Award-winning documentary, *Who Are the DeBolts and Where Did They Get 19 Kids?* The John Korty film is a record of how Dorothy and Bob DeBolt and their nineteen children became a well-integrated family of fulfilled individuals even though eight of the children are severely physically handicapped. The film is so moving that some viewers find it impossible to discuss it immediately after seeing it.

While its sequel, *Stepping Out*, may lack some of the emotional impact of the first film, it is still well-worth seeing. The year 1980 proved to be one of great change and challenge for the DeBolt children. The activities necessary for independence such as cooking, cleaning, and walking to school, and even walking "faster," assume a critical importance for the teenagers still at home, as they work toward providing for themselves. J.R., paralyzed and blind, struggles to move from a school for the blind into regular school. Twe, the blind Vietnamese girl, tells the horrifying story of the death of her mother and the disappearance of her father and brother from her life. (She finally hears from them.) All of the children work courageously toward their own identity and independence. John Korty's affection and admiration for the family shines through this film as it does in its predecessor. It is a beautiful film for language arts, special education, guidance, and family living classes.

THE STRINGBEAN
(17 min, c, $330/45, Films, Inc., 1964)

In this lovely bit of visual poetry, an old woman lives in a bare, stark apartment with little around her except her sewing machine on which she makes small purses. The rooms are dark and the water tap is in the hallway, shared by the other tenants. Determined to have something living, the old woman plants a stringbean seed in a flower pot which she places carefully on the window sill. She tends it affectionately until she transplants it into the majestic public park nearby. Surrounded by brilliant flowers, the stringbean is unseen by passersby, but the old woman visits it daily to steal quick, surreptitious glances at it.

One day she watches in anguish as the gardener notices her plant, hesitates a moment, and throws it in his trash cart. Quickly she retrieves one of the pods, removes a seed, and goes home to start the process again.

The filmmaker uses black and white film contrasted with color film to delineate the line between the woman's private world of loneliness and longing, and the world of light, flowers, people, and dogs that she encounters in the park. This Academy Award winner is a deceptively simple film that usually appeals only to students who have the maturity and empathy to understand the difference between being fully human and merely existing. Although it is nonverbal, the filmmaker's message is clear: to be fully human is to be life-affirming.

THE SUN DAGGER

(Full version: 58 min, c, $850/85, Bullfrog Films, 1982;
edited version: 29 min, c, $400/50, Bullfrog Films, 1982)

Chaco Canyon lies in a remote region of New Mexico once inhabited by the Anasazi Indians, who, after several centuries of compulsive building of superb temples, multifamily dwellings, and roads, inexplicably abandoned them about 1,200 years ago. Although anthropologists and other academicians have long been interested in these magnificent ruins, it was not until June 29, 1977, that a visiting Washington artist, Anna Sofaer, discovered the significant but controversial ancient Pueblo celestial calendar, now known as the Sun Dagger. This astronomical find, which ranks with Stonehenge and the Pyramids in importance, is the subject of this fascinating documentary, narrated by Robert Redford.

At first, experts believed Ms. Sofaer's discovery accidental because they doubted the Anasazis's ability to construct anything of such complexity. After repeated trips to Chaco Canyon, Sofaer and her scientific colleagues revealed that the calendar not only marked the summer solstice, but also the winter solstice, the spring and fall equinoxes, and the nineteen-year-cycle of the moon. Eventually, scientists affiliated with England's Oxford University Symposium on Archeoastronomy verified the Chaco Canyon calendar as the only known site in the world to mark both cycles of the sun and the moon.

Technically, it is a beautiful film, particularly the time-lapse photography which shows the sun dagger marking the summer solstice on barren, inhospitable Fajada Butte. The film has unique educational value. It uses modern technological equipment and scientific explanations to describe the dagger's complexity. Classes are introduced to the concepts of astronomy, physics, anthropology, geology, and archeology as they are integrated with Indian religion and mythology. Although these subjects are not usually taught in secondary schools, students should be aware of this part of their cultural heritage. *The Sun Dagger* is essential for school districts and public libraries.

SURVIVAL RUN

(12 min, c, $325/45, Pyramid Films, 1981)

This film is a brilliant cinematic achievement featuring a sighted runner, Mike Restani, and his blind partner, Harry Cordellos, in California's grueling marathon Dipsea Race over 7.1 miles of tortuous Marin County terrain. Trees, roots, stones, steps, steep inclines and declines are overcome as the blind runner responds smoothly and skillfully to his companion's grunted instructions. Incredibly, he stumbles only once.

The relationship between the two men soon arrests attention. The complete trust shown by the blind runner is awesome. The sighted runner is equally amazing in his willingness to assume the handicap. Inspiring in their affection, effort, and teamwork, they make the simply structured film engrossing.

Although it may be of particular interest to physical education or special education classes, *Survival Run* is superb for any class using values clarification because many concepts are demonstrated: trust, affection, adaptability, courage, generosity, and success.

The film deserves the many awards that it has received, including the Grand Prize of the International Rehabilitation Festival.

TRAVELLING HOPEFULLY
(28 min, c, $480/50, Films, Inc., 1982)

Roger Baldwin, one of the principal founders of the American Civil Liberties Union (ACLU), lived to a remarkable 97 years of age. Throughout his productive career that was frequently involved in tumult and change, he "travelled hopefully" toward a world he envisioned of freedom, equality, and justice. Before his recent death, he said that he had seen significant progress toward realization of his dream. In this fine documentary, Academy Award-winning director John Avildsen follows Baldwin's career through nearly sixty years of leadership in the protection of civil liberties.

As a young man, Baldwin seemed an unlikely candidate for the post. Gentle, soft-spoken, born into a family of privilege, he seemed destined to be a business executive. But when he founded the ACLU with a small group of friends, it quickly became his life's focus.

From eighteen hours of recorded material, director Avildsen extracted the essence of Baldwin's life and work, from his happy marriage to a woman who was a lawyer, Socialist, and feminist to the ACLU's defense of important social issues: the Scopes Trial, the organizing rights of labor, and the civil rights of unpopular organizations such as the American Nazi Party and the Ku Klux Klan. In each case he lived to see the position of the ACLU upheld by the Supreme Court. The film also features conversations with Edward Kennedy, historian Arthur Schlesinger, Jr., producer Norman Lear, and author Gail Sheehy.

In an era when positive role models are urgently needed, Roger Baldwin's life of service and devotion to civil liberties is exemplary. Although he professed no religious beliefs himself, he repeatedly said that Jesus's message of love toward one's fellow man was humanity's most important declaration. To that goal he dedicated his life.

In an era when polls show that 65 percent of the citizens of this country would no longer support the Bill of Rights, Roger Baldwin's message is urgent. Classes in history, government, humanities, sociology, and language arts find it superb.

VIETNAM REQUIEM
(52 min, c, $800/75, Direct Cinema, Limited, 1982)

Albert "PeeWee" Dobbs, Duane Maybee, James McAllister, Raymond Baker, and Kenneth Patterson are veterans of the Vietnam war. All were decorated for heroism; all fought honorably for a cause they believed in; none had ever been in trouble with the law before going to Vietnam. Now all are in prison for terms of two years to life, with no possibility of parole, for crimes ranging from second-degree assault to aggravated rape. As the film demonstrates, such stories are not unique among returning Vietnam veterans.

Hundreds of thousands of veterans who saw heavy combat have been arrested since the war's end at a rate twice that of nonveterans of the same age. Although accurate figures on the number imprisoned are not available, a Veterans Administration study concluded that the greater the vet's exposure to heavy combat, the greater was the likelihood of his being arrested.

In this disturbing documentary, the personal stories of the five men are intercut with scenes of actual combat. Albert Dobbs is shown in combat on the same day that he killed an innocent Vietnamese family, the atrocity that made him suicidal. The others tell their stories of rejection and alienation, which have their roots in the Vietnam conflict.

Vietnam Requiem makes clear the differences between the veterans of Vietnam and those of World War II: the average age of the Vietnam veterans was seven years younger, the Vietnam troops spent much more time in continuous combat, and they were met with a hostile or indifferent reception when they returned home, usually alone, on a commercial jet forty-eight hours after being in jungle combat. An unsparing film, it points out chillingly the human costs of war that are seldom recognized or discussed. A superb film for classes in psychology, sociology, humanities, and history.

THE VOYAGE OF ODYSSEUS
(27 min, c, $495/50, Churchill Films, 1982)

The visual beauty and imaginative richness of Pieter Van Duessen's screen interpretation of Homer's *Odyssey* is extraordinary.

Van Duessen began his film by asking himself this question: If Homer had an audience of film-viewers to play to and a half-an-hour to tell his story, how would he have described the homeward journey of his favorite hero?

Van Duessen chose as the setting of the film a potter's workshop in which a muse (played by Julie Harris) unfolds the epic tale. As she narrates, the visual story comes to life through the artifacts surrounding her.

Since the ancient Greeks often told stories by painting figures on pottery, the filmmaker devised ways to make figures appear and disappear on vases. Zeus, Athena, and Odysseus appear as classical sculptures that are outside the confines of the vases. Throughout the film, vases, sculptures, and models seem suspended in a misty world of fire and water. Ordinary vases are transformed by light and shadow into the land of Homer's narrative. The melding of man-made artifacts with nature gives the film its mythic quality.

The Voyage of Odysseus is a rare combination of a literary masterpiece and extraordinary filmmaking. It will stimulate student interest in reading the classics. Filmmaking classes will find it rich in original techniques and special effects. Many teachers interested in returning to a more academic approach will find *The Voyage of Odysseus* to be a superb aid to them.

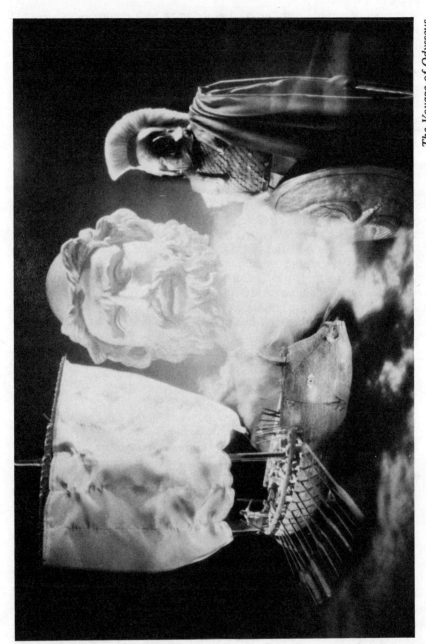

The Voyage of Odysseus
Photograph courtesy of Churchill Films

THE WEAVERS:
Wasn't That a Time!
(78 min, c, $195, rental, Films, Inc., 1982)

The Weavers celebrates the 1980 Carnegie Hall reunion of the four legendary performers. Renowned for their invention of folk music in the 1950s and 1960s, the Weavers saw their careers temporarily destroyed by the political paranoia of the McCarthy era. Interviews with Studs Terkel, Harry Reasoner, singer-composers Mary Travers and Arlo Guthrie, as well as the Weavers' manager Harold Leventhal, confirm the group's overwhelming influence on American folk music.

The film begins with a backyard picnic at the home of Weaver Lee Hays. Though ill and having suffered the loss of his legs from the complications of diabetes, Hays's account of organizing the picnic and the event itself is marvelously funny. At the picnic Pete Seeger approaches the group with the idea of a reunion with him at Carnegie Hall. Hays is reluctant but game. Ronnie Gilbert, the only female in the group, is fearful and eager. Fred Kellerman reflects Seeger's attitude of unassuming self-confidence. The Carnegie Hall reunion is a triumph. The Weavers' voices are still filled with youthful enthusiasm and elan. The audience rises to its feet in a prolonged, deafening ovation.

With its portraits of four remarkable human beings, especially the witty, courageous Lee Hays, its historical reminder of the McCarthy era, and most of all the Weavers's stirring hits, "Goodnight, Irene," "Kisses Sweeter Than Wine," and "If I Had a Hammer," the film should be seen by young Americans.

THE WORKPLACE HUSTLE
(30 min, c, $520/100 wk. (applied to purchase),
available only from the distributor, MTI Teleprograms Inc., 1980)

The drive for equality must not be slowed down by the failure of the Equal Rights Amendment. Education regarding the historical oppression of women sexually, politically, and economically is more urgent than ever. *Workplace Hustle* has demonstrated its effectiveness to change attitudes and increase understanding, particularly about sexual harassment in the marketplace.

Narrated by Lou Grant, the film features Lyn Farley, author of *Sexual Shakedown*, who traces the battle women have fought against sexual harassment at work. Such harassment is demeaning and illegal; it is also systemic in the business world, difficult to define, and even harder to prove. As the men and women in the film talk candidly of their feelings about sexual equality, we begin to understand the social and emotional forces that have shaped their thinking. Suggestions are made for legal recourse for women who are victims.

Widely used by business and the military, the film is also very effective for use with older secondary students, many of whom, if they know of the subject at all, treat it as a joke.

Psychology, sociology, women's studies, language arts, personal living, and career and business education classes should give *Workplace Hustle* a high priority. Secondary school is terminal for many students, and this film offers valuable information to take with them into the marketplace.

5 ANNOTATED FILMOGRAPHY

Some very fine films, because of their subject matter or intellectual depth, do not have as broad application as those in the study guides or film reviews. Although their use may be more limited, teachers should be aware such films are available.

There are also a number of films of Academy Award caliber about which teacher opinion is sharply divided. Some teachers use them with great success while others react very negatively.

Occasionally a fine film appeals only to a particular group of students, a gifted class or a remedial one. Some films can only be used for very specific purposes: for example, for a filmmaking class or a sex education class.

The annotated filmography includes the kind of films just described. It is my hope that teachers will study them and order those for preview which best meet the needs of a particular class.

AM I NORMAL?
(24 min, c, $425/45, New Day Film Co-op, 1979)

Am I Normal? is a light-hearted comedy about the experiences boys go through during puberty. Using three fictional characters, it presents facts about male sexual development, while raising important issues about masculinity, identity, and peer pressure. It is an important contribution to helping young men to develop healthy attitudes about themselves and their sexuality. A companion piece to *Dear Diary* that covers the same ground for young women, it is ideal for junior high school students. It was a Blue Ribbon winner at the American Film Festival.

AMERICAN PARADE:
Song of Myself
(30½ min, c, $530/74, BFA Films, 1976)

Actor Rip Torn is engrossing as Walt Whitman in this CBS News production of his life. Whitman reminisces about his life from the time he began *Leaves of Grass* until he returned, a paralytic, to the family home. The question of Whitman's homosexuality is mentioned but not sensationalized. His poetry, beautifully read by Torn, is the focus of the film.

Students interested in poetry are fascinated by the power of Whitman's language and by the gifted and tormented poet as portrayed by Torn. An ideal film for students studying poetry, *Song of Myself* is also a good starting point for mature students who are not particularly interested in poetry because in the skilled hands of Rip Torn, Whitman comes through as an intrinsically interesting human being.

ANGEL AND BIG JOE
(27 min, c, $450/40, Learning Corporation of America, 1975)

"What's your name, kid?" asks Joe. "Angel," answers the engaging fifteen-year-old Hispanic, as he draws an imaginary halo around his head. Joe, a mature telephone lineman, soon learns that Angel is a young person of great resourcefulness along with his beguiling personality. Ultimately Angel is forced to choose between responsibility to his migrant family and the security and friendship that Big Joe offers. Dadi Pinero and Paul Sorvino are engaging as Angel and Big Joe in this moving Academy Award-winning film.

ANIMATION PIE
(26 min, c, $375/37.50, Film Wright, 1976)

For a teacher who would like to excite students about filmmaking, this film is a marvelous resource. Filmmaker Bob Bloomberg's high school class illustrates a variety of animation techniques: flipbooks, drawing on film, pixilation, cut-outs, and working with clay. During the process, the students comment on what they are doing and the value of being responsible for all phases of their productions.

APPLE DOLLS
(19 min, c, $330/33, Wombat Productions, Inc., 1980)

Canadian artist Urve Buffey demonstrates the art of making dolls from apples, following the process from the apple to the finished product. The result is a delightful doll with clothes, hair, and painted features. As enjoyable as the subject matter is, Ms. Buffey's obvious delight in her life and work is even more winning. A superb film for demonstrating the importance of art in an individual's life, and for anyone who would like to teach the art of making dolls from apples.

BARN BURNING
(41 min, c, $747, rental, inquire Perspective Films, 1980)

Abner Snopes, a poor, proud tenant farmer in the late nineteenth century South, burns his employer's barn in revenge for an imagined slight. His son, Sarty, is torn between love for his father and aversion to his father's unrelenting, violent nature. When Snopes is once again offended by a new employer, the boy betrays his father by giving warning of his father's destructive intentions.

William Faulkner's complex Southern world of class divisiveness, alienation, and hostile family relationships is the backdrop to Sarty's attempts to become a man by liberating himself from the milieu of hatred and poverty represented by his father. It is for advanced literature classes.

BEGINNINGS
(9 min, c, $185/20, National Film Board of Canada, 1980)

A beautifully animated, poetic film in which all the forms of nature — clouds, sky, earth, and water — constantly metamorphose, suggesting human shapes that float effortlessly. At the end, snow falls gently down to melt into the earth. Completed after the death of the filmmaker, it is a lovely commentary on birth, life, and death that is wonderful for any class in which imaginative writing is encouraged.

BEING PART OF IT ALL
(24 min, c, $450/50, Filmakers Library, 1981)

It is easy to see that Gary and Barbara Young, two mentally handicapped young adults with strong affection for each other enjoy their married life.

Their transition from the institution when they met to independent living was accomplished with the support of personnel from the mental health agency in the couples' home town. The film demonstrates the viability of such marriages if other circumstances are appropriate: family affection and help, aid from social workers, and government subsidies. It is far less expensive than institutional care and much more emotionally satisfying. It is a superior film for classes in special education, psychology, sociology, family living, and guidance.

BERNICE BOBS HER HAIR
(47½ min, c, $832, rental, inquire Perspective Films, 1977)

Shelly Duvall is perfect as Scott Fitzgerald's heroine, Bernice, who is transformed from an ugly duckling into a sought-after vamp by her manipulative cousin, Marjorie. When Bernice begins to snare Marjorie's dates, Marjorie traps her into bobbing her hair. Shorn, Bernice loses all of her new-found seductiveness, but in a delightful, ironic twist she gets her revenge. No deep insights are to be found in the film, but it is marvelous for giving students a feel for the style and morés of the Fitzgerald era. It is highly recommended for classes in the short story.

BETWEEN A ROCK AND A HARD PLACE
(59 min, c, $100, rental, First Run Features, 1982)

The film takes us into the coal mines of Appalachia and into the lives of three men who work them. Rather than focusing on labor interests and labor-management struggles, it provides a unique vision of the workplace and the divided emotions of the men who shaped it. Tracing the varied responses of each man to his labor, the film documents the changing meaning of work in this country. It is an important resource for American history, economics, sociology, and industrial education.

BIG BOYS CAN CRY:
The Changing American Man
(28 min, c, $495/75 (applied to purchase), MTI Teleprograms Inc., 1982)

This informative documentary examines the impact of the changing roles of men on careers, sexuality, personal relationships, and parenting. Case histories of a two-career couple, a single adult male, a divorced father, and a house-husband illustrate how men and women are adjusting to the changes. A valuable film for sociology, psychology, language arts, and parenting classes.

BIG HENRY AND THE POLKA DOT KID
(33 min, c, $450/40, Learning Corporation of America, 1977)

This Emmy Award-winning film is based on *Luke Baldwin's Vow* by Morley Callaghan and promises to become a classic short film. A young orphan wins his battle to save the life of an old blind dog by convincing his stubborn uncle (Ned Beatty) that there arc values other than practical ones. Estelle Parsons brings warmth to her portrayal of an understanding neighbor. It is recommended for junior high students for classes in language arts, values, and guidance.

THE BOY WHO LIKED DEER
(18 min, c, $350/35, Learning Corporation of America, 1975)

Vandalism is one of the public school system's most urgent problems. In this film, a boy learns in personal terms the pain that vandalism can inflict. In retaliation for a much-deserved punishment, Jason and his friends vandalize their teacher's room, making sure that they destroy the teacher's much-prized first edition of e.e. cummings. When Jason inadvertently sees the teacher's tears, he runs blindly from the emotional realization of the pain he has caused. He soon discovers that through another act of vandalism, he has destroyed the deer that he loved as the teacher had loved his book. It is recommended very highly for all students in grades seven through nine.

CHALLENGE OVER THE ATLANTIC
(14 min, c, $350/35, Pyramid Films, 1982)

Fifty years after Colonel Charles A. Lindbergh made his historic flight across the Atlantic, three Albuquerque businessmen made the same journey in a balloon they called the "Double Eagle Two." Two prosperous, middle-aged men, Ben Abruzzo and Maxie Anderson, together with young Larry Newman, undertook the daring voyage with skill, teamwork, and determination. As one of them says, "When we stop crossing frontiers or achieving new goals, we stagnate and move backward instead of forward. Moving forward was, for me, the long hidden motive of our journey." The film stimulates discussion and encourages motivation.

CLAUDE
(3 min, c, $110/35, Pyramid Films, 1965)

Claude is a small animated boy who lives in an opulent house owned by his materialistic, cliché-ridden parents. Constantly told, "You'll never amount to anything," Claude and the little black box he carries around with him have the last word. The sardonic surprise ending is a commentary on the results that occur when parents stifle creativity. For language arts and psychology.

CLAYMATION
(18 min, c, $310/45, Pyramid Films, 1978)

Academy Award-winning animator Will Vinton and his staff take the viewer inside their studio for a whimsical demonstration of their clay animation techniques. Using scenes from *Closed Mondays, Mountain Music,* and *Martin the Cobbler*, they illustrate the complexities of their work. They mix colors, mold movable characters, compose and record music, and produce the live-action film that serves as the animation guide. Marvelous for filmmaking classes.

DANCE ON A MAY DAY
(11 min, c, $200/25, Learning Corporation of America, 1978)

Ballet star, Jacques D'Amboise founded the National Dance Institute in 1976 to give boys an opportunity to dance. In May, 1977, the boys gave an exciting performance for their parents and friends at New York City's Lincoln Center. Interspersed with their performance are interviews with the boys, who candidly discuss both dance and their instructor. The energy of the boys as they dance is infectious. As D'Amboise says, "Wouldn't it be wonderful if America would be a nation of people who danced?" It is a marvelous film for breaking down the stereotype of male dancers as feminine or of dancing as only for sissies.

DEAR DIARY
(25 min, c, $425/45, New Day Film Co-op, Inc., 1981)

Dear Diary is an amusing, educational film about female puberty presented in a situation comedy format. Like its companion film for boys, *Am I Normal?*, it both raises and answers the questions young adolescents have as they enter puberty. Information about body changes and maturation is presented with humor and reassurance. The important issues of self-image, peer pressure, and the pressure to date are presented effectively. A good film for the junior high or younger group.

DEATH BE NOT PROUD
(99 min, c, $1,150 (lease)/90, Learning Corporation of America, 1974)

Teenage idol Robby Benson stars in this moving story of the death of Johnny Gunther, son of John Gunther. Victim of a brain tumor, Johnny was determined to cram a lifetime of living into the time he had left. This account of the last few years of his life shows him going to school, setting future goals for himself (even though he was aware that he would not live to accomplish them), maintaining his friendships, and trying for normality. It is an inspiring

Claymation
Photograph courtesy of Pyramid Films

film for students because Johnny Gunther is a marvelous example of a teenager facing difficult circumstances with grace and courage. For language arts, psychology, and guidance.

DOES ANYBODY NEED ME ANY MORE?
(29 min, c, $400/35, Learning Corporation of America, 1975)

This film is a good introduction to the women's movement for students who have received no other exposure to it. Maureen Stapleton plays Connie, a middle-aged woman whose life has been filled with caring for her children and her husband. Now the children are gone, time drags, and she feels useless and unattractive. Paul Sorvino plays her hardworking husband who cannot understand her dissatisfaction with life. But Connie finds a solution on her own, a job that enables her to use the skills she has acquired as a homemaker. The film is adapted from the feature film *Tell Me Where It Hurts*, which was made for television. For language arts, psychology, women's studies, family living, guidance, and values.

DR. HEIDEGGER'S EXPERIMENT
(22 min, c, $330, rental, inquire Britannica Films, 1974)

Nathaniel Hawthorne's short story is about a group of oldsters given the opportunity to be young again. In an appealing science-fiction format, it explores two of the author's major themes: the consequences of tampering with nature and of rejecting conventional morality. Since the film is more cinematic than many filmed short stories, it is useful for filmmaking classes as well as for language arts, psychology, and guidance classes.

DREAMSPEAKER
(75 min, c, $995/100, Filmakers Library, 1979)

A learning-disabled, violent boy is institutionalized for arson. Confined, Peter reacts to the benign attitude of the institution's staff with mute hostility.

Escaping the institution, he runs away to the Vancouver forests where he encounters an Indian Shaman. The Shaman's tolerance and humor disarm Peter completely, and for the first time he plays with enthusiasm, his laughter reverberating through the forest. The Shaman convinces him he can control his violent behavior. Tragedy results when the authorities locate Peter and return him to the institution. *Dreamspeaker* is a serious film that should only be used by students interested in psychology or by adults interested in the treatment of mentally disturbed juveniles.

EMILY DICKINSON:
A Certain Slant of Light
(29 min, c, $445/50, Pyramid Films, 1977)

Emily Dickinson was an eccentric figure to her contemporaries in Amherst, Massachusetts. Not until long after her death did the world realize that a major poet had lived in this quiet New England town. Actress Julie Harris brings to life the artist behind the legend by reciting Dickinson's incomparable poetry and reading her letters as she strolls through the poet's house and garden. The beauty of the landscape is captured in the poetry. Ms. Harris's narration shows how poetry enlarged Emily Dickinson's world. Red Ribbon, American Film Festival.

THE END OF ONE
(7 min, c, $165/20, Learning Corporation of America, 1970)

In this simple but compelling film, the camera watches seagulls soaring, swooping, and scavenging for food above a huge garbage dump. At a distance a dying bird limps along a polluted stretch of beach, while in the distance the other birds raucously compete for food. The film ends on a close-up of the dying bird's eye as it shuts for the last time. A powerful ecological message for classes in language arts, ecology, and values.

EVERY CHILD
(6 min, c, $185/35, Pyramid Films, 1980)

Made by the National Film Board of Canada for UNICEF, this animated film creatively combines humor and pathos to illustrate every child's right to an identity and a place in society. It is the story of a nameless infant who is shunted from doorstep to doorstep. But no one really wants a child without a name or background. For classes in psychology, filmmaking, family living, child development, and sociology. Won an Academy Award for 1980.

THE FABLE OF HE AND SHE
(11 min, c, $225/25, Learning Corporation of America, 1976)

Sex stereotyping is the theme of this delightful film based on a story by Marie Winn. Creative clay animation by Elliott Noyes, Jr., depicts the tale of the "hardibars" and the "mushamels" who discover that the traditional male and female roles can be reversed without loss of identity or self-esteem. *Fable* is ideal for women's studies, language arts, psychology, and sociology. Blue Ribbon, American Film Festival.

FALL LINE
(12½ min, c, $325/45, Pyramid Films, 1981)

This exciting film looks at the high-risk sport of extreme skiing. On a peak in the upper regions of Wyoming's Grand Tetons, once considered too hazardous to climb, a skier braves first the climb and then the fall line—the steepest line of descent between two points on a slope, the course a falling rock would follow if unobstructed. His breathtaking descent from the rocky tip of the mountain down a nearly vertical slope is a stunning affirmation of the will to succeed despite danger. Academy Award nominee.

THE FLASHETTES
(20 min, c, $400/40, New Day Film Co-op, Inc., 1981)

An improved sense of self-esteem, better health, and a feeling of camaraderie are some of the benefits reaped by the Flashettes Track Club, an organization of young urban women who have banded together to develop themselves through sports. The film is effective in combatting sexism in the athletic world and in the sports training of girls and women. An ideal film especially for minority students. For classes in physical education, guidance, and values.

FLIGHT OF THE GOSSAMER CONDOR
(27 min, c, $425/50, Churchill Films, 1978)

This is the exciting story of Dr. Paul McCready who made aviation history by building a man-powered aircraft capable of flying a difficult prescribed course and of pilot Bryan Allen who kept the "Gossamer Condor" in the air. Especially useful to encourage motivation. Academy Award winner.

THE FLY
(3 min, c, $95, Perspective Films, 1981)

A fly's-eye view of the world. The fly buzzes in from the countryside, flies through an open window, buzzes from room to room. Footsteps! Panic! Faster and faster he flies until the ultimate swat occurs. A nonverbal film with marvelous animation, it is useful for teaching point of view, irony, and filmmaking. Academy Award winner.

GLASS
(12 min, c, $215.25, CRM/McGraw-Hill Films, 1952)

Glass is a short film classic, a lyrical cine-poem that contrasts the ancient art of glassblowing with modern mechanical processes for making glass bottles. The pride of the glassblowers in their art is evident. It is a superb blending of visual imagery and imaginative soundtrack. Academy Award winner.

GRAVITY IS MY ENEMY
(26 min, c, $450/50, Churchill Films, 1977)

Quadraplegic Mark Hicks becomes a superlative artist using only his lips to hold his brush. He sees his art, his life, and others' perceptions of him clearly. The film is useful in special education, art, guidance, and motivation. Academy Award winner.

GREAT MOVIE STUNTS:
Raiders of the Lost Ark
(49 min, c, $750/145, Films, Inc., 1983)

Harrison Ford, star of *Raiders of the Lost Ark*, takes the viewer through a pit containing ten thousand snakes, great walls of fire, high waterfalls, exploding trucks and airplanes, and bullwhip fights. Tracing the origin of these famous stunts, the film also offers action sequences from early Saturday matinee cliff-hangers. Stunt coordinator for *Raiders*, Glenn Randall, and Harrison Ford's double, Terry Leonard, demonstrate some of the technical difficulties and hazards involved. Stunts, as old as the movies themselves, are the real stars of this film.

HORSE LATITUDES
(43 min, c, $600/60, Wombat Productions, Inc., 1978)

Based on an incident that actually occurred during an around-the-world sailing race to and from England, a vainglorious yachtsman falsifies his log and his radio signals to win. When circumstances dictate that he cannot appear to be the winner, he must confront his moral failure and despair. An absorbing film for classes in psychology, humanities, and values.

HOW COULD I NOT BE AMONG YOU?
(29 min, c, $525/55, Benchmark Films, 1972)

A very moving film about the death of a young poet, Ted Rosenthal, who was told at age 30 that he had leukemia and had six months to live. His initial reactions of rage and despair gave way to a new resolve to devote himself each day to the things that he valued most. Rosenthal's 93-page paperback, with the same title, is distributed at no charge with the film. A Blue Ribbon winner at the American Film Festival.

HUNGER
(12 min, c, $190/20, Learning Corporation of America, 1975)

Filmmaker Peter Foldes uses computer-assisted animation to create this allegory about man as the devourer. As he eats and eats, his gluttony swells him to grotesque proportions and brings on a nightmare in which he is consumed by the starving people of the world. *Hunger* is not a film for everyone. Some viewers are repelled, but others admire the film very much. It should definitely be used only with students who enjoy challenge and by a teacher who sees its merits. An Academy Award nominee.

I HEARD THE OWL CALL MY NAME
(78 min, c, $1150 (5-year lease)/110 rental,
Learning Corporation of America, 1973)

Unaware that he has only a short time to live, a young Anglican priest is sent by his bishop to a remote Indian village in Canada, ostensibly to help them, but really to learn enough about life to be ready to die. At first the priest, movingly played by British actor Tom Courtenay, attempts to change their ways and is met with polite hostility. When he finally understands that the Indians are living in harmony with nature and themselves, he apologizes for his efforts to bring them "the ways of the white man." He becomes a respected, loved, and loving friend of the Indians. When the "owl calls his name," a summons to death, the bishop's plan has succeeded. The performance of Tom Courtenay and the quiet dignity of the Indian villagers make this film a beautiful experience for everyone.

I WILL FIGHT NO MORE FOREVER
(106 min, c, $1200/150, Films, Inc., 1975)

A very moving account of the efforts of Chief Joseph of the Nez Perce Indians to negotiate with the white man for the freedom of his people. When all of his efforts failed, he tried to fight his way to freedom in Canada. Chief Joseph's story, one of the most poignant in American history, is brought to life by a very good cast headed by James Whitmore. For classes in American history, values, and any group interested in Indian history.

THE IMMIGRANT EXPERIENCE
(38 min, c, $450/40, Learning Corporation of America, 1973)

Over 35,000,000 people came to America between 1820 and 1920. Their story is told in this moving portrayal of one family who comes to the United States from Poland in 1907. The hopes and conflicts of all immigrants are seen through the eyes of the boy, Janek. In a warm scene near the end of the film, Janek, now grown old, sees his dreams fulfilled through his grandchildren. For classes in language arts, history, and family living.

IN THE REGION OF ICE
(38 min, b & w, $425/35, Phoenix Films, 1977)

This adaptation of an unusual short story by Joyce Carol Oates concerns the relationship between a nun, who teaches in a Catholic college, and a brilliant, but troubled, male student that ends in the student's death. It is a subtle exploration of student-teacher relationships and of the limitations of idealism in dealing with problems. Although the film won the Academy Award, it is recommended only for high-achieving students who are seriously interested in literature or psychology.

IS IT ALWAYS RIGHT TO BE RIGHT?
(8 min, c, $180, Churchill Films, 1970)

"There once was a land where men were always right," begins this fast-moving parable that highlights the divisiveness in our society. Stressing the need for our complex age to establish a spirit of interdependence, the film is designed to provoke discussion without alienating any particular group. Although made in 1970, it is surprisingly contemporary and is a good investment for any film library. For classes in language arts, sociology, psychology, and values.

THE JILTING OF GRANNY WEATHERALL
(57 min, c, $895, rental, inquire Perspective Films, 1980)

On her deathbed, a stubborn and once-domineering matriarch faces the long-suppressed realization that the accomplishments of her life cannot compensate for the day that, as a young women, she was left waiting at the altar.

Katharine Anne Porter's compelling story has as its theme our propensity toward self-deception. Granny, in spite of her independence, had passively accepted and rationalized what life had brought her, rather than actively seeking fulfillment. For classes in language arts, psychology, and women's studies.

JOCELYN
(28 min, c, $425/50, Filmakers Library, 1981)

Jocelyn is a seventeen-year-old girl with such enormous spiritual resources that she is able to face her remaining days and her untimely death with equanimity. Unlike most films about the dying, *Jocelyn* does not concern itself with physical suffering. It is a sensitive portrayal of a loving family, faithful friends, and a girl's courageous spirit. Her parents see their role as three-fold: to explore all medical advances, to encourage Jocelyn to live each day as fully as possible, and to help her accept her coming death. It is an unforgettable example of a family unafraid to deal openly with emotions. For classes in psychology, family living, and values.

JOHN MUIR'S HIGH SIERRA
(21½ min, c, $385/40 (school version), Churchill Films, 1982)

This soothing film follows the trail of the great naturalist and environmentalist. As we enjoy the beauty of the Sierra Nevada mountains, we hear his radiant prose. The serenity of the film is surprisingly appealing to secondary students. Marvelous for classes in language arts, biology, ecology, and for students interested in forestry as a vocation. An Academy Award nominee.

A JOURNEY
(12 min, b & w, $205/20.50, Wombat Productions, Inc., 1977)

A train journey becomes a metaphor for life in this strangely compelling nonverbal film. As the train starts its journey, various symbolic types are aboard—a nun, a guitar player, a prostitute, and others. One by one, as the train plunges into darkness, each disappears. The train continues down the track, its passengers gone, its cab empty. *A Journey* is helpful for teaching symbolism.

THE JUGGLING LESSON
(14 min, c, $295/35 (3-day rental), Little Red Filmhouse, 1982)

An itinerant street juggler teams up with a personable instructor whose personal goal is to teach everyone in the world to juggle. Together they hand out equipment to a diverse group of students, ranging in age from seven to seventy, and lead them through the basic moves of juggling. They correct common errors, give helpful hints, and continuously reinforce the learning process. An ideal film to teach the rudiments of juggling to beginners.

KARL SHAPIRO'S AMERICA
(13 min, c, $235/35, Pyramid Films, 1976)

Pulitzer Prize-winning poet Karl Shapiro's personal statements are woven into this visualization of his poems about commonplace objects and everyday life. Several of the poems demonstrate his belief that free verse is a natural and direct way of responding to the environment. The film opens the viewer's eyes to the world and helps one to find meaning in the most ordinary occurrence or object. As Shapiro says, "You can write a poem about anything, even manhole covers," and he proceeds to do so. It is a good film for students who think they don't like poetry.

KITTY—A RETURN TO AUSCHWITZ
(73 min, c, $970/125, Films, Inc., 1981)

When Kitty Felix Hart was a teenager, she was #39934 at Auschwitz. Although she survived this terrible ordeal, thirty members of her family and many of her friends did not. She speaks of her horrifying past from her present home in England and from Auschwitz where she returns with her grown son thirty-four years after her liberation. Her personal dynamism makes this exploration of her past absorbing to the viewer. (Kitty Hart's book of the same title is described in the study guide for *Night and Fog*.)

LARRY
(80 min, c, $700/70, Learning Corporation of America, 1973)

Larry is the tragic true story of a healthy young man, committed by error to an institution for the mentally retarded as an infant, who assumed the appearance and behavior of the patients with whom he was raised. Through the efforts of an alert psychologist, he was restored to normal living at age 23. Fredric Forrest, who won an Emmy for his stunning performance as Larry, is so good one has difficulty believing he is an actor. The film has tremendous impact for students and is unparalleled for psychology.

LEISURE
(14 min, c, $325/40, Pyramid Films, 1976)

Leisure traces the history of man's leisure time from the caveman's first moments of play to our present concept of providing a suitable environment for our leisure hours in an affluent society. Superbly animated, *Leisure* is a witty and stylish production. Useful for filmmaking, recreation classes, and language arts. Academy Award winner.

THE LUCK OF ROARING CAMP
(27 min, c, $550/50, Learning Corporation of America, 1982)

A new production of Bret Harte's classic story about the orphaned baby who is adopted by a shabby group of miners. Dubbed "The Luck" because the miners find gold, fortune soon turns against them, and the baby drowns. The miner (Randy Quaid) who discovers gold, dies when "The Luck" is taken from him.

MAKE IT HAPPEN
(22 min, c, $375/40, Mobius International, 1982)

Make It Happen is a film about recognizing and breaking out of the traditional reward patterns experienced by women and girls: being valued for being pretty, good, and feminine; becoming the supporting cast when they enter the work force; taking much more responsibility for home and children than the husband though both work. It is not a particularly creative film, but the message is important and clearly stated. High school girls should view it before they make decisions about their lives.

THE MAKING OF "RAIDERS OF THE LOST ARK"
(58 min, c, $895 6-year print license/75 secondary school rental,
Direct Cinema, Limited, 1982)

An exciting documentary about the making of one of the most successful films in film history. There is all the drama of filmmaking on an epic scale: the problems, the places, the personalities. A product of George Lucas's strong interest in helping students understand all aspects of filmmaking—acting, directing, art design, etc.—it is invaluable for teaching filmmaking, film appreciation, or for the entertainment of general audiences.

MANIMALS
(29 min, c, $425/45, Phoenix Films, 1978)

Although filmmaker Robin Lehman begins humorously, it is soon apparent that he is examining serious problems concerning pet owners in New York City. Do people have pets for the wrong reasons? Should animals be considered as conversation pieces? Is it desirable for animals to acquire human traits? Do pets reflect their owner's neuroticism? These ideas and others form Lehman's amusing but provocative commentary on society's attitude toward nature. For classes in language arts, psychology, sociology, biology, and values.

MARK TWAIN:
Beneath the Laughter
(58 min, c, $750/75, Pyramid Films, 1979)

Mark Twain is one of America's best-known but least understood authors. This film focuses on the tragedy or folly that often provoked Twain's humor. Expertly played by Dan O'Herlihy, the writer reflects on his life and work during a time of personal tragedy. A scholarly, well-researched film, *Beneath the Laughter* is important for the serious study of literature.

MINDSCAPE
(8 min, b & w, $210/35, Pyramid Films, 1976)

A painter steps into the landscape he is painting and travels the regions of the mind. We enter the places of our own interior landscape in a dreamlike journey strewn with symbols and fueled by images that shift across the screen. The moving images of this film were created by manipulating 240,000 pins on a perforated screen. Highly recommended for nature students in language arts, film study, and psychology.

MOIRA:
A Vision of Blindness
(24 min, c, $395/30, Direct Cinema, Limited, 1979)

Moira is a moving account of a nine-year-old blind girl being mainstreamed in a junior high school in Garden City, New York. Encouraged by her parents, Moira participates fully in life; she leaps from a diving board, climbs a tree, and makes apple pies. The American Foundation for the Blind considers *Moira* "one of the outstanding films about blind persons; it has warmth, sincerity, and most of all, integrity." A Blue Ribbon winner at the American Film Festival.

MOTHER, MAY I?
(23½ min, c, $420/50 (school version), Churchill Films, 1982)

Distressed because she mistakenly believes herself to be pregnant, sixteen-year-old Michelle is unable to talk to her parents, who are themselves embarrassed to talk to each other about their daughter's sexuality. Michelle's ten-year-old sister inadvertently learns of the possible pregnancy and shares Michelle's worry. The film emphasizes the need for family communication in problem-solving, and perhaps, indirectly, the need for sex instruction at a younger age. For classes in family living, sex education, guidance, sociology, and values.

MOVING MOUNTAINS
(27 min, c, $500/50, Mobius International, 1981)

A documentary about women exploring their options and succeeding in what have traditionally been considered men's jobs: trucking, dynamiting coal, and driving heavy equipment. A good film for breaking down stereotypes. The strong reaction of students to this film makes it very useful to start discussions. For classes in psychology, sociology, women's studies, and guidance.

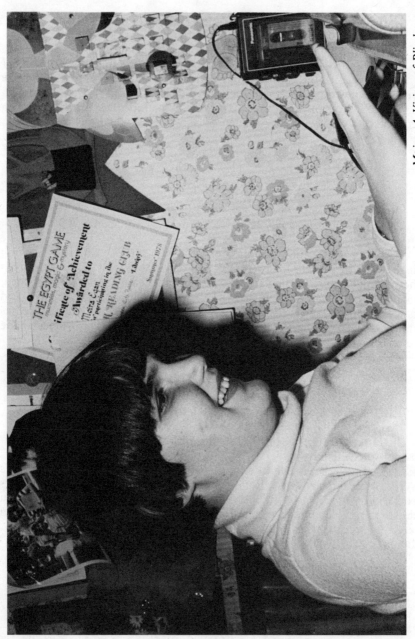

Moira: A Vision of Blindness
Photograph courtesy of De Nonno Pix Inc.

THE MUSIC OF AUSCHWITZ
(16 min, c, $325, rental, inquire Carousel Films, 1980)

Fania Fenelon recalls the German atrocities committed when she was a young woman prisoner at Auschwitz. Because the Germans needed calming music for their horrendous duties, the life of Fania, an accomplished musician, was spared. The film contains actual footage taken during the Holocaust of the camp orchestra. Fania Fenelon's experiences were the basis for the recent, disturbing television production of the same name, starring the controversial British actress, Vanessa Redgrave. It is a very good film in a unit on the Holocaust.

THE MUSIC SCHOOL
(30 min, c, $553, rental, inquire Perspective Films, 1977)

John Updike's metaphorical short story about a writer who struggles to find meaning in life has been beautifully written and directed by Academy Award-winning filmmaker John Korty. It is a difficult but brilliant film. Students who do not like challenge will usually not make the effort, but high-achieving students find it rewarding. Especially good for advanced placement classes.

THE NEEDLE'S EYE
(27 min, c, $395/25 wk., Paulist Productions, 1982)

Ron Howard of TV's "Happy Days" and Jerry Houser star as two medical students on an adventure trip across North Africa. When their jeep breaks down near a small village, they discover a clinic run by a dedicated woman physician. Although the two friends have always planned on having a lucrative medical practice together, one feels an urge to stay in Africa. He must choose between service to the needy or the pursuit of wealth. Although the plot is somewhat improbable, the film arouses strong responses in students who also feel the conflict between materialism and idealism. Good for assignments in the language arts.

NEVER GIVE UP
(28 min, c, $425/40, Phoenix Films, 1975)

Famed photographer Imogene Cunningham is the subject of this highly personal documentary about a woman whose art and spirit kept her alive until her death. The film is inspiring because Ms. Cunningham never gave up. Shortly before her death, she was still practicing her art. Beautiful and informative for classes in photography, psychology, gerontology, humanities, women's studies, and language arts.

THE NEW MAID
(35 min, c, $300/40, Learning Corporation of America, 1981)

Maria, a recent Central American immigrant, is hired by the McGraths, a well-to-do couple with two mischievous boys, to be their new maid. A warm friendship develops between Maria and the younger boy, Joey, because she gives him the attention that he lacks from his mother. The relationship (and Maria's popularity with the father and the other son) threatens Mrs. McGrath, and she forces Maria to leave. The film is an interesting look at family relationships, particularly as they are affected by jealousy. For classes in psychology, language arts, and values.

NICK MAZZUCCO:
Biography of an Atomic Vet
(22 min, c, $400/30, Green Mountain Post Films, 1981)

Brooklyn-born Nick Mazzucco was drafted into the army in 1955, shipped under secret orders to the U.S. Atomic Proving Grounds, and ordered to view eighteen atomic explosions from trenches as close as one-and-a-half miles with no protective gear. Nick Mazzucco talks about his experiences and the mounting confusion, anger, and fear he felt as he realized the enormity of his situation. It is a powerful and provocative film that will interest everyone interested in the experiences of veterans, nuclear power, the health effects of radiation, the history of the atomic age, and human rights.

NIGHTLIFE
(12 min, c, $250/25, Phoenix Films, 1976)

Academy Award-winning filmmaker Robin Lehman made this beautiful exploration of the exquisite forms in the depths of the ocean. Filmed in the Irish Sea, it brings the viewer close to dazzling creatures and forms and is accompanied by a delightfully humorous soundtrack. Excellent for classes in filmmaking, photography, and zoology.

NO LIES
(16 min, c, $295/30, Direct Cinema, Limited, 1972)

A young actress sits in her dressing room preparing to leave after a performance. As an unseen interviewer questions her insistently, he strips away the defenses that she has built to protect herself from the trauma of acknowledging that she has been raped. As she breaks, she turns on the interviewer, and we learn exactly what the experience has done to her. The actress playing the role is unusually convincing; it is difficult to believe it is not a *cinema verite* film. It is superb as a delineation of a woman's feelings. For psychology, sociology, law enforcement, and guidance.

NO OTHER LOVE
(58 min, c, $700/70, Time-Life Films, 1979)

Janet Michaels (Julie Kavner) is a slightly retarded young woman who has been overprotected all of her life by her concerned parents. In a home for young retarded adults, she meets an equally retarded, but much more self-reliant man, Andrew Madison (Richard Thomas). They fall in love and want to marry, but first they must convince their worried parents that they are ready for such a responsible and intimate relationship. It is an ideal film for classes in special education, psychology, sociology, language arts, and parenting.

NUCLEAR WAR:
A Guide to Armageddon
(25 min, c, $450/50, Films, Inc., 1983)

Using the black and white footage of the Hiroshima-Nagasaki films as well as animation, the film shows the development of the bomb. The horrifying effects of the fallout from a one-ton megaton bomb on London are graphically portrayed. It is not a film to be used with young students.

NUCLEAR WATCHDOGS
(13 min, c, $250, rental, inquire Carousel Films, 1979)

To discover the truth about safety in nuclear construction, CBS News went to one of the largest projects being constructed in the United States, the South Texas Nuclear Project. This disturbing documentary found that most of the safety inspections certified to the Nuclear Regulatory Commission had been done by company employees rather than government inspectors as required by law, or had not been done at all, and the records had been falsified. Since the film was made there have been many documented instances of inadequate safety inspection, particularly in California's Diablo Canyon Project. A strong film to accompany a unit on atomic energy.

ONE OF OUR OWN
(55 min, c, $700/75, Filmakers Library, 1979)

David McFarlane, whose life is described in *David: Portrait of a Retarded Youth*, plays a mentally handicapped man who must learn to live apart from his family if he is to gain independence as an adult. The film documents the problems as well as the rewards in making the transition and emphasizes the need for strong professional and family support if it is to be successful. For classes in special education, guidance, and family living. A Blue Ribbon winner at the American Film Festival.

ONLY THE BALL WAS WHITE
(30 min, c, $495/55, Films, Inc., 1980)

This is an interesting history of the black baseball players who were excluded from major league play until Jackie Robinson broke the color barrier. Vintage film clips, photographs, and interviews with Satchel Paige, Roy Campanella, Don Newcombe, and other stars of the black leagues make an absorbing thirty minutes. A good film for building pride among black students and for anyone interested in the history of baseball.

THE OUTSKIRTS OF HOPE
(54 min, c, $695/70, New Day Film Co-op, 1982)

Who are the poor in America today? How are they surviving the 1980s? In Minnesota, South Carolina, Indiana, Pennsylvania, and California, six Americans tell their stories in an unforgettable way. The film examines the successes and failures of the war on poverty and the impact of recent federal budget cuts. It is narrated by Maya Angelou — author, lecturer, poet, and artist.

PAUL'S CASE
(54½ min, c, $812, rental, inquire Perspective Films, 1980)

Eric Roberts plays a young man who longs to leave his hometown and enter the sophisticated world of New York City in this beautifully mounted production of Willa Cather's well-known short story. Sensitive and romantic, a failure at school and at work, he escapes to the city using money stolen from his employer. Briefly he lives his illusion until reality brings tragedy. A Red Ribbon winner at the American Film Festival.

THE PHANS OF NEW JERSEY
(49 min, c, $700/65, Films, Inc., 1980)

As members of an upper-middle-class family, the Phans had prospered in Vietnam. Now the nineteen-member refugee family lives on welfare in a lower-middle-class neighborhood in Jersey City, New Jersey. But Colonel Phan and his family pursue the American Dream as ardently as any native and, although it happens after the completion of the film, their efforts are extremely successful. The dedication to excellence in school and work characteristic of all the Phans is amazing to American students and is the principal reason to use the film. For classes in language arts, history, guidance, and values.

PIECE OF CAKE
(26 min, c, $400/50, Learning Corporation of America, 1980)

The need to create a fantasy as a protection against the losses of old age is the theme of this moving film about two lonely old men, Jack and Bert, living in a small rural town in Australia. Unable to buy a goose for Christmas dinner, and expecting his married daughter from overseas, Jack persuades the reluctant Bert to help him "catch" one. The escapade doesn't work out as planned, but before it is over, Bert has gently helped his friend to accept the fact that his daughter is dead. For classes in psychology, sociology, gerontology, and language arts.

THE POWERS OF TEN
(9 min, c, $225/40, Pyramid Films, 1979)

Formerly done in black and white, this is an updated version of Charles and Ray Eames's classic film about the relative size of things in the universe. It appeals even to those who don't understand it well because the film techniques themselves are so interesting. Very good for classes in filmmaking, mathematics, and language arts. French, German, Swedish, and Spanish versions are also available.

A PRIVATE LIFE
(31 min, c, $425/50, Museum of Modern Art, 1980)

As people grow older, forming new relationships becomes more difficult. Margot, a fun-loving older woman, a recent German-Jewish emigré, works part-time and looks forward to the future. She forms a relationship with Karl, who returns her interest, but spends much of his time dwelling on the past. When Karl's son invites him to live with him in another town, Karl, unable to face a future where he must accept responsibility for his own life and happiness, accepts his son's offer, leaving Margot alone again. *A Private Life* is a lovely film for psychology, gerontology, sociology, and language arts.

RADIANCE:
The Experience of Light
(22 min, c, $395/55, Pyramid Films, 1978)

Radiance is a journey from the light in nature to the spirit in all life. Using a stunning array of mandalas, video images, and religious art, the filmmaker shares her own experience with the phenomenon of inner light. A beautiful film for anyone interested in religion, humanities, women's studies, or psychology. It should not be used with groups who have had no introduction to metaphysics, or who would be unreceptive or uncomfortable with it. A very special film, it is accompanied by a twenty-page guide explaining its many uses.

A RAINY DAY

(35 min, c, $400/40, Learning Corporation of America, 1979)

Mariette Hartley stars as a famous actress going home for her father's funeral and remembering, with her mother, an over-regulated, over-protected childhood that now seems a horror. The film is about a mother determined that her daughter would succeed; about a kind and ineffectual father; and about a women who comes to grips with her hostilities. For classes in language arts, psychology, and family living.

RANSOM OF RED CHIEF

(27 min, c, $450/40, Learning Corporation of America, 1978)

Based on the well-known O. Henry short story, this film is fun for everyone. Sam and Bill, somewhat inept con men, decide that it will be easy money to kidnap the banker's son for ransom. But young Johnny ("Red Chief" and "terror of the plains") is so obnoxious that they abridge the kidnapping and rush to get the money, only to find the tables turned again. Good for teaching classes in short story and especially good for teaching irony.

THE RIVER

(29 min, c, $425/40, Phoenix Films, 1978)

A strange, disturbing short story by Flannery O'Connor about a lonely boy who is taken to the river for a healing service by his babysitter. Returning to his home where he finds the remains of a party his parents have just given, his deeper loneliness drives him back to the river where the story ends in tragedy. It is a compelling film for students interested in Flannery O'Connor, but it is not recommended for those who are not seriously interested in literature.

ROCK-A-BYE, BABY

(30 min, c, $450/40, Time-Life, 1977)

This film demonstrates the critical importance of mothering in the first three years of the baby's life. Touch and movement are crucial to young children. Monkeys raised in isolation from their mothers develop human-like schizophrenia and become violent toward each other and themselves. Children raised in orphanages without mothering become listless and withdrawn. It is an important topic that all secondary students should be made aware of. It won the prestigious Emily Award at the American Film Festival. A Spanish-language version is also available.

ROCKING HORSE WINNER
(30 min, c, $450/40, Learning Corporation of America, 1977)

This absorbing production of D. H. Lawrence's famous psychological drama stars British actor Kenneth More as the uncle and confidant of a young boy whose family conflicts lead him to develop a strange ability to pick racetrack winners. The film builds to its powerful climax as the boy predicts his last winner. Recommended for those students interested in the serious study of literature.

ROSIE GREER:
The Courage to Be Me
(23 min, c, $395/40, Churchill Films, 1976)

Ex-professional football player Rosie Greer explains how he overcame shyness, rejection, and failure to achieve success in football and to serve young people. Rosie Greer is a very positive role model, especially for black students. He is not the stereotypical jock, despite his athletic achievements. The film opens with Rosie doing needlepoint. He demonstrates that a "real man" can be interested in many things, not just sports or the opposite sex, and can feel the pain of failure. It is a simple film in format, but it has many valuable ideas for students.

RUNAWAY
(54 min, c, $740/75, Media Guild, 1981)

Public Broadcasting System commentator Robert MacNeil narrates this hard-hitting documentary about the one million children, who are ten to seventeen years old, who run away from home each year. Their stories are told by the runaways themselves, their parents, police, juvenile authorities, counselors, and social workers. Filmed on location in various parts of the United States, *Runaway* alerts young people to the dangers of running away and the resources available to them if they do. It provides concerned adults with the facts about why teenagers run away, what runaways experience, and how they survive. For classes in psychology, guidance, contemporary problems, sociology.

SEE WHAT I SAY
(24 min, c, $450/50, Filmakers Library, 1982)

Holly Near, folksinger and caring citizen, shares the stage with Susan Freundlich, recognized interpreter of American Sign Language, who incorporates mime and dance into her translation of the lyrics. Their synchronized performance heightens feminist Holly Near's vision of a better world. As the film ends, Holly, Susan, and the audience sing and sign "Harbor

Me," a song about women supporting each other. *See What I Say* ends with a sense of shared communication between hearing and deaf cultures. An Academy Award nominee and winner of a Blue Ribbon at the American Film Festival.

A SENSE OF PURPOSE
(13 min, c, $270/30, Learning Corporation of America, 1972)

Excerpted from the feature film *Drive, He Said*, and directed by screen star Jack Nicholson, the film is about basketball superstar Hector Bloom. Indifferent to the rhetoric of success surrounding him, he contemplates his future with little expectation of finding happiness or meaning. The film strikes a responsive chord with many students who seem uncertain about how to establish personal goals or achieve fulfillment. Useful for classes in language arts, psychology, and values.

SIGN OF VICTORY
(22 min, c, $450/45, Filmakers Library, 1981)

All the players on this competitive basketball team are deaf girls who have overcome the isolation of their handicap by participating in the world of sports. They ask for no quarter nor do they give any. The team's enthusiasm is contagious, and when they finally win the championship, the crowd goes wild. For classes in special education, physical education, motivation, guidance, and values.

SNOWBOUND
(32 min, c, $450/40, Learning Corporation of America, 1979)

Attractive, self-confident Tony (one of the high school "ins") offers a ride to plain, plumpish Cindy (one of the "outs") to spite his girl friend. When the two of them are caught in a life-threatening blizzard, it is Cindy's resourcefulness and stamina that save them. Tony eyes Cindy with new appreciation. Students learn about courage, survival, and the value of not judging on appearances alone. Entertaining, but thought-provoking, *Snowbound* is excellent for language arts, psychology, women's studies, and values.

SPOON RIVER ANTHOLOGY
(20½ min, c, $415/62, BFA Films, 1976)

Using music, authentic settings, and period photography, a talented cast of four brings to life the lyrical realism of Edgar Lee Masters's poetry of small-town America. It is presented as a concert reading interspersed with transitional music. Even students who are unreceptive to poetry are captured by the directness and clarity of Masters's work.

STRANGE FRUIT
(33 min, c, $400/40, Learning Corporation of America, 1979)

Inspired by Lillian Smith's famous novel of the same name, this is the story of Henry Brown, a black house painter in a small rural town in Georgia. Refusing at first to become involved in a voter registration drive, Henry does so when an organizer is killed. He tries to vote, is beaten, then hanged. It is a sensitive, powerful film that should be used carefully. Unaware of the lynchings, burnings, and beatings of blacks in the United States before the civil rights movement, students are often shocked to learn of them. An Academy Award nominee.

SUNSHINE'S ON THE WAY
(30 min, c, $450/40, Learning Corporation of America, 1981)

Bobba June Strang, a young employee of the Sugar Hill Nursing Home, encourages the residents to form their own jazz group. Despite her mother's objections, Bobba June herself wants to be a great jazz drummer. Finally she must tell her mother that she and the residents' jazz band are going to Hollywood to appear on the "Tonight Show." It's a finger-snapping film that dispels many myths about age. For classes in language arts, human relations, sociology, psychology, and gerontology.

SURVIVORS:
A Film about Japanese-American Atomic Bomb Victims
(58 min, c, $850/100, First Run Features, 1983)

Survivors is the first film in English in which Japanese-Americans who were trapped in Hiroshima and Nagasaki during the war speak for themselves about the trauma they endured. It exposes the political struggles of the survivors for justice and depicts the aftermath of nuclear war. "Harrowing," "heartbreaking," "deeply disturbing," "compassionate"—these are some of the words critics have used to describe the film. Excellent for classes in history, psychology, science, filmmaking, language arts, and sociology, and to accompany the film, *Hiroshima-Nagasaki, August 1945.*

Sunshine's on the Way

Photograph courtesy of Learning Corporation of America

SWEET SIXTEEN AND PREGNANT
(29 min, c, $450/75, Media Guild, 1982)

Five teenage women who have been pregnant tell how the event affected their lives. Carol, sixteen, married her child's father and lives with his family while he is in the military. Jackie, seventeen, lives with her grandmother and two-year-old daughter and is struggling to finish high school. Renee, sixteen, was forced to give up the child for adoption or leave her parents' home. Debbie, seventeen, opted for abortion, which she faced alone. Denise, pregnant at twelve and a mother at thirteen, faces a very uncertain future. Hosted by actress Sally Kellerman, the film reveals the sadness, abandonment, indecision, and anger resulting from teenage pregnancy. For sex education and family living classes.

TAKING CHANCES
(22 min, c, $450/50, Mobius International, 1979)

Taking Chances frankly illustrates the role of attitude in teenage use of contraceptives. The film follows the relationship of a couple as seen through the eyes of Kathy and her girl friend. As they talk, the viewer becomes aware that Kathy is conscious of the need for contraceptive information. In an excellent, nonthreatening sequence she visits a clinic for counseling. The role of the teenage boy who wants to be a responsible sex partner is explored also. An excellent film for sex education, family living, or biology classes.

TEEN MOTHER:
A Story of Coping
(24 min, c, $480/50, Mobius International, 1981)

Rosie, a nineteen-year-old mother has been "surviving" (as she puts it) with her son George since she was seventeen. The film is somewhat unusual in that it shows some of the pleasures as well as the difficulties of being a teenage mother. The unusually good study guide that accompanies it was made possible by a grant from the Children's Aid Society of the Metropolitan Toronto Foundation.

TEENAGE FATHER
(30 min, c, $465/50, Mobius International, 1979)

This Academy Award-winning film engages the interest of many secondary students probably more than any other film on the same subject. It is difficult to understand the reason for this, but it may be because everyone that surrounds Kim, fifteen, who is pregnant, and John, seventeen, the baby's father, offers counsel. Their involvement reflects the need to help Kim and John out of their confusion and uncertainty. After painful searching, Kim makes her decision.

TEENAGE SUICIDE
(60 min, c, $780/75, Films, Inc., 1983)

Eighteen young people, who are ten to twenty-one years old, kill themselves each day in the United States. Suicide is now the second leading cause of death among this age group. Narrated by Tim Hutton, who won an Academy Award for his portrayal of a suicidal teenager in *Ordinary People*, this is a frank examination of the lives and deaths of four teenagers. Can suicide be prevented? What can we learn from the victims and their families? A sobering look at a difficult problem, *Teenage Suicide* should lead to the discussion of this crucial issue.

THINGS IN THEIR SEASON
(79 min, c, $750/75, Learning Corporation of America, 1974)

A splendid cast, headed by Patricia Neal, makes this story of a Wisconsin dairy family that must face the death of the mother from leukemia totally absorbing. Ed Flanders plays the husband, an inarticulate man unable to express his love to his wife until the crisis. Conflict between father and son (Marc Singer) is clarified and resolved. The film demonstrates that tragedy can sometimes be a catalyst for happiness. *Things in Their Season* is very appealing to students. For classes in language arts, psychology, sociology, and family living.

THIS ONE'S FOR DAD
(18 min, c, $280/25 wk., Paulist Productions, 1982)

David idolizes his father who has always dreamed that David will one day be a champion cross-country runner. Now his father is dying. Trying to escape the realization of his impending death, David isolates himself from his friends and his running. He also turns off his emotions; nothing can reach him. After his father dies, he begins to run aimlessly until he drops to the ground in exhaustion. Finally he realizes that his father had always wanted him to be a winner. Returning home, he again takes up racing and wins his next time out. As he wins, he is finally able to weep for his father. He has accepted his death and can participate in life again.

THE UGLY LITTLE BOY
(26 min, c, $450/40, Learning Corporation of America, 1977)

The first story by Isaac Asimov ever brought to the screen, this poignant film pits science against morality in a futuristic world. British actress Kate Reid is superb as a humanistic nurse in charge of a child who has been brought forward in time from the Neanderthal Age. She is in conflict with the scientists responsible for the child's return because they have forgotten the human element in their research. Many teachers report that *The Ugly Little Boy* is unusually good for stimulating discussion and writing.

UP IS DOWN
(6 min, c, $110/35, Pyramid Films, 1969)

This classic, small gem of a film is the animated story of a boy who walks on his hands, and illustrates with wit and clarity the conflict between conformity and creativity. Examined by experts who give him prolonged treatments, the boy finally stands on his feet, only to reject his new perspective and walk away on his hands. For classes in sociology, psychology, language arts, child development, and values.

WAR OF THE EGGS
(27 min, c, $445/35, Media Guild, 1972)

Michael Crichton, author of *The Andromeda Strain*, wrote this film about one of the country's most distressing problems, child abuse. Bill Bixby and Elizabeth Ashley are effective as the parents of a young child who is hospitalized several times due to injuries inflicted by one of them. Part of the interest of the film is that we do not know which of the parents is guilty, although psychological clues are offered as the film progresses. *War of the Eggs* is enlightening and provocative. Splendid for classes in psychology, family living, sociology, and language arts.

WAR WITHOUT WINNERS II
(28 min, c, $480/50, Films, Inc., 1978)

This film explores the danger of nuclear war from the scientific, political, and military points of view. It also examines it from the viewpoint of the Americans and Russians who express their fears and hopes in an age in which civilizations can be wiped out in minutes. An updated version of *War without Winners*, it is a good film to use with other films on nuclear conflict.

WOMEN IN SPORTS
(Full version: 58 min, c, $750/75, Pyramid Films, 1980; edited version: 26 min, c, $445/50, Pyramid Films, 1980)

James Michener reviews the history of women in sports and examines the current status of women athletes and women's athletics. Rare footage of historic firsts and fascinating conversations with pioneers and present superstars, such as Chris Evert Lloyd and Nancy Lopez, highlight the film. For classes in sociology, physical education, women's studies, and teacher education.

YOUTH TERROR:
The View from behind the Gun
(48 min, c, $695/70, CRM/McGraw-Hill Films, 1978;
also available in two parts: Part I: 29 min, $480; Part II: 19 min, $335)

This controversial documentary, produced by ABC News, examines the lives of alienated young criminal offenders in the Bronx. They explain why they break the law, how they choose their victims, and their feelings toward them. The film is particularly effective for students who have never seen the area in the Bronx where these people live. Many students cannot believe that such a place exists in the United States. The film is exceptionally good to use with students that share some of the alienation and despair expressed by the delinquents, even though their feelings have not produced the destructive behavior of the young people of the Bronx.

Appendix A
FILM DISTRIBUTORS

There are many fine distributors of short films in the United States. Because each is unique in size, personal philosophy, and services offered to education, public libraries, business, and industry, all of the distributors mentioned in this book were asked if they wanted to submit a short statement to be reprinted here. This appendix contains the statements of the companies that responded. The addresses of the other distributors are found in appendix B.

BFA Films (See **Phoenix Films**)

Benchmark Films, Inc.
145 Scarborough Road
Briarcliff Manor, New York 10510   (914) 762-3838
The emphasis at Benchmark is on a small list of fine films for schools, colleges, and public libraries. Because of our high standards, we release only about four or five films a year. The president of this small company is Mike Solin, who had fourteen years experience at McGraw-Hill Film Division in production and was in charge of all acquisitions before founding Benchmark in 1967.

Bullfrog Films, Inc.
Oley, Pennsylvania 19547
Bullfrog Films is the number one distributor of films on energy and the environment. We produce many of our own titles, and represent other independent producers, and the National Film Board of Canada. The guiding theme of our collection is to help people appreciate the gift of life on our garden planet, and to behave accordingly. When someone sees a Bullfrog Film, we hope they will be motivated to take some positive action, whether it's to build a solar greenhouse, or to bake a loaf of whole grain bread.

Among our best-selling titles are *The Solar Promise, Getting the Most from Your Garden, Estuary, Diet for a Small Planet, The Home Energy Conservation Series.* Besides a large number of films on renewable sources of energy, our collection includes films on agriculture and land use issues; peace education; self-reliance; gardening and nutrition; and the work of E. F. Schumacher (*Small Is Beautiful*) and energy analysts Amory and Hunter Lovins (*Lovins on the Soft Path*).

CBC Enterprises (The Canadian Broadcasting Company)

Box 500, Terminal A

Toronto, Ontario, M5W IE6

Marketing in the United States, through a number of distributors, is centered at CBC Enterprises, 245 Park Avenue, New York, New York 10167.

The Canadian Broadcasting Company has been internationally known for decades as one of the world's largest producers and broadcasters of radio and television programs.

In recent years, this nationally owned organization, Canada's largest employer of performing and production talent, has become almost as well known as a source of quality audiovisual material, honored by almost every major festival. Nonbroadcast distribution of selected programs from the large volume of CBC television programs has become worldwide.

Although its broadcast productions cover the spectrum, CBC programming is best known among audiovisual users as a source of enrichment material — films and videocassettes — in the categories of sociology, health, natural life and environmental and ecological issues, with a recent trend to interesting coverage of business and technological subjects.

CRM/McGraw-Hill Films

P.O. Box 641

Del Mar, California 92014

CRM is the film division of McGraw-Hill Book Company. We specialize in training films, multi-media modules and programs for business and industry (which we produce and acquire), as well as educational films (which we acquire).

We prefer to acquire films that are thirty minutes or less, are good quality, and are based on a core curriculum subject.

We distribute approximately 700 films on the following subjects: The arts, business/staff development, communications, biographies, guidance, health and safety, home economics, history, language arts, psychology, science, social studies and special education. We offer free previews, of course, and a free instructor's guide is included with every rental, preview, and sale.

California Newsreel

630 Natoma Street

San Francisco, California 94103   (415) 621-6196

California Newsreel is a nonprofit distributor of films and supplementary instructional materials on social concerns. It specializes in two areas. California Newsreel's *Media at Work* program is the most widely used, nonmanagement source of films on labor, work, and the economy of the country. The films are selected to prepare students to participate more fully and effectively in the economic decisions that affect their lives, both in the workplace and in the community. Similarly, Newsreel's Southern Africa

Media Center is the country's most prestigious source of films on apartheid and life in that embattled part of the world. All of California Newsreel's films are available to secondary school teachers at a 50 percent discount.

Centron Films (See Coronet Films)

Churchill Films
> 662 North Robertson Boulevard
> Los Angeles, California 90069

Churchill Films, being a smallish company, is readily available for teachers' questions or problems. We think our films are thoughtful and imaginative, and generally of high quality. The collection is particularly strong in health at all levels. And strong in language arts, science, social studies and guidance.

We're also careful about the titles we acquire from outside. We take a few, with emphasis on quality, and interesting and provocative points of view.

Clarity Productions
> 4560 Horton Street
> Emeryville, California 94608   (415) 655-7150

Clarity Productions is a nonprofit producer and distributor of educational media, both film and print. Our primary areas of concern in the products we produce are social issues of both domestic and international concern—such as women's issues, labor issues, and Third World development.

Clarity Productions is the producer and distributor of the widely acclaimed film *The Life and Times of Rosie the Riveter* and the book of the same title.

Coronet Films (Perspective Films, Centron Films)
> 65 East South Water Street   (312) 977-4011
> Chicago, Illinois 60601   Toll Free (800) 621-2131

Since 1939, Coronet Films has brought the finest in instructional media to educational systems worldwide. As one of the pioneers in the educational field, Coronet has, from the very start, been an innovator in instructional design, technical quality, and marketing programs. Coronet was the first to release an entire collection in color and worked closely with the educational community to establish many of the film libraries in the United States. The Coronet collection excels in film series with strong curricular content such as the award-winning *World Culture and Youth, The Human Body*, and *The Biological Sciences.*

In 1973, Perspective Films was established to bring Coronet expertise to the noncurricular areas of the educational film market such as colleges and public libraries. Perspective has since built a reputation for unrivalled quality with such acclaimed titles as *The American Short Story Series, Picasso: A Painter's Diary*, and *Eisenstaedt: Germany.*

Centron Films & Video, with its collection of over 250 educational titles, has 35 years of producing award-winners like *Leo Beureman* and *What Do You See, Nurse?* for business and industry. Centron Films & Video was acquired in January 1982.

Coronet Films is proud of its number one position in the industry. No matter how you add it up—total dollar sales; total number of titles; total experience in production, distribution, and marketing—Coronet is Number One!

De Nonno Pix
    7119 Shore Road
    Brooklyn, New York 11209
Tony De Nonno's films are human portraits of many kinds of people from celebrities such as Itzhak Perlman and Fleetwood Mac to an eleven-year-old blind girl and a baker who loves his work. The films, which all emphasize our common humanity, are appreciated by people of all ages and are widely used in schools and libraries.

Direct Cinema, Limited
    P.O. Box 69589
    Los Angeles, California 90069   (213) 656-4700
Background: Formed in 1978 to represent independent filmmakers, from George Lucas to unknowns, who wanted to control their own distribution, it has grown to represent over forty filmmakers, three Hollywood studios (for selected films), a few Fortune 500 companies, a great many nonprofit educational organizations and one national government.
    A Commitment to Excellence: Over three-quarters of our eligible films have won awards from the Educational Film Library Association, five films have been selected as outstanding films for young adults by the American Library Association, and most of our films have been selected for review by *Booklist, Media and Methods*, and *Choice*. We distribute two Academy Award-winning documentary short films and one Academy Award-winning animated short. In 1982 three of our films were nominated for Academy Awards.
    Service: Our films are available for free preview to educational film libraries. All prints are provided on estar base at no extra charge. Various ownership plans are available for prints and video copies.

Documentary Films, Ltd.
    159 West 53rd Street
    New York, New York 10019   (212) 582-4318
Documentary Films, Ltd. offers award-winning, critically acclaimed films emphasizing important issues of social concern. Among these important films featured in its library are *Best Boy* (Academy Award winner), *Fighting Back* (International Emmy Award winner), and several classic documentaries by such directors as John Huston (*Let There Be Light*), John Ford (*The Battle of Midway*), and William Wyler (*Memphis Belle*). Each film has been selected not only for its ability to convey its subject matter in an interesting and informative way for all audiences, but also for its intense emotional impact. Feature-length and short films in 16-mm are available to rent and purchase, with time payment plans for the purchase of feature films. Some subjects are also available in ½-inch and ¾-inch videocassette formats.

Filmakers Library
   133 East 58th Street, Suite 703A   (212) 355-6545
   New York, New York 10022   (212) 356-6545
   Filmakers Library specializes in thought-provoking films for use at the high school and college levels. We have many award-winning films in the area of political and social documentary, as well as in the areas of psychology, the life cycle, and the handicapped. Many of our titles are produced by Canadian Broadcasting Corporation and Granada Television and show the technical and informational resources of a large production unit. Others are independently made and reflect a fresh perspective or an interesting point of view.
   We are a small company and are eager to learn the needs of our clients and make recommendations for programming.

First Run Features
   144 Bleecker Street
   New York, New York 10012
   First Run Features brings a new concept to independent film distribution. Established and directed by filmmakers, it presents only the finest in independently produced American feature films — documentaries and narratives, comedies and dramas, all made with purpose, passion, and a commitment to ideas.
   The First Run collection includes film from every region of the United States: films about politics and social justice; films about history told by those people who lived it and shaped it; and personal films in which people intimately share their lives.
   Our catalog reflects the complete spectrum of themes and styles found in the American independent film movement today. The films have won recognition and awards at major film festivals in London, Cannes, New York, and Los Angeles — including Academy Award nominations. The critical acclaim accorded First Run Features' collection heralds the vitality and growth of independent film in the United States today.

IFEX Films/International Film Exchange Limited
   159 West 53rd Street
   New York, New York 10019   (212) 582-4318
   Outstanding foreign films, important documentaries, and unique short films are the keynote to "The Collection," the latest 16-mm films from the catalog of IFEX Films. Emphasizing Russian films such as *Moscow Does Not Believe in Tears* (Academy Award winner) and the film version of Goncharov's classic novel, *Oblomov*, the IFEX library also includes such notable titles as Fred Schepisi's *The Devil's Playground* and Francis Mankiewicz's *Le Bons Debarras*. CBC's *Sharing the Secret, Snow*, and *Dead Bunnies* are among the documentaries and shorts in the IFEX Film Collection. All titles are available for 16-mm film rental, and some titles are available for purchase in 16-mm and videocassette.

Kinetic Film Enterprises, Ltd.
781 Gerrard Street East
Toronto, Canada M4M 1Y5

How does one compete with five years of *Sesame Street* and *Sixty Minutes*? At Kinetic Films we believe that the answer lies in the comprehensive utilization of audiovisual material that has been specifically designed for the education process in that it provides entertainment through enlightenment, not vice versa, always bringing the viewer to new perceptions of self and the surrounding world.

Sports and women's issues ... cruelty to animals and child abuse ... the far North ... the aged and disabled; children today have all been confronted with these subjects through television. They are significant, and yet the child's perceptions are left untutored for the most part, and only the image is grasped. Lingering perceptions fade to a jumble. Learning it is not only watching. The same subjects presented coherently, with direction, open the student to a degree of comprehension that is reinforced with each new similar experience, even of television viewed in his or her own living room. *Television has become more significant in North American culture than even the worst early predictions.* As a result, it has become the duty of the modern teacher not only to help the student in the perception of this overwhelming force in our lives, but most significantly, in his or her ability to analyze the almost fantastic quantities of information available to them.

The overwhelmingly visual orientation of the modern student must be dealt with constructively. Kinematic films will help.

Our material is for sale and rental in 16-mm and all video formats with a free preview to consider purchase. We ship to U.S. customers from our lab in Massachusetts.

Learning Corporation of America
1350 Avenue of the Americas
New York, New York 10019   (212) 397-9330

Learning Corporation of America is a long-time leader in the production and distribution of high-quality programs for education, television, community, and government. Our success is evidenced by more than 600 major awards earned in little over a decade — including 48 Emmy Winners and 10 Academy Awards. Commited to the idea that media in education is as important as a good book or a good teacher, LCA specializes in producing language arts, social science, literature, and values films.

LCA is also dedicated to media education and is the only educational film company to have a full-time educational consultant on staff. The company also produces an on-going supply of comprehensive leader's study guides and support material including a videotape workshop on film utilization and a handbook on how to teach effectively with film.

In the words of William F. Deneen, president of LCA, "We believe in the necessity of film in education today. We believe in our own ability to produce and distribute perhaps as no one else can."

Mass Media Ministries
2116 North Charles Street
Baltimore, Maryland 21218   (301) 727-3270

Mass Media Ministries is well known for its personalized customer service, as well as its excellent collection of short films from around the world. In addition to films that inform, inspire, or entertain, MMM specializes in visual parables that transcend boundaries of culture, language, age, etc., by focusing on a universal theme. Another specialty is the discussion film that serves as a catalyst for group interaction in church, school, or community organization.

The Media Guild
11526 Sorrento Valley Road
Suite J
San Diego, California 92121
The Media Guild distributes films from a number of sources including John Wiley & Sons, the National Film Board of Canada, CBS/TV, ABC/TV, The Research Press, Paulist Productions, the British Open University/BBC-TV, Thames Television, and several independent filmmakers. The catalogue collection includes films for elementary, secondary, college, and adult audiences, with strong emphasis in guidance, high school science, psychology, and the language arts areas. A complete program of college-level academic films, produced by BBC/TV for the Open University, is included in a separate "University Media" catalogue. In addition to catalogues and special brochures through the mail, The Media Guild has personalized telephone sales and service, and its sales people meet customers at the leading national, regional, and state conferences. The Media Guild was founded in 1976 by Preston Holdner, who had been manager of CRM Films, and held various sales positions with McGraw-Hill Films. In 1981, Jim LeMay joined the company after twenty years in key management posts with Coronet Films.

The Media Project
P.O. Box 4093
Portland, Oregon 97208   (503) 223-5335
The Media Project, founded in 1974 by filmmakers and teachers, is a nonprofit organization designed to stimulate awareness of and support for the work of independent film and video workers in the Northwest. The film program catalogue represents award-winning film/video work of independent Northwest artists. Many films explore the Northwest region, its history, heritage, and people. Others examine the work and lives of poets, artists, and craftspeople. Animated and experimental films express the creative range of media technology.
Films are available for purchase and rental in 16-mm and ¾-inch videocassette. (See our catalogue for exceptions.) Films are selected by an annual programming panel according to artistic merit, production values, and originality.
The Media Project offers free senior center showings, discounts on multiple bookings, guest appearances of media artists, and workshops with film/video makers on such techniques as lighting and animation.

Mobius International
P.O. Box 315
Franklin Lakes, New Jersey 07417   (201) 891-8240

Mobius International is the distribution division of Mobius Productions Limited, a company producing and distributing educational films — documentaries, dramas, docu-dramas, animated shorts, and video and slide-tape productions. We distribute American films in Canada and Canadian films in the United States and abroad. Our American collection has been the recipient of more than thirty-five individual awards. Good to excellent reviews have appeared in *Booklist, The School Library Journal, Media and Methods, VOYA, Choice,* and *Sightlines.* We specialize in films on health and social issues currently of interest to educators. Study guides accompany many of our films. Free preview-to-purchase and rental arrangements can be made through our office in Franklin Lakes, New Jersey.

Museum of Modern Art
11 West 53rd Street
New York, New York 10019   (212) 956-6100
The Circulating Film Library sells, leases, and rents 16-mm films. It will shortly begin distributing independently produced videocassettes. The collection spans the history of cinema and has special strength in the silent film, the avant-garde film (European and American), and the documentary.

National (Audiovisual) Center
National Archives and Records Service
General Services Administration
Reference Section SS
Washington, D.C. 20409   (301) 763-1896
The National (Audiovisual) Center is the central information and distribution source for more than 12,000 films, videocassettes, filmstrips, audio/slide sets, and other media produced by or for the United States Government. It was established, in fact — under the aegis of the National Archives and Records Service of the General Services Administration — to serve as *the central clearing house for all Federally produced audiovisuals.*

Subject concentrations within the collection are as varied as medicine and mechanics, space exploration and social issues, military battles, and energy conservation. And the list of Agency producer/sponsors is equally diverse — from the National Park Service to the National Aeronautics and Space Administration, the International Communication Agency (formerly USIA) to the National Institutes of Health, the Small Business Administration to the Department of Defense.

The initial production of Government audiovisuals is funded by tax dollars, and as a public service, the National Audiovisual Center ensures that you will have continuing access to all the materials through our collection — *and at the most reasonable prices possible.*

Virtually every prevalent audiovisual format is offered for purchase through the Center — and media conversion to special formats is available by request on an individual title basis.

Many 16-mm films, which represent 80 percent of the Center's collection, are available to you through our rental program at very nominal fees.

A trained staff will respond quickly to telephone or written requests.

New Day Film Co-Op, Inc.
    P.O. Box 315
    Franklin Lakes, New Jersey 07417   (201) 891-8240
    New Day is a cooperative of independent filmmakers who distribute films
about social change. We began in 1972 as a distribution cooperative for
feminist films. Over time, it became clear that feminism was more than the
domain of women or "women's issues" alone. The lives of both men and
women needed to be explored and changed. As feminists, we are attempting to
transform all of society, from daily relationships between people to social,
political, and economic institutions. We now include films on a broad range of
issues: families, history, marriage, aging, single parenting, worker's health,
labor history, women artists, and sexuality.
    Why do we distribute our own films? If filmmaking is a way of sharing
ideas and discoveries with others, then our work cannot stop when a film is
completed—this is only half the process. The other half is distribution. We
wanted to create an alternative to the traditional distribution process in which
filmmakers are cut off from their audiences. Through our direct involvement
in distribution, we can be responsive to the needs of all our viewers, whether
they be in theaters, college classrooms, high schools, libraries, churches, union
halls, or living rooms.
    We are New Day—independent filmmakers working together with a
common vision. We believe in the importance of cooperative action in
bringing about social change. New Day means personal commitment,
responsibility, and a desire to create a society responsive to human needs.

Paulist Productions
    P.O. Box 1057
    Pacific Palisades, California 90272   (213) 454-0688
    Paulist Productions was founded in 1960 by Father Ellwood Kieser, CSP,
a Paulist priest who continues as its chief executive.
    The purpose of Paulist films is to communicate human values with Gospel
relevance through use of the media. [All of the Paulist films communicate
values. However, they maintain two categories of films: those suitable for
public schools and those that may be used by religious schools. If you write for
their catalogues, be sure to specify which you are interested in.]
    The *Insight* series is seen on domestic and foreign television by over 100
million persons each year. We also supply films and videocassettes to
educators and clergy. We sell our film to religious media centers, as well as to
public schools and libraries.
    Paulist Productions has won numerous awards, including two Emmys.
    Additionally we offer a rental service to schools and churches through our
national distributor, Audience Planners, Inc.

Perspective Films (See **Coronet Films**)

Phoenix Films (BFA Educational Media)
    468 Park Avenue South
    New York, New York 10016

Nine years ago what is now Phoenix/BFA Films was an idea. It was created by two people, Barbara Bryant and Heinz Gelles, to create a "full service" distribution house with a high level of quality and service to both customers and producers. For eight years, in good times and not so good times, Phoenix continued to grow at an astonishing rate. A little over a year ago the company acquired BFA and is now one of the stronger companies in the field and continues its growth.

The integrity of both lists has been maintained so that customers can know exactly what to expect. Both divisions of the company are continuing to produce and acquire exceptional products. BFA continues its emphasis on quality curriculum film, and Phoenix continues its production and acquisition of the more open-ended, creative-type film.

Classics such as *Peege, Portrait of Grandpa Doc,* and *Mandy's Grandmother* are being joined by new productions like *A Boy, a Dog, and a Frog* and *Remarkable Riderless Tricycle,* etc.; from Phoenix, and an impressive list of new curriculum titles are joining the BFA list. The production schedule for 1983 is a full one and looks impressive indeed.

Pyramid Films (Pyramid Film & Video)
P.O. Box 1048
Santa Monica, California 90406
David Adams started Pyramid Films in 1960. Success with emergency medical films led to other subjects. Now ninety percent of its films come from other producers, many from other countries. The search for films of a certain level of cinematic quality has ensured the long life in distribution of many of the most popular films in the list of more than five hundred titles in current catalogues.

The short-film market continues to change through the years. There is no longer the dependence upon only school and library usage since films have become integrated into the media practices of corporations and government departments. Cable television is opening the short-film field to a wider public, sufficiently to occasion the change to the name: Pyramid Film & Video. And foreign film usage in the smaller countries and the Third World is increasing. Among the films in distribution are more than forty Academy Award nominations and winners. And the new films enter more than sixty festivals around the world each year.

Texture Films
P.O. Box 1337
Skokie, Illinois 60076   (312) 256-4436
Texture Film's Library consists of independent film and video productions that are exceptionally well crafted and fill the needs of one, or many, educational markets.

Our films range widely over varied subjects and are directed at age groups from preschool to adult.

Texture is famous for its classic children's films (*Anansi the Spider*), its health education films (*About Sex*), its specialized features (*Ulysses, Portrait of the Artist as a Young Man, The Quiet One*), and films of general interest (*Islam: The Prophet and the People*).

We both sell and rent.

Visucom Productions, Inc.

    P.O. Box 5472

    Redwood City, California 94063   (415) 364-5566

    Visucom Productions, which was founded in 1976, currently distributes over 70 titles in the following areas: highway safety (6); school bus driver and passenger training (10); industrial health and safety (5); management training (26); sales training (23); literature (1); and spouse abuse (1). With the exception of the management and sales training films, Visucom has been involved in the writing, producing, and directing of all its titles.

    Visucom's commitment is to change behavior by providing the viewer with high-quality visuals. Believing that most of today's viewers are highly sophisticated AV "freaks," we must offer films of the highest quality to achieve maximum viewer impact. The goal of most of our films is not only to impart information, but to actually change behavior.

    Visucom does not have a specific catalogue. Because of its variety of subjects, individual sheets describing the films are available. Previews are available for as long as 30 days if ordered by an organization with intent to purchase.

Wombat Productions, Inc.

    Little Lake

    Glendale Road

    P.O. Box 70

    Ossining, New York 10562   (914) 762-0011

    Since 1970, Wombat Productions has been providing films and video-cassettes that affirm human values and explore with insight the human condition. We attempt to reach people of all ages by selecting films that are honest — films that don't polarize, preach, or frighten. We strongly believe in the affective and emotional development of human beings and distribute films that reflect that belief in such areas as language arts, social studies, social issues, drug abuse education, family living, and the arts. Every Wombat title is available for preview/rental in 16-mm and for purchase in 16-mm as well as any video format. Feel free to call us with your requests and questions.

Appendix B
ADDRESSES OF OTHER DISTRIBUTORS

Barr Films
3490 East Foothill Blvd.
P.O. Box 5667
Pasadena, CA 91007

Beacon Films
1250 Washington St.
P.O. Box 575
Norwood, MA 02062

Best Films
P.O. Box 725
Del Mar, CA 92014

Brigham Young University
Audio Visual Services
290 HRCB
Provo, UT 84602

Britannica Films
425 North Michigan Ave.
Chicago, IL 60611

Carousel Films
1501 Broadway
New York, NY 10036

Cinema Five
1500 Broadway
New York, NY 10036

Films, Inc.
733 Green Bay Rd.
Wilmette, IL 60091

Film Wright
4540 18th St.
San Francisco, CA 94114

Green Mountain Post Films
P.O. Box 229
Turners Falls, MA 01376

Icarus Films/Cinema Perspectives
200 Park Ave. South
Suite 1319
New York, NY 10003

Little Red Filmhouse
666 North Robertson Blvd.
Los Angeles, CA 90069

MTI Teleprograms
3710 Commercial Ave.
Northbrook, IL 60062

Media Five
3211 Cahuenga Blvd. West
Hollywood, CA 90068

National Film Board of Canada
1251 Avenue of the Americas
New York, NY 10020

New Front Films
1309 Willow St.
Minneapolis, MN 55404

Teleketics
1229 South Santee
Los Angeles, CA 90015

Time-Life Video
1271 Avenue of the Americas
New York, NY 10020

United Artists
729 Seventh Ave.
New York, NY 10019

Appendix C
FILM RENTAL DEPARTMENTS OF COLLEGES AND UNIVERSITIES

Many of the films recommended in this book are also available, sometimes at a lower fee, through film rental departments of universities and colleges. Interested readers should call or write directly to these institutions and request a catalogue.

Arizona State University
Central Arizona Film Co-op
Audiovisual Center
Tempe, AZ 85287
(602) 965-5073

Boston University
Krasker Memorial Film Library
765 Commonwealth Ave.
Boston, MA 02215
(617) 353-3272

Brigham Young University
Educational Media Center
290 Herald R. Clark Building
Provo, UT 84602
(801) 374-1211, extension 3456

Central Washington University
Film Rental Center
Ellensburg, WA 98926
(509) 963-1221

Fitchburg State College
Massachusetts Film and Media
Service Co-op
Fitchburg, MA 01420
(617) 345-0166

Florida State University
Instructional Support Center
Film Library
Seminole Dining Hall
Tallahassee, FL 32306
(904) 644-2820

Indiana University
Audio Visual Center
Bloomington, IL 47405
(812) 337-2921

Iowa State University
Media Resource Center
121 Pearson Hall
Ames, IA 50011
(515) 294-1540

Kent State University
Audio Visual Services
330 Library Building
Kent, OH 44242
(216) 672-3456

Oklahoma State University
Audiovisual Center
Stillwater, OK 74074
(405) 624-7216

Pan American State University
Edinburg, TX 78539
(512) 381-3851

Pennsylvania State University at
  University Park
Audiovisual Services
Special Services Building
University Park, PA 16802
(814) 865-6315

Portland State University
Office of Continuing Education
1633 Southwest Park Ave.
Portland, OR 97207

Rhode Island College
Film Center
600 Mt. Pleasant Ave.
Providence, RI 02908
(401) 831-6600

Southern Illinois University
Learning Resources Services
Morris Library
Carbondale, IL 62901
(618) 453-2258

Syracuse University
Film Rental Center
1455 E. Colvin St.
Syracuse, NY 13210
(315) 479-6631

University of Arizona
Film Library
Media and Instructional Services
  Division
Audiovisual Building
Tucson, AZ 85721
(602) 626-3856

University of California
Extension Media Services
2223 Fulton St.
Berkeley, CA 94720
(415) 642-0460

University of Colorado
Educational Media Center
Folsom Stadium 364
Boulder, CO 80302
(303) 492-7341

University of Connecticut
University Center for Instruc-
  tional Media and Technology,
  U1
Storrs, CT 06268
(203) 486-2530

University of Georgia
Film Library
Georgia Center for Continuing
  Education
Athens, GA 30601
(404) 542-1184

University of Illinois
Visual Aids Services
1325 South Oak St.
Champaign, IL 61820
(217) 333-1360

University of Iowa
Audio Visual Center
C-5 East Hall
Iowa City, IA 52242
(319) 353-5885

University of Kansas
Audio Visual Center
746 Massachusetts St.
Lawrence, KS 66044
(913) 864-3352

University of Michigan
Audio Visual Education Center
416 Fourth St.
Ann Arbor, MI 48103
(313) 764-5360

University of Minnesota
Audio Visual Library Service
3300 University Ave., Southeast
Minneapolis, MN 55414
(612) 373-3810

University of Missouri
Film Rental Library
505 East Stewart Rd.
Columbia, MO 65201
(314) 882-3601

University of Nebraska
Instructional Media Center
421 Nebraska Hall
Lincoln, NE 68566
(402) 472-1011

University of Nevada
Film Library-Getchell Library
Attn: Ruth Hart
Reno, NV 89557
(702) 784-6037

University of New Hampshire
Department of Media Services
Diamond Library
Durham, NH 03824
(603) 862-2240

University of South Carolina
Film Library
Instructional Services Center
Columbia, SC 29208
(803) 777-2858

University of Southern California
Division of Cinema Film Library
University Park
Los Angeles, CA 90007
(213) 741-2238

University of South Florida
Film Library
4202 Fowler Ave.
Tampa, FL 33620
(813) 974-2874

University of Utah
Educational Media Center
207 Milton Bennion Hall
Salt Lake City, UT 84112
(801) 581-6112

University of Washington
Instructional Media Services
  DG10
Room 35D Kane Hall
Seattle, WA 98195
(206) 543-9909

University of Wisconsin
Bureau of Audio Visual
  Instruction
1327 University Ave.
Madison, WI 53706

Washington State University
Film Rental Center
Pullman, WA 99163
(509) 335-4535

Wayne State University
Center for Instructional
  Technology
77 West Canfield Ave.
Detroit, MI 48202
(313) 577-1980

Other Rental Sources

Viewfinders Inc.
Box 1665
Evanston, IL 60204

Index of Themes

MARITAL INSTABILITY

MARITAL INSTABILITY

A Social and Behavioral Study
of the Early Years

JOSEPH VEROFF,
ELIZABETH DOUVAN,
and SHIRLEY J. HATCHETT

PRAEGER

Westport, Connecticut
London

306.810973
V599m

Library of Congress Cataloging-in-Publication Data

Veroff, Joseph.
  Marital instability : a social and behavioral study of the early
years / Joseph Veroff, Elizabeth Douvan, and Shirley J. Hatchett.
       p.   cm.
  Includes bibliographical references and index.
  ISBN 0–275–95031–X (alk. paper)
  1. Marriage—United States—Longitudinal studies.   I. Douvan,
Elizabeth Ann Malcolm.   II. Hatchett, Shirley.
  III. Title.
  HQ536.V398   1995
  306.81'0973—dc20   94–42825

British Library Cataloguing in Publication Data is available.

Library of Congress Catalog Card Number: 94–42825
ISBN: 0–275–95031–X

First published in 1995

Praeger Publishers, 88 Post Road West, Westport, CT 06881
An imprint of Greenwood Publishing Group, Inc.

Printed in the United States of America

The paper used in this book complies with the
Permanent Paper Standard issued by the National
Information Standards Organization (Z39.48–1984).

10 9 8 7 6 5 4 3 2 1

CONTENTS

FIGURES AND TABLES

PREFACE

In conducting research on the quality of life of the American population, time and again we came to the conclusion that for most adults the cornerstone of a solidly constructed satisfying life free from overwhelming tensions is a happy and stable marriage.

With this observation we were eager to do a prospective study of marriage—what makes for commitment, stability, and happiness in married couples. A grant from the National Institute of Mental Health (MH 41253) enabled us to follow up this wish. The grant underwrote a collection of data from newlyweds right after they were married and for three successive years thereafter. The Early Years of Marriage study was launched.

The results reported in this book are based on this study. In multiple ways we examine the determinants of marital stability over the four years. This is a data-saturated book, meant for scholars and researchers who are interested in marriage or close relationships generally. The data are especially complex, since we, like Jesse Bernard, feel there is a his and her marriage, and black couples and white couples hold very different expectations for how marriage scripts should be played out. Men and women's reactions and commitments to marriage are not the same, just as men and women differ in many other aspects of life. Black couples interpret their marital experiences in the context of their social worlds, their communities and kin, their economic situations—all within a backdrop of institutional racism. White couples also interpret their experiences contextually, but they are bound to be different from the black context. As a result we have to present results separately for blacks and whites and separately for men and women. This does not make easy reading for the lay person, but we hope we have highlighted enough of the meaning of the results so that the complexity does not overwhelm the reader who is less well-versed in the details of multivariate statistical analyses.

Data gathering and data analyses for this study were not simple. We needed the help of a large group of interviewers and coders and their supervisors, as well as a large staff of researchers and research assistants. Clerical work, typing, and table construction all demand collaborative effort. For these various steps we are especially indebted to: Linda Acitelli, Hiroko Akiyama, Toni Antonucci, Zoanne Blackburn, Letha Chadiha, Elizabeth Chase, Sue Crohan, Kay Davis, Kelly Everding, Diane Holmberg, Halimah Hassan, Donna Henderson-King, Heather Hewitt, Doug Leber, Ruth Lenchek, Janet Malley, Bruce Medbury, Dina Moreno, Jean Oggins, Terri Orbuch, Robert Ortega, Joan Peebles, Ann Ruvolo, John Siebs, Abby Stewart, Lynn Sutherland, Lawrence Thompson, Jackie Thornsby, Jody Veroff, and Monica Wolfert.

We want especially to acknowledge the 373 couples who agreed to offer their married lives up for study. This is a brave act, not well compensated by the respondent payments we offered for participation. This book is dedicated to them.

1

INTRODUCTION

No matter how threadbare their public and private lives are, most people in the United States are still confident that a fulfilling life comes from formal connections to the significant people in their lives. Even while policy makers and religious leaders bemoan the demise of marriage and family values, men and women still take marriage vows in large numbers. Dire statistics predict that most marriages begun now, as we approach the end of the twentieth century, will end in divorce. However, this does not stem the tide of men and women engaging in this most basic of social institutions. Do they think they will beat the odds? Or is this form of intimacy so fulfilling that they don't even think in those terms? Just having such a relationship may be so basic to their sense of well-being that getting married is worth the risk. Regardless of the reasoning behind this behavior, it is clear that in this ever changing world such relationships have become very fragile.

But then being married has never been an easy task. Two individual lives have to be forged into a satisfying and functional unit. Perhaps in earlier times, when the implicit and explicit rules governing marriage were clearer, husbands and wives had an easier time of it. During the Victorian era, middle class mores began to emphasize the importance of motherhood as the critical role for women. They were supposed to stay out of the work force and be subservient to their husbands who held positions as breadwinners. This structure enforced certain ways of being in a marriage that made the transition to being a couple less ambiguous for men and women. Similarly, more traditional societies than ours gave newlywed couples clearer boundaries for their feelings and behaviors.

These days, life is not so simple. Gender roles have become ambiguous. Social movements of the twentieth century as well as post-industrial economic

transition have dictated new normative and organizational family structures. Adaptation to the modern and post-modern world has changed but not destroyed family values. Women now work as well as raise children. Men are being pressured to participate more equally in parenthood and in household chores in addition to their jobs. The expansion of women's public sphere has made a complementary expansion of men's private sphere imperative. Who does what, and when, and how important it is, were rarely questioned before. Now, what we once took for granted is being illuminated and energized by visions of new possible lives and worlds.

An increasing emphasis on individual expression, finding one's self, and changing over the life span to meet one's potential, which began among a few devotees of the potential movement at mid-century, is fast becoming the norm for men and women. These views have filtered into the value systems of the majority of young Americans and, as a result, are now persistent concerns among couples. Under these conditions, "being a couple" is an ever changing elusive phenomenon. The fact that any couple attempts and succeeds at forging a stable and mutually gratifying relationship must be looked upon as the exceptional miracle. How do they do it? Why do some marriages persist while others fail?

The answers to these questions are bound to be complex. Every couple is made up of a man and woman who are different from any other man and woman. And yet there must be some regularities, some ways that couples come together even with idiosyncratic histories and varying expectations. And, these regularities must foster functional relationships. They must have something to do with the way that couples in good marriages interact with each other, think about each other, and generally approach their lives together as workers, parents, and lovers. This book is a search for such regularities. We do this in a study of 373 couples interviewed first in 1986, a few months after their marriage. During the next three years, we annually tapped into their lives as couples and as individuals. By the end of the fourth year, we knew which marriages had failed or appeared to be failing. Our quest has been to find out why. Thus, this book is a systematic examination of factors that are involved in understanding successes and failures in marriages. We have done this in a longitudinal study of a relatively representative sample of urban couples in their first marriages.

Since this is not the first time that researchers have tried to find the equilibrium of marital success, we are able to build on other studies. Beginning with Raush, Barry, Hertel, and Swain's (1974) examination of the role of communicating affective messages in various conflict styles in the transition to marriage, there have been a number of longitudinal studies analyzing the early years of marriage. Each had different emphases. Although Raush et al. (1974) started with the simple idea that the more open a couple is about communicating feelings in marriage when conflicts arise the happier

the marriage would be, they ended with a more conditional view. They found that marital harmony in the early years depended on compatibility of communication orientation. Cowan and Cowan (1992), guided by a family systems perspective, looked at young couples over time through the transition to parenthood and asked how that transition affects individual spouses who have divergent goals. A third set of studies has come out of the longitudinal analyses of Huston and his colleagues (Huston, McHale, & Crouter, 1985; MacDermid, Huston, & McHale, 1990) who have studied the transition to marriage and parenthood. Their emphasis has been on relatively direct measures of couples' activities both individually and together. They find that over the early years there are changes in a couple's activities and that these are correlated with the ebbs and flows of marital well-being.

One other longitudinal study of early marriage is noteworthy. Kurdek (1989, 1991), like Huston's group, gathered a sample of couples from marriage licenses and obtained written responses to a variety of questionnaires. Kurdek emphasizes individual differences in a set of various orientations: loving, liking, trust, quality, social support, instrumentality, and expressiveness. Kurdek finds that some of these individual differences have far more effect on marital quality than demographic factors have. Although Johnson, Amoloza, and Booth's (1992) longitudinal study of marriage covered a similarly wide range of marital qualities, their study does not focus exclusively on the early years.

With these studies as backdrop, we entered our study with multiple options for considering factors that might affect marital instability and how to assess these factors. We borrowed from these studies and others that were either not longitudinal or were focussed on individual spouses rather than on couples. The uniqueness of our efforts lies in an attempt to extend these borrowed efforts to a systematic analysis of early marriage among black couples as well as white couples. Most studies have focussed on white respondents who were often highly educated. Our study will be more representative of the urban population in general. Furthermore, by borrowing from others and creating some assessments of our own, our study will be especially comprehensive. We will cover many different types of factors of marital experience as well as assessment orientations to measure these factors.

Most important in our work will be the distinction we make between stability in marriage and well-being. A number of relationship theorists (e.g., Kelley, 1983) and marriage theorists (e.g., Cuber & Harroff, 1965) wisely point out that to be committed to a stable marriage does not necessarily mean that marriage is particularly gratifying or vital. This book will deal with one way of defining success—whether a marriage is lasting (stability) as opposed to whether a marriage is particularly happy (well-being). We will use other measures of marital well-being to help understand the bases of stability.

We will devote chapters in this book to different sets of factors that might

be critical in understanding how the marriages have fared. We will consider each set of factors by itself and then in connection with other factors. For example, there will be a chapter devoted to interaction, ways in which couples interact that may be helpful in understanding failures in marriage (Chapter 3). In this chapter we will enumerate the interactive factors we observed, indicate how we measured them, what we expect about them given the literature available on the topic, and what the predictive power of each is in the context of all measures of interaction. We will especially highlight those predictors that are significant in regression analyses. In each chapter we will also present data to show how significant interactive factors compare with other predictors that had been considered significant. By this last procedure, we are recognizing that factors like interaction are also related to other factors that are being considered. For example, it seems quite clear that marital interaction is interrelated with personality factors, which we will investigate. Interaction may be a function of the personality styles of individual partners. We will analyze the data to detect whether there is some connection of personality to the kinds of interaction that lead to the stability and well-being in marriages. Thus, we can begin to plot a general causal sequence for how factors are related to each other and which ones stand out on their own in predicting marital stability.

A Conceptual Framework for Thinking About Marital Stability

Over the four years of the study we asked couples a large array of questions about themselves and their marriages. Each year of questioning could be seen as an assessment of additional factors in the dynamic processes that ultimately affect a marriage. Even the exact questions asked in Year 1 and Year 2 of the study could be reflecting different phenomena that capture the experience of the couples in the different preceding years. Thus, the longitudinal nature of the data collection permits some degree of organization of the causal chain to be considered. Some of the same factors will reappear in different years.

Beyond this, what causal picture do we have of regularly appearing factors that affect marital stability and well-being? These are listed schematically in Figure 1.1. There are five types from the analysis of the first year of marriage: premarital factors, personal factors at the time of marriage, interpersonal marital factors describing multiple kinds of experiences that couples have during their first year of marriage, external stresses, and summary marital feelings that integrate the composite of factors. For subsequent years assessments of some of these factors will be repeated, so that we will be able to gauge how much more information we gain from considering these factors at later times in the marriage. In addition, certain assessments were added to each of the factors in subsequent years, so that we might know about a given

Figure 1.1
General Framework for Considering Factors Affecting Marital
Well-Being and Stability

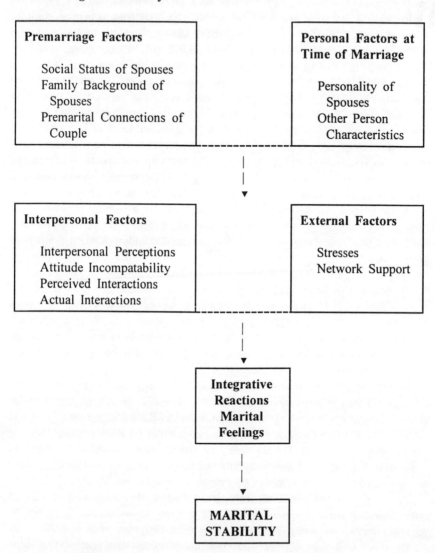

factor in just one of the years.

We will not go into each of the factors in detail at this point. Subsequent chapters will be explicit about how these factors will be assessed and the

rationale for including them. Nevertheless, we should spell out the general framework we are using in thinking about the interconnections of these multiple factors. This was a framework first developed in Hatchett, Veroff, and Douvan (in press), but we are making it more extensive in this book. As presented in Figure 1.1, we see three levels of antecedents to marital stability and well-being. First, there are <u>premarital factors</u>. Among these, we see as critical: the social status of the partners, their family backgrounds, and their own premarital history as a couple. We see these premarital factors as interacting with another type of factor that at a causal level has to be considered as prior to the marriage itself, that is the personality and other personal factors of the spouses as individuals (e.g., religion). Together these provide the antecedents of what goes on in the marriage.

At the next level are the <u>marital factors</u> which include both interpersonal factors (perceptions, attitudes, and actual interactions as they affect the interpersonal environment of the couple) as well as external factors (stresses and experiences as well as support they receive from their network). Finally at the third level, we see the qualitative sense that the couple makes of their life together—<u>marital integrative feelings</u> which can be both specific and general. We assume this chain of three levels underlies the stability or instability of a marriage.

To illustrate these ideas further, we have listed in Figure 1.2 assessments we have made for each of these factors in Year 1 of the study. We will not discuss the specifics of the assessments here, but the list will give the reader some sense of the intended nature of the somewhat abstract concepts introduced in Figure 1.1. We will give more details about each of the assessments and each of the factors as we systematically consider them in the chapters to come.

Since this is a longitudinal study, marital factors and marital integrative feelings constantly interweave over time. Feelings in one year set the stage for the marital factors in the next which in turn affect the feelings in that year and so on. We would be hard-pressed to depict the exact causal linkages, but we are willing to state that feelings are integrative of other marital factors, and these in turn set the tone for the next stage in the couple's development. This overall conception is schematically represented in Figure 1.3.

The multitude of potential factors revealed in this scheme portends an overwhelming sorting task for us and the reader. However, we hope by the analyses we adopt to simplify that task in three different ways.

First, we will highlight only factors that work as statistically significant predictors and not dwell on those that do not. Of course, if the non-significant findings are theoretically surprising or inconsistent with previous results we will discuss them, but otherwise they will be ignored.

Second, the regression analyses that will be used will enable us to detect redundancy in concepts and the ways that factors measured at one level of

Figure 1.2
Factors Affecting Marital Instability Assessed in the First Year of Marriage

YEAR 1

Premarriage
Factors

Social Status Situation

•Father's education
•Mother's education
•Own education
•Personal income
Discrepency in Educational
    attainment
       (Husb/Wife)
Poverty ratio
Race

Family Background
•Broken home background •Number of siblings •Presence of older sibs

Premarital Situation
•Cohabitation •Premarital pregnancy/child •Length of time as couple

Personal Factors

Personality
•Zest vs. depression •Neuroticism •Ambitiousness •Power orientation •Cooperativeness

Figure 1.2
(continued)

Other Personal Factors

•Attractiveness
•Age
•Being Catholic
•Church attendance
•Alcohol problem

Marital Factors:
Cognitions

Interpersonal Perceptions

•Perceived similarity re: sex life
•Perceived similarity re:
    conflict reactions
•Understanding other re:
    sex life
•Understanding other re:
    conflict reaction

Attitudinal Incompatability

Educational discrepancy
Incomparability re:
    •importance of religion
    •attitudes towards
     conflict
    •ideal pace of life
    •openness to new
     experience
    •sex roles
    •rules for ideal
     marriage

8

Figure 1.2 (continued)

Marital Factors:
Interactions

> **Perceived Interactions As Couple**
>
> - Shared time
> - Relaxed time
> - Positive sex
> - Negative sex
> - Frequency of conflict
> - Range of disagreement
> - Husband's power

> **Perceived Interactions As Individuals**
>
> - Spouse not easy to talk to
> - Disclosing communication
> - Affective affirmation
> - Destructive conflict reaction
> - Constructive conflict reaction
> - Avoidant conflict reaction

> **Actual Interaction**
>
> - Degree of husband influence
> - Collaborative style
> - Confirming style
> - Collaborative\Confirming style
> - Conflictual style

External Factors

> **Stresses**
>
> - Worry about money
> - Job interfering with marriage
> - Job dissatisfaction

Figure 1.2
(continued)

Network

Support of families
Support of friends
Closeness to families

Integrative Factors

Marital Feelings

•Marital happiness
•Marital competence
•Marital control
•Marital equity
•Marital tension
•Concern with relational affects

•Measured separately for each spouse

Figure 1.3
General Framework for Factors Affecting Marital Instability

Year 1 Year 2 Year 3 Year 4

Premarriage Factors
\
Marital Factors
\
Integrative Factors
\
Marital Factors
\
Integrative Factors
\
Marital Factors
\
Integrative Factors
\
Marital Factors
\
Integrative Factors

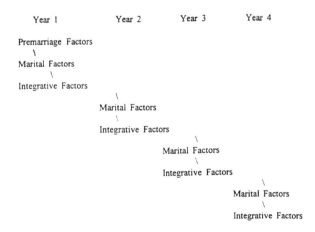

analysis are embedded in variables at another level of analysis. For example, we will be measuring income as a determinant of marital stability. If low income couples are more prone to fight (perhaps instigated by their financial situation), then we can plot the connection between income and fighting on marital stability and see the way that these two levels of analysis form a unified picture of marital stability rather than two separate sources. Third, to the extent that we will be adding comparable variables from successive years of the first four years of marriage, we will add new variables from these successive years to the predictive chain only when they represent changes in predictive power. If the experience of marital competence as measured in Years 1, 2, 3, and 4 predict marital stability, we will highlight only the Year 1 measure if Years 2, 3, and 4 are very much related to Year 1. If a change in the experience of marital competence at a subsequent year adds to the prediction of instability, we will of course note that.

THE STUDY

In 1986, the Wayne County (Michigan) Clerk's Office agreed to cooperate with our research team in listing couples who applied for marriage licenses during a set period of time (April–June). Critical to the study was the potential for parallel investigations of black couples and white couples. Wayne County is a primarily urban county with metropolitan Detroit as its core and surrounding small city satellites adjoining. There is a large concentration of blacks in Detroit and its vicinity. As a result, it was an excellent opportunity to initiate a systematic longitudinal study of black marriages in tandem with a study of white marriages. A random sample of white couples applying for marriage licenses and a complete census of black applicants were sent a letter from the Survey Research Center (see Appendix p. 188) announcing that they had been chosen to participate in the study. Few other specifics were given beyond suggesting that it was important to know about marriage, given the rising number of divorces.

There were three limitations we set for the sample. Each member of the couple had to be in a first marriage. It was not that we found remarriages uninteresting. Quite the contrary. But we did want to disregard the particular complexities that remarriages entail, given that we would have a somewhat small sample to begin with. The same reasoning went into our second limitation for the sample. We only selected couples in which the wife to be was thirty-five years of age or younger. We wanted issues about having children to be part of the picture for the couples. Although we were tempted to limit the sample to couples without children, a pretest questionnaire revealed that a large proportion of couples enter first marriages with a child of one or both spouses. Since it was so prevalent, we decided we needed to have

premarital parenthood/pregnancy as part of the study if we wished to get an
adequate picture of first marriages in modern urban society. The third
limitation was to exclude interracial couples. We wanted our analysis not to
be burdened by the complexity of these marriages.

Three hundred seventeen white and 377 black couples were designated as
the sample.[1] Interviewers followed the Survey Research Center's general
tracking policy to enlist cooperation. Couples were offered $25 for
participating in the first year. For this study we matched interviewers with
couples with respect to race. At the County Clerk's office, we had couples fill
out a screening form which included race. If they failed to do this, the clerks
checked the appropriate racial designation. Race was not listed on the
marriage license itself. For the initial interviewing 199 black and 174 white
couples participated, the rate of response being 65% (66% white; 65% black),
with 22% active refusals to participate, and 13% who were not located or
otherwise not interviewed. We find this an acceptable response rate since two
members had to agree to participate for interviews not only for 1986 but for
subsequent years as well. We interpret the 65% response rate for couples as
approximately an 80% response rate for individual spouses. Based on other
studies of response rate (DeMaio, 1980; Hawkins, 1975) we have to recognize
that we perhaps undersampled some middle income couples and couples who
are particularly suspicious. The race matching of interviewer with couple was
undoubtedly critical in our attaining such a relatively high response rate from
black couples.

Interviewers were part of the regular trained interviewing staff of the
Survey Research Center. All interviewers were women, varying in age but
generally middle-aged. There were a few more interviewers in their twenties
on the telephone staff than on the field staff. Following the Survey Research
Center standard procedures, interviewers were given particular respondents to
interview. Different interviewers were assigned the Spouse Interview and the
Couple Interview, which we will describe below. Interviewers were carefully
trained on the study, given a study guide, and then were required to pretest
some interviews with study staff feedback. The study guide gives detailed
ways of handling various exigencies or questions asked by respondents. In the
first year, each spouse was interviewed separately on what we will designate
as the Spouse Interview. This interview lasted on the average ninety minutes
and covered a wide range of topics. In addition, there was a Couple Interview
in which the husband and wife were interviewed together. Eight percent of
black couples and 2% of white couples were not interviewed together on the
Couple Interview, primarily because of scheduling difficulties. The Couple
Interview included two different procedures: one asked the couple to tell a
relatively spontaneous story of their relationship from its inception to the
present and future (see Veroff, Sutherland, Chadiha, & Ortega, 1993, for
details); another was a procedure in the which couples reconciled their

differences on a set of attitudes about rules for marriage. Both procedures were tape-recorded. This book will draw on data from both the Spouse and the Couple Interviews but rely more heavily on the Spouse Interview.

In the second year, all couples who participated in the first year were recontacted by phone and given a short telephone interview[2] that covered the spouses' evaluations of their marital well-being as well as stresses and interferences they had experienced over the year.

The procedure for the third year repeated the procedure for the first with each spouse individually interviewed, and the couple interviewed together for another narrative and another rules for marriage procedure. Couples were again given $25 for participating. Most of the questions repeat what was asked in earlier years. If a couple had indicated in a prior year that they were divorced or separated, they were not recontacted in the third or fourth year.

The fourth year was again a telephone interview of each spouse. Again there were a few new questions asked, but by and large questions asked in Year 4 repeated prior questions. If the couple had indicated in Year 3 that they were divorced or separated, they were not recontacted in Year 4.

Aside from the procedures used in the Couple Interview, coding was done by the Survey Research Center's professional coding staff. Open-ended questions were carefully checked for coding reliability by the study staff. The Couple Interview had procedures that required unusual coding. Graduate students were trained to use specific coding schemes for the couples' narrative data. Agreement of 80% between a coder and the professional staff person was established as the minimum standard (for details, see Veroff, Sutherland, Chadiha, & Ortega, 1993). Each year couples were sent anniversary cards along with some information about the results of the study and a tracking postcard to be returned if their address or status had changed since we last were in touch with them. The feedback reports were straightforward presentation of largely demographic data (e.g., how many have children) to minimize effects in subsequent interviews. After the fourth year, the anniversary card presented a more detailed and thoughtful account of major results.

The attrition rates from the original sample appear in Table 1.1. There was attrition due to divorce or separation, attrition due to refusals to participate in Years 2, 3, or 4, and attrition due to couples not being located or not being available. These are all differentiated in the table. For whites, the overall attrition is surprisingly low—only 23% from Year 1 to Year 4. However, for blacks, attrition was a more serious problem—55% from Year 1 to Year 4. Blacks divorce at a higher rate than whites (21% of the original set of black couples compared to only 8% of the white couples) which accounts for some of the differential attrition in blacks compared to whites. Nevertheless, it does not account for all of it. By Year 4 we had lost 15% of the white respondents who, for reasons other than known divorce or separation, we could not

interview; for black respondents, the same figure was 34%. Tracking blacks was considerably more difficult, many leaving without a way to trace them, but many also clearly resisted being interviewed by breaking appointments and generally making it difficult to set up a time for an interview. We would suggest that this differential was partially a function of the greater difficulty that black couples were facing in their marriages. Resistance to being interviewed often comes from couples who are having considerable difficulty.[3] We thus think that we have a somewhat attenuated sample of marriages by Year 4, especially among black couples. These will likely be marriages in reasonably good condition, with more foundering ones having decided not to participate. This makes our search for relationships between marital factors and stability somewhat more difficult, since we assume that some of the extremely distressed couples are not part of the continuing sample. Results that are significant perhaps should be considered even more robust than they appear, given this problem of attenuation.

Table 1.1
Response and Attrition Rates by Year

Number of Respondents Interviewed	Percent Responded	Percent Refused	Percent Not Located	Cumulative Attrition	Number Divorced/ Ineligible Sample
YEAR 1					
1148	65%	22%	13%	—	—
YEAR 2					
746	93%	3%	4%	9%	(34)
YEAR 3					
681	85%	8%	7%	25%	(56)
YEAR 4					
559	90%	5%	5%	34%	(24)

*This figure represents doubling of the number of couples who are involved in a divorce during the prior year in order to get the number of individuals who are in that status. In some instances a divorced or separated individual has been interviewed; in other instances, they have not. These individuals whether interviewed or not were not part of the eligible sample for the subsequent year, and hence are computed into the attrition rate for the next year.

Profile of the Sample When First Married

Table 1.2 presents descriptive information about the sample in 1986 when couples were first interviewed. Socioeconomic and demographic

characteristics of black couples and white couples are presented separately to call attention to ways they may differ. On average, the couples were in their mid-twenties, had attained educational levels beyond the high school degree and beyond the educational level of their parents. White husbands were more highly educated than black husbands. This is reflected in their work. Many more white husbands are in professional, managerial, or sales occupations while many more black husbands are in service occupations. Practically all the men are employed, and the majority of the women are. More black women consider themselves unemployed, and surprisingly 16% of the black wives and 18% of the white wives consider themselves homemakers. White couples have much higher household incomes. Nevertheless, it is clear, looking at the socioeconomic data, that the sample covers a spectrum of statuses and is not limited to the college educated professional groups that often dominate samples of research on marriage. None of the socioeconomic distributions in this sample would lead us to believe that we had a limited sample in this regard, but there are no data available from census information which would allow us to test whether the sample is different from urban newlyweds in general. Many of the couples lived together for some period before marriage, the black couples (66%) more than the white couples (41%). Related to that is the fact that 55% of the black couples and 22% of the white couples entered their first marriages as parents. This may explain why such a large proportion of these newlyweds consider themselves homemakers.

One final fact in Table 1.2 is that a much larger percentage of the white couples compared to black couples grew up with both parents in their household. This should be remembered as we approach the study of instability of marriages in this next generation.

ANALYSIS PLAN

In each subsequent chapter, we will consider a different set of predictors by themselves and then coordinately with other sets of predictors. In addition, for each set of factors we present analyses telling us whether predictors operate differently for black couples and white couples. Although initially we will rely on multiple regression analyses for the total group, we will later conduct these analyses separately for black and white couples. We will combine across sets of factors by selecting significant predictors from each set and building other regression analyses. We will thus use successive regression analyses to isolate the critical set of factors that help us understand sources of marital instability. Hierarchical regression analyses will be used to the extent that the factors are at theoretically different time points in the causal process. For example, in the first year there will be three levels of predictors analyzed

Table 1.2
First Year Socioeconomic and Demographic Characteristics of Black and White Couples

	Blacks			Whites		
	Husbands	Wives	Couple	Husbands	Wives	Couple
Mean Age	27.3	24.8		25.6	24.0	
Mean Age Difference			2.4			1.6
Mean Education Difference			−0.3			0.3
Mean Father's Education	11.2	11.2		11.8	12.1	
Mean Mother's Education	11.9	12.3		11.8	11.9	
Mean Number of Months Cohabited Before Marriage			14.7			6.9
Cohabitation						
No			59%			34%
Yes			41%			66%
Employment Status						
Working	90%	63%		93%	72%	
Laid Off	3	2		3	1	
Unemployed	5	16		3	1	
Homemaker	—	16		—	18	
Student	1	3		—	—	
Other	1	1		—	—	
	100%	100%		100%	100%	
Both Work			56%			65%
Combined Income						
$0 – $9,999			16%			2%
$10,000 – $19,999			21			14
$20,000 – $29,000			25			21
$30,000 – $39,000			16			25
$40,000 – $49,000			11			19
$50,000 +			11			19
			100%			100%

Table 1.2 (continued)

	Blacks			Whites		
	Husbands	Wives	Couple	Husbands	Wives	Couple
Occupation						
Professional/Technical	11%	10%		20%	16%	
Managerial	6	5		11	5	
Sales	2	2		5	4	
Clerical	8	32		6	33	
Crafts	15	1		23	1	
Operatives	21	0		22	2	
Laborers	6	0		3	0	
Farmers	0	0		0	0	
Service	21	14		8	11	
(Not working, missing data)	10	36		3	29	
	100%	100%		100%	100%	
Parental Status						
No children			45%			78%
All by spouse			27			17
Some by someone else			28			5
			100%			100%
Number of Children						
One			58%			82%
Two			26			18
Three or more			16			—
			100%			100%
Grew up with Both Parents	50%	41%		80%	71%	

hierarchically: the first level, premarital factors; the second, marital factors; and the third, integrative feelings. Successive levels will be added from the second, third, and fourth year assessments. Integrative sections in each chapter will bring together the set of predictors most prominent overall from these successive hierarchical analyses. The final chapter will offer the best model from the data for understanding the cumulative predictability of marital instability. How these overall models may differ for black and white couples will be highlighted as we move along.

In a certain sense, this is a highly empirical procedure. We are filtering out those assessments that work in prediction equations. It is a highly inductive approach, one that will help us integrate the clearest factors affecting the first years of marriage. For simplicity, we will be downplaying factors and assessments that do not significantly predict instability or marital quality. We will attend to these only when they are dramatically different from expectations or other patterns of findings. Nevertheless, we realize that these negative results are useful for theorists of marriage and interpersonal relationships.

While there is some arbitrariness to this procedure, we were generally guided by the order of variables outlined in the framework above. More than that we were guided by other researchers' previous results and thinking in that we included many of their measures in our battery. As we designed this study, we decided to put together an eclectic array of predictors without any overarching grand theory of marital relationships.

If we were to select one conceptual view as a major guide for our predictive study, it would be the one developed in Oggins, Veroff, and Leber (1993), and Veroff, Douvan, and Hatchett (1993), that focuses on the process of affective affirmation. We simply suggest that to have a good marriage each individual has to be affectively affirmed by the other. A wife has to feel that her husband makes her feel that she is a lovable person; the husband has to feel that his wife cares for him and the kind of person he is. However, simple as it sounds, it is a complex affective communication that occurs subtly in the way two people look at each other, talk to one another, and treat each other in the heat of conflict or sexual embrace. As a result, many different factors may contribute to the process, and many different factors can be affected by the process. The self is strengthened in relationship; the individual feels strong in communion. Although dynamic dialectical tension is hard to measure directly, we think it underlies marital fulfillment; therefore, we suggest that it will play a pivotal role in understanding the layers of regression analyses that we present.

Measuring Marital Instability

While there were many couples from the original sample who separated or

divorced (fifty-seven), there were undoubtedly some, who in spite of being in relatively unstable marriages, remained together. In order to tap the full range of instability in that sense, we took advantage of a single item asked in each year of the study, one developed from the work of Booth, Johnson, and Edwards (1983). Booth et al. suggested people should be asked directly about stability and instability. Their item asked whether the person had any thoughts about leaving: "In the last few months, how often have you considered leaving your wife/husband? often, sometimes, rarely or never." Therefore, using the fourth wave of data collection, we constructed an instability measure based on this item and whether or not the couple was actually divorced or separated. The scale appears below:

5=Divorced/separated at any point during the study

4=Husband and/or wife answers "often" to thoughts of leaving question

3=Neither answers "often" but husband and/or wife answers "sometimes" to thoughts of leaving question

2=Neither answers "often" or "sometimes," but husband and/or wife answers "rarely" to thoughts of leaving question

1=Neither answers "often," "sometimes," "rarely," but husband and/or wife answer "never" to thoughts of leaving question

In this scale, the couple is assigned the more unstable response if the husband and wife disagree with the logic that the marriage is as unstable as the more unstable member feels. If we had an interview with only one respondent, we accepted that person's answer as describing the couple's instability. If there were missing interviews from a couple in Year 4, and we had their responses in Year 3, we used third year assessments from the thoughts of leaving

Table 1.3
Distribution of the Index of Marital Instability of Couples

	Score*	Percent
5	Separated/Divorced	19%
4	One or both spouses say they "often" thought of leaving	4%
2	One or both spouses say they "rarely" thought of leaving	17%
1	One or both spouses say they "never" thought of leaving	53%

*Couple is assigned highest applicable score. If neither spouse was interviewed in Years 2 and/or 3, and the couple was not known to have divorced or separated, then the couple was coded as Not Ascertained on this scale. Fifty-two couples were considered Not Ascertained.

question to measure that couple's instability. Table 1.3 below presents the distribution of the measure of instability. It should be noted that while there are 19% who are in the extreme instability category of having been divorced or separated, 53% of the couples are at the opposite extreme (highly stable), having said they have never thought about leaving the relationship.

SUMMARY

Introducing a study on the early years of marriage and their effects on marital instability, we described the procedures used in gathering the sample of newlyweds who will be the focus of the inquiry and the kinds of data that will go into the analyses from annual interviews with the couples over their first four years of married life. Important to the analyses will be a measure of instability that accounts not only for actual divorce or separation but also for how much thought the couple has given to leaving the marriage. The analysis strategy to be followed will call for examining each year's data separately and within each year looking at sets of predictors that reflect common theoretical issues. The strongest predictors for each set and year will be sifted out as a way of identifying critical factors that comprise the dynamics affecting marital instability. Parallel analyses will be run for the white couples and black couples since early in our analyses we discovered that quite different findings emerged for white couples compared to black couples. The analysis and results will promote a contextual approach to understanding marital instability.

Enough by way of introduction. Let us move on to the results.

NOTES

1. In addition to the couples chosen for the study sample, we selected forty-five white couples and forty-five black couples to serve as a control sample. These couples were contacted in the first year but were never given the full interview. They were contacted again in Year 4 and compared to couples who had participated throughout the study. In this way we were able to assess the effect that participation had on the study couples. This research appears in Veroff, Hatchett, and Douvan (1992) and shows that while there was a trend for some negative consequences of participation in the early part of the study, by the fourth year there seemed to be positive consequences for the relationship for the couples who did participate.

2. Half of the black couples were interviewed face-to-face as part of the methodological investigation of differences between face-to-face and telephone interviewing on the distribution of responses among blacks, given that face-to-face interviewing identifies race matching but the telephone interviewing does not. In fact, there was little race matching for the telephone interviewing. No significant differences between the two groups in response distributions were evident.

3. An analysis of those respondents who in Years 2, 3, and 4 were not interviewed or refused to be interviewed indicated that they, compared to those who did consent to being interviewed, were more likely to be among those respondents who said they were in unhappy marriages in the prior year of contact (Veroff, Hatchett, & Douvan, 1992).

2

PREMARITAL FACTORS IN MARITAL INSTABILITY

The new trends in modern relationships and marriages have made formal and informal premarital counselling play a larger role in the helping and pastoral professions. The goal of such counseling has been to screen couples who are clearly mismatched to avoid the painful process of later separation and/or divorce. Because it does not sanction divorce, the Catholic Church has long provided this service to its members. Other denominations appear to be following this practice in less formal ways. Such counselling usually emphasizes religion's role in marriage and values that should be expressed in the marriage bond. Issues of compatibility between the prospective spouses along these lines may also be addressed. Still, most modern couples are not exposed to this type of premarital reflection and evaluation. In light of the current cultural confusion about the nature of families and relationships, some form of guidance seems imperative to help couples make what might the most important decision in their lives.

Do we know enough about marriage to address this need? What are the critical passages that couples must negotiate in the first years of marriage? Knowledge of the issues raised in these early years could help couples assess their readiness for marriage as well as prepare them for what follows as they progress through the family life cycle. Couples could then preview marriage—what life will be like and what sacrifices have to be made. We undertook the research described in this book to provide a basis for the development of such guidelines. The usefulness of these guidelines will depend upon whether or not they have direct meaning for couples' lives. This can be accomplished by relying on what really happens as two individuals attempt to adjust to life as a couple instead of religious or popular visions of

what married life should be.   To this end, a prospective research design seemed most appropriate. We wanted to tap into the perceptions and feelings of each spouse as various life events unfolded. Overall, we wanted to find the ingredients for marital well-being and stability as revealed by black and white couples in a changing and complex urban environment.

This chapter will address the issues faced by couples which may derive from their particular and unique histories as individuals and as a couple prior to marriage. We have delineated five sets of what we see as premarital factors affecting   marital   stability.   They   are: social   status   of   each   spouse, characteristics of their families of origin, premarital experiences and cohabitation, and personality traits and other personal characteristics of each spouse. We will consider each of these in turn.

Social Status Factors

How much is one's success in marriage conditioned by one's success in the world at large prior to marriage? Most of us harbor some romantic notions about couples in love disregarding differences and overcoming economic adversity. Such notions are based on the myth that people can survive on love and passion alone. However, in the real rather than fictive world, these things do matter. We live in a world of competition for life's valued and scarce resources—wealth, power, and prestige. There are "haves" and there are "have nots." To be a "have not" engenders comparison and feelings of relative deprivation. Husbands and wives have better or worse jobs, make more or less money, can afford to live in better or worse housing, and can consume more or less of the goods of society for themselves and their children depending on their social status origins and their current social positions. In World of Pain (1976), Lillian Rubin documents how working class marriages founder on the economic deprivations couples feel, on the lack of dignity husbands feel about their low-status work, on the overload and lack of leisure that wives feel when they need to work to make ends meet. Such feelings can emerge from having been and/or continuing to be in lower status positions in a society that generally values success and upward mobility. There is much more that goes into a marriage than economic security, and there are perhaps as many lower status marriages that are solid and stable as there are those that have difficulties.   Yet couples from such backgrounds should be aware of the financial burdens of marriage.   The best counsel might be for them to recognize the inherent obstacles and to know what is in store, so that they are not automatically set up for the experience of dashed expectations in marriage.

How do we assess a person or a couple's social status? We use such indicators or proxies as: their education and the education of their families while they were growing up; their incomes and jobs, and regrettably, their race. In American society, nonwhites, especially blacks, are still seen as lower in value than other Americans. This differentiation along race and ethnic lines is seen in all areas of life: segregation and discrimination often doom most

blacks to lower education, joblessness, and poverty (Massey & Denton, 1993).

Social status, race, and ethnicity have taken on even more importance in modern post-industrial societies in determining life chances. Economic restructuring has displaced many from their former low skill yet high paying jobs. The competition for resources and the American dream has become more fierce. Indeed, in the current bitter debate around family structure and family values, race and inequality have taken on new meaning. Socioeconomic disadvantage is seen by some as a major factor in current patterns of declining marriage, and increasing divorce, out-of-wedlock births and other social ills such as joblessness, substance abuse, and crime (Wilson, 1987). Others blame the lack of values or changing individual and family values on continuing socioeconomic disadvantage (Murray, 1986). As empirical investigations of the links between inequality and changing family structure and function unfold, more evidence suggests that what we are seeing are adaptations to larger, social structural dynamics. So the best counsel for low socioeconomic and nonwhite couples may be to recognize problems such as those cited by Lillian Rubin for what they are—problems often not of their own making, problems often arising out of their life situation that should not necessarily impugn their marriages or their character. Only then might such couples avoid being set up for the experience of dashed expectations in marriage.

So we will use education, family and personal income, occupation, childhood social status, and race to gain some insight into how these factors, alone and together, contribute to marital instability. White's (1990) recent review of the determinants of divorce in research during the 1980s covers studies showing the importance of race (black Americans are more likely than white Americans to divorce) and socioeconomic status (there is a negative association between income or other measures of socioeconomic status and divorce). As shown in the first regression analysis presented below in Table 2.1, race as a status variable in its own right is a very powerful predictor of marital instability in our overall sample. In fact, the table reveals that race is by the far the strongest status predictor of marital instability. This finding confirms what other studies have shown: that even when income and education are simultaneously considered as joint predictors with race, black marriages run a greater risk than white marriages in being unstable and/or ending in divorce. For the most part, all the analyses presented in this book will be done for blacks and whites separately. Nevertheless, race is clearly related to other status variables. And to the degree it interacts with other variables in our understanding of instability, we will often interpret such findings as resulting from the oppressed status of blacks relative to the privileged one of whites in this society.

Social Status Measures

A number of different direct measures of socioeconomic status will comprise what we will denote as social location or social status factors. Using

Table 2.1
Summary of Multiple Regression Analyses Predicting Marital Instability from Status Differences

Predictor	Total Group (N=321)†		White Couples (N=166)†		Black Couples (N=155)†	
	B	beta	B	beta	B	beta
Wives						
Mother's Education	.03	.05	-.06	-.11	.06	.08
Father's Education	-.03	-.05	.07+	.17+	-.09*	-.16*
Own Education	.01	.01	-.08	-.12	.12	.12
Personal Income	-.06**	-.19**	-.05+	.20+	-.07*	-.20*
Husbands						
Mother's Education	-.07+	-.10+	.02	.04	-.18**	-.23**
Father's Education	.05+	.10+	-.01	-.02	.15**	.24**
Own Education	-.14**	-.18**	-.13*	-.22*	-.14+	-.16+
Personal Income	-.04	-.12	-.07+	.28*	.04	.12
Couple						
Difference in Education	.09	.07	.13+	.13+	.01	.01
Income Adequacy	.12	.13	.31**	.43**	-.22	-.21
Race (1=white, 0=black)	-.94***	-.30***	(—)	(—)	(—)	(—)
Adj R²	.18***		.13***		.15***	

+=p<.10
*=p<.05
**=p<.01
***=p<.001

†Reflects the average number of couples on predictors in which there are no missing data.

years of education of each spouse's mother and father as the measure of family of origin social status, and the husband's and wife's own education as a measure of the couple's social status, we will be able to test the relative impact of status experienced during childhood and adolescence to that obtained during adulthood. Instead of creating a socioeconomic index, we will use education, income earned in the year prior, and occupation separately. These variables have different implications.

The assessments of status that we used are listed in Table 2.1. Like all such tables in the rest of the book, the exact wording of the questions used to assess each measure, or the details of the way an index is constructed appear in the Appendix. The items and the indices are arranged alphabetically according to their titles.

Examine the predictors of social status that are listed in Table 2.1. We have mentioned all but two. One is the Income Adequacy, an index of how adequate the household income is for the couple adjusted for the needs of members of the household (this index takes account of the number and ages of the members of the household the couple lives in, including children that the couple has who live with them); and the other is the discrepancy between the educational attainment of the husband and wife. The latter is not so much a direct measure of status as it is a measure of the compatibility of the partners' statuses.

Table 2.1 presents not only the summary of the multiple regression analysis applied to these measures of status predicting marital instability for the whole group, as mentioned above, but also two others: one for the black couples and the other for the white couples. These parallel analyses for blacks and whites will be the basic pattern of data presentation for the remainder of the chapters exploring marital instability.

For simplicity, in this and similar tables to follow, only the bs and the standardized regression coefficients (Beta weights) are presented along with the Adjusted R-squared. Unless otherwise indicated measures are at the couple level. For example in Table 2.1 wives' own education and own personal income are listed separately from their husbands' education and personal income, but poverty ratio and educational discrepancy are listed by themselves, unidentified as wives' or husbands', indicating that these are measures of the couple's poverty ratio and educational attainment discrepancy.

RESULTS: PREDICTING INSTABILITY FROM SOCIAL STATUS

In only a few sections of the book will we present regression analyses for the entire group. We did it at this beginning point to demonstrate the place of race differences in accounting for marital instability, which, as we noted above, is very powerful. But since race is so important to this study, we will want

primarily to concentrate on results about instability considered separately for black couples and white couples. These separate analyses also appear in Table 2.1 for social status factors. In dealing with the regression analyses broken down separately for the two sets of couples, we can see how certain effects may be true for both groups, some for only one group or the other, or stronger in one group than the other. Getting and staying married undoubtedly has some different meanings for the two groups, and we want to be alert to them. In running parallel analyses we will also be able to highlight any effects that are clearly prominent in both groups. We will return to regression analysis for the total group to see whether more psychological variables about marriage and reactions to the world in general help us account for the strong race effects noted above.

Let us turn to other results about status predictors of instability found in Table 2.1, both for the total group and for blacks and whites separately. Surprisingly, for the total group, status as measured through wives' incomes has clearer prediction to stability than status as measured through husbands' income. These results become clarified when we note in the regression for the black couples that the income earnings of husbands during the year prior to marriage have little to do with the eventual stability of their marriages. Could it be that many black males have such fluctuations in their earnings that their potential for financial security cannot be detected reliably in a single year prior to marriage?

A man's educational attainment prior to marriage is an important status predictor of marital stability for both blacks and whites, albeit not as important as race. Men with higher educational attainment are in more stable marriages. There are no significant results for women relating their education to instability, not for the total group or for either race group separately.

If we examine the effects that status background measured through parents' education has on predicting marital instability, we immediately have to take race into account. Results are very different for black couples and white couples, and all the differences are statistically significant.[1] The results make an especially interesting pattern for blacks. For them, their opposite sex parents' educational attainment was negatively related to instability, but their same sex parents' educational attainment was positively related to instability, although this latter result was only a weak trend for black women. Let us consider these results carefully.

The less educated the black women's fathers were, the less stable were these women's marriages, and the less educated the black men's mothers were, the less stable their marriages were. The latter results are in keeping with the general idea that socialization from a lower status parent will undermine potential stability of a marriage. But why the opposite effect from the same sexed parent for blacks, particularly for men? The only speculation we have to offer is that in achieving a higher education a same sexed parent can serve

as a role model for more autonomous coping and being on one's own after a potential separation. To the degree that the level of one's education also reflects the prestige of a potential job that one will hold, then a same sex parent's education tells the child how far he or she could strive to go in the occupational world. And to the degree that personal ambition can interfere with marital commitment, so this line of reasoning might go, socialized goals for higher achievement might disrupt marital stability.

None of the above helps explain why there is a trend for white women whose fathers had higher educational attainments to be in more unstable marriages. Perhaps white women identify more with the occupational attainments of their fathers than their mothers, for whom educational attainment had only minor connections to their occupational roles. Many white women's mothers did not work even when they had a college education. So it may be that white women turn to their fathers to gauge their own potential for autonomy through a career. This is merely speculation but worthy of testing in long-term longitudinal studies of women. Surprisingly, two other status variables operate as significant predictors of instability in white marriages but not in black marriages: Income Adequacy and the differential in education for husbands and wives, although the latter is just a trend. The positive association between income adequacy and marital instability among white couples is indeed puzzling. We would have expected the opposite, and also that the relationship would appear in black couples more than white couples, given our stereotypes of the special economic difficulties black families face.[2] This stereotype is true of black couples in this study compared to white couples. The mean Income Adequacy for blacks is 2.50[3]; the mean for whites is 3.58. This difference is statistically significant (F = 79.46, df 1,707; p <.001). What accounts then for the reversal from expectations that we found in results showing a relationship between marital instability and income adequacy among white couples? The only explanation we have is that since personal income itself for both white husbands and wives operates as a significant predictor of marital stability as expected, the effect measured in the remaining variance of income adequacy index is mostly the contribution of families of origin or other sources of independent income, particularly rentals on properties. These additional sources of income may be levers of disruption if they are seen in the early years of marriage as the means by which one spouse or the other gets an upper hand in joint decisions about finances in the family. For black couples sources of additional income might be ADC, food stamps, and unemployment benefits or the like, which may not as easily be construed as sources of income that give one partner greater power over the other.

The fact of the educational discrepancy between husbands and wives being predictive of marital instability for whites but not blacks was also surprising, although the black-white difference in regression coefficients is not statistically

significant. The stereotype is once again that this factor is stronger in black couples, and the data from our study supports this stereotype. The mean educational discrepancy for the black couples is 1.52 years of schooling; the mean for white couples is 1.26. This difference is also statistically significant ($F = 4.06$; df = 1, 370; $p < .05$). Perhaps educational discrepancies, being more prevalent in black families, become part of the black experience of oppression and, hence, less dramatically disruptive of marriage in these early years. White marriages may be more immediately stressed by educational differences between husbands and wives, perhaps because that condition is less generally normative in worlds in which men and women have not experienced as individuals or as a group the oppression of being barred from realistic opportunities for success merely on the basis of skin color.

These latter results highlight why we have decided to depict the relationships between sets of predictors of marital instability separately for blacks and whites. There are critical differences in the patterns of results. We will not always have ready answers to why these differences exist, but we feel it is critical to present them, discuss them, and permit readers to think about the nature of marriage for blacks whose experiences have been largely ignored in systematic longitudinal investigations of marriage.

When we begin combining across sets of predictors in the hierarchical regression analyses, we will include as variables those showing different relationships for blacks and whites, as these latter results describe, as well as those that show parallel relationships for both groups.

Structural Factors in Families of Origin

One of most provocative theories coming out of the clinical treatment of families has been the family systems approach (see Goldenberg & Goldenberg, 1980) which suggests that a couple entering marriage and establishing a new family brings with them the baggage of unresolved tensions, styles of communication, fantasies, and myths that each learned from his/her family of origin. The couple joins together families for better or worse and not just themselves as husband and wife. The empirical evidence for this proposition is scanty, but the assumption of strong family ghosts remaining with a couple is common in our systemic views of family dynamics (see Bowen, 1978). Thus, the structure of families of origin may play an important role in our understanding of marital instability.

Measures of Family Structure

We measured a few aspects of the structure of the families of origin of the

men and women in our study. The most crucial one was whether the marriages of the respondents' fathers and mothers were themselves stable. A critical assessment of this was whether or not the husbands and wives experienced a breakup in their parents' marriage while they were growing up (before the age of sixteen). Most evidence advanced on this question is reasonably conclusive with respect to women's family experience (see McClanahan & Booth, 1989), but there is less research available on this aspect of men's family background. There can be a variety of theories advanced for why this transmission of marital instability occurs for women. One clear idea is that the broken home experience occurs more frequently in lower status families, and so we must be careful to control for status background in doing research on family origins of marital instability. Another is a straightforward theory of role modeling. Watching one's own parents divorce increases the legitimacy of such action for the self. A third rests on the reasoning that in broken homes there is poorer socialization of children to the major accepted norms of the society, including the institution of marriage. Additional theories pivot around the concept of the dysfunctional family that one may assume is more applicable to families in which divorce occurs than to families which remain intact. In these theories, one can postulate that the modus operandi of a dysfunctional family gets transmitted to the next generation as well.

Other assessments of family structure can come from the size of families of origin, birth order experiences in the family of origin, and somewhat more complicated discrepancies between husband and wife in these experiences. To grow up in a large family requires some adjustment that may not occur for a person growing up in a small family. Similarly, if one is an only child or a firstborn, one's entire schema for thinking about interpersonal relationships can take on the perspective of being from that preeminent position in the family constellation, which should be very different from someone who grew up having an older sibling to contend with. Thus, one can hypothesize that, with regard to a wife's and husband's family of origin, it would be discrepancies in size and birth order position that would be most important for understanding marital instability. It should be noted that we assessed only two structural facts about families of origin: how many siblings each spouse had and whether or not each spouse had older siblings. More refined assessments might have led us to more provocative hypotheses about family structure, but we are limited to these two features.

In regression analyses, we could include a measure of the discrepancy in size of family along with the size of family of origin of both husbands and wives, because it was a measure of the absolute difference in size and hence not completely determined by the size of the husbands' and wives' families of origin. This was not possible with birth order, since the simple assessment of birth order (has older sib/does not have older sib) for each spouse completely determines the birth order discrepancy measure. Because we were more

interested in discrepancy, we included the wife's birth order measure and the discrepancy measure, and omitted the husband's birth order assessment for one analysis, and then repeated the analysis leaving out the wife's birth order but including the husband's along with the discrepancy.

RESULTS: PREDICTING INSTABILITY FROM STRUCTURAL FACTORS OF FAMILIES OF ORIGIN

The only family structural variable that works convincingly in predicting marital instability is a broken home background, and that works for white wives only. That result can be seen in the regression analyses using structural factors of families of origin as predictors, reported in Table 2.2. This result confirms what has been generally found in prior literature. The results are not at all clear for the effects of broken home backgrounds assessed for black women, although the difference in regression coefficients for white wives and black wives is not statistically significant, and there is no evidence for the effect of a broken home background on the stability of men's marriages. These are important additional pieces of information to weave into our understanding of marital stability.

Contrary to our hypotheses, discrepancies in family size of the couples and discrepancies in their birth order position did not predict marital instability. Wives' having an older sib and husbands not having an older sib tended to be more characteristic of unstable than stable marriages among the white couples, but these were not highly significant results. Since these results did not show up in the black couples' data, and since we have no clear hypothesis about why this should be true in understanding the stability of the white couples' marriages but not the blacks, we question the importance of these findings. These may be leads for social researchers who are particularly interested in unravelling the potential meaning of birth order effects.

The Couple's Premarital Situation

It would be a truism to say that couples in the study started their married lives on different footings. We have already discussed socioeconomic background differences. If a couple is well off, it enables them to start marriage feeling secure; if a couple is impoverished, it often forces them to worry about their future married life together. But beyond status, are there experiences the couples have together before they are married that might make a difference in what marriage will mean for them? There are undoubtedly many, but we limited ourselves to three: how long before they were married a couple were committed to each other (the length of their relationship);

whether or not the couple lived together before marriage (cohabitation); and whether or not the couple started marriage as parents[4] (parental status). Each of these factors may color the way a couple sees their marriage.

Not much research has investigated the effects of the length of prior commitment to a relationship to the eventual stability of a marriage. Earlier in the century, advocates of lengthy engagements argued that the couples needed time to be both committed and to consider carefully what they were undertaking. Engagement periods were tests to safeguard committed marriages, but this is not the era of lengthy engagements, and so length of commitment to a relationship has to be assessed more informally. One might expect that there would be a correlation between the length of premarital commitment to a relationship and the commitment to a marriage as measured by its stability.

There has been a great deal of research on the effects of cohabitation on marital quality and stability, most of which finds that couples who have lived together before marriage have lower marital quality and are more likely to divorce than those who have not cohabited (see Bennett, Blanc, & Bloom, 1988). The results seem perplexing at first blush since many couples profess that they live together before marriage as a test of their compatibility for marriage, and so we could assume that those who then went on to marry would feel especially confident about their future together. However, most studies examining the consequences of cohabitation fail to control for some critical differences between cohabiters and non-cohabiters. For example, non-cohabiters are more likely than cohabiters to be religiously committed couples, who, in turn, would feel a stronger commitment to the institution of marriage.

Martin and Bumpass (1989) have plotted recent trends in marital disruption and offer clear evidence that premarital childbearing has negative consequences for marriages. Since so many of the couples in our sample started marriage as parents (55% of the black couples; 22% of the white couples), we assumed that this would be an important factor to consider in our depiction of the determinants of marital instability in this urban sample.

RESULTS: PREDICTING INSTABILITY FROM COUPLES' PREMARITAL SITUATION

One factor stands out in Table 2.3 for both black and white couples as a factor from the couples' premarital situation predicting marital instability: whether or not they bring children into the marriage. And that seems to be an important disruptive factor. The result is clearer for whites than blacks, but the difference between the two groups is not statistically significant. These results confirm Martin and Bumpass's (1989) demographic analyses showing that having children before marriage makes for difficulties in some households.

Table 2.2

Summary of Multiple Regression Analyses Predicting Marital Instability from Family Background Factors

(Within White Couples and Black Couples)

Predictor	White Couples (N=158)[†]		Black Couples (N=155)[†]		Sign. of W/B diff.
	B	beta	B	beta	
Wives					
Number of Siblings	.05	.08	-.02	-.03	NS
Has older sibling	.91+	.03+	.26	.07	NS
Broken home background	.58*	.20*	.34	.10	NS
Husbands					
Number of Siblings	.00	.01	.05	.10	NS
Has older sibling	-.19	-.07	-.24	-.06	NS
Broken home background	-.38	-.10	-.18	-.04	NS
Couple					
Family size discrepancy	.02	.03	.01	.01	NS
Sibling order discrepancy	-.23	-.09	.54	.15	*
Adj. R^2	.015 NS		.00 NS		

+=p<.10
*=p<.05

[†]Reflects the average number of couples on predictors in which there are no missing data.

34

Table 2.3

Summary of Multiple Regression Analyses Predicting Marital Instability from Premarital Situation (Within White Couples and Black Couples)

Predictor	White Couples (N=168)[†]		Black Couples (N=155)[†]		Sign. of W/B diff.
	B	beta	B	beta	
Cohabitation	-.01	-.09	-.01	-.04	NS
Parental Status	.79**	.27**	.42+	.13+	NS
Length of Time as Couple	.05	.09	-.10*	-.17*	**
Adj. R²	.05**		.03*		

+=p<.10
*=p<.05
**=p<.01

[†]Reflects the average number of couples on predictors in which there are no missing data.

We checked to see whether the results could be mostly attributed to couples who brought into their marriages children conceived in relationships with men or women other than their spouses, but we found no significant difference in instability for that group compared to the group of couples who had children together before marriage.

The fact that cohabitation does not predict instability when parental status and length of time as a couple are also considered is an important finding. We have no evidence that cohabitation has good or bad effects on marriages, even without critical controls for status or religious commitments. It could be that it might have either benefits or problems for certain specialized groups, but overall there seems to be nothing in the data to warrant considering it an important general variable for understanding marital instability.

In black couples there is a significant effect of the length of time the couple was committed to each other, showing greater instability among couples who had shorter premarital commitments. This effect was significantly different from the counterpart effect among white couples who, if anything, showed the opposite trend, having greater instability among couples who had longer premarital commitments.

Personality Characteristics of Spouses

Husbands and wives not only have personal histories in families and with each other prior to getting married, they also have recognizable personal characteristics that could help shape the direction that a marriage takes. We will consider two groups of these personal characteristics. The first will be labelled personality characteristics because we assume they summarize general traits of spouses that could have dynamic significance for how they might relate to each other and to their marriage in general. The second group will be a catchall list of other personal characteristics for which there are data or at least hunches about their relevance to marital instability.

Among the personality characteristics, there are two that reflect traits of general emotionality: Anxiety (or neuroticism) and Zest. The first one is featured in Eysenck's (1975) scheme of basic personality and has been shown time and time again to have critical bearing on people's lives. In particular, a measure of neuroticism has been found to be a strong predictor of marital well-being in longitudinal investigations of married couples (Kelly & Conly, 1987). The specific measure in our study is a scale developed by Gurin, Veroff, and Feld (1960) from their factor analytic study of psychophysical symptoms that they label as Anxiety but that captures the conceptual meaning of neuroticism. We will call it Anxiety. The second assessment of emotionality comes from four items of the Zung (1965) scale to measure depression. Since these items are all phrased in the positive, it has been

labelled as the opposite of depression or <u>Zest</u>. The heuristic value of this scale is reported in <u>The Inner American</u> (Veroff, Douvan, & Kulka, 1981). This scale picks up facets of confidence in one's self that are part of Eysenck's second basic personality factor, extroversion-introversion. We make no claim that the scale measures extroversion directly, but it should have some relation to it.

Three other measures of personality come from judgments about how "ambitious," "cooperative," and "bossy" each spouse is. The measures are sums of the person's self judgments and his/her spouse's judgments of him/her on each of these traits. Thus the measures reflect both self perceptions and the judgment of another, perhaps making them more generalized measures of personality. This triumvirate of personality comes close to the basic concerns (achievement, affiliation, and power) that McClelland and his colleagues have emphasized in their research on personality predictors of behavior (Smith, 1992). If we were to follow the proposition that men and women who fulfill traditional gender roles would have more successful marriages, we would suggest that men who are particularly ambitious and bossy, and women who are cooperative and not ambitious or bossy would more likely be in stable marriages. This represented our general expectations, but we recognized that this was a simple formulation, and much more complex associations were plausible.

RESULTS: PREDICTING INSTABILITY FROM PERSONALITY CHARACTERISTICS

Table 2.4 summarizes the regression analyses grouping these five personality characteristics of each spouse as predictors of marital instability. There are remarkably different patterns for black couples and white couples. In white couples, the only relatively strong predictor is the wife's cooperativeness, which significantly predicts stability in marriage. In itself, the result is not remarkable, but the fact that it only emerges for white wives and not for black wives or for either group of husbands perhaps tells us how much a "feminine" compliant style indeed plays a functional role in maintaining marriages for the dominant ethnic group in our society. By contrast among the black couples, wives' zest plays a positive role in marriage. If we interpret zest to mean optimism and to some degree extraversion, as we suggested above, then it is not black women's compliant style that is critical to their marriages but their active, positive capacity to cope with life with a certain joy. Perhaps marriage among oppressed groups in our society requires women to be hopeful supporters of the family, especially when their husbands' face obstacles to successful achievement. In this respect, it is important to realize that <u>Ambitiousness</u> in black women has negative consequences for their

Table 2.4

Summary of Multiple Regression Analyses Predicting Marital Instability from Personality Characteristics (Within White Couples and Black Couples)

Predictor	White Couples (N=168)[1]		Black Couples (N=155)[1]		Sign. of W/B diff.
	B	beta	B	beta	
Wives					
Zest	-.01	-.02	-.19**	-.22**	*
Anxiety	.04+	.12+	.00	.00	NS
Ambitiousness	.02	.07	-.00	-.01	NS
Bossiness	.02	.05	-.00	-.06	NS
Cooperativeness	-.10*	-.22*	-.03	-.06	NS
Husbands					
Zest	-.10+	-.16+	-.01	-.01	NS
Anxiety	.01	.03	.12**	.23**	**
Ambitiousness	.00	.01	-.02	-.04	NS
Bossiness	.03	.08	.02	.06	NS
Cooperativeness	.00	.01	-.06	-.11	NS
Adj. R²	.07*		.09**		

+=p<.10
*=p<.05
**=p<.01

[1]Reflects the average number of couples on predictors in which there are no missing data.

marriages.   Thus, for black women to be very concerned about personal achievement evidently stands in the way of their being in stable marriages. And so among black couples there may be an important distinction between being a wife who is an assertively hopeful supporter in her family and being a wife who assertively takes on achievement goals for herself.   The former is stabilizing; the latter is disrupting.

This pattern seems characteristic of black couples but not white couples. The difference between the relevant regression coefficients in the black versus white regression analysis is statistically significant.   This suggests that black men may be especially vulnerable to feeling inadequate because of their wives' ambitiousness and especially likely to feel adequate because of their wives' optimism.   Perhaps for these men, their own possible lack of accomplishment in the world, particularly as a family provider, makes them especially sensitive to their wives' personal characteristics that either support or question their accomplishment.   In this connection, it is revealing that black husbands who are particularly anxious are those who are in marriages that are more unstable. This is not so for white couples, with the difference between whites and blacks again being statistically significant.   This characteristic anxiety may be just the factor that makes men overly sensitive to what their wives do or do not do as a commentary about their own adequacy.

Among white couples there was a trend for women's Anxiety to be a destabilizing influence in their marriages.   If we follow the same reasoning as we did with the black males above, we might suggest that white wives could be particularly vulnerable to feelings of adequacy depending on what their husbands do or don't do.   And if they are generally anxious, then they are particularly vulnerable to such feelings.

Scanning over the different pattern of results for black and white couples we are impressed with how much we have to take cultural context into account before understanding how personality factors may have an impact on a long term interpersonal relationship like marriage.   Couples do not exist immune from the expectations that reference groups may have for them.   And those expectations can translate into different sensitivities to different personality styles of husbands and wives in different groups.

Other Personal Characteristics of the Spouses

Personal characteristics other than personality often enter into men's and women's choices of partners, and once chosen can play a part in how their marriages are shaped.   High on a list of such factors that may be important are a person's attractiveness, age, and religion.   Let us discuss each in turn.

In our society being physically attractive can be a benefit for a marriage since, all other things equal, it can be a force for keeping a marriage together

in the spouse who is benefitted. Since we have sexist double standards about physical attractiveness, it being especially critical in evaluating women, men may be concerned about this benefit more than women. As a result we could suggest that on the basis of benefits to a marriage it is more likely that women's attractiveness will be a predictor of marital stability than men's attractiveness.

On the other hand, one's physical attractiveness can make one more eligible for other relationships. Not only are other men and women especially interested in a married woman or man who is physically attractive, and under certain conditions attempt to lure the woman or man into alternative relationships, but the physically attractive man or woman can also easily count on successful pursuit of alternative relationships if his or her own marriage becomes problematic. This line of reasoning would suggest that attractive husbands and wives would be in more unstable marriages. Thus we had no firm prediction about how physical attractiveness would relate to marital instability. The effects of these two opposing forces could very well cancel each other out and result in no association between physical attractiveness and marital instability.

One mark of general couple compatibility might be the degree to which they match each other in their attractiveness. As a result we also included in the regression analyses of personal characteristics the absolute discrepancy between husband's and wife's physical attractiveness.

The measure of physical attractiveness used in our study was the combined (multiplied) ratings of each spouse's physical appearance on a five-point scale made by two independent interviewers during the first year, one the spouse interviewer and the other, the couple interviewer. If the couple was not interviewed in a couple interview or if the spouse interviewer and the couple interviewer was the same person, then the single judge's rating was used. These comprised less than 10% of the ratings of the couples. And so, for the most part the measure of physical attractiveness combined across two different judgments of what is attractive. There was some reliability in judgments of Attractiveness although it was higher for the white women (.40 for women; .19 for men) than the black women (.14 for women; .22 for men), an interesting finding in itself.

A second personal characteristic that entered into our analyses was the Age of the husbands and wives. Maturity at the time of marriage can possibly be relevant for later marital stability. Compared to older couples, younger couples perhaps marry more impulsively, the stereotype being that they respond more to their passions than their rational judgments of compatibility. Indeed Martin and Bumpass (1989) conclude that in the early years of marriage, age at marriage is the most critical demographic predictor of divorce. Another way to think of the importance of age is in terms of discrepancies

between spouses. As a result we entered not only the age of each spouse but also the absolute difference in their ages as independent predictors of marital instability.

Two other characteristics considered in the analyses concerned religion. One was whether or not the spouse is Catholic and hence, pledged to a faith that opposes divorce. We would assume that being Catholic might thus affect couples' decisions about divorce, which in turn might be reflected in our measure of instability. The other characteristic regarding religion assessed was the frequency of church attendance. Veroff, Douvan, and Kulka (1981) had found Church Attendance a strong positive predictor of marital well-being. We will be using another question asked about religion, how important it is in each spouse's life, as a basis for measuring religious attitude compatibility, which will be considered in the next chapter.

The final characteristic we examined in this set of personal characteristics was how much of a problem alcohol (or drug) use was for each spouse. The measure is based on the reports from the person and his/her spouse on how frequently drinking alcohol or getting high caused problems for family or friends. Each spouse was asked about himself/herself and his/her spouse. The measure for each spouse was based on the combined self- and spouse- reports about each, multiplied together. While the phrase "getting high" permitted individuals to think about drug usage other than alcohol, our guess is that most spouses were thinking of alcohol. We will label this variable as a measure of a husband's (or wife's) Alcohol Problems. We have every reason to believe that this variable may be a highly significant predictor of marital difficulties. Alcoholism in a partner ranks high as one of the complaints offered by divorcing people in accounts of problems in their marriage leading to the decision to divorce (e.g., Cleek & Pearson, 1991).

RESULTS: PREDICTING MARITAL STABILITY FROM OTHER PERSONAL CHARACTERISTICS OF THE SPOUSES

The twelve predictors reflecting personal characteristics other than personality factors are listed in Table 2.5. Only two predictors are significant for white couples: the wife Being Catholic, which is associated with marital stability and the husband having Alcohol Problems, which is associated with instability. The latter is significant as a predictor for black couples as well, but along with that predictor are four others: the wife's Attractiveness, Age, the husband's Church Attendance, all predicting stability; and wife's Alcohol Problems, which like husband's Alcohol Problems predict instability.

The fact that black women's Attractiveness predicts stability, but white women's Attractiveness does not is a significant interaction effect. How do we account for this? We would suggest that with the marriage market very

favorable for eligible black men and distinctly more favorable than for eligible white males, black husbands are more likely than white husbands to consider alternative relationships if their wives are not particularly attractive. On the flip side, highly attractive white women may have more alternatives for their marriages if they face problems in their relationships than highly attractive black wives do. As a result, there may be less counterforce keeping attractive white women in unsatisfactory marriages than black women. At any rate the inference would be that wives' Attractiveness would be a clearer positive predictor for black marriages than white marriages.

For the other significant predictors for black marriages the trends in the white marriages are parallel although not significant. Could it be that black marriages are somewhat more dependent on the nature of the individual husbands and wives? The Adjusted R-squared for predicting marital instability from these personal characteristics is .13; this is nearly double the predictive power compared to only .07 for the white couples. We should keep this in mind when we present results in the next chapter which show that the white couples' instability is better predicted by couple interaction patterns than black couples' instability. This repeats a pattern that Veroff, Chadiha, Sutherland, and Leber (1993) found in examining the affects that these couples expressed in their spontaneous narratives about their relationship, as well as how they interacted in the telling of the stories. The black couples seem more individualistic; the whites, more interdependent. The blacks seem more focussed on the individual persons; the whites, more on the couple's relationship. This may be what is occurring in these regression analyses of personal characteristics and why we find so many interactions that differentiate what seems important in understanding marital instability for black couples and white couples from the set of variables measuring aspects of their histories and the kind of individuals they were when they came into marriage.

The fact that Being Catholic helps us understand marital instability for whites more than blacks is not surprising considering the differences in numbers of Catholics in the two groups. There are so few black Catholic wives in the sample (compared to the white group) that there was little opportunity for this assessment of religion to generate correlations with instability or any other factor for the black couples. Contrariwise, Church Attendance by black husbands is a significant predictor for black husbands but not for white husbands, but this difference in predictability based on regression coefficients is not statistically significant. Religiosity in general may be especially critical to black marriages. The fact that it is black men's Church Attendance and not women's that matters is an interesting result. Black males' participation in church may represent a highly personal decision, and hence have special significance for their everyday reactions to their intimate lives. Black women's participation may be more for social bonding and have less carryover into their intimate worlds.

Table 2.5
Summary of Multiple Regression Analyses Predicting Marital Instability from Other Personal Characteristics (Within White Couples and Black Couples)

Predictor	White Couples (N=162)†		Black Couples (N=151)†		Sign. of W/B diff.
	B	beta	B	beta	
Wives					
Attractiveness	−.02	−.02	−.39*	−.23*	*
Age	−.06	−.18	−.15+	−.35+	NS
Being Catholic	−.42*	−.17*	−.41	−.06	NS
Church Attendance	−.27	−.09	.18	.05	*
Alcohol Problems	.21	.11	.31+	.14+	NS
Husbands					
Attractiveness	.09	.08	.06	.04	NS
Age	.02	.08	.08	.21	NS
Being Catholic	.22	.09	−.25	−.04	NS
Church Attendance	−.46	−.10	−.71*	−.16*	NS
Alcohol Problems	.21*	.19*	.23*	.17*	NS
Couple					
Attractiveness Discrepancy	−.04	−.03	−.19	−.08	NS
Age Discrepancy	.03	.05	−.04	−.08	NS
Adj. R^2	.07*		.13**		

+=$p<.10$
*=$p<.05$
**=$p<.01$

†Reflects the average number of couples on predictors in which there are no missing data.

Combining the Effects of Significant Premarital Factors

Now that we have examined within each set of premarital factors what the significant predictors are for black and white couples, we face the task of combining across these sets to examine the way that the significant effects we have been discussing separately, may in fact covary and thus represent common predictive themes. The ideal analysis would add factors one at time and note the change in covariance patterns. This would also be a gargantuan task. To circumvent that problem, we followed an arbitrary procedure: first, we limited ourselves to factors that in either the individual sets for the black couples or for the white couples, the ones we just examined, were significant at least at the .05 level of confidence; secondly, we put all those factors for blacks screened in our first step together in one regression analysis for blacks and another one for whites. We realized that in this procedure we were not precisely following through on the predictive models generated from the multiple regression models tested in the separate sets. This new combination of variables thrown together may yield very different results as the patterns of covariation are distinctly different from what was present in the regression models thus far tested. Nevertheless, we felt that this procedure would isolate those factors that have especially strong potential as predictors of marital stability and would help us generate an overall model across levels of analysis and time of assessments, which is one of the main goals of our inquiry.

In Tables 2.6 and 2.7 we present the summaries of the two regression models combining across significant premarital predictors of marital instability for white couples and black couples, respectively. We are again impressed with the different patterns for blacks and whites. We selected a completely non-overlapping set of predictors for black couples and white couples. We are impressed further with what we noted earlier, that many more premarital factors are more powerful predictors for blacks than for whites. The Adjusted R-squared for the black couples is .29; the adjusted R-squared is .19 for the white couples.

We have begun to formulate a rationale for why this may be. Most all of the significant predictors for the black couples are either status variables (particularly social status assessed by black spouses' parents' educational attainment) or personality factors. The status variables have more to do with the background socialization of the couple, a background that in the urban midwest cannot fail to connect with issues of racism in our society. The viability of marriage for many black couples may be firmly rooted in the way that marriage has been interpreted along with other institutions for this oppressed group. And these interpretations may be conditioned by the particular social status backgrounds from which a man or woman comes. The particular models of one's parents' status attainment may be especially meaningful for an oppressed group in interpreting whether one should get

married, and whether one should stay married and under what conditions. It may be that the marriage market being what it is for black women, it is the issue of men becoming and staying committed to marriage that is at stake. And in that respect cues that men and women use from their parents' relationship and how it may have been conditioned by their social status may be highly salient. Not that these factors are irrelevant for white couples. It is just that racism is likely to foster learning to adapt to deprivation of status, to play by the rules of what to expect, and to limit one's goals to avoid disappointment. These rules as they apply to marriage are often learned from the models that parents provide. Whites also learn rules of adaptation from their parents and their parents' examples. But there is nothing built into their ultimate adaptation that is as powerful as the rules learned about being black in a white society. And that's where early socialization about status would be especially important for black men and women, perhaps not only with respect to marriage but with respect to any major social role in which economic and achievement opportunities are so important in guiding the course of that role performance.

The fact that personality variables play a stronger role in predicting instability in black marriages than in white marriages can be interpreted from a different standpoint, one we discussed in the section on personality factors. That is, black marriages may depend especially on the functioning of two individuals as individuals who somehow get along and remain committed because of their natures while white marriages are focussed more on the styles of interacting that couples have with each other which may or may not depend so much on their individuality or personality characteristics. We will see in the next chapter that the style of couple interaction plays an especially important part in predicting white marriages, more so than black marriages. And so we make the following tentative interpretation: black husband-wife relationships are structured more around the paradigm of individualism; and white husband-wife relationships are structured more on the paradigm of relationship. We will look for further corroboration of this interpretation in analyses in later chapters. We also want to make clear that we are speaking about the husband-wife bond rather than the parent-child bond and other kin bonds, which in black families may especially reflect the relationship rather than the individual paradigms.

Would growing up black in our culture have anything to do with why individualism might be especially prominent in black husband-wife relationships? We would say yes. Experiencing oppression sets up a wariness about relationships, especially with the dominant culture, a protection against the possibility that the social world governing opportunities for blacks in our society might ultimately undo what a couple might try to develop in their lives together. Individualism in marriage is a protection against commitments that may be difficult to nourish, if opportunities for success in the occupational

Table 2.6
Summary of Multiple Regression Analyses Predicting Marital Instability from Significant Premarital Factors (Within White Couples)

Predictor	White Couples (N=149)[†]	
	B	beta
Wives		
Broken home background	.19	.07
Being Catholic	−.28	−.11
Cooperativeness	−.11***	−.24***
Husbands		
Own education	−.12*	−.19*
Personal income	−.06*	−.22*
Alcohol problems	.17*	.16*
Couple		
Income adequacy	.19*	.26*
Parental status	.43+	.15+
Adj R²	.19***	

+=p<.10
*=p<.05
***=p<.001

[†]Reflects the average number of couples on predictors in which there are no missing data.

Table 2.7
Summary of Multiple Regression Analyses Predicting Marital Instability for Significant Premarital Factors (Within Black Couples)

	Black Couples (N=158)[†]	
Predictor	B	beta
Wives		
Father's education	−.09**	−.17**
Personal income	−.06**	−.17**
Attractiveness	−.21*	−.13*
Zest	−.16**	−.19**
Husbands		
Mother's education	−.16**	−.20**
Father's education	.15**	.23**
Alcohol problems	.14+	.10+
Church attendance	−.60*	−.14*
Anxiety	.12***	.23***
Couple		
Number of years as couple	−.12**	−.20**
Adj. R^2	.29***	

+=p<.10
*=p<.05
**=p<.01
***=p<.001

[†]Reflects the average number of couples on predictors in which there are no missing data.

47

world or for attainment of economic security are limited.

As for the specific significant findings in these combined regressions listed in Table 2.6 and 2.7, most of them have been fully discussed in their initial presentations in Tables 2.1–2.5. What we should attend to at this point, however, are those status and other premarital variables that no longer linger as significant effects under our new combination of pooled significant effects. We will discuss these below.

Most interesting is the decreased predictive power of parental status. In fact, in the context of social status variables, parent status, if anything, is a predictor of <u>stability</u> for black couples. The result suggests that parental status, known to be a predictor of divorce, may often have been a proxy for social status, and that in itself it may not contribute to marital instability.

The same might be said of the reasons why for white wives' <u>Broken Home Backgrounds</u> and <u>Being Catholic</u> no longer contribute significantly to marital instability in the pooled regression analysis for white couples.

The only really puzzling change is that women's <u>Personal Income</u> no longer is a significant predictor in this new pooled regression context for either black or white couples, although the trends are still there. We can only suggest that taking account of women's parental status simultaneously with their personal income washes out the effect of both variables. Being a mother interferes with the earning potential of women in our society. The zero-order correlations between <u>Personal Income</u> and <u>Parental Status</u> are −.36 for white wives and −.28 for black wives. Putting the two variables into the same regression equation may undo the apparent significance of each. It would be wise to keep this in mind and not entirely dismiss the importance of either.

Premarital Factors and Race Differences in Marital Instability

We began our regression analyses using the total group and immediately recognized the preeminence of <u>Race</u> in predicting marital instability. Although we have run our analyses since then separately for blacks and whites, we had earlier stated that we would return to the analysis of the total group and see whether we could begin to account for the strength of the race predictor. Can any of the significant premarital factors we have thus far examined in parallel analyses for black and white couples be used to mitigate the strength of the race effect?

To answer that question, we followed the following arbitrary procedure. First, we performed the simple regression of instability on <u>Race</u>. Then we performed a series of multiple regressions, each including <u>Race</u> and one other factor as predictors of instability. For each of these multiple regressions we paired <u>Race</u> with one of the other factors that met the following criteria:

1. It proved to be a significant predictor of instability (at least at the .05 level) for either the black couples or the white couples, or both.
2. It produced beta weights for the black couples and white couples that were in the same direction.
3. The factor significantly correlated with the race variable.

Using these criteria we selected five factors: two reflected social status (wife's Personal Income and husband's Own Education); two reflected religious orientation (Being Catholic and husband's Church Attendance); and one reflected family background (wife's Broken Home Background). If any of these factors in multiple regression with race significantly reduced the B weight of the contribution to instability, we could argue that it was a mediator of race and could be partially used to explain the effect of race on marital instability.

Table 2.8 summarizes the results. What is startling is that none of these potential moderators had significant effects (see rows 1–6). Furthermore, putting all of these variables together with Race as predictors did not significantly reduce the contribution of Race to the multiple correlation (see row 7). We are thus impressed that the race effect cannot simply be dismissed as nothing but social status, premarital, or personality differences in blacks and whites. Either something must go on during the marital relationship and experience in the two groups that helps account for the results or the experience of blacks and whites is so fundamentally different with regard to the meaning of marriage that certain factors that may appear as frequently in blacks and whites affect the two groups differently. Of course, both of these alternatives may be true. As we proceed with analyses of the marital experience itself in the next chapters we may uncover critical mediators of the race effect. But we have already encountered certain factors that affect one group or the other and that factor is not any stronger or weaker in one group or the other. Wife's lack of zest and husband's feelings of anxiety are more likely to affect instability in black couples than white couples. These characteristics are not significantly different in the two groups. Furthermore, both husband's mother's education and wife's mother's education have opposite effects on instability in the two groups, although there is no mean difference in reported education of the mothers. It's that the implication of these background differences are just different for black couples and white couples, as we discussed in earlier sections. As we proceed therefore we should be on the lookout for both possibilities—mediators of race effects, and qualities in the black experience of marriage and in the white experience of marriage that help us understand instability in the special terms of each group. We shall soon discover that the search for mediators of the race effect is futile, since the predictors of marital instability for the two groups will by and large be highly distinctive.

Table 2.8
Summary of Regression Analyses Predicting Marital Instability in Search of Moderator Effects for Race Within Premarital Factors

Regression model Predictor(s)	Beta Weight For Race Effect	S.D.	Significance of Drop in Beta Weight
1. Race (0 = Black/ 1 = White)	−1.03	.17	—
2. Race, Wife's Personal Income	−.96	.16	NS
3. Race, Wife's Broken Home Bkgd	−.96	.17	NS
4. Race, Wife Being Catholic	−.94	.18	NS
5. Race, Husband's Education	−.95	.16	NS
6. Race, Husband's Church Attendance	−.96	.17	NS
7. Race, W's Pers Income W's Brk Hm Bkgrd W's Being Catholic H's Education H's Church Attnd	−.77	.17	NS

SUMMARY

Analyses of five different types of premarital factors that theoretically have some bearing on marital stability were examined, first separately and then together.

Regression analyses of status factors yielded such strong race effects that we adopted the strategy of examining all subsequent analyses separately for white couples and black couples.

The strongest status effects for white couples involved husbands, for whom more education and high income reduced the risk of instability. The strongest effects for black couples involved their parents' educational background, with couples whose wives' fathers and husbands' mothers had more education were at less risk for instability. Two perplexing results were that black husbands whose fathers had higher education were in marriages that were prone to be unstable, and it was not the husbands' incomes that were protective of marriage for the black couples but the wives' incomes.

Other structural analyses of couples' premarital situation offer few significant predictors. Structural factors in families of origin yielded only one major result: white women from broken home backgrounds were more likely to be in unstable marriages. The only result coming out of examining aspects of the couple's premarital situation that was predictive of marital instability was among black couples for whom a longer relationship prior to marriage was predictive of greater stability. There was a trend for white couples to be more unstable if they entered this, their first marriage, as parents.

The analyses of different types of personal characteristics that could be part of the premarital situation contributed some insights about proneness to instability in couples. Certain personality characteristics and other personal characteristics yielded the following as characteristics related to instability: among white couples, wives being low on Cooperativeness, and husbands having Alcohol Problems; among black couples, wives being physically unattractive and being low in zestfulness, husbands being high in Anxiety, and, like the white husbands, having Alcohol Problems. Aside from the fact that men's Alcohol Problems predisposes marriages to instability, whether among black or white couples, a different set of personal factors seems to predispose white marriages in contrast to black marriages. This is a pattern of results that will characterize the rest of this book.

NOTES

1. Here and in other sections of the book, to test the significance of the difference between black and white couples with regard to how a particular variable predicts marital instability in a given multiple regression analysis, with the aid of the standard deviation for the beta (unstandardized coefficients) we established confidence intervals for the beta emerging in the analysis for the blacks, and did the same for the whites. We asked the question, at what confidence level does the white beta fall into the same distribution from the white regression analysis. We conservatively adopted the significance level which was less as the one representing the difference in betas.   That significance level is indicated in the table. The same analysis is identical with standardized coefficients.

2. It is true that income adequacy is negatively related to marital instability for black couples, but it is only a trend at the .18 level of significance.

3. See the Appendix for a complete description of parameters that go into measuring income adequacy, which is basically the ratio of household income to the needs of the members of the household.

4. Some couples may not have been parents at the time of their wedding, but we considered them to be parents if at the time of the first interview (4 to 7 months after their wedding) they were parents.

3

THE FIRST YEAR OF MARRIAGE: INTERPERSONAL ATTITUDES, PERCEPTIONS, AND INTERACTIONS

A complex web of interpersonal perceptions and interactions governs the marital processes that describe the experiences of newlyweds as they undertake their lives together. The fact that they are newlyweds perhaps makes the first year more complex than any other year they will have together. Whether or not they have lived together in their pre-marriage days, the new husband and wife have to learn how to adapt to being a couple that has publicly committed to remain intact until separated by death. That's no small undertaking especially when the clues to what it takes to stay together are not well mapped out. As a result, what husbands and wives learn to think of each other in this new married condition, how they begin to respond to each other's styles and passions, and how they learn to accommodate to what they think each other wants or demands may set the tone of their married life for years to come.

In this chapter and in Chapter 4, we will explore a set of attitudes, perceptions, and interactions which are part of adaptation to married life to try to ascertain which ones significantly predict marital instability. This chapter will concentrate on attitudes, perceptions, and interactions relevant to the couple's relationship to each other, factors that describe their experience within their own intimate connections to each other. The next chapter will examine first the stresses and then the supports felt by the couple from <u>outside</u> the relationship. In Chapter 5 we will also examine overall integrative feelings that the couple has about their married life during the first year.

As in the previous chapter, we will describe several sets of relevant factors, first examining each set separately and then adding the significant factors from these separate analyses into one overall model. However, we have no clear-cut causal schema for integrating these factors in a single model. Each one seems potentially interrelated with the others. Therefore, we will give each set equal causal priority in our attempts to understand marital instability. Again, we

perform our analyses on black couples and white couples separately.

The sets of factors we will be exploring are summarized in Table 3.1.

Table 3.1.
Sets of Interpersonal Perceptions and Interactions Explored Regarding the First Year of Marriage

Attitudes and Perceptions

Attitude incompatibilities
Interpersonal perceptions regarding conflict
Interpersonal perceptions regarding sexual interaction

Interactions

Perceived interaction styles of the self
Perceived couple interaction styles
Actual interaction styles

Attitude Incompatibilities

Do certain general attitudes that husbands or wives hold about issues that are in one way or another intertwined with their lives as couples have significant impact on the stability of their marriages? Attitudes that might come to mind could include men's "sexist" attitudes towards marriage, women's repressed feelings about sexuality, and husbands' or wives' negative attitudes about voicing points of sharp disagreement between them. Yet, for each set of these attitudes, one could suggest that the similarity of attitudes between spouses could promote stability rather than instability. Thus, if men who held sexist attitudes were married to women who also had sexist attitudes, or those where women who had repressed feelings about sex were married to men who were equally repressed about sex, and those with couples who agreed about not communicating too much about their disagreements, the marriages could be quite stable.

We were thus led to a general proposition: it is not a couple's attitudes per se but a couple's attitude incompatibility that fosters marital instability. However, research on this issue is scarce. The best example we know of comes from Vannoy-Hiller and Philliber's (1989) findings on a large urban sample of couples in Cincinnati which showed that congruence between a

husbands' and wives' work/family ideologies is associated with marital well-being, not the specific attitudes themselves. Attitude incompatibility is also implied in research on the intermarriage of men and women of different religious faiths. By and large, the results suggest that these intermarriages are more vulnerable (Washington, 1970).

Measures of Attitude Incompatabilities

From the spouse and couple interviews in our own study, we developed six different measures of attitude incompatibility. Three are based on single attitude items measuring the absolute discrepancy in husband and wife ratings of: the importance of religion ("how important is religion for you personally?"); preferred pace of life (whether they wanted life to go faster, slower, or did they judge it to be just right); and openness to new experiences (prefer trying new things as opposed to doing what one is used to). The remaining three are based on summed absolute discrepancies on items reflecting: attitudes towards conflict (five items; e.g., "Couples should try to avoid disagreements"); sex roles (six items; e.g.,"Both men and women should share equally in childcare and housework"); general rules for marriage (sixteen items covering such topics as cooling off in an argument, each spouse having some private time, understanding each other's sexual needs). All of these items were specifically tailored for this study.

It would not be difficult to justify any one of these measures of incompatibility of attitude as a potential source of marital instability. The discrepancy in rules for marriage is an omnibus general measure covering many different topics, and as such, should have been our best measure. Unfortunately these rules for marriage were only evaluated on a two-point scale (very important/not very important) since these "rules" were used in the couple interview not so much for assessing attitudes as they were for quickly locating attitudinal disagreements for a conflict resolution task.

RESULTS: PREDICTING INSTABILITY FROM ATTITUDE INCOMPATIBILITY

Table 3.2 summarizes the multiple regression analyses that examine the effects of attitude incompatibility predictors on marital instability first for white couples and then for black couples. Neither the multiple Rs nor the individual betas in these two analyses are particularly impressive, although the multiple correlation is significant for white couples but not for black couples. Nevertheless, the couples' incompatibility on the single item reflecting preferred pace of life is significant in both groups. During the first year of

marriage undoubtedly, all the differences in norms and values have not yet surfaced. This is an extended honeymoon period in a sense. However, it would be difficult to avoid differences in general attitudes and approaches to life, such as one's preferred pace. We thought differences in openness to new experiences would also surface early in the marriage as a major issue to be resolved. But evidently it is a less critical issue for young couples. In fact, one could argue that it is in a discrepancy between openness to experience that a couple may balance each other, the wife may be impulsive, the husband conservative or vice versa. This complementarity can keep their life together as a couple functioning well. Two impulsive souls may lead to mayhem; two conservative souls, to boredom.

The other measures of incompatibility may play a stronger role in understanding marital instability when we assess them in the third year of these couples' marriages. By then, after the honeymoon period, these more specific incompatibilities may have not only surfaced in their lives more openly and frequently but also led to many difficulties.

Interpersonal Perceptions Regarding Conflict and Sexual Interaction

We thought two areas of married life were highly susceptible to different appraisals: how couples are getting along in their sexual lives and how they deal with conflict. Therefore, we constructed measures of similarity for each spouse's perceptions for both of these interactions (actual similarity). Previous research has suggested, however, that it may be more important to get at assumed similarity rather than actual similarity (Levinger & Breedlove, 1966; Acitelli, Douvan, & Veroff, 1993). For a number of issues, we had included each spouse's guess as to how their spouse would have answered a given question. This enabled us to get a measure of perceived similarity or dissimilarity in perceptions of couples' sex lives and conflict styles. We could see how similar a husband's actual responses were to the way that his wife thought he was and how similar a wife's actual responses were to the way her husband thought she was. Generally, we thought that the greater the assumed similarity between spouses, the greater the shared frames of reference and empathy, and hence the greater the chances for a stable relationship.

Asking each spouse how they felt the other one would answer a given question about their physical intimacy or actions during conflict also allowed us to gauge how close spouses came to accurately describing their spouse's answer to the same questions. Thus, we systematically explored the degree of overlap between a husband and wife in predicting what the other said about himself or herself regarding sex and conflict. We call this measure Understanding after Acitelli, Douvan, and Veroff (1993) and Acker and Veroff (1991); our measures are derived from their work. Again we would posit that

Table 3.2

Summary of Multiple Regression Analyses Predicting Marital Instability from Incompatibilities (Within White Couples and Black Couples)

Predictor	White Couples (N=158)[†]		Black Couples (N=155)[†]		Sign. of W/B diff
	B	beta	B	beta	
Differences in					
Importance of Religion	.21	.10	.37	.11	NS
Attitudes: Conflict	.07	.10	-.05	-.05	+
Preferred Pace of Life	.16+	.15+	.25*	.17*	NS
Openness to Experiences	.02	.02	-.05	-.03	NS
Sex Role Attitudes	.07	.12	-.03	-.04	+
Rules for Marriage	.04	.07	-.02	-.03	NS
Adj. R²	.04*		.01		

+=p<.10
*=p<.05

[†]Reflects the average number of couples on predictors in which there are no missing data.

the greater the understanding the spouses have of each other, the greater the marital stability.

Questions of social cognition in interpersonal interaction have played a central role in social psychology (see Sillars, 1985; Kelley, Berscheid, Christensen, Harvey, Huston, Levinger, McClintock, Peplau, & Peterson, 1983), particularly in earlier symbolic interactionists' thought (e.g., Laing, 1971; Goffman, 1959). But systematic application of this framework to predicting marital stability or quality is minimal.

Acker and Veroff (1991) studied parallel interpersonal perceptions about how caring the spouses were towards each other and found that understanding the level of caring was important in predicting marital quality over and above how caring the spouse actually was. Acitelli, Douvan, and Veroff (1993) also found that understanding of a spouse with regard to conflict styles was useful in predicting marital happiness. Assumed similarity was also important but to a lesser extent. Acitelli et al. found that they had to distinguish between interpersonal perceptions with regard to positive conflict styles (e.g., listen to the other's point of view) as opposed to destructive styles (e.g., yell or insult). In a similar vein, Acker and Veroff (1991) found that perceptions of each other's views about their sex lives had different implications for the marriage if they further differentiated perceptions of positive sexual experience from perceptions of negative sexual experience. In other words, the implications of interpersonal perceptions like assumed similarity and understanding may be different depending on whether the behavioral context for measuring them is a positive or a negative one.

Measures of Interpersonal Perceptions

We took Acker and Veroff's and Acitelli et al.'s leads and kept positive versus negative behavioral context distinctions in the assessments we used in our analyses. Thus, for sexual interactions there were eight measures: a husband's assumed similarity with and understanding of his wife with regard to how enjoyable sex is for her (measures 1 and 2); a wife's assumed similarity with and understanding of her husband with regard to enjoyable sex (measures 3 and 4); a husband's assumed similarity with and understanding of his wife with regard to how upset she is about their sex life (measures 5 and 6); and a wife's assumed similarity with and understanding of her husband with regard to how upset he is about their sex life (measures 7 and 8). Parallel measures of assumed similarity and understanding of each other with regard to positive conflict styles and negative conflict styles resulted in eight interpersonal perceptions for conflict styles.

Separate regression analyses were run for interpersonal perceptions regarding conflict and interpersonal perceptions regarding sexual interactions.

RESULTS: PREDICTING INSTABILITY FROM INTERPERSONAL PERCEPTIONS OF CONFLICT

The most striking result found in predicting instability from interpersonal perceptions of conflict (See Table 3.3) is that these perceptions are much more significant for predicting instability among black couples then they are among white couples. Twenty-one percent of the variance is explained in the case of the black couples, compared with 5% among the white couples. And even the one significant predictor for the white couples is significantly higher among the black couples. We will hold off commenting on this difference until we look closely at what the specific results were.

Most of the significant predictors operate in a direction that one would assume: the more understanding of the spouse and the more perceived similarity about conflict styles, the less the instability. In the case of the black couples, both understanding and perceived similarity about negative conflict styles operate as predicted from assessments from both husbands and wives. In the case of the white couples, only the assessment of husbands' understanding of their wives' negative conflict style operates as predicted.

Among the black couples, however, we find that two significant predictors operate in a direction opposite to predictions: the greater the understanding and perceived similarity, the greater the instability. The direction of the parallel results for white husbands is the same and not significantly different from the black husbands' data. What do we make of these puzzling findings? Our only speculation is that both understanding and perceived similarity by husbands of these apparently positive responses to conflict may represent somewhat distanced appraisals of what happens when the couple is in conflict. Both couples may be denying much in the way of emotional reactions to conflict, which if appraised by the husband may mean that he has pulled out of the fighting and sees only rational interaction. Couples who fight in this distanced way may be pulling back from the relationship in general. This is highly speculative and deserves closer attention in future analyses, especially in the parallel examination of the third year interpersonal perceptions about conflict (see Chapter 7).

Why should any of the above be more apparent in predicting the instability of black couples than predicting the instability of white couples? We again return to a theme that we were beginning to develop in the second chapter: black couples are more wary about the interdependence of their marital relationship and react more to each other as individuals. A black couple's perceptions about how they as individuals deal with their conflicts are more likely to affect their stability than their interactions as a couple or what they think of each other as a couple. When these perceptions correlate with reality (in essence what we measure in the assessments of understanding and assumed similarity), then interpersonal perceptions about conflict can play a

particularly strong role in maintaining or interfering with the stability of black marriages. The husband or wife will be sensitive to each other's perceptions because they are reading each other as individuals and not looking at the relationship in "relationship" terms. We suggest that this may be more characteristic of black couples than of white couples.

RESULTS: PREDICTING INSTABILITY FROM INTERPERSONAL PERCEPTIONS OF SEXUAL INTERACTION

The results in Table 3.4 predicting instability from interpersonal perceptions of sexual interactions are not consistent with the results using interpersonal perceptions of conflict. By and large, these interpersonal perceptions are not as powerful predictors for either white or black couples. Only one result is anything more than a trend. White males' perceived similarity with their wives about positive sexual experience is associated with couple instability. We can only suggest that this represents some white males' insensitive projections of their own sexual gratification on to their wives, who are perhaps finding it difficult to get much positive excitement from sexual activity. Any such misperception might lead to greater discord under these circumstances. There was a trend indicating that when white males do actually understand their wives' positive sexual reactions, their marriages tend to be more stable.

By contrast, black males' perceived similarity about such matters predicts couple stability. Perhaps assumed similarity about sex does not reflect as much defensive projection on the black males' part. Furthermore, their wives may be less generally inhibited about sexuality than white wives, and hence, when assumed similarity represents misperception on the part of black husbands, there may be cause for marital enhancement rather than discord. The black-white difference in the relationship of husbands' perceived similarity of positive sexual interaction to marital instability is highly significant.

Perceived Interaction Styles of the Self and Perceived Couple Interaction Styles

Oggins, Veroff, and Leber (1993) analyzed all the perceptions of marital interaction that were gathered in the first year in the Spouse Interview. Thirty-eight items were initially identified as having to do with the way husbands and wives see their own way of interacting with their spouses, as well as how their spouses' interactions make them feel. By and large, the items were essentially self-reports rather than reports about their spouses, which was what we covered in the previous section. The items asked about a broad range of interaction,

Table 3.3

Summary of Multiple Regression Analyses Predicting Marital Instability from Interpersonal Conflict Behaviors (Within White Couples and Black Couples)

Predictor	White Couples (N=158)[†] B	beta	Black Couples (N=155)[†] B	beta	Sign of W/B diff
Wives' Perceptions					
a. Positive Conflict Behaviors					
Understanding	-.15	-.08	-.01	.00	NS
Assumed Similarity	-.12	-.06	.21	.10	*
b. Negative Conflict Behaviors					
Understanding	-.48	-.23	-.40*	-.18*	NS
Assumed Similarity	.00	.00	-.35+	-.16+	+
Husbands' Perceptions					
a. Positive Conflict Behaviors					
Understanding	.18	.09	.40*	.17*	NS
Assumed Similarity	.16	.08	.50*	.21*	NS
b. Negative Conflict Behaviors					
Understanding	-.21**	-.11**	-.56*	-.22*	+
Assumed Similarity	.01	.00	-.62**	-.25**	**
Adj. R^2	.05*		.21***		

+=$p<.10$
*=$p<.05$
**=$p<.01$
***=$p<.001$

[†]Reflects the average number of couples on predictors in which there is no missing data.

from conflict management and sexual interactions, as above, to approval reactions, communication, and power styles. All of them were submitted to factor analyses, some were omitted subsequently because they were loading definitely on any factor, and the remaining were factor analyzed again for husbands and wives separately. From these factor analyses six factors emerged that were common to both husbands and wives (<u>Disclosing Communication, Affective Affirmation</u> by the <u>Spouse of the Self</u>, <u>Destructive Conflict Management Style</u>, <u>Constructive Management Style</u>, <u>Negative Sexual Interaction</u>, and <u>Traditional Role Regulation</u>). One was specific to husbands (<u>Avoidant Conflict Style</u>) and another specific to wives (<u>Positive Coorientation</u>).

Measures of Perceived Interactions

We used these factor analyses as a basis for selecting measures of perceived interactions that could be predictors of instability in this book. Some were scales based on the factors; some were single items that covered interaction issues that did not factor out simply or uniformly across husbands and wives. In particular, issues of power and affiliative styles of relating to each other seemed to be very different for men and women. As a result, we sometimes used only single items to represent certain issues or took the liberty of breaking off part of a factor that was different for men and women. To make a long story short, we pulled together fourteen measures of important perceptions of interaction and made these the bases of the analyses of this section.

Of these fourteen, six were direct self-reports about how the individual was interacting or reacting to the interactions of the spouse. Three had to do with conflict styles: destructive (e.g., yelling, insulting); constructive (e.g. trying to understand, listening); and avoidant (e.g., leaving to cool off). Another three had to do with how easy spouses found it to relate to each other in general: finding one's spouse non-supportive (as measured by the report that it is easier to talk to someone other than the spouse); disclosing communication style (e.g., frequency of revealing intimate things); feeling affectively affirmed by what the spouse does (e.g., reports that spouse makes person feel good about his/her ideas). The other eight were reports about their interaction as a couple: how much they shared activities; how much relaxed time they have together; frequency of particularly enjoyable sexual interaction (positive sexuality); frequency of negative sexual interaction (negative sexuality); frequency of conflict; range of topics on which they disagree; how much power the husband has in decision making; and how much role sharing they do (a summary code of attitudes and behaviors regarding work obligations and household task assignments). Since both husbands and wives reported on these interactions

between them, we used the product of their judgments as the couple score. This pooled judgment, while still in the realm of self-reports, may approximate the couple's interactive behavior.

RESULTS: PREDICTING INSTABILITY FROM PERCEIVED INTERACTION STYLES OF THE SELF AND PERCEIVED COUPLE INTERACTION STYLES

Table 3.5 summarizes regression analyses for spouses' self-reports of their own interactive style with their partners, as predictors of instability; Table 3.6 summarizes the regression analyses for the couples' pooled judgments of their interactions as couples, as predictors of instability.

Among the spouse's reports of his/her own interactive style with his/her partner, only one consistently predicts instability across race and gender: whether or not a person reports using destructive styles of reacting to conflict. This consistency mirrors what many researchers of marital well-being have discovered, that negative reactions to conflict, particularly when reciprocated, are good predictors of marital disruption (Gottman, 1993). Furthermore, the fact found in Table 3.5 that the frequency of conflict reported by couples is also a solid predictor of marital instability probably reflects scenes of destructive interchanges between people. People remember as fights those situations where bitter words and raised voices are exchanged. These almost become the defining characteristics of conflict for many couples.

We had expected Affective Affirmation of husbands and wives by their partners to be strong predictors of instability. Surprisingly, only the Affective Affirmation of husbands by wives seems to matter for understanding stability. It is highly significant when black husbands feel affirmed, and only a trend when white husbands feel affirmed (p = .11). Nevertheless, the direction is clear for predicting instability for both black and white couples. Why not with respect to wives' feelings of affirmation by their husbands?

Oggins, Veroff, and Leber (1993) had found that Affective Affirmation by husbands was especially important for women's marital happiness in the first year. Evidently this does not hold for marital instability. This may be an important finding. It could be that most women who feel unaffirmed in their marriage may be relatively unhappy in the relationship but do not put the kind of pressure on a marriage that would result in disruption. It is almost as if many women come to feel that it is part of the bargain to feel non-affirmed in marriage. They therefore put up with these circumstances and seek affirmation in other relationships (friends, children, and extended family). Men, when feeling unaffirmed by their wives, also are unhappy (as Oggins, Veroff, and Leber found), but we can speculate that, unlike women, this may be all they need to set into motion activities (affairs, drinking, abusive reactions generally)

Table 3.4

Summary of Multiple Regression Analyses Predicting Marital Instability from Interpersonal Perceptions of Sexual Interaction (Within White Couples and Black Couples)

Predictor	White Couples (N=158)†		Black Couples (N=155)†		Sign of W/B diff
	B	beta	B	beta	
Wives' Perceptions					
a. Positive Sexual Interaction					
Understanding	−.10	−.07	−.07	−.03	NS
Assumed Similarity	.00	.00	.25	.08	NS
b. Negative Sexual Interaction					
Understanding	.01	.00	−.09	−.07	NS
Assumed Similarity	−.17	−.12	−.16	−.10	NS
Husbands' Perceptions					
a. Positive Sexual Interaction					
Understanding	−.26+	−.18+	−.05	−.03	NS
Assumed Similarity	.64**	.27**	−.55+	−.16+	***
b. Negative Sexual Interaction					
Understanding	.14	.13	−.09	−.07	+
Assumed Similarity	.05	.03	−.08	−.07	NS
Adj. R²		.06*		.02	

+=p<.10
**=p<.01
***=p<.001

†Reflects the average number of couples on predictors in which there is no missing data.

that will ultimately disrupt the marriage. Many researchers (e.g., Veroff, Kulka, & Douvan, 1981) have shown that men are more solely dependent on their wives for support than women are on their husbands. When marital support goes bad for men, it thus has more dire consequences for their commitment to marriage. This set of speculations seems worthy of further testing in these longitudinal data.

Table 3.5 further indicates that two other interactive styles have different implications for stability, depending on whether it is the self-report of husbands or wives. Both have to do with communication. For women, finding it easier to talk to someone other than their husbands is associated with instability. This is not true for the men. And for men, having a self-disclosing style of communication is associated with instability. This is not true for the women. Not finding the husband's ease of talking to his wife as a factor in marital stability makes sense only if such talking is seen by men to mean instrumental talking. Men often would prefer talking to their buddies about sports, their colleagues about their work and affairs of state. Not finding it easy to talk with their spouses about these issues may not be a serious matter about their relationship. Women, however, often want more talk with their husbands as a way to validate their ideas and legitimacy, as well as a way to maintain an affiliative connection and derive emotional support. There is a higher correlation between ease of talking with spouse and Affective Affirmation for women (.38) than for men (.28).

It is more difficult to think of reasons why men's having a Disclosing Style would interfere in a relationship. Much of popular literature would have us think otherwise for both men and women. If communication in disclosures is about positive feelings only, the results are indeed perplexing. But if the communication is largely about negative or resentful feelings or about ways in which the couple is not getting along, disclosure could reflect troubles in the marriage. We would suggest that this may be the case for men, who are generally uncomfortable about talking about relationships, but who might be prompted to talk in the heat of emotional fighting. By contrast, women may be used to disclosing feelings, both positive and negative ones, so that even when they discuss problems in the marriage, it may have less disruptive significance for them.

Our regression analyses point to certain marital interactions that predict stability or instability only for black couples: husbands' use of constructive styles of dealing with conflict (see Table 3.5) and the couples' reports of husbands' power in decision making (see Table 3.6). We consider that these results reflect the same phenomenon. There has been some suggestion that one of the pitfalls for black men in modern urban society is that they are in a tenuous position as economic provider for a family. Joblessness has increased among black men over the last thirty years. A number of analysts suggest that this trend is due to industrial restructuring which has eliminated many low

skill, high paying jobs. The competition for jobs over all has increased with black men being at the end of the hiring queue as the opportunities for good jobs have diminished. In the next chapter, we will see that black husbands' worrying about financial matters has more to do with marital stability than does such worry from white husbands or from women. What could stabilize a black husband's sense of well-being under these circumstances is some sense of traditional power being available to him in the family. And that is why we think the measure of husband's power in decision making has some significance in predicting the stability of black marriages but not the stability of white marriages. Among white couples traditional power is automatically granted the husband in his readily available opportunities for economic success. There is less pressure on white marriages to compensate for a husband's lack of economic power by granting him greater power in marital decision making.

If we are right about our analysis of the need for black husbands to feel traditionally in control of their marriages, then it might help us explain why a constructive conflict management style by black husbands significantly predicts marital instability. The style can be interpreted as appeasing and granting a partner equal status in conflict. While this may be beneficial for conflict resolution, it may not be beneficial to a person desiring to be the person in charge.

One remaining result about perceived interactions that should be briefly noted is the predictive power of negative sexual interaction experienced in the first year in understanding marital instability in both blacks and whites. Sexual frustration is clearly an important factor in understanding marital dissolution. While Henderson-King and Veroff (1994) found that both positive and negative sexual interactions were predictors of different dimensions of marital well-being, only the negative experiences of sexual interactions were relevant for understanding marital stability. This suggests that marital partners may maintain relationships even when their sexual lives are not markedly gratifying as long as there were no significant problems. There will evidently be cause for marital trouble when marital sexual experience is seen as problematic, either because of its frequency or lack of frequency or because of other problems leading to sexual dissatisfaction. It will be interesting to see whether reports of negative sexual interactions are maintained as significant predictors when they are combined with the other significant predictors emerging from our analysis of the marital processes during the first year of marriage.

A final observation should be made about Table 3.5, which focuses on couple interactions as predictors. This set of predictors is more useful in understanding the overall variance of marital stability in white couples (Adjusted R-squared = .26) than in black couples (Adjusted R-squared = .08). As before, we would observe that this set has a focus on the couple as a unit

Table 3.5
Summary of Multiple Regression Analyses Predicting Marital Instability from Interaction Styles of the Self (Within White Couples and Black Couples)

Predictor	White Couples (N=168)†		Black Couples (N=155)†		Sign of W/B diff
	B	beta	B	beta	
Wives					
Easier to Talk to Other	.37*	.17*	.31+	.13+	NS
Disclosing Style	.02	.02	.06	.06	NS
Affective Affirmation	.01	.02	.01	.01	NS
Destructive Conflict Style	.11**	.24**	.07	.10	NS
Constructive Conflict Style	-.05	-.11	.04	.07	*
Avoidant Conflict Style	-.02	-.03	.08	.10	NS
Husbands					
Easier to Talk to Other	.06	.02	-.08	-.04	NS
Disclosing Style	.20***	.28***	.14+	.14+	NS
Affective Affirmation	-.10	-.13	.32**	-.34***	**
Destructive Conflict Style	.07+	.15+	.10	.15+	NS
Constructive Conflict Style	.00	.00	.18***	.33***	***
Avoidant Conflict Style	.01	.02	.02	.02	NS
Adj. R^2	.218****		.225****		

+=p<.10
*=p<.05
**=p<.01
***=p<.001

†Reflects the average number of couples on predictors in which there is no missing data.

Table 3.6
Summary of Multiple Regression Analyses Predicting Marital Instability from Measures of Couple Interaction (Within White Couples and Black Couples)

Predictor	White Couples (N=158)[†]		Black Couples (N=155)[†]		Sign of W/B diff
	B	beta	B	beta	
Shared Time	–.01	–.01	.01	.04	NS
Relaxed Time	–.03	–.09	–.04	–.07	NS
Positive Sexual Interaction	.00	.02	.00	.02	NS
Negative Sexual Interaction	.14	.30***	.08	.14	NS
Frequency of Conflicts	.13	.32***	.12	.27**	NS
Range of Disagreements	.00	–.01	–.02	–.07	NS
Husband's Power	–.01	–.02	–.09	–.14+	NS
Role Sharing	–.06	–.11	–.08	–.12	NS
Adj. R^2		.26***		–.08*	

+=p<.10
*=p<.05
**=p<.01
***=p<.001

[†]Reflects the average number of couples on predictors in which there is no missing data.

rather than individuals, and, as such, should be more relevant to the orientation we have posited as more characteristic of white couples than of black couples.

Actual Observed Couple Interaction

During the couple interview two procedures were used which enabled us to obtain measures of actual interaction. One procedure asked couples to tell the story of their relationship. The couples told the stories together with little prompting from the interviewer although they were asked to follow a general story outline. The story was tape-recorded and interactions were identified as any change in voice from one spouse to another. Each interaction sequence was then coded for its presumed social impact on the other spouse. The procedure is outlined in Veroff, Sutherland, Chadiha and Ortega (1993).

Measures of Observed Couple Interaction

Four categories of observed interactions were used for the present regression analysis of predictors of marital instability: interactions whose effects were Collaborative (i.e., indicated a further extension of the ideas of his/her spouse); interactions whose effects were Confirming (i.e., indicated approval of what his/her partner said); interactions that were Conflicting (i.e., indicated disagreement with the spouse); interactions that were both Collaborative and Confirming (i.e., indicated both approval and extension of ideas). These were not the only categories coded but the ones appearing with sufficient frequency to warrant systematic analysis. The simple assessments used were the proportion of the husbands' total number of interactions that fit each of the four categories and the proportion of the wives' total interactions that fit these categories. As a result, there were eight measures in total from the story procedure used in the multiple regressions in this set.

One other assessment was derived from a second procedure used in the couple interview. Having been asked to rank the importance of sixteen rules for marriage (e.g.,"share equally in household chores"), couples were asked to reconcile differences they had in a consensual ranking. This ranking was then compared to each spouse's individual ranking, and an evaluation was made in terms of husband's relative power in bringing about the consensus. That is, a high score was given to a couple if the correlation of the husband's initial ranking to the consensus ranking was much higher than the wife's initial ranking; a low score was given to a couple if the correlation of the wife's ranking was much higher than the husband's initial ranking, and so on.

Our predictions were that the more collaborative, confirming, or collaborative and confirming a couple was in working out the story of their

relationship, the more likely they were to have a solid basis for their marriage during the first year. Alternately we assumed that the more conflicting they were, the more difficulty they would have establishing an agreed upon basis for their married life. We were more exploratory about the observed husband's power in decision making. If our couples were highly traditional, more power vested in the husband's decisions might enhance the relationship; if our couples were more egalitarian, this might signify possible problems they needed to work through in their interactions.

RESULTS: PREDICTING INSTABILITY FROM ACTUAL OBSERVED COUPLE INTERACTION

By and large, the actual couple interactions observed in the two procedures yielded little that was useful in predicting marital instability, as can be seen in Table 3.7. The overall multiple regressions were insignificant for both black couples and white couples. Two types of interactions measured in the observations of the black couples were significant predictors and in the expected direction: the more black wives were collaborative with their spouse or both confirming and collaborative, the more stable the marriages. The parallel measures for black husbands' observed interaction were significant predictors of marital instability also but in the direction opposite to our expectations. The predictive power of these two variables among both black husbands and black wives was significantly different from the predictive power of these variables among their white counterparts.

The results are puzzling. Why should a collaborative orientation in the behavior of husbands towards their wives be associated with being in a marriage that was later to be unstable? We hesitate even speculating about this, given the lack of overall significance in the regression. If we were to venture any guesses, it would be in the direction of seeing collaborativeness on the part of black men as being accommodative to the power of their wives. Earlier we argued many black husbands may need to feel in control of their marital lives as compensation for power insecurity in the public spheres of their lives. But given this explanation, why did the measure of husband's power in decision making not turn out to be a significant predictor for black couples? All in all, we must chalk up these results as curious findings which likely will not remain as significant predictors of instability when we put them into a larger regression analysis with other measures of marital processes that were significant predictors in previous sections.

Combining the Effects of Predictors from the First Year of Marriage: Marital Perceptions and Interactions

The multiple regressions for white and black couples appearing in Tables 3.8–3.10 summarize the combined predictive effects of the significant predictors of marital instability we found in this chapter. As in the previous chapter, we selected those predictors that were significant at the .05 level for either the black couples or the white couples, but used the same overall set in each multiple regression analysis. We were again liberal and included individually significant predictors even if the particular multiple regression in which it was embedded was not significant.

Because there were so many significant predictors, we broke them up into sets of perceptual factors and interaction factors. The results using perceptual variables as predictors appear in Table 3.8; the results using interactive variables appear in Table 3.9; and the results using only those significant effects found across Tables 3.8 and 3.9 are summarized in Table 3.10.

In Table 3.8, we learn that husbands' understanding of their wives' Positive Constructive Conflict Style is no longer significant when considered along with assumed similarity about positive sexual interactions. Perceptions about constructive styles of conflict management and perceptions about positive reactions to sexuality are evidently getting at similar kinds of things, and the assumed similarity about positive sexuality seems to be the only predictor we need to consider. In addition, incompatibility on preferred pace of life no longer remains a significant predictor. It stands to reason that this very general incompatibility in orientations may be made up of a number of interpersonal perceptions that are captured in the measures that remain significant in Table 3.8.

From Table 3.9, we learn that we cannot drop any of the measured interaction variables. Perceived individual interaction behavior, perceived couple interactions, and actual interactions observed continued to be significant predictors in the combined analyses for black couples and white couples separately as well as the total sample.

When we include the significant predictors from Tables 3.8 and 3.9 together in the multiple regressions of Table 3.10, one more predictor filters out: wife's finding it easier to talk to someone other than her husband. This variable, found to be a predictor for white couples only, has a significant and moderately high correlation (−.27) with white women's collaborative interactive style. As a result, with these both in the same prediction equation, neither one has sufficiently strong associations with instability to produce significant effects for the white couples.

We are impressed with the number of remaining significant predictors. The overall R-squared for the first year of marriage interpersonal variables is .36 for the white couples and .45 for the black couples. This difference in R-

Table 3.7
Summary of Multiple Regression Analyses Predicting Marital Instability from Measures of Actual Interaction Observed (Within White Couples and Black Couples)

Predictor	White Couples (N=134)†		Black Couples (N=136)†		Sign of W/B diff
	B	beta	B	beta	
Wives					
Collaborating	1.84	.24	-3.42	-.38*	***
Confirming	.01	.00	-2.91	-.13	NS
Conflicting	-.16	.00	.58	.02	NS
Collaborating/Confirming	.15	.01	-5.36	-.23*	*
Husbands					
Collaborating	-.74	-.11	-2.53	.27+	*
Confirming	.17	.01	-.18	-.01	NS
Conflicting	2.90	.05	-1.12	-.03	NS
Collaborating/Confirming	-1.36	.09	3.99	.25*	**
Power Rank	.09	.07	.13	.08	NS
Adj. R^2	00,NS		00,NS		

+=$p<.10$
*=$p<.05$
**=$p<.01$
***=$p<.001$

†Reflects the average number of couples on predictors in which there is no missing data.

Table 3.8

Summary of Multiple Regression Analyses Predicting Marital Instability from All Significant Interpersonal Perceptions (Within White Couples and Black Couples)

Predictor	White Couples (N=150)†		Black Couples (N=158)†		Sign of W/B diff
	B	beta	B	beta	
Wives					
Understanding H's Negative Conflict Style	-.48**	-.24**	-.35*	-.16*	NS
Husbands					
Understanding W's Positive Conflict Style	.08	.04	.24+	.12+	NS
Assumed Similarity W's Positive Conflict Style	.12	.06	.64***	.27***	**
Understanding W's Negative Conflict Style	-.22	-.12	-.68***	-.27***	**
Assumed Similarity W's Conflict Style	.03	.02	-.69***	-.28***	***
Assumed Similarity Positive Sexual Interaction	.38*	.16*	-.57*	-.16*	***
Couple					
Discrepancy, Pace of Life	-.02	-.02	.06	.04	NS
Adj. R^2	.08**		.24***		

+=p<.10
*=p<.05
**=p<.01
***=p<.001

†Reflects the average number of couples on predictors in which there are no missing data.

Table 3.9
Summary of Multiple Regression Analyses Predicting Marital Instability from All Significant Interpersonal Interactions
(Within White Couples and Black Couples)

Predictor	White Couples (N=150)[†]		Black Couples (N=158)[†]		W/B diff
	B	beta	B	beta	
Wives					
Ease of Talking to Others	.28*	.13*	.28*	.12*	
Destructive Conflict Style	.08*	.18**	.06	.09	
Collaborative Style	.71	.09	-2.00**	-.22**	***
Collaborative/ Confirming Style	-.32	-.02	-4.22**	-.18**	**
Husbands					
Disclosing Style	.15**	.20**	.12*	.12*	
Affective Affirmation	-.02	-.02	-.32****	-.35****	****
Constructive Conflict Style	-.01	-.02	.18****	.33****	****
Collaborative Style	.66	.04	3.53***	.23***	*
Couple					
Negative Sexual Interaction	.11**	.23**	.05	.09	
Frequency of Conflict	.11***	.28***	.10**	.21**	
Adj. R^2	.33****		.31****		

*p<.05
**p<.01
***p<.001
****p<.0001

[†]Reflects the number of couples in which there are no missing data on any of the predictors.

Table 3.10
Summary of Multiple Regression Analyses Predicting Instability from All Significant Interpersonal Perceptions and Interactions (Within White Couples and Black Couples)

Predictor	White Couples (N=150)[1]		Black Couples (N=158)[1]		W/B diff
	B	beta	B	beta	
Wives					
Understanding Husband's Negative Conflict Style	-.08	-.04	-.52***	-.23***	
Ease of Taking to Stress	.22	.11	.08	.03	
Destructive Conflict Style	.08*	.18*	-.01	-.01	
Collaborative Style	.80	.10	-2.30****	-.25****	****
Collaborative/Confirming Style	.15	.01	-4.56***	-.20***	***
Husbands					
Perceived Similarity of Positive Conflict	-.06	-.03	.60*****	.25****	****
Understanding Negative Conflict	.02	.01	-.54***	-.21***	***
Assumed Similarity Negative Conflict	-.03	-.01	-.44*	-.18*	*
Disclosing Style	.13**	.18**	.09	.09	
Affective Affirmation	-.01	-.01	-.31*	-.34****	****
Constructive Conflict Style	-.02	-.05	.19****	.34***	****
Collaborative/Confirming Style	.72	.05	9.56*****	-.20****	***
Couples					
Negative Sexual Interaction	.12***	.26***	.00	.00	***

Table 3.10 (continued)

Predictor	White Couples (N=150)[†]		Black Couples (N=158)[†]			W/B diff
	B	beta	B	beta		
Frequency of Conflict	.10***	.26***	.07*	.15*		
Perceived Similarity Positive Conflict	.51***	.21***	−.34+	−.10+		***
Adj. R²	.36****		.24***			

+p<.10
*p<.05
**p<.01
***p<.001
****p<.0001

[†]Reflects the number of couples in which there are no missing data on any of the predictors.

squared indicates once more that something different may go into the processes that destabilize white marriages compared to black marriages. If we were to select a set of factors emerging in this analysis that differentiates the two groups, it would be the finding that black husbands' feelings of affective affirmation from their wives is important for stable marriages. Among white husbands, these feelings are not a strong predictor of stability for white couples. White husbands evidently need far less reassurance from their wives than the black husbands in order to make a go of their marriages.

A number of the other variables describing interaction yield results contrary to our predictions for black husbands. We guess further, that there is an enormous sensitivity to appearing vulnerable and powerless among black husbands, which makes their marriages responsive to defensive strategies of interaction. The fact that black husbands' reports of using constructive conflict styles and their observed interactions of being collaborative in conflict situations are both positively related to marital instability in the prediction equation makes us realize how reactive black couples are to subtle meanings of marital interaction. These subtle meanings could very well be instances where husbands protest too much about their accommodation and communicate to their wives and to themselves that their marriages may falter.

SUMMARY

In this chapter we dealt with the attitudes, perceptions, and interactions that may be relevant in the first year of marriage for establishing a close interpersonal bond between husbands and wives that would obviate any thoughts about separation or divorce, and instead would commit the partners to a stable marriage. Examining attitude incompatibilities was fruitless although there was a trend for both black and white couples who had incompatible preferences about their pace of life to be in unstable marriages. Examining spouses' perceptions of one another with regard to sexuality was also not generally fruitful but, with regard to conflict styles it was fruitful, particularly for black couples. We interpreted the special importance of social perceptions regarding conflict styles in understanding black couples' marital stability to reflect the importance of sizing each other up as individuals among black couples and avoiding any focus on interdependence or the nature of the relationship, which we suggest is the central focus of concern for white couples in the first year of marriage.

Analyses of spouses' reports of the marital interaction styles of the self as well as reports of couple interactions and actual interaction observed each produced important findings for understanding how first year marital interaction may affect marital instability. Only one result was common in both black and white couples. Reported frequency of conflict is associated with

marital instability, a result that is not too surprising. More interesting was the fact that reports of negative sexual interaction in white couples was important in predicting the instability of the white couples but not the black couples. For the black couples, by contrast, evidence of their not having collaborative and confirming styles of interaction in telling the story of their relationship was especially critical in predicting their marital instability, as was the report that black husbands felt not affectively affirmed by their wives.

There were many assessments in this chapter that were effective predictors of instability beyond those we have just summarized. Some are straightforward; some are more puzzling. The patterns present many possibilities for interpretation and speculation, particularly in building a conception of how black couples growing up and living in a racist society have to confront different norms and styles for establishing a committed marital relationship as compared to couples growing up and living with white privilege.

4

THE FIRST YEAR OF MARRIAGE:
EXTERNAL FACTORS

In a search for factors affecting marital instability in the first year of marriage, we wanted to look beyond the couple's relationship and what they are like as individuals. We wanted to consider the external world and how it helps shape marital adjustment. That external world could impose undue stress or provide support. In this chapter we will consider stresses and support.

STRESSES

Among the many potential stresses that young newlyweds face, perhaps the most common and crucial are those having to do with finances, financial pressures, and the creation of an acceptable balance between work and family life. The beginning stages of marriage coincide for most part with the very years when spouses are establishing their individual careers or work patterns, and thus, setting trajectories that will influence their social status attainment. Dealing with these external matters at the same time that they are learning how to be a family on their own, responding to the needs of an intimate relationship, and gaining recognition and validation as a social unit can create high levels of stress for the partners and the marriage.

Husbands, in particular, face heavy pressure from the work and financial realm. It is still the case in our culture that masculinity is intricately tied to the ability to provide for one's family. Hence, most men feel they should establish a viable work life even if it sometimes interferes with their marriage or family life.

Other stressors that can affect the newly established marital relationship include pressures from friends and family. Involvement in these social networks can generate competing demands on the time and energy of young

couples and deny them the time and privacy they need in order to work out their own norms and establish their own identity as a family. In the second year of our study, we asked spouses whether they had experienced interference from their families and friends since we interviewed them. The impact of these sources of stress on marital instability will be assessed later in Chapter 6. In the first year, work and the financial arena are the only external stressors we measured.

The questions asked included frequency of worry about being able to meet financial needs (pay the bills), job dissatisfactions, and the extent to which demands of the job interfere with family life. Question wording and response categories appear in the Appendix of measures.

We expected that worry about finances or stresses of work, either unhappiness and dissatisfaction on the job or excessive work demands experienced as interference with family life, would create stress on the marriage and thus lay the groundwork for marital instability and dissatisfaction. Kanter (1977), Piotrkowski (1978), Voydanoff (1987), and other theorists who have worked at the intersection of work and family life stress the critical effects work life has on other areas of experience and particularly on satisfaction and performance in family roles. For women, assuming a role in the paid labor force is associated with increased power in family decision making. Voydanoff and Majka (1990) summarized the heavy effects that unemployment of the husband/father has on family functioning. Quinn and Shepherd (1974) documented more subtle effects of various aspects of work satisfaction or stress on families. Numerous research studies have shown the critical effects of job and financial insecurity on the lives of the unemployed and underemployed, effects ranging from direct physical health disturbance to mental health problems and family conflict and breakdown. Wilson (1987) in particular has described the ways in which African-American men and their families are affected by the severe unemployment and underemployment that confront African-Americans in the occupational world.

RESULTS: STRESSES AFFECTING MARITAL INSTABILITY

Findings from the regression of marital instability on each of the stressors appear in Table 4.1. We find significant results only for black husbands for whom worrying about money and saying that their work interferes with their family life both increase marital instability. In both of these instances, the difference in the predictive power of husband's response is greater for black couples than for white couples. The Multiple R-squared for all stressors' effects is significant for black couples but not for white couples. None of the three stress reports by either black wives or white wives predicts instability in the marriage. There is a curious difference between the predictive power of black and white wives' reports of Work Interference: for white wives, Work Interference shows a slight positive relationship to instability while for black wives, it is negatively related to instability (i.e., seems to increase stability).

Since neither relationship is significant in itself, however, we are reluctant to say much about it.

What do we make of these findings? Why the clear relationship of black husbands' stress and marital instability when equivalent relationships do not appear for stressors in any of the other three race/gender groups? If the stress factors had been uniformly non-predictive in all groups, we might have interpreted this as a phenomenon of early marriage. Stressors that affect individuals and their relationships in other circumstances and at other times in the life cycle are not, we might have speculated, sufficient to outweigh the general glow or positive aura of the honeymoon period. Even though they have money worries and job worries, even though they feel that work interferes with their family time, couples in the earliest stage of marriage, we might have suggested, remain optimistic about their chances for a long and satisfying marriage because the relationship has brought them so much pleasure and satisfaction.

For some couples, the fact that there is no relationship between work and financial concerns and the stability of their marriage may also stem from the belief that having to work too much or having too little money is a temporary condition that will eventually dissipate. If one or both spouses are full-time students, their anticipated future would include financial security and more leisure. Being poor doesn't feel such a heavy burden when it is known to be temporary and in the service of one's education or one's future earning power.

In some cases, present financial problems may be less severe because the couple knows that their parents or other relatives would help them if things got too bad. Any of these ameliorating conditions can relieve some of the tension that might otherwise be created in a relationship by financial worries or heavy work demands.

Perhaps this is what happens in young white couples. It may be true for black wives as well. But how to account for the differential effect of black husbands' concern about finances and the interference between work and family life?

Much has been written about difficulties committing to a long term relationships among young black men. Analysis of the marriage ratio in the black community has led theorists to suggest that the marriage option has greater value for black women because the pool of eligible black males is small (Fosseti & Kiecolt, 1993; Tucker & Mitchell-Kernan, in press). The scarcity of eligible black males means that their value is high and options available to them outside of marriage may gain relative value. A more fundamental reason may be that black males experience considerable labor market vulnerability (Wilson, 1987). Both historical and contemporary discrimination have kept young black males in the most vulnerable and conflicted position in the occupational world. Historically, even under slavery, black women have been more readily employable than black males, albeit in domestic work and other undervalued and underpaid occupations. And young black women were often encouraged to stay in school when their brothers had to drop out to work, the case in many working class families.

Table 4.1
Summary of Multiple Regression Analyses Predicting Marital Instability from Stressor Variables (Within White Couples and Black Couples)

Predictor	White Couples (N=158)†		Black Couples (N=155)†		Sign. of W/B diff
	B	beta	B	beta	
Wives					
Worry About Money	.15	.11	.12	.06	NS
Job Satisfaction	.04	.03	-.02	-.01	NS
Work Interference	.08	.10	-.10	-.08	*
Husbands					
Worry About Money	.01	.01	.40**	.25**	**
Job Satisfaction	-.08	-.05	-.12	-.06	NS
Work Interference	.04	.04	.28**	.23**	*
Adj. R^2	.00		.10		

*=p<.05
**=p<.01
**=p<.001

†Reflects the average number of couples on predictors in which there are no missing data.

In contemporary America, young high school educated black males have essentially been dealt out of the occupational world. With the closing down of heavy manufacturing as the main thrust of American enterprise, semi-skilled and skilled factory jobs in industries protected by unions have decreased drastically. Unless a young person is educated to use language in service jobs or has skills for high technology occupations, he will be restricted in his occupational options to low paying service jobs. More troublesome is the fact that in most areas of this country employers place black men at the end of the hiring queue (Neckerman & Kirschenman, 1991). In addition to the psychological damage that discrimination causes, the real deprivation that such limited and low paying occupational possibilities lead to is that many young black men are not able to support a family. Wilson (1987) describes cases of young men working two jobs to make enough money to live on. With long hours and distant commutes, they have neither enough money to support a family nor enough leisure to meet potential mates.

The pressure of scarce finances, long hours, and feelings of job insecurity at work may, then, be an order of magnitude greater for black husbands than for the white husbands or for either group of wives. When they say that they worry about whether they can pay their bills or that their work interferes with family time, they may be speaking of concerns that are extremely serious and that create heavy tensions in their relationships. Since our culture defines manhood in part as the ability to provide, the threat to a young man's self-esteem that results from his inability to find decent employment may be especially severe.

It may also be that young African-American husbands, having especially high value as a scarce resource, have more problems forming stable attachment in marriage. When, then, their self-esteem is beset by the strain of un- or underemployment, the marriage commitment may be the first point of vulnerability, the first victim of dislocation.

SOCIAL SUPPORT

We allude above to the cushioning effect of family support when young couples face difficult conditions at work or in their financial security. And research over the last decade has built a strong case for the effectiveness of social support as a buffer against all kinds of difficult life circumstances, ranging from illness to widowhood to the depredations of aging and the isolation of parenting young children (Antonucci, 1990). We wanted to look at the effects of social support on young couples' marital stability and also ask whether the presence of a support system does in fact cushion the effect of work and financial stressors when they occur in the lives of young married couples.

We had three measures of social support in our first year's information. We asked each partner how close they felt to their own family and their spouse's family. We derived one measure from the product of the husband's closeness to his family and the wife's closeness to her family (couple's Closeness With Families). We asked each partner how many family members they thought they could turn to for help and again derived a measure by taking the product of the two spouses' estimates (Family Support). And our third measure came from the product of each spouse's estimate of the number of friends they could turn to for help (Friends' Support).

We expected that social support would cushion the early marriage relationship from external stresses like financial hardship and work-related problems. Having people to turn to—even just for advice and comfort—should decrease the corrosive effect of such stress on the couple's relationship to each other. But we did not think we could predict in advance that a strong support network would necessarily strengthen the relationship irrespective of the presence of stress. Close family and friendship ties might contribute to the solidarity of the couple—particularly if each partner is close to the family and friends of the other partner. But what about cases where each partner has a strong individual support system but these do not overlap or include the partner in their supportive attentions? McGoldrick (1980) and Anderson (1982) have studied the effects of various network structures on the development of couplehood, and both McGoldrick (1980) and Slater (1963) have theorized about the important task of consolidating networks. Slater describes the social systems that develop to counterbalance the young couple's tendency to withdraw into dyadic isolation. Reminding the couple that they have ties and obligations beyond their couplehood can in some cases create tension for the young spouses as noted earlier. Marital troubles are often provoked by parents who continue to make subtle or blatant demands on one of the pair, in a sense contradicting the inviolability of the marital bond or by friends who insist on maintaining a unilateral relationship with one of the spouses. Such pressures from family and friend networks can present strains and invasive pressure in the life of the couple just as easily as they provide support.

RESULTS: SOCIAL SUPPORT AFFECTING MARITAL INSTABILITY

What we find in our analysis (see Table 4.2) is that only Family Closeness relates to marital stability, and this occurs only in the black couples and not for the white couples. Family Closeness is a strong predictor of marital stability for the black couples and is significantly different in its predictive for white couples.

Combining the stress and support factors in an overall regression does not

Table 4.2
Summary of Multiple Regression Analyses Predicting Marital Instability from Support Factors (Within White Couples and Black Couples)

Predictor	White Couples (N=158)[†]		Black Couples (N=155)[†]		Sign. of W/B diff.
	B	beta	B	beta	
Closeness with Family	.01	.08	−.04**	−.26**	***
Family Support	.02	.06	−.02	−.04	NS
Friend Support	−.02	−.06	−.01	−.04	NS
Adj. R²	.00		.06**		

**=p<.01
***=p<.001

[†]Reflects the average number of couples on predictors in which there are no missing data.

change the results we have reported. That is, the same effects appear for the two stresses reported by black husbands (Worry About Money and Work Interfering With Family Life): in both cases, these stresses on black husbands predict instability in marriage (see Table 4.3). And Closeness to Family predicts marital stability for black couples but not for white couples. The Adjusted R-square for the combined effects of stress and support is significant for the black couples and not for the white couples.

How do we interpret these findings? We rely on our original interpretation of the special vulnerability of young black men who face uncertainty in the economic/occupational realm and the prospect of appearing inadequate in the conventional construction of "manhood." And at the same time recognizing his relative scarcity and high value in the marriage market, the young black male may develop a tentativeness about long term commitment that strains the marriage. To the extent that closeness to their families may also reflect a pressure on the young husband to stick by his commitment, it may bolster the couple's marriage stability.

Combining Stress and Support Predictions with Reports of Perceptions and Interventions

Do these external sources of stress and support add anything to our understanding of instability beyond what we have learned from considering the internal dynamics of the marital relationship during the first year of marriage, discussed in Chapter 3?

We ran an additional regression analysis for black couples only, since it was only for them that stressor or support information yielded any significant effects. The only new factor that emerged over and above the last chapter had to do with Job Interference. For men, this variable's partial correlation with instability was .29 (p<.001) with all other significant perceptual and interactive variables partialled out.

Thus, black men's job and provider stresses are critical for understanding black marital instability. These are stressors that do not have immediate psychological mediators in our assessments of marital quality.

SUMMARY

Surprisingly, assessments of external stresses and supports experienced by young married white couples in their first year did not emerge as critical factors affecting the stability of their marriages. There was some indication for the black couples, however, that external family support does matter in maintaining marital stability, as does the absence of external stress experienced

Table 4.3

Summary of Multiple Regression Analyses Predicting Marital Instability from Significant Stressor and Support Variables (Within Black Couples)

Predictor	Black Couples (N=195)[†]	
	B	beta
Couples		
Closeness with Family	-.04***	-.22***
Husbands		
Worry About Money	.39***	.25***
Work interference	.23**	.18**
Adj. R²	.15	

**=p<.01
***=p<.001

[†]Reflects the average number of couples on predictors in which there are no missing data.

by men in the provider role. Black men who worry about finances and find that their jobs interfere with their marriage are more likely to be in unstable marriages. We speculate that in the early years of marriage white couples are able to ride out waves of external stress or the absence of support during a honeymoon period when love may be seen as conquering all. The special disadvantage of blacks in the job world may make black men who are attempting to adopt the provider role in marriage particularly susceptible to financial and job stress as forces countering their commitment to marriage, and both they and their wives may need the closeness to their families to sustain them during this period.

5

THE FIRST YEAR OF MARRIAGE: INTEGRATIVE MARITAL FEELINGS

The tentative model presented in Chapter 1 dealing with the chain of causation that links variables describing couples' experience in the first year of marriage to marital instability assigns a prominent role to overall marital evaluations or integrative marital feelings for that year. The model suggests that these evaluations consolidate and integrate the specific interactions and perceptions, the stresses and supports, and as such, help us think about how the variables assessed in the previous two chapters might be connected to marital instability. Before we attempt to use this model, we should clarify what is meant by marital integrative feelings, how they are distinct from marital instability, and how we measured them in the present study.

Integrative marital feelings are overall judgments of how well the marital relationship is going. Although we have encountered evaluations of the marital relationship in certain variables we have analyzed in previous chapters, each of these preceding variables assessed a specific facet of marriage (e.g., sexual interactions, frequency of fighting, and the like). In this chapter we will be dealing with broader evaluations, ones that cut across specific domains.

Four of the measures are derived from the (Crohan and Veroff, 1989) factor analysis of overall evaluations, discussed in Chapter 1: (1) Marital Happiness, a three-item scale asking about overall feelings of satisfaction and happiness in marriage; (2) Marital Competence, summarizing overall feelings of adequacy and lack of guilt about role performance; (3) Marital Control, a two-item scale reflecting how much the person feels he/she can influence his/her partner's happiness; (4) Marital Equity, a two-item scale measuring the degree of equity the person feels exists in the marital relationship. These are all broad gauged evaluations; happiness, competence, control, and equity define feelings that require a person to make judgments across a number of domains of marriage. Presumably a person would not feel particularly happy

about his/her marriage if he/she was happy about one facet but not happy about other facets. The same would apply to the other three measures. It is in this sense that we view them as integrative feelings.

Crohan and Veroff found that these factors were interrelated but not so highly interrelated as to preclude differential relationships with other variables. We expected that the Marital Happiness measure would be the most powerful predictor of stability because Crohan and Veroff found that it had the strongest covariance with the other three factors.

Two other measures of overall feelings about the marriage were Marital Tension and Relational Affect. The measure of Marital Tension picked up general negative feelings about the relationship focussing on resentments, irritations, and feelings of being upset about fighting. The measure of Relational Affect was based on the narrative procedure (Veroff, Sutherland, Chadiha, & Ortega, 1993); it was the frequency with which the couple spoke of themselves as a unit having feelings or needs that focussed on relationships (e.g., "we were in love," "we wanted to make my family feel comfortable at the wedding"). As such, it was an overall orientation to operate affectively as a couple in relation to themselves and the rest of the world. We see this measure of Relational Affect as an integrative commitment to their relationship. It is a subtle measure of integrative feelings, a non-conscious statement that the couple is making in the way they tell their story.

We expect that each of the measures of integrative feelings should be related to our measure of marital stability, but none should be identical to it. Crohan and Veroff (1989) had been surprised that there was not a separate factor of stability in their factor analysis, since there were three items in their battery that were devoted to issues of perceived stability of the marriage. Those three items, however, loaded clearly and unequivocally with the happiness factor.[1] They then reasoned that in the early years of marriage, most couples do not distinguish between happiness experienced in the marriage and commitments to stay in the marriage. Only when a marriage has some history, and each partner becomes committed to the partner merely because their bond has a history, might evaluations of marital happiness and perceived stability in the marriage begin to pull apart as separate dimensions. Factor analysis of the marital evaluations in the fourth year still found stability items loaded with the happiness items (Crohan & Veroff, 1989). Thus, the differentiation of the two in the minds of couples may take longer than four years to develop.

RESULTS: PREDICTING MARITAL INSTABILITY FROM INTEGRATIVE MARITAL FEELINGS

We were surprised to find that the pattern of significant predictors of

marital instability from the set of variables measuring integrative feelings was quite different for black couples and white couples (see Table 5.1). While we would have thought that different marital perceptions, attitudes, interactions, stresses, and supports might be critical for one group and not the other as we did in the previous two chapters, we had not anticipated that the general evaluative feelings would have different predictive consequences for marital instability.

The most striking difference found in multiple regression analyses, was that while black husbands' evaluations of their marital happiness in the context of the other evaluations had <u>negative</u> associations with instability for black couples, as we expected, white husbands' evaluations had <u>positive</u> associations with instability. This difference between black and white couples was highly significant. We must remember that the zero-order correlation between husbands' evaluations of marital happiness and marital instability (.03) is not in this unexpected direction for white couples. Thus, it is only in the multiple regression procedure where we take account of the variance that <u>Marital Happiness</u> shares with other measures that we find this anomalous result for the white couples.

This result forces us to consider that part of white husbands' evaluation of their marriage may be a strong component of reactive idealization. Some white husbands may be telling themselves and the interviewers that everything is just wonderful in their marriages when they may, in fact, be struggling with difficulties they are encountering. This kind of reactive denial may be especially characteristic of white males who may find the affective negotiation of becoming a couple, the transaction of inevitable conflicts, especially threatening to ideals of being rational and unemotional. Black males may be more comfortable with their affective reactions to their marriage, and so their expression of marital happiness may be a more direct translation of their inner feelings.

Two other significantly different patterns of results appear in comparing black and white couples. Wives' feelings of equity seem more important for understanding the stability of white couples than for black couples, and wives' sense of marital control seems more important for understanding the stability of black couples than it does for white couples. Both equity and control are in some sense issues of power. The balance of power in equity terms may be especially salient for white women who only in recent years have become highly conscious of their relative power in marriage. Power in control terms may be a more subtle power expression which may be particularly important for a person who is trying to minimize the power that she implicitly holds. Black women have been important providers for their families and have thereby assumed more public displays of power. To make that dimension of power less salient, black women who focus on controlling positive outcomes for their husbands' feelings about the marriage may engender commitment

Table 5.1

Summary of Multiple Regression Analyses Predicting Marital Instability from Integrative Feelings (Within White Couples and Black Couples)

Predictor	White Couples (N=158)[†]		Black Couples (N=155)[†]		Sign. of W/B diff.
	B	beta	B	beta	
Wives					
Happiness	-.06	-.04	.19	.11	NS
Competence	-.32*	-.22*	-.02	-.01	NS
Control	.05	.04	-.29+	-.15+	NS
Equity	-.24+	-.13+	.17	.08	*
Marital Tension	.38**	.24**	.29	.13	NS
Relational Affects	-2.70*	-.22*	-.94	-.06	NS
Husbands					
Happiness	.32*	.19*	-.57**	-.31**	***
Competence	-.11	-.06	-.07	-.03	NS
Control	-.21*	-.15*	-.12	-.06	NS
Equity	.00	.00	.23+	.14+	NS
Marital Tension	.19	.13	.21	.09	NS
Relational Affects	.77	.06	-1.59	-.09	NS
Adj. R^2	.22***		.14***		

+=p<.10
*=p<.05
**=p<.01
***=p<.001

[†]Reflects the average number of couples on predictors in which there are no missing data.

from their husbands. Notice in Table 5.1 that white husbands' sense of marital control also has positive repercussions for the stability of their marriages. Might not a parallel thing be going on for them as we suggest is going on for the black wives? Might it not be that when white husbands who, granted more public power, focus on their affective control as a way of feeling power, they contribute to the enhancement of their wives' commitment to the marriages? These are speculations that might be useful to keep in mind as we tackle other variables that have implications for the public versus private enactment of marital power.

Aside from the curious positive association between black husbands' experience of marital equity and _instability, the remaining significant predictors in Table 5.1 are all in the expected direction. Most of them are first year integrative feelings experienced by white women—their sense of competence, their reports of marital tension, and their orientation to relational affects—all of which independently predict marital instability four years later. White women may be the most differentiated about their feelings and reactions to marriage. It is curious that overall Marital Happiness is not the strong predictor for them, but these other general feelings may feed into their sense of marital well-being.

Why should white women's integration of their marital feelings be more powerful in relationship to marital instability than the integration of marital feelings experienced by other groups? Might this be the most subtle power of all that white wives wield? Their refined affective reactions to marriage evidently have considerable impact on the stability of their marriage. Perhaps it is not that white wives themselves act directly on these feelings to destabilize a marriage, but that their husbands are very sensitive to them and begin to pull away from the relationship if the feelings are negative or become more committed if the feelings are positive. Or, perhaps white wives early on are prescient about the viability of a marital relationship. As a result, some of these integrative feelings reflect their own gratification or frustration about the stability of the marriage.

Is there any evidence that integrative feelings mediate the significant predictors of marital perceptions, interaction stresses, and supports uncovered in the previous two chapters? To answer this question, we performed two hierarchical regression analyses using the significant predictors reflecting integrative feelings with and without the aforementioned predictors, one tailored for the white couples and one for the black couples.

In the case of the black couples, the sole integrative feeling measure that was significant by itself—men's Marital Happiness—is completely eliminated as a significant predictor in the hierarchical strategy. This suggests that the perceptions, interactions, stresses, and strains measured among blacks are sufficient for understanding their marital instability. Furthermore, if our model is right, there may be few other important first year variables to consider. And

indeed the Adjusted R-squared is high without assessing integrative feeling—.48 (see Table 3.9 in Chapter 3).

For white couples, the results are a little different. There is some indirect evidence that two of the measures of integrative feeling may be mediating certain perceptions and interactions occurring in the first year. The wives' Marital Tension and the husbands' Happiness no longer are significant predictors when integrative feelings are combined with the other significant predictors. We suggest that these two variables are integrating what we have been measuring in first year perceptions and interactions and reflect little else. Marital Tensions in particular could well be an integrative reflection of frequency of conflicts and other perceptions and evaluations of conflict styles. Husbands' Happiness may no longer have the negative net impact it had in the regression set of integrative feelings when Disclosing Communication is also included as a predictor. The reader should recall that Husbands' Disclosing Communication among white couples is a significant predictor of instability. Our interpretation of that result was very much like our interpretation of the net negative impact of Happiness. Both measures may be picking up some defensive denial about difficulties in the marriage. Among the white couples, however, the analyses indicate that three of the integrative feelings remain as strong predictors of instability independent of the significant marital interaction and perception measures. This suggests, if our model is right, that the measures of integrative feelings also reflect marital experiences not explicitly tapped in our assessment of first year interactions, perceptions, stresses and strains. The model that includes all significant predictors for whites had an Adjusted R-squared of .31 (see Table 3.8 in Chapter 3).

SUMMARY

Do Integrative Feelings Add Much to Our Understanding of Marital Instability?

We began our search for factors affecting marital instability with a model that suggested that overall integrative feelings were summary feelings consolidating what husbands and wives experience in their perceptions and interactions with each other. If such is the case, and if we have done an adequate job of assessing factors internal and external to the marriage in the first year, then our measurements of integrative feelings that significantly predict instability should be reduced in their predictive power when we add the factors assessed in Chapters 3 and 4.

To some extent, our hypothesis was borne out. For white couples and black couples separately, we selected those factors in Chapters 3 and 4 that

significantly predicted instability and added them to those integrative feelings that were found to be important, and we discovered that the following integrative feelings for white couples were no longer significant: Wife's Marital Tensions and Husband's Happiness. This would suggest that these were indeed integrative reactions to perceptions, attitudes, and interactions that we had assessed in previous chapters. For black couples, a parallel strategy would have us conclude that the only major integrative feeling that was important—Husband's Marital Happiness—was indeed an integrative feeling, as we would predict, because like the results for the white couples, it no longer remained significant when the significant variables from the previous chapters were also included in the regression model.

There were, however, three integrative feelings that remained significant even when we added the significant variables from the previous chapters. These were for the white couples: wife's sense of marital competence and use of relational affects in her story-telling and the husband's sense of marital control. We would conclude that these integrative feelings either depend on phenomena in marital perception and interactions that we did not assess, or that these feeling states are experiences that are quite apart from marital perception and interactions. We prefer to think it is a matter of not having assessed everything and to stick with the idea that evaluative feelings serve the function of integrating marital interactions and perceptions and, as such, affect marital instability.

NOTES

1. To avoid an artifactual overlap between the measure of marital happiness and the index of marital instability used in the analyses in this book, we removed the three items asking directly about marital stability that, given the results of the factor analysis, would have produced an especially reliable and strong index of marital happiness.

6

THE SECOND YEAR OF MARRIAGE: STRESSORS, INTERFERENCE, AND INTEGRATIVE FEELINGS

The first year of marriage is filled with challenge: joining two social worlds and two world views, adapting to the tastes and rhythms of the partner, establishing one's new family unit as an independent entity, developing shared norms about life, love, and expressiveness and about the transparency or clarity of individual and couple boundaries. All of these take time and energy, and they are the focus of negotiation in the benign climate of romantic tenderness and sexual passion of the honeymoon period. What about the period after the honeymoon, the year after the wedding when norms are in place and the ordinary dailiness of life takes over? What are the issues and challenges young couples contend with then? Huston, McHale, and Crouter (1985) speak of the honeymoon period being over for the couples they observed at eighteen months. Various dissatisfactions begin to set in.

The reader will remember that in the second wave of our study covering this post-anniversary period we obtained only as much information as we could gather in a fifteen minute telephone call with the spouses. Our main concern was to find out whether the couple was still together, how satisfied they were with their marriage, and something about the life events—things like births, job changes, moves, illness, unemployment—they had experienced during the preceding year. We also asked a few questions about their marital interaction and their worries and concerns.

In this chapter, we will look in turn at external stressors and the way they affect marital instability. Then we will consider interferences from family, friends, and work demands that have implications for the stability of the marriage. Finally, we will consider the effect of the few integrative factors we measured in the second year—their effects on marital stability. In these analyses we are looking for effects of the stressor (or interference or integrative feeling) net of its effect in the first year. We do not expect this net

effect to be very large.

STRESSORS

The stressors we tapped included husband's and wife's worry about money (do you ever worry that you won't have enough money to pay all your bills?) and the following major life events: the birth of a baby, a period of unemployment for one of the partners, a death in the family or friendship circle, a serious illness of one of the partners or a member of the couple's social group, and a geographic move.

Overall, the second year stressors listed in Table 6.1 account for a small segment of the variance in marital instability, a contribution that is marginally significant for white couples (R-squared = .03; p <.10) and clearly significant for black couples (R-squared = .17; p <.01).

Many more of the individual stressors relate to instability among the black couples than among white couples. The only one that shows the same kind of effect in both groups is husband's worry about finances. In both cases, this factor shows a significant relationship to marital instability. The husband's anxiety about money evidently creates tension in the relationship and some degree of uncertainty about the marriage itself. As we have indicated earlier, our culture's conflation of male adequacy (manliness) with the ability to earn enough money to support a family places young males in a highly vulnerable position in the intimate marital relationship.

With Year 1 financial worry controlled, the contribution of husband's Year 2 worry about finances to instability drops out for African-American couples (p <.35). The relationship was strong in the first year of marriage so that adding the financial worry item for the second year does not significantly change the effect on marital stability. For white couples, there was no significant first year effect of the husband's financial worries on marital instability, so that the second year effect is, in essence, a new relationship. Apparently financial worries build during the first two years of marriage or the strong romantic involvement of the first year buffers the couple's relationship from the deleterious effects of financial worries.

Major life events also show differential effects on black and white marriages. The birth of a baby and a period of unemployment for one partner both show strong relationships to marital instability for blacks. In each of these instances, the difference between the two racial groups is significant. And it is a most striking difference in the case of the birth of a baby. For the white couples, a new baby seems to have a positive, though non-significant effect on the marriage. That is, birth of a baby relates negatively to instability (beta = −08), while for the black couples, the birth of a baby has a strong negative effect on stability. That is, birth of a baby relates positively to

Table 6.1
Summary of Multiple Regression Analyses Predicting Marital Instability from Second Year Stressors
(Within White Couples and Black Couples)

Predictor	White Couples (N=150)[†]		Black Couples (N=163)[†]		W/B diff
	B	beta	B	beta	
Wives					
Worry About Money	.06	.05	.16	.09	
Husbands					
Worry About Money	.25*	.18*	.21	.12	
Worry About Money (YR 1)			.20**	.24**	
Couple					
Someone Unemployed	.00	.01	.35*	.18*	***
Had Baby	−.22	−.08	.66*	.18*	***
Someone Died	−.05	−.04	−.29**	−.20**	
Someone Seriously Ill	.30	.13	−.31	.09	
Moved	.02	.01	.33	.09	
Adj. R^2	.03+		.17**		

+p<.10
*p<.05
**p<.01
***p<.001

[†]Reflects the number of couples in which there are no missing data on any of the predictors.

instability (beta = +19). The difference between the groups is highly significant (p < .001).

A death in their social circle or a serious illness of one of the partners or someone close to them both have interesting though small effects on marital instability and effects that are different in black and white couples. For white couples, the effect of either of these events is insignificant, but the direction is different for the two events. A serious illness in their social circle seems to increase (though not significantly) instability, while the death of someone close decreases instability (i.e., strengthens the relationship). For black couples, both of these apparently harsh life events increase the stability of the relationship. In the case of death, the relationship is significant. In the case of illness, the effect is not significant, but the difference in the relationship for black and white couples is significant.

The overall effect of the life event stressors seems to be larger for African-American marriages, and we think we detect a differential impact of internal and external events. By internal events we mean those things that happen in the relationship between the partners, and by external events we mean problems or events imposed from the outside (e.g., illness or death of a relative or close friend) with which the young couple must somehow cope.[1] The internal events seem to strengthen the bond between the partners while the external ones (Unemployment, Worry About Finances) increase strain and instability.

The main thing we can say about the effect of stressors on white marriages is that Financial Insecurity or Financial Worry seems to have an increasing effect on these marriages over the course of the first two years. Whereas black couples' relationships showed the effect of financial anxiety in the first year of marriage (and continue to show the effect), the young white couples seem to have been buffered against these effects until the second year of their marriages.

Demands That Interfere with Marriage

One of the critical areas in which the young couple must develop shared norms is the primacy of the marriage in relation to both time and commitment. When other demands from work or family of origin or friends or civic, voluntary organizations compete for the young spouses' time, thought, resources, or commitment, there must be some shared understanding of where in the list of priorities the marriage and partner demands stand. If the young husband spends all of his discretionary time at work and each member of the couple understands that he is doing it in order to establish his business so that their future will be secure, and he can spend more time at home when they have children, the impact will be benign compared to a situation in which the

husband spends all his discretionary time at work because he is basically introverted and finds solitude comfortable. If this was not clear during the courtship, the couple will have significant adjustments to make in order to reach some shared expectations and understandings. Otherwise, they will very likely be in for big problems.

We asked each of the spouses how much their own job interfered with their marriage and how much there was interference from each of their (i.e., their own and their spouse's) friendship and family circles. For our measure of the wife's family's tendency to interfere, we combined the response of the husband and wife about this; we combined their estimates of the husband's family's interference in the same way; and for each spouse's friends' interference, we also combined their responses.

Using these indicators of interference to predict marital instability led to the following results summarized in Table 6.2: interference from job demands does not play a large part in marital instability, but interference from friends and/or family plays a more or less disruptive role in young marriages in all four of our analysis groups. Neither husband's job demands nor wife's job demands contribute significantly to marital tension or instability. In fact, the only relationship this factor showed to our instability measure—and even here it was only marginal ($p < .10$)—is in the opposite direction. When black wives report that they feel their jobs sometimes interfere with their marriages, their marriages are marginally more stable than other black marriages. In no other group is there any relationship between job interference and marital instability.

The slight relationship we find for black wives may be worth some speculation. It is likely, first of all, that the feeling that one's job sometimes interferes with one's family life is most common among people in professional, high demand jobs. And it is probably also the experience of people who hold a quite demanding conception of the marriage role, who expect a lot of themselves as spouses. Both of these possible meanings of the response could potentially contribute to marital stability. In black marriages, the wife's holding a job that is demanding (i.e., a career line job with significant status and pay) could relieve the young husband of some of the financial anxiety that has such a corrosive effect on marriage, perhaps compensating for the fact that he is not the major supporter of the family. And the young wife's holding demanding expectations for her performance in the wife role (very likely traditional expectations) would fit with earlier findings to the effect that a more traditional construction of the authority and power distribution characterized more stable marriages among the black couples.

Interpersonal demands from family and friends clearly create stress for young couples. For both white and black couples, the tendency of the wife's friends to interfere in the relationship is strongly related to marital instability; and in white couples, the husband's friends' interference shows a similar

Table 6.2

Summary of Multiple Regression Analyses Predicting Marital Instability from Second Year Interferences (Within White Couples and Black Couples)

Predictor	White Couples (N=167)[†]		Black Couples (N=191)[†]		W/B diff
	B	beta	B	beta	
Wives					
Job Interferences	-.05	-.07	-.15+	-.13+	NS
Family	.10	.13	-.04	-.04	NS
Friends	.27***	.31***	.43***	.33***	NS
Husbands					
Job Interferences	.05	.08	.05	.06	NS
Family	-.03	-.05	.33**	.29**	***
Friends	.14**	.21**	.05	.06	NS
Adj. R²	.22***		.19***		

+p<.10
*p<.05
**p<.01
***p<.001

[†]Reflects the number of couples in which there are no missing data on any of the predictors.

though smaller relationship to instability. Black husbands' friends' tendency to interfere with the relationship is not apparently critical to the stability of their marriages, but in the black husband's network, it is his family's tendency to interfere that seems to lead to marital instability. Interference from the wife's family does not relate to marital instability; nor does family interference by white husbands' families seem to affect the stability of the white marriages.

Establishing the boundaries of their new family is one of the critical tasks for any newly married couple, as we have discussed before. Asserting their claim to an independent existence, space, and privacy is both a crucial and delicate task since it means asserting claims that involve limiting the claims of other established relationships. Saying no to an old friend who calls to see if she can drop by for a visit or—even more delicate—somehow letting friends and family members know that you expect a phone call before anyone "drops by" are issues that require tact and assertion of one's own tastes and limits. These are the issues that fill advice columns because they are hard to handle yet cannot be ignored.

Since women are traditionally the socioemotional experts who invest in personal relationships and have more interpersonal ties than men, it is not surprising that they might face these issues more frequently than men and that, again because of their own and their women friends' socialization to the interpersonal realm, they might face them in a form that is both more subtle and more difficult to handle. So the fact that the wife's saying that her friends tend to interfere in her marriage relates to marital instability makes sense. It is in all likelihood harder for the young wife to establish boundaries and independence from her friends. Her friendships are more intimate and her boundaries have been more permeable. Since her husband has not had friendships of equivalent intimacy, it may be particularly hard for him to understand why his wife can't just put her foot down and insist that her friends respect their limits and need for privacy. Such differences in perception and interpersonal style are fertile ground for tension and conflict.

It could also be that letting her friends interfere with her marriage is a sign that the young wife is not fully committed to the relationship or has some conflict about it. Family members are a special case because even if they interfere in one's marriage, they cannot be dismissed. But with friends, one might expect that if they continue to interfere in the marriage, the young spouse would eventually cool the friendship. Friendship is, after all, a voluntary association that must at some level meet the expectations of and provide some pleasure to both partners.

The fact that black husbands' family interference is associated with marital instability was not unexpected since in early analyses of sources of conflict in the first year of marriage we had found evidence that family interference was an important point of contention for young couples—and particularly, interference from the husband's family. We were more struck by the fact that

the relationship to instability did not appear for white men in the present analysis. Instead, we find that it is their friends' interference that relates to marital instability for white males, much as it is for women in both racial groups.

This is a paradoxical finding, given considerable evidence that men, and particularly white men, are less deeply involved in friendships than women are. For most married men, their interpersonal network consists largely of the spouse—it is their wives to whom they confide and from whom they gain their social support. Perhaps it is the very rareness of the man's having close friends that creates tension in his marriage. Since he is not expected to "cleave to his friends," closeness itself may seem a burdensome interference and create tension in the marriage.

The finding about family interference needs at least one other point of clarification. This concerns the fact that interference from the wife's family does not relate to instability. Evidence from our study indicates that the chance of her family interfering is greater than the chance of his family doing so. Spouses usually indicate that they are closer to the wife's family and see more of her family compared to his family. So presumably they would also be in a position to interfere more often. But apparently the greater familiarity—even closeness—the young husband has with his wife's family (compared to her acquaintance with his family) acts as insulation against his feeling resentful toward them.

Integrative Feelings in the Second Year

The contribution of individual measures of integrative feelings in the second year is not highly significant over and above their contribution during the first year of marriage (see Table 6.3). Happiness with the marriage reported by wives is highly related to marital stability for both the black and white couples and Husband's Marital Happiness is marginally related to stability for white husbands. Husbands' reports of tension in the marriage is also related to instability.

The most interesting findings in this group of analyses have to do with Control and Equity. Black husbands' report that their marriages are equitable (who gets more out of your marriage, you or your wife or both the same?) is significantly related to instability in their marriages. With first year Equity controlled, the relationship is only marginal (p < .16), but the finding is worth noting because it reinforces the first year relationship in which it seemed that Equity between the partners tended to threaten black marriages while it tended to strengthen the marriages of the white couples.

The finding about Control occurs in the group of black wives where the wife's indication that she can influence what happens in the marriage is

Table 6.3

Summary of Multiple Regression Analyses Predicting Marital Instability from Integrated Feelings (Within White Couples and Black Couples)

Predictor	White Couples (N=146)[†]		Black Couples (N=138)[†]		W/B diff
	B	beta	B	beta	
Wives					
Happiness	-.60***	-.49**	-.62***	-.38***	
Control	.16	.10	-.25+	-.13+	**
Equity	-.19	-.05	-.06	-.01	
Marital Tension	.07	-.05	.16	.08	
No Privacy	.15	.13	.06	.04	
(Happiness YR1)	.24+	.14+			
Husbands					
Happiness	-.36*	-.21*	-.10	-.06	
Control	.08	.05	.05	.02	
Equity	.02	.01	.53*	.14*	*
Marital Tension	.25	.16	.37*	.14*	
No Privacy	-.08	-.06	.07	.04	
Adj. R^2	.38***		.37***		

+$p < .10$
*$p < .05$
**$p < .01$
***$p < .001$

[†]Reflects the number of couples in which there are no missing data on any of the predictors.

marginally related to stability in the marriage. The difference between white and black wives is highly significant since the woman's sense of Control is associated (though not significantly) with instability in the white sample. Controlling for the influence of first year sense of Control, the difference is still marginally significant ($p < .13$).

Again, we take this as evidence of the special burdens black marriages face because of the structural conditions imposed by a racist society. With his position in the labor market threatened by discrimination and his adequacy in the traditional role of provider brought into question, the African-American male seeks reassurance of his masculine power in a traditional construction of the marital roles. So long as he feels that he is in a position to make choices and decisions in the marriage—that in this sphere he enjoys a dominant voice—the relationship is stable. For him, however, equality between the partners—though it may in fact be the reality—is not the ideal marital relation for the black male.

SUMMARY

Husbands' financial anxiety in the first year of marriage, found to be prognostic of instability among black couples, becomes prognostic of instability among white couples in the second year of marriage. However, there were other external stresses during the second year that come into play as indicators of instability among black couples: unemployment and having a baby. That someone dies during the second year was interestingly a stressor that enhanced the marital bond among black couples. The overall effect of external stress seems to play a stronger role in understanding the stability of black couples than it does among the white couples.

Interferences from friends of the wife are clear predictors of instability in couples; a parallel effect can be seen only in interferences from white husbands' friends but not from black husbands' friends. Interferences from black husbands' families seem to be disruptive of the stability of black marriages. This is not so for the white marriages nor for the impact of the wives' families for either group of couples. We speculate that the greater closeness to wives' families insulates the couple from resentments about interference.

The contribution of integrative feelings experienced in the second year of marriage does not seem to be different from the contribution of such feelings in the first year, as described in the last chapter. Most provocative was the further reinforcement of results previously found suggesting that equity in the marital relationship experienced by black husbands may be disruptive of the stability of their marriages.

NOTES

1. Unemployment can be seen as either an internal or external event but is at least more susceptible to an interpretation that holds the unemployed person responsible for the situation (e.g., blaming him/her for not finding other employment).

7

THE THIRD YEAR OF MARRIAGE

Each successive year in a marriage can bring new issues. This is undoubtedly clearest with respect to changes in family composition as children are added to the family or as spouses' job situations begin to consolidate or change in character. These external changes are perhaps most dramatic during the early years. This is not to say that internal dynamics of a marriage do not change in successive years. One might expect that the first year, crucial as it is to setting the rules and standards for what the marriage will be like for some time to come, is still, after all, a honeymoon period. Evaluations of what goes on during that year and the effects such evaluations may have on the eventual course of a marriage might be distorted because of the aura of that transition. As couples continue in their marriage, they may become more realistic about what is going on and what the consequences of their relationship are for their lives, which of their partners's foibles they can discount and learn to live with, and which are long standing and injurious to their well-being.

In the third year of marriage we returned to face-to-face interviewing of each spouse as well as the couple. Most of the measures used in the first year were included in the third year interviews. As a result, we could see whether there were any changes from Year 1 to Year 3 in the way a given factor in the marriage predicted marital instability. In addition, we asked some questions and derived some measures that were new in Year 3. We either inserted these new measures in one of the sets of measures we had established for Year 1 (e.g., incompatibilities in attitudes, interpersonal perceptions of conflict, couple interaction), or we established new sets of measures that we will describe below.

NEW MEASURES IN YEAR 3

Marital accommodation. From Ruvolo's (1990) work we introduced into the present study of marital instability a measure of marital accommodation, the degree to which spouses moved from their perceptions of themselves in the first year of marriage in the direction of goals that their spouses had for them. These goals were defined by discrepancies that spouses had between their ideal and actual ratings of their partners on a series of adjectives. The more a person changed from Year 1 to Year 3 in the direction defined by a discrepancy felt by the spouse in Year 1, the more we assumed that person was accommodating to the spouse's ideals. Such a measure was obviously not available in Year 1 because it depends on examining the patterns of self-perceptions from Year 1 to Year 3.

Expressing love. In Year 3, a respondent was asked directly how often he/she tells his/her spouse that she/he loves the spouse. Many married couples complain that their spouses are reluctant to speak spontaneously of their affections. It was our guess that this would be positively tied to marital stability.

Role sharing. Three subscales reflecting egalitarian role structuring in marriage were combined to form a new index we called Role Sharing. The subscales were: (1) how egalitarian the couples say they should be in their household and work tasks; (2) how many tasks they actually do share; and (3) how nontraditional the couples say they are about housework. Both husbands' and wives' responses were merged to create the measure. Hence, Role Sharing orientation is assessed at the couple level since each item comprising the scale is formed by the product of the husband's and the wife's responses to the same item. The internal consistency of this scale is relatively high (alpha = .65) considering that both attitudes and behaviors make up the items that go into the subscales.

Similar items were asked in the first year but not as many. Hence, we only used items in Year 3 to get at role sharing orientation. We also suggest that it is not until the third year or thereabouts that the couple gets a firm idea about their role sharing propensity.

Solving couple dilemmas. In the third year, we asked couples how often they followed certain prescriptive rules for marriage. We had asked how important these rules were in the first year, but only in the third year did we also ask how much they behaved in accordance with these rules. Some of them concerned having certain feelings about the marriage. And these will appear below in the new measures of specific feelings. Some have to do with each of their interpersonal styles, and these were included in a new set of measures about interpersonal styles. But others of these rules deal with how the couple accommodates issues of jointness in their marriage—joint task sharing at home, joint sharing of space, friends, and money. These four items,

along with one which asked whether they had an equal say in their marriage, constituted a new group of items we will analyze together as couple behaviors regarding couple dilemmas. In addition, from the spouse interview we also had their evaluation of how much leisure time they shared with one another. Where relevant, we combined both the husband and wife appraisals of the item (e.g., both husband and wife appraisals of the joint leisure item).

A major theoretical conception we held in entering this study was that marriage involved a dilemma of balancing individual and couple goals. The way that couples solve this dilemma should, we thought, be diagnostic of the capacity of the marriage to withstand inevitable tensions and conflicts. Without room for the individual to express his or her needs separate from the relationship, there could be little reserve for the person to turn to in times of couple tension. Without a couple commitment, in addition, there would be little reason for the couple to maintain a relationship when they encounter interpersonal tension between them.

Interpersonal styles. Two interpersonal styles were assessed in the spouses' judgments of themselves and each other on the following marital ideals: one should control one's anger (Control of Anger) and one should always speak one's mind (Speaking Up). These two are somewhat inconsistent personality styles in the interpersonal realm although not completely independent. Indeed we found significant negative correlations between the two for both black and white men and women. We used the composite of the couple's assessment of each spouse. We would anticipate that controlling anger and not always speaking one's mind would be beneficial for maintaining a marriage. They are mirror images of an accommodative style that generally helps preserve marital interaction.

Another interpersonal style, Independence, was measured in the list of self- and other perceptions that had been the basis of the measures in the first year of marriage of the personality characteristics of Bossiness, Cooperativeness, and Ambitiousness (see Chapter 2). We had added this to the list of characteristics, since it seemed to be a more direct assessment of the agentic mode in contrast to the communal mode in personal orientations that might be basic forces in marital interaction.

Specific feelings. In the third year we added to the list of feelings about which the couple reported: Jealousy (being worried about a relationship or attraction to someone else); Lack of Understanding (feel spouse does not understand self); Not Understanding One's Spouse; Satisfaction with Home (how satisfied the person feels about his/her home)[1]; Satisfaction with Leisure (how satisfied person feels about time for personal leisure); Feelings of Sexual Understanding; Feelings that Spouse Not Critical; Feelings of Faithfulness. Feelings of Privacy was continued from Year 2.

Attitudes towards marriage and divorce. A number of questions in the third year were added to get a fuller picture of the couples' attitude structure

with regard to marriage and divorce in general. From a list of items, three were used in our analysis of instability: (1) how much positive orientation to marriage each spouse had; (2) how favorable the person's general attitude towards divorce was; and (3) how many different grounds for legitimate divorce each person endorsed. To measure the positive orientation to marriage, each person was asked how a person's life was changed by getting married. Two particular answers to that question (it makes life happier and fuller) were combined to measure general attitudes towards marriage. In the same way agreement with two statements about divorce—that divorce is an acceptable solution to problems and that divorce does not reflect badly on the people involved—were combined to form attitudes towards divorce. Finally the couples were asked a series of questions about specific acceptable grounds for divorce (an extramarital affair, alcoholism, abuse, etc.). The number of these reasons endorsed by the person was taken as a measure of the Range of Grounds For Divorce the person accepted.

Social support. In the third year, we added four factors about the social networks in which the couples were embedded that could potentially be parameters on which social support and social integrative feelings of the couples could depend. Many network theorists speak of the importance of density of networks as a characteristic that may bind a couple more to the norms of the community. By density theorists have meant how interconnected all the members of a network are. Presumably the more interconnected, the more stringent the rules for conformity become, but the more cushion there may be for handling any stress that comes up. The more a network knows each other, the more likely they will be informed about any pressures the couple is experiencing, and the more likely a member of the network will be available for helping with those pressures. Thus, predictions about the value of dense networks are not straightforward. (Dense networks cushion stress but also apply more pressure for conformity.) To approximate density, we asked whether a couple's friends tended to know one another and how well the husband's family and the wife's family knew each other. The products of each spouse's responses were used to derive these indices.

Two other measures of social support came from asking couples about how close to the couple their families live and how often they see their families. For each measure both families were combined to make joint indices for the couple as a unit.

RESULTS: ATTITUDES AND PERCEPTIONS

Attitudes Towards Marriage and Divorce

While we had expected that positive general attitudes towards marriage and

negative general attitudes towards divorce would be correlated with the stability of one's own marriage, we were in for a surprise. There were only trends in the regression analyses, and those occurred only among the black couples. Table 7.1 indicates that black wives who have a positive orientation to marriage, and black husbands and wives who do not easily endorse divorce as a solution to marital problems tend to be in marriages that are more stable. None of these findings is robust. We are thus impressed with the general absence of relationships between how stable a couple's marriage is and the general attitudes a husband and wife hold either about the value of marriage in a person's life or about the virtue of divorce in faltering marriages.

For many people, it seems, the ideals about marriage and divorce do not follow directly from their own personal experience. Positive ideals can be maintained in spite of difficulties, and negative general attitudes can emerge even if one's own experience has been a happy one. A rearrangement of attitudes may occur at crisis points in marriages. Attitudes may then become aligned to behavior as individuals actually take the step towards separation. The fact that people do not leave a troubled marriage, that they think about leaving but hang in there, may in part be understood as being a function of holding positive attitudes towards marriage and negative feelings about divorce.

Attitude Incompatibilities

The same measures used in Year 1 to measure attitude incompatibilities were used again in Year 3 as potential predictors of marital instability. Aside from differences in preferred pace of life that were found to be significant in understanding marital instability in both white and black couples, no other measure of attitude incompatibility was a significant predictor (see Chapter 3). The results are slightly different by Year 3. Table 7.2 reveals that for both black couples and white couples incompatibility with regard to pace of life is no longer related to marital instability. Nor are any of the other attitude incompatibilities for white couples. For the black couples, however, three measures of attitude incompatibility are relevant to marital instability. Differences in the importance of religion and differences in sex role attitudes both are predictors of instability for black couples; and surprisingly, differences in openness to new experiences is correlated with stability rather than instability.

Why are significant results generated only for the black couples, and why does a couple's incompatibility about openness to new experiences relate positively to marital stability? A number of social researchers and commentators have suggested that religion figures strongly in the lives of blacks to solidify their ties to community (Taylor & Chatters, 1991). Thus any discrepancy in religious orientation between husbands and wives among black

Table 7.1
Summary of Multiple Regression Analyses Predicting Marital Instability from Third Year Attitudes Toward Marriage and Divorce (Within White Couples and Black Couples)

Predictor	White Couples (N=133)†		Black Couples (N=115)†		W/B diff.
	B	beta	B	beta	
Wives					
Positive View of Marriage	-.02	-.04	-.15+	-.19+	
Positive View of Divorce	.07	.06	.26+	.17+	
Range of Grounds for Divorce	.02	.07	.03	.05	
Husbands					
Positive View of Marriage	-.08	-.12	.00	.00	
Positive View of Divorce	-.05	-.04	.20	.15	*
Range of Grounds for Divorce	.03	.10	.04	.08	
Adj. R²	.01		.10**		

+p<.10
*p<.05
**p<.01
***p<.001

†Reflects the number of couples in which there are no missing data on any of the predictors.

114

Table 7.2

Summary of Multiple Regression Analyses Predicting Marital Instability from Attitude Incompatibilities in the Third Year (Within White Couples and Black Couples)

Predictor	White Couples (N=128)[†]		Black Couples (N=112)[†]		W/B diff.
	B	beta	B	beta	
Differences in					
Importance of Religion	−.21	−.10	.66*	.18*	
Attitudes	.01	.01	−.12	−.12	
Conflicts					
Preferred Pace of Life	−.05	−.05	.13	.09	
Openness to Experience	.07	.08	−.33**	−.24**	*
Sex Role Attitudes	.03	.05	.16*	.24*	*
Rules for Marriage	.01	.03	−.04	.05	
Adj. R²	.00		.12**		

+p<.10
*p<.05
**p<.01
***p<.001

[†]Reflects the number of couples in which there are no missing data on any of the predictors.

115

couples may be a stronger signal of their difficulties in integrating their lives in their community and maintaining their couplehood than it would among white couples.

While discrepancies in sex role attitudes might be a problem for any husband and wife, it should be especially problematic among couples where the power relationship between husbands and wives is a touchy issue. We have earlier argued that maintaining the public image of masculine power may be especially important for black couples. If we are right, then incompatibilities about sex role attitudes might undermine a comfortable adaptation in black couples more than it would in white couples.

More difficult to comprehend is why a discrepancy about openness to new experience might be correlated with a positive adjustment for black couples. These results were strong both in the multiple regression analysis and in the zero order relationship $(-.22)$. We can only speculate that for black couples a degree of complementarity about seeking a steady life or seeking adventure is adaptable. A wife who seeks the familiar while the husband seeks out new stimuli, and vice versa, may protect each from one extreme or the other—from risky adventure and from stale sameness. Why this should be true only for black couples is a mystifying question and is well worth pursuing in follow-up research.

RESULTS: INTERPERSONAL PERCEPTIONS REGARDING CONFLICT AND SEXUAL INTERACTION

Interpersonal Perceptions Regarding Conflict

While many results indicated that interpersonal perceptions about conflict in Year 1 were relevant to the stability of black marriages, such was not the case in Year 3. These perceptions seemed irrelevant, as can be gleaned from scanning Table 7.3A. By contrast, for whites a number of results involving husbands' perceptions of their wives' conflict styles in the third year were associated with marital instability—results that were absent in the first year. Furthermore, white women's understanding of their husbands' destructive behaviors in a conflict situation, a significant predictor in the first year, was no longer a significant predictor of marital stability in the third year.

New to the third year is the association between husbands' capacities to understand what their wives are trying to do both destructively and constructively in conflict resolution (Understanding of Negative and Positive Conflict Behaviors) and marital stability. We could speculate that there has been some learning on the husbands' part. Perhaps they are developing some empathy over time about what their wives are attempting to do when fights occur—an empathy that puts them in better touch with feelings being

Table 7.3A

Summary of Multiple Regression Analyses Predicting Marital Instability from Interpersonal Perceptions of Complex Behaviors (Year Three)

Predictor	White Couples (N=130)[†]		Black Couples (N=100)[†]		W/B diff.
	B	beta	B	beta	
Wives' Perception					
a.Positive Conflict Behavior					
Understanding	.13	.06	.32	.13	
Assumed Similarity	.03	.01	−.20	−.08	
b.Negative Conflict Behavior					
Understanding	−.67**	−.30**	−.44	−.18	
Assumed Similarity	.34+	.20+	−.05	−.02	
Husbands' Perception					
a.Positive Conflict Behavior					
Understanding	−.53*	−.21*	.00	.00	
Assumed Similarity	.02	.01	.07	.03	
b.Negative Conflict Behaviors					
Understanding	.01	.01	−.20	−.09	
Assumed Similarity	−.27+	−.16+	−.42	−.17	
Adj. R^2	.11**		.05, NS		

+p<.10
*p<.05
**p<.01
***p<.001

[†]Reflects the number of couples in which there are no missing data on any of the predictors.

expressed than they had before they were married. Women may thus socialize men to be empathic over time. And when socialization is successful, this may be helpful to the marriage.

There was also a trend for less stability in white marriages in which husbands portrayed their destructive reactions to conflict as being like their wives' (Negative Assumed Similarity). Many of these cases would be cases where the husbands said neither of them reacted destructively. It is our guess that in many of these instances men were denying that any negative reactions occur. This kind of denial must ultimately be problematic for maintaining the communication required to keep a marriage at an equilibrium. To the degree that the result also reflects husbands' seeing both members of the couple as equally destructive, one might guess that the pattern reflects an awareness of reciprocated hostility. The fact that the same assumed similarity about destructive means of coping with conflict did not apply to the women's perceptions would argue still that the trend for men came primarily from the assumed similarity in lack of destructive styles.

Interpersonal Perceptions of Sexual Interaction

Unlike the first year analysis of interpersonal perceptions of sexual interaction, there are no significant findings in the parallel analysis in the third year. Table 7.3B yields not a single significant result, not even a trend. It very well could be that the interpersonal perceptions about sexual life that develop after the first year are those that come from attempts to adapt to difficulties as much as they are reflections of an empathetic marriage. The first year reactions were perhaps more immediate and reflect more spontaneous reactions to the couples' sexuality.

RESULTS: INTERACTIONS

Perceived Individual Interactions

Table 7.4 summarizes the multiple regression analyses predicting marital instability from perceptions of individual interaction. In Year 1 a consistent finding for all couples was that when wives found it easier to talk to someone other than their husbands, they were more likely to be in unstable marriages. We interpreted this to mean the lack of communication that women might experience in not being able to talk easily with their husbands was disruptive of their conceptions of a good marriage and relationship. Since the result did not hold for husbands when they found it easier to talk with someone else, one might have concluded that it was specifically a woman's issue in marriage. We would have been mistaken, for lo and behold, the results are completely

Table 7.3B

Summary of Multiple Regression Analyses Predicting Marital Instability from Interpersonal Perceptions of Sexual Interactions (Year 3) (Within White Couples and Black Couples)

Predictor	White Couples (N=131)[†]		Black Couples (N=115)[†]		W/B diff.
	B	beta	B	beta	
Wives' Perceptions					
a.Positive Sexual Interaction					
Understanding	−.24	−.18	.00	.00	
Assumed Similarity	.22	.09	−.08	−.03	
b.Negative Sexual Interaction					
Understanding	.00	.01	−.18	−.11	
Assumed Similarity	−.12	−.09	−.36+	−.17+	
Husbands' Perceptions					
a.Positive Sexual Interaction					
Understanding	.02	.01	−.08	−.05	
Assumed Similarity	−.14	−.05	−.24	−.07	
b.Negative Sexual Interaction					
Understanding	.07	.06	−.14	−.09	
Assumed Similarity	−.12	.08	.17	.10	
Adj. R²	.06,NS		.08,NS		

+p<.10
*p<.05
**p<.01
***p<.001

[†]Reflects the number of couples in which there are no missing data on any of the predictors.

Table 7.4

Summary of Multiple Regression Analyses Predicting Marital Instability from Individual Interactions in the Third Year (Within White Couples and Black Couples)

Predictor	White Couples (N=123)[†]		Black Couples (N=91)[†]		W/B diff.
	B	beta	B	beta	
Wives					
Tell Spouse Love	−.46	−.16	−.46	−.15	
Easier to Talk to Other	.23	.13	.00	.00	
Disclosing Style	.08	.11	.04	.04	
Affective Affirmation	−.05	−.07	−.08	−.13	
Destructive Conflict Style	.03	.12	.09	.13	
Constructive Conflict Style	.06	−.12	−.02	−.03	
Avoidant Conflict Style	.08	.10	−.04	.04	
Accommodation	.01	.07	.00	−.02	
Husbands					
Tell Spouse Love	−.18	−.07	.53	.21	
Easier to Talk With	.69	.23	.53	.21	
Disclosing Style	.01	.02	−.13	−.14	
Affective Affirmation	.09	.15	−.03	−.04	
Destructive Conflict Style	.06	.12	.12	.19	
Constructive Style	.06	.12	.12	.19	
Avoidant Conflict Style	.08	.10	.01	.02	
Accommodation	.02	.19	.00	.02	
(First Year Destructive Conflict Style)			.05	.08	
(Second Year Constructive)			.08	.15	
Adj. R^2		.22		.23	

+p<.10
*p<.05
**p<.01
***p<.001

[†]Reflects the number of couples in which there are no missing data on any of the predictors.

reversed for the third year of marriage. Wives' finding it easier to talk to someone else, while on its own is still a significant predictor of instability, in the third year is no longer a significant predictor in the multiple regression analyses (see Table 7.4). By contrast, husbands' finding it easier to talk to someone else in the third year analysis becomes a significant predictor in the regression analyses for both black and white couples.

How to account for this crossover from Year 1 to Year 3 on this aspect of communication? We suggest that women who have looked forward to an intimate communicative relationship may be bitterly disappointed during the first year of marriage when their relationship is less than expected, and that disappointment can be diagnostic about their orientation to their marriages in general. Over time, some women may learn to adapt to that problem, seek out other sources of intimate communication, and become resigned to that condition of marriage, especially as they discover that it is normative. As a result, whether women feel that they have an easy communicative relationship with their husbands may become less diagnostic of their orientations to their marriages in general.

The reverse may be true for men. They may enter marriage with few expectations about intimate communication with their wives through talk. As a result, the question of whether they find it easier to talk with someone other than their spouse may not be at all diagnostic about the way they feel about their marriage. Their buddies may be the group to whom they feel most comfortable talking, and that is probably the way they like it. Over time, however, as friendships usually diminish in centrality for married men, and as their wives socialize them to the need for intimate talk in a marriage, many men would begin to rely more on their wives as their sole source of support. Veroff, Douvan, and Kulka (1981) have clear evidence that most husbands only talk to their wives about personal problems and to no one else, while wives talk about personal problems with many in their network in addition to their husbands. This could create a situation in which men would recognize that if they find it easier to talk with someone other than their wives, something indeed must be wrong with their marriages.

Other results in Table 7.4 highlight gender differences as well. Particularly striking is the result showing that black men who say they frequently tell their wives that they love them are less likely to be in stable marriages. So much for the power of those three little words. In all of the other race by gender groups the direction of relationship was as one would expect, and it was significant in the case of the white women. It could be that some black husbands use protestations of love as a way to reduce conflicts they may be experiencing with their wives, at least more than white husbands. And we find that there is a much higher correlation between the frequency with which black men report they tell their wives they love them and the reported frequency of constructive behaviors used to deal with conflict, than there is for white

husbands. Furthermore, black husbands' reported use of constructive styles of dealing with conflict is also predictive of instability in marriage, and that result is significant even when we control for the first year assessment of the same thing, which had itself been a significant predictor. We might suggest, therefore, that black husbands may self consciously do the right thing in their interactions with their wives as a way to reduce trouble between them. And it may be that these procedures do not deal with the problems that their marriages are facing, and in fact, quite to the contrary, avoid dealing with them. We would suggest that the pattern of results indicates that there is some socialization of these styles over time that may ultimately be dysfunctional to maintaining stable marriages.

The same pattern may be going on for white males but in a more subtle form. As can be seen in Table 7.4, white husbands who accommodate to their wives' wishes are in more unstable marriages. In keeping with our analysis of black husbands, we would suggest that these accommodations are changes evoked through conflict and pressures. These are often changes which reflect men's feeling that they need to accommodate to preserve the marriage, rather than changes out of positive enrichment of the relationship. In our sexist world, men are supposed to be autonomous. Any acceding to pressures to change can be read as emasculation. Interesting is the fact that in the third year a destructive style of conflict resolution did not remain as strong a predictor of marital stability, and even the significance found for black males in this measure as a predictor is reduced considerably once the first year measure of reported use of destructive style of conflict resolution is simultaneously entered into the prediction equation. This pattern of results suggests that there may be an adaptation to destructive styles over time that may not interfere with marital stability. Husbands and wives get used to each others' insults, and so their appearance in later years of a marriage may be less diagnostic of a faltering marriage than it was when it first appeared. Indeed, those who were most destructive in their styles may well have gotten divorced before the third year assessments. We are reminded of Albee's play, Who's Afraid of Virginia Woolf?, in which insulting bickering was the modus vivendi of the marriage, a style of relating that was at least reassuring because it was familiar to the couple.

Individual Interactive Styles

There is some evidence that an accommodative style in both husbands and wives is associated with preserving marital stability among white couples but not at all among black couples. Table 7.5 indicates that anger control among white women and not speaking one's mind among white men are significant predictors of those couples who in the fourth year have more stable marriages. There are not even any comparable trends for the black couples. Rather, the

Table 7.5

Summary of Multiple Regression Analyses Predicting Marital Instability from Individual Interactive Styles in the Third Year (Within White Couples and Black Couples)

Predictor	White Couples (N=117)[†]		Black Couples (N=89)[†]		W/B diff.
	B	beta	B	beta	
Wives					
Control Anger	-.19+	-.18+	-.07	-.05	
Speak Mind	.06	.06	-.01	-.01	
Independent	-.01	-.02	-.02	-.04	
Husbands					
Control Anger	.08	.08	.03	.02	
Speak Mind	.26*	.25*	.16	.13	
Independent	.00	.00	-.11+	.20+	*
Adj. R²		.05*		.00	

+p<.10
*p<.05
**p<.01
***p<.001

[†]Reflects the number of couples in which there are no missing data on any of the predictors.

interactive style that was predictive of stability for them was how independent the husbands were seen to be. The more independent the husbands are, the more stable their marriages are.

The results for the white couples are as predicted. Accommodative styles should be conducive for stability. Controlling one's anger is often a way of accommodating to what one's spouse has said or done. And evidently such accommodation by women pays off in a harmonious marriage, while such accommodation in men has no significant effect. "Speaking one's mind" is a way of talking about a person in interaction who disregards the cues that others would find inhibiting. "Speaking one's mind" often means saying hurtful things in the course of disagreeing with someone and having the last word in demonstrating one's power. The virtue of honesty can be the sin of inconsiderateness. And that seems to be the case with regard to the men's behavior among white couples.

Controlling one's anger and speaking one's mind are in some ways mirror images of each other. And indeed these two behaviors are significantly related to one another for both men and women among both black and white couples. The results show that white women who control anger and white men who don't speak their mind are in stable marriages. We suggest that the especially important channel of interpersonal accommodation for women is in the way they regulate affect (controlling anger) while the important channel of interpersonal accommodation for men is in the way they deal with power such as in relinquishing control of a situation (not speaking one's mind). It is as if women and men who are willing to give up gender stereotyped assertive behaviors (getting angry for women; speaking one's piece for men) impress their spouses with their accommodative styles.

We can ask whether we are picking up anything new in observing that white wives who reported controlling their anger were in more stable marriages than wives who reported that they did not control their anger. Recall that from the personality assessment in the first year, we learned that white wives who were "cooperative" were in more stable marriages. Is controlling one's anger just a manifestation of cooperativeness? We reran the regression analyses using interactive styles as predictors and also included the assessment of white wives' Cooperativeness. In the new model both Controlling Anger and Cooperativeness were significant predictors. Thus, we conclude that Cooperativeness covers much more than holding back one's anger when upset. It most likely also entails doing proactive things to make the relationship happy.

Why did it not apply to the black couples? We would suggest that not speaking up and not expressing angry feeling are norms for interpersonal considerations that are stronger in the majority culture. Kochman (1981) has found evidence that expression of feelings, especially feelings in conflict situations, may be more normative and even often playful in black society.

Thus both controlling of anger and speaking up might on occasion have quite the opposite meanings for judging one's spouse's commitment to a relationship. The paradoxical meaning of the phrases may thus lead to their overall insignificant power in understanding marital commitments among black couples.

Why is a black husband's <u>Independence</u> such a positive predictor of marital stability among black couples? Results are beginning to coalesce around a general pattern indicating that black males, engulfed in marriage by their own collaborative commitment to a highly interdependent style of marriage, may need space to withdraw. Interdependence may accent the importance of their wives in maintaining not only the financial but also the emotional security of the family. Thus, a relatively high degree of autonomy may be required by black husbands to avoid this threatening interdependence and to allow them to feel okay about themselves. Without it, their potential failures as providers are psychologically accentuated.

Couple Interactions

<u>Perceived couple interactions</u>

When we look at perceived couple interaction, we find some curious and provocative changes occurring between the first and third years in the relationship between these variables and marital instability. These results are in Table 7.6. It will be recalled that negative sex and frequent conflict reported in the first year were predictive of marital instability in both black and white couples. For black couples, the husband's power in the relationship was associated with marital stability.

<u>Negative Sex</u> in Year 3 does not predict instability for either group of marriages although the first year report of <u>Negative Sex</u> is still marginally related to instability in white couples (beta = .16; p = .069). When we consider the fact that dissatisfaction with sex is among the main contributors to marital instability in the first year and that the couples most unhappy with their sexual relationship have probably already divorced or separated by Year 3, we are not surprised that <u>Negative Sex</u> has less predictive power for the remaining sample in Year 3. Furthermore, those who were experiencing problems in the sexual relationship in the early years but did not construe the sexual relationship as paramount to a good relationship may continue in a stabler relationship but consider other factors as critical in judging their commitment to the marriage.

<u>Frequency of Conflict</u> shows slightly different patterns between first and third years in our two co-culture groups. For white couples, the first year report of frequent conflict is predictive of instability and continues to have an effect when we enter third year reports of conflict into the regression. But

Table 7.6
Summary of Multiple Regression Analyses Predicting Marital Instability from Couple Interaction in the Third Year (Within White Couples and Black Couples)

Predictor	White Couples (N=131)†		Black Couples (N=126)†		W/B diff.
	B	beta	B	beta	
Couple Shared Time	-.05	-.09	.03	.04	
Couple Relaxed Time	-.06*	-.19*	-.04	-.08	
Couple Positive Sex	.05	.15	.01	.03	
Couple Negative Sex	.02	.06	.05	.10	
Couple Frequency of Conflict	.01	.02	.17***	.40***	
Couple Range of Disagreement	-.03	-.10	-.10*	-.21*	
Husbands' Power	-.05	-.11	.01	.02	
Couple Role Sharing	-.11	-.12	-.30**	-.27**	
First Year Couple Negative Sex	.07+	.16+			
First Year Couple Frequency of Conflict	.15***	.38***	.03	.06	
Adj. R²	.25***		.27***		

+p<.10
*p<.05
**p<.01
***p<.001

†Reflects the number of couples in which there are no missing data on any of the predictors.

third year Frequency of Conflict does not add anything to the predictive power of the first year.   In the black couples, third year Frequency of Conflict predicts instability in the fourth year.   When first year Frequency of Conflict is put into the regression with third year conflict, the power of first year conflict drops out.   Conflicts in the first year, if they are worked out, apparently do not jeopardize the stability of the marriage.   Only in cases where conflicts continue, where no mechanisms or strategies have developed for resolving them, do they have deleterious effects on the stability of the relationship.

The range of disagreements a couple reports has predictive power in the black couples but, surprisingly, it predicts stability rather than instability.   A broad rather than narrow range of areas of disagreement may indicate an open style in which any and all areas are permissible for discussion and argument, or it may also indicate that no single issue is so critical that it focusses all of a couple's negativity or difference.

An interesting relationship appears for the first time in the third year data for black couples: there is a relationship between Couple Role Sharing and marital stability.   Given our interpretation that black men thrive best in marriage when power is clearly in their control, how do we account for this result?   First we should note the fact that Husband's Power in the marriage, predictive of marital stability in black couples in the first year, has dropped out by the third year.   To us, this indicates a significant reversal in emphasis in the relationship between the young black husband and wife: whereas early in the relationship it seemed important to uphold an image and ideal of patriarchal power in the marriage, by the third year the reality of a mutual and more egalitarian relationship has asserted itself.   Reassured of his power in the relationship in the earliest stage of marriage, the young male can relax and interact with less concern for power issues.   The fact that there may now be children to care for can also be seen as a factor urging a more egalitarian relationship.

In the white couples, having relaxed time together is a new predictor in the third year.

Solving couple dilemmas

Establishing equity in decision making for a couple seems to be an important ingredient for stability for both black and white couples.   The measure of Equity Input, which we should remember is based on both the husbands' and wives' appraisal of having an equal say, related to marital stability for both black and white couples (see Table 7.7).   We have discovered that these common predictors for black stability and white stability are rare.   Thus, although the significance of equity as a predictor is marginal in both groups ($p = .07$, whites; $p = .06$, blacks), we are impressed with its replication

Table 7.7

Summary of Multiple Regression Analyses Predicting Marital Instability from Solving Couple Dilemmas in the Third Year (Within White Couples and Black Couples)

Predictor	White Couples (N=124)[†]		Black Couples (N=94)[†]		W/B diff.
	B	beta	B	beta	
Equity Input	−.04+	−.17+	−.06+	−.24+	
Share Chores	.00	.02	.04	.15	
Has Privacy	.02	.10	.02	.10	
Take Time for Friends	−.02	−.12	.05+	.23+	
Leisure Together	−.05**	−.30**	.01	.04	
Separate Money	−.00	−.02	.00	.03	
Adj. R²	.11**		.09**		

+p<.10
*p<.05
**p<.01
***p<.001

[†]Reflects the number of couples in which there are no missing data on any of the predictors.

in the two groups. To have equal say thus allows people to feel as if their individual needs are being negotiated in a marriage when conflicts occur. This may be one of the most important examples of how the dilemma is solved. It says nothing of the style of negotiation nor the general trappings of one's style. Only that each has a say in what goes on in the marriage.

The other two significant results in Table 7.7, one for white couples and one for black couples, speak of different facets of the same general norms. The black couples have more stable marriages if the couple asserts that they take relatively less time for their own friends. Separation of the couple in their individual contact with friends thus seems to be a detrimental solution to the couple dilemma for black couples. By contrast, the white couples have more stable marriage when they say they are satisfied with their leisure together. Thus the white couples focus on the benefits of togetherness; the black couples focus on the difficulties of separation. These may be reflections of the same phenomenon: that the couple needs relaxed time together spent in satisfying ways, perhaps especially in the early years of marriage when they are forging their own identity as a couple separate from friends and family, and when the couple perhaps finds leisure time and private time hard to come by.

RESULTS: INTEGRATIVE FEELINGS

Specific Feelings

Of all the new measures of specific feelings about marriage assessed in the third wave of the study, none was more revealing about potentially differential marital dynamics in black and white couples than the measure of Jealousy. Jealousy reported by wives was more characteristic of unstable white marriages; jealousy reported by husbands was more characteristic of unstable black marriages (see Table 7.8). Jealousy reported by white husbands and black wives was not significantly related to the stability of their marriages. Why is that so?

We might suggest that the differential dynamics of jealousy among black couples compared to white couples are partially related to differential mate availability among blacks and whites. Among whites, there may be a relatively balanced sex ratio with regard to potential other partners for husbands and wives should the marriage dissolve. Nevertheless, the ratio may be in favor of men having more possible choices since white males have the most resources (money, education) for living alone and establishing new liaisons. In that case, women recognizing their husbands' roving eyes might spell greater potential disaster for the marriage than if the men were jealous. Furthermore, white females' jealousy might reflect perceptions of a real situation to be concerned about compared to white males' jealousy which may

Table 7.8

Summary of Multiple Regression Analyses Predicting Marital Instability from Specific Feelings in the Third Year (Within White Couples and Black Couples)

Predictor	White Couples (N=116)[†]		Black Couples (N=97)[†]		W/B diff.
	B	beta	B	beta	
Female					
Sat with Home	.01	.00	−.18	−.08	
Sat with Leisure	−.13+	−.16+	.02	.02	
Jealousy	.30+	.16+	.03	−.02	
No privacy	.14	.11	.17	.09	
Feels Spouse Doesn't Understand	.07	.05	.11	.05	
Feels Spouse Understands Sex Needs	−.12	−.09	−.01	−.00	
Feels Spouse is Not Critical	.03	.02	.12	.07	
Feels Spouse Would Not Deceive	−.15	−.06	−.26	−.15	
Male					
Sat with Home	.12	.07	−.35	−.15	*
Sat with Leisure	.10	.12	.01	.01	
Jealousy	−.22	−.10	.35+	.19+	***
No Privacy	.16	.12	.08	.04	
Feels Spouse Doesn't Understand	.17	.12	.12	.07	
Feels Spouse Understands Sex Needs	−.10	−.07	−.11	−.06	
Feels Spouse is Not Critical	.22	.14	−.13	−.07	*
Feels Spouse Would Not Deceive	−.53*	−.20*	.11	.06	**
Adj. R²	.16**		.06*		

+p<.10
*p<.05
**p<.01
***p<.001

[†]Reflects the number of couples in which there are no missing data on any of the predictors.

more likely be possessive paranoia not in tune with the ongoing marital situation.

For black couples, there is a distinctly greater imbalance in favor of more choices for males (Tucker & Mitchell-Kernan, in press). Such being the case, it may be that many black women learn to adapt to a situation of an open marriage more easily than white women. Jealousy certainly would be there, but the consequences for the marriage may be less severe. When black males are jealous they may be coming from a position of being more vocationally and economically vulnerable than both their white counterparts and their more educated wives. Thus, their jealousy could very well reflect their anxiety about their dependence on their wives, which can be a powerful force in their wanting to get out of the situation. Even if the jealousy had no clear grounds in reality, it would be especially threatening to be jealous when there was no easy way for a man to offer a woman the security that men are traditionally expected to achieve.

Besides issues of jealousy little else about specific feelings helped us understand marital instability. Indeed, we were particularly surprised by that fact since the specific feelings we assessed seemed so close to what would produce overall feelings of contentment in marriage. For the white couples, husbands' feeling that their wives would not deceive them was a significant predictor of stability. This variable, which understandably was significantly correlated negatively with the amount of jealousy the husbands experienced (−.28), is different from jealousy in that it gets at general trust as well as relational trust and puts the burden of the feeling squarely on the spouse, unlike jealousy. White males perhaps enter marriage with an enormous idealization of their wives; anything that disillusions them may become a considerable obstacle to their commitment.

The one other specific feeling that showed connection to marital instability for the white couples was a trend showing that white wives who were satisfied with how they spent their leisure tended to be in more stable marriages. Our guess is that Leisure Satisfaction in this case means having just the right amount of satisfying time to be with one's spouse on a relaxed basis. It is again curious why such a variable should not be significant for blacks or for white males. It may be that these groups define ideals for leisure as being more separate than white women do.

General Feelings

Table 7.9 summarizes the multiple regression analyses predicting marital instability from the same measures used to assess general marital integrative feelings in previous chapters covering Years 1 and 2. By and large, the measures found to be significant are ones that were important in the previous years as well: among white couples, women's marital happiness and men's and

Table 7.9
Summary of Multiple Regression Analyses Predicting Marital Instability from Third Year Integrative Feelings
(Within White Couples and Black Couples)

Predictor	White Couples (N=127)[†]		Black Couples (N=106)[†]		W/B diff.
	B	beta	B	beta	
Wives					
Happiness	.00	.00	−.28	−.17	
Competence	−.01	−.01	.17	.08	
Control	.19	.11	−.41	−.23	*
Equity	.03	.02	.25+	.14	
Marital Tension	.12	.06	.11	.05	
Happiness Year 2	−.62	.45***	−.57	−.35	
Control Year 1			−.08	−.04	
Husbands					
Happiness	.34*	.18*	.00	.00	
Competence	.04	.02	.10	.06	
Control	−.04	−.03	.11	.06	
Equity	.06	.04	−.12	−.07	
Marital Tension	.48**	.25**	.08	.04	
Happiness Year 2	−.34*	−.21*			
Marital Tension Year 2	.07	.04	.46**	.22	
Adj. R^2	.39***		.39***		

+p<.10
*p<.05
**p<.01
***p<.001

[†]Reflects the number of couples in which there are no missing data on any of the predictors.

women's lack of marital tension are related to marital stability; among black couples, women's happiness and sense of control in the marriage, along with men's lack of marital tension are predictors of stability. To ascertain whether some of these results were especially potent during the third year, we ran additional regression analyses. If second year versions of significant third year variables had themselves been significant, they were also introduced into the prediction equation. In these new analyses, two results remain strong for the third year: marital tensions experienced by white husbands; marital control experienced by black wives. Evidently, newfound tensions during the third year add to white husbands' concerns about their marriage in general as do black women's feelings that they lose some control of how to make their marriages work.

For some clues about why these two results stand out as third year factors in understanding marital instability, we can refer back to the results on specific feelings during the third year that are significantly associated with marital instability. Jealousy reported by white women was a significant predictor of marital instability for white couples; jealousy reported by black men was a significant predictor of marital instability for black couples. The emergence of jealous reactions, whether they are real or imagined, can spark tension or loss of feelings of control in one's spouse. Why jealousy occurs in these groups at this time we cannot speak to, especially since we did not have comparable assessments in the previous two years. Whether it was a persistent trait of these white women or black men to be jealous or whether it was something that emerged because of new relationships developed during this particular year would be hard to determine with the data. Nevertheless, jealousy, whenever and however it emerges, should be psychologically related to tensions and feelings of being not in control of one's partner.

RESULTS: STRESSORS AND INTERFERENCES

Stressors

By Year 3 the only set of stressors of the entire group we considered that had some significant association to marital instability had to do with the experience of alcohol problems. These results are in Table 7.10. If a wife, black or white, was identified by the couple as having an alcohol problem, the couple tended to be more unstable. This was also the case for a recognition of alcohol problems for black men. However, such was not the case for a recognition of alcohol problem for white men, although the trend was certainly in the same direction. Since this was not as prominent in the first year of marriage, one can speculate that there is considerable amount of enabling that couples perform for each other in the first years that keep couples from having

Table 7.10

Summary of Multiple Regression Analyses Predicting Marital Instability from Stressors Year 3 (Within White Couples and Black Couples)

Predictor	White Couples (N=135)[†]		Black Couples (N=120)[†]		W/B diff.
	B	beta	B	beta	
Couple Stress					
Baby	.25	.09	.31	.08	
Unemployment	.08	.04	.09	.05	
Death	−.02	−.02	.03	.02	
Moved	.17	.07	.13	.04	
Serious Illness	.09	.05	.00	.00	
Wife Stress					
Worry Re: Money	−.05	−.04	.01	.01	
Alcohol Problems	.23**	.29**	.26*	.21*	
Husband Stress					
Worry Re: Money	.10	.07	.17	.11	
Alcohol Problems	.04	.09	.10*	.21*	
Adj. R^2	.06*		.11*		

+p<.10
*p<.05
**p<.01
***p<.001

[†]Reflects the number of couples in which there are no missing data on any of the predictors.

an accurate awareness of the problem. As a marriage progresses, however, it may become more and more difficult to deny the problem and the tension that it may be causing in the marital relationship.

By the third year, it is also apparent that the importance of worrying about finances for black husbands, salient as a predictor of instability in Years 1 and 2, no longer remains a significant predictor. Those couples for whom this anxiety became a symptom of difficulties and tensions most likely had already separated. Those that remain in the third year may be couples who worked out that worry or did not let that worry interfere with the way they got along. One can speculate that a black wife's awareness of provider concerns in her husband could lead a couple to discuss matters, lend support to each other, and underscore their commitments. Earlier those concerns might have been passed over or exaggerated with blame, thereby threatening the harmony of the relationship.

Interferences

In the second year, we were able to detect some association between perceived interferences couples have with their lives and how stable their marriages are. In particular, interferences experienced from friends seem to be associated with unstable marriages. That was true for friends of the wives and friends of the white husbands, but not the black husbands. The curious thing about the third year results is that the pattern is somewhat reversed (see Table 7.11). In the third year interference by black husbands' and black wives' friends is associated with instability, but such interference is no longer associated with instability in the white couples. We can only suspect that many of the white couples began to comply with the felt interference and dropped some friendships or the demands from the friendships. Under these conditions there may still be some underlying resentments but at least the complaints about friends would diminish. Among the white couples, those that still experienced interferences from friends may have been more moderate in their concerns. For the black couples, on the other hand, interferences from friends persist as potentially destabilizing forces and indeed become more salient. To the degree that black couples find it difficult to take a "couple attitude" about their marriage and are concerned about their own individual friendships, they may continue to find interferences from the demands of friends problematic in their relationship.

Family interferences experienced by the black couple with regard to the husbands' families were the only interferences from families that were associated with instability in the second year. This result persists in the third year (see Table 7.11), and it is significant predictor over and above the same interferences experienced in the second year.

Table 7.11

Summary of Multiple Regression Analyses Predicting Marital Instability from Perceived Interference in the Third Year (Within White Couples and Black Couples)

Predictor	White Couples (N=131)[†]		Black Couples (N=113)[†]		W/B diff.
	B	beta	B	beta	
Wives					
Job Interference	−.01	−.06	−.02	−.05	
Family Interference	.01	.04	.00	.02	
Friend Interference	.06	.13	.07*	.18*	
Husbands					
Job Interference	.05	.29**	−.03+	−.15+	***
Family Interference	.01	.04	.08*	.25*	
Friend Interference	.03	.13	.07*	.19*	
Couple					
Work Interference	−.02	−.06	.12*	.21*	
Adj. R^2	.13*		.24***		

$+p<.10$
$*p<.05$
$**p<.01$
$***p<.001$

[†]Reflects the number of couples in which there are no missing data on any of the predictors.

RESULTS: SOCIAL SUPPORT

The major result found for social support assessments in Year 1 were replicated in Year 3: black couples who were close to their families were still more unlikely to be in unstable marriages than were black couples who were not close to their families. These findings are in Table 7.12. The result is no longer significant when we include first year closeness to family as an additional predictor, suggesting that it was the general sense of support from the family that was important and not something special that emerged in the third year of marriage.

Of the new measures of support network introduced in the assessment of the third year of marriage, one proved to be of interest for white couples and another one for black couples. The results for whites in Table 7.12 were particularly interesting, defying all intuitions. Those white couples who live closer to relatives were in more unstable marriages than those couples who live at some distance from their families. A post facto account of this result would run something like this: couples who manage to establish their own turf and act independently from their families of origin lay deeper roots for the continuance of their own marriage. Their identity as a couple is on firmer ground since their intermingling with the larger family system is minimal, requiring them to dispel fewer family myths and ghosts. Having said that, we realize it is purely post facto since we could have well argued the opposite. We could have argued that with close family connections available there was a generally more favorable climate for generating a strong family system. Thus, our interpretation of the result should be thought of as mere speculation. We have a provocative, but not a firm, convincing finding. The fact that interferences from family are not significantly related to instability for white couples suggests that the negative features of having a family close by for white couples are not from increased interference but from something more psychological and subtle.

For black couples, the density of the friend network turned out to be a positive feature of their network for facilitating marital stability. To the degree that density reflects a greater integration into a social network for black couples, we would argue that the result reflects an implicit social support that comes from stable black couples being tied into their communities. Another possible but highly speculative interpretation might be that black couples who experience dense networks may find less need to depend on each other for their personal lives. Such being the case, the black husbands, in particular, may not feel as entrapped in the marriage and may be more comfortable with a less intense relationship.

Table 7.12
Summary of Multiple Regression Analyses Predicting Marital Instability from Social Support in the Third Year
(Within White Couples and Black Couples)

Predictor	White Couples (N=123)[†]		Black Couples (N=114)[†]		W/B diff.
	B	beta	B	beta	
Marital Instability					
Friend Density	.04	.12	−.11*	−.24*	
Sum Closeness with Family	.01	.08	−.02	.11	
Family Support	−.02	−.06	−.06	.09	
Friend Support	−.01	−.05	−.01	−.03	
Family Density	−.05	−.13	.03	.05	
How Close Family Lives	.01	.16	.03	.12	
Contact with Family	.01	.07	−.00	−.04	
Sum Closeness with Family (Second Year)			−.03	−.19	
Adj. R^2	.07,NS		.10*		

+p<.10
*p<.05
**p<.01
***p<.001

[†]Reflects the number of couples in which there are no missing data on any of the predictors.

SUMMARY

There were many findings from the third year interviews that were different from the parallel analyses from the two previous years. And there were new findings emerging that stem from assessments that were introduced in the third year and were unavailable in previous years.

Among those that showed different patterns from previous years were results relevant to spouses' reliance on each other as major supports. Whereas this was critically important in women who were found to be in stable marriages in Year 1, such was not the case in Year 3. And, to make things symmetrical, whereas this was not important in men who were found to be in stable marriages in Year 1, it was important in Year 3. This cross-over is interpreted to mean than men are socialized to seek their major support from their wives, and this takes time, and women are socialized over time not to expect support from their husbands. A similar adaptation may be going on in the discovery that the use of destructive conflict by spouses no longer is so clearly tied to instability. We suggest that both men and women learn to adapt to conflict styles, even those that are apparently destructive. Evidently, what was devastating in the first year of marriage becomes part of the turf for many couples by the third year.

Issues of sexuality, both experiencing problems with sex and the degree of insight that spouses had of each others' sexual feelings, waned in importance as factors affecting the stability of marriage in the third year. Some perspective on the importance of sexuality for the marital relationship evidently begins to develop as the marriage progresses beyond the honeymoon period.

Black couples and white couples continue to differ with each other with respect to third year factors found to predict marital instabilty, and that is especially clear with respect to the regulation of conflict. These issues are important for understanding the stability of white couples, but not for understanding the stability of black couples. It is suggested that black couples are more sanguine about absorbing conflict as a way of relating and can even think of it at times as a demonstration of commitment.

New to the third year was a finding that only among black couples incompatibilities about religion and sex role issues had negative associations with stability. Traditionalism about religious commitments and sex role issues are thought to be especially salient in black communities. However, there are two counter-indicators about sex role traditionalism among the black couples. One is that, like the white couples, black couples who think that each spouse has an equal say in decisions tend to be the stable couples. And the other is that black couples who are higher in the index of <u>Role Sharing</u> between husband and wife are in more stable marriages. We suggest that the discomfort with sex role equality in marriage for black couples is a major factor in the initial instability for black couples, but for couples who remain

past the first two years, there is likely going to be greater accommodation to sex role equality.

The white couples showed the curious finding from new third year data that those who lived close to their families were most at risk. Such was not the case for the black couples, who, quite the contrary, showed that highly dense family networks were associated with marital stability. Black couples and white couples clearly have different dynamics for relating most satisfactorily to the families of origin.

Other new third year data not available in earlier analyses suggests that jealousy plays an important role in marital instability, but somewhat differently in black couples and white couples. For the black couples, the wife's jealousy seems disruptive, but not the husband's jealousy. The results are reversed for the white couples. Interpretations make use of ideas about which spouse has more currency in the marriage market, which we suggest is different for whites and blacks.

Finally, new data about attitudes towards marriage and divorce introduced in the third year yield no results to suggest that these attitudes are correlated with the stability of the marriage.

NOTES

1. <u>Satisfaction with home</u> was assessed in Year 1 but not analyzed because we thought the couples had had too little time in their marriage to assess this aspect of their marriage reliably.

8

THE FOURTH YEAR OF MARRIAGE

For each of the analyses of the previous years we were able to pinpoint factors in the year of marriage under consideration that contributed to marital instability with the knowledge that an important aspect of the measure of instability was whether the couple had divorced or separated at some later point. With the analyses of the marital experience in the fourth year we have a much more attenuated research issue. Since the questions asked in the fourth year were asked only of couples in intact marriages in the fourth year, the measure of instability only reflects how frequently either of the partners had thought about leaving the marriage "in the past few months." The measure is either the husband's reported frequency or the wife's depending on which was higher. As such, this is a more limited analysis. Nonetheless, it speaks to the factors that contribute to psychological uncertainty about remaining in the marriage.

As in Year 2, there were three broad categories of factors analyzed: stressors, interferences, and integrated feelings. Since Year 4 like Year 2 was a short telephone interview, only a limited number of questions could be asked. We did not anticipate that there was anything unique about the fourth year of marriage. In general we expected that the experiences with problems and gratifications of married life would gradually accrue without any special issues engendered by the fourth year. Of course, additional couples became parents for the first time, and maybe some for the second or third time. This would mean that more couples than in previous years had to face juggling family responsibilities and holding down jobs, or leaving the work arena to have and tend children. And of course, with each succeeding year there is an increased likelihood that some new stressor (like death of a loved one or a serious illness) might occur as the couples' parents and family age. Furthermore, the fourth year was 1990, and the economy of the country was

sputtering. The ramifications of economic downturns place special stresses on couples trying to integrate work and family goals. Nevertheless, we entered analyses of the fourth year data with no special expectations.

STRESSES

The only new measure of stress introduced in the fourth year was wife's or husband's report of having been involved in an extramarital affair or reporting that their spouse had been. The questions were very direct:

"Did your (husband/wife) have an affair?" (Yes/No)

"Did you have an affair?" (Yes/No)

The product of the husband's and the wife's answers to these questions were used to measure the appearance of an affair as a stress. Thus, more weight was given to the appearance of an affair if both wife and husband report the affair. As one might guess, very few couples admitted to either partner having had an affair. In this sample 3% of the white women report that they have had affairs or their husbands have had affairs. The comparable figures for white men, black women, black men are 5%, 5%, and 4%, respectively.

In Table 8.1 are the regression analyses for stresses reported in Year 4 as predictors of marital instability. It is clear in that table that reports of affairs are indeed associated with couple instability. This is true for black couples and for white couples. While this is not surprising, what should be underscored is that the reports of a wife's infidelity had stronger association with marital instability than reports of a husband's infidelity. The double standard on that issue evidently still prevails. Men's affairs may be disruptive to a marriage, but perhaps not as catastrophic as women's affairs. It remains an open question whether a spouse's affair causes as much grief in women as it does in men, but that grief does not as quickly translate into thoughts of leaving the relationship. Again it is not clear that women are more forgiving or that they experience more dependence on the relationship and fear moving out of it more than men do when confronted with their partner's infidelity. A closer look at these processes is in order.

Another result, parallel in both black and white couples, shows that a husband's concern about not having privacy was associated with marital instability. This is the first time that this measure has shown any connection to marital instability. And it is curious that the disruptive nature of this feeling occurred for men and not for women. Could it be that it takes this long a period for the build-up of concerns about independence to occur in a man's life in our modern American arrangements? The commitment to marriage undoes independence. That may be understood by both men and women for the first stages in marriage. Then, as the day-in, day-out interdependence and responsibility of lives joined together becomes more evident, maybe especially

Table 8.1

Summary of Multiple Regression Analyses Predicting Marital Instability from Fourth Year Stressors with Third Year Controls (Within White Couples and Black Couples)

Predictor	White Couples (N=123)[†]		Black Couples (N=91)[†]		W/B diff.
	B	beta	B	beta	
Couple Stress					
Had baby	−.05	−.02	−.41	−.11	
Moved	.04	.01	−.02	.06	
Someone Unemployed	.36*	.19*	.29	.09	
Death	−.06	−.05	.03	.02	
Serious Illness	.22	.08	−.07	−.01	
Wife Stress					
No Privacy	−.05	−.04	.01	.01	
Worry Re: Money	.22*	.18*	.22	.12	
Had Affair	4.25***	.41***	2.82***	.41***	
Alcohol Problems	.04	.03	−.27+	−.19+	*
Husband Stress					
No Privacy	.30**	.23**	.28*	.18*	
Worry Re: Money	.00	.00	.16	.10	
Had Affair	1.03*	.24*	.64+	.14+	
Alcohol Problems	.00	.00	.20*	.32*	**
Third Year Husbands					
Alcohol Problems	—	—	.06	.12	
Adj. R^2		.49		.45	

+p<.10
*p<.05
**p<.01
***p<.001

[†]Reflects the number of couples in which there are no missing data on any of the predictors.

as children became more prominent on the scene and invade not only their individual privacy but their couple privacy for intimacy, then there may be a greater toll on men. Husbands have been generally less socialized than their wives to the value of interpersonal interdependence and more socialized than their wives to the value of individual autonomy.

Other stresses that were significantly disruptive of marital stability for the white couples were not the same as the stresses significantly disruptive for the black couples. For white couples, either the wife or husband being unemployed during the year was associated with instability, as well as wives' Worrying About Money. These economic stresses, although associated with marital instability in the same direction for the black couples, were not significant predictors for them. It might well be that the economic stresses that were there as significant predictors for black couples in the earlier years are prominently associated with actual divorce and separation. During this fourth year analysis, the divorced/separated group is omitted from the analysis. Perhaps it is as if economic issues take their toll on black marriages earlier, and once the couple remains together, other phenomena become more prominent. The economic issues may take a longer time to penetrate the vulnerabilities of white couples. It is as if the threshold of economic vulnerability of marriage is much lower in black couples. We have reason to believe that black couples with the same household income as white couples experience greater vulnerability, because the safety net provided by families is financially weaker for black couples. Many more black couples emerge from families with small assets to support their children in time of stress or to assist them in such matters as getting together a down payment for a house or car. White couples fare better in these respects. As a result, economic vulnerability has a greater impact on black couples early on, and there may be some lag before it has an impact on the white couples.

Black husbands' drinking continued to have a strong effect on marital instability in the fourth year, over and above the effect noted in the first year. It might very well be that this drinking pattern is symptomatic of financial stress, and, as such, mutes the predictive power of the economic variables in the fourth year. Indeed, black husbands' Alcohol Problems is correlated with Worrying About Money both on the husbands' part (.20) and the wives' part (.35). The comparable correlations of Alcohol Problems are .18 to white husbands' Worrying About Money and .14 for white wives' Worrying About Money. However, only the correlation difference for the wives is significant, and it is the white wives' worrying about finances that is significantly associated with instability for the white couples.

The most curious result is the trend for black wives having alcohol problems to be in marriages of stability rather than instability. This is a masked result since the correlation between wives' Alcohol Problems and the measure of instability is positive, albeit small (.08). However, when the other

correlates of wives' <u>Alcohol Problems</u> are also considered (especially the highly correlated husbands' <u>Alcohol Problems</u>), then the unique variance remaining evidently reflects a commitment to the marriage either on the husband's part or the wife's. It might very well be that when husbands are aware that their wives' alcoholism might have been brought on by their own abuse of alcohol, as it often is, husbands may develop greater commitments to stay in the marriage. In any event it is a curious result and worth some future detailed exploration focusing on the interpersonal dynamics of substance abuse in marriage.

Interferences

We were surprised to find that there was one set of perceived interferences experienced by couples that was associated with instability for both black couples and white couples, and that had to do with perceived interferences from the husbands' families (see Table 8.2). In analyses of the prior year, this was true only for the black couples. In these analyses of the fourth year, once controls were introduced from parallel variables from prior years, interferences from white husbands' families also had negative associations with marital instability.

Our speculations about why a husband's family interferences may be problematic for marital stability center on the stereotyped notion of the wife's mother-in-law being a difficult relationship for the wife to transact. Mothers' attachments to sons can be intense, and vice versa. Women's jealousies are often more about husbands' emotional attachments than are men's jealousies. And if husbands cater to their mothers, or express considerable concern for them, women's jealous concerns about their attachments may come quickly into the picture.

With all other perceived interferences, the results diverged for black and white couples. For white couples, perceiving that wives' friends interfered was associated with marital instability, even controlling for parallel results found for white couples from the Year 2 data. This suggests that changes in how wives' friends interfere since the second year also have some impact on marital instability. Wives' friends may become involved in supporting women in their complaints about their husbands. If these involvements become expressed either to the wife or to the husband or to both, the couple may perceive that as interference with the couple's life. For the white couples, there was an additional significant effect found for interferences experienced from husbands' friends but when the previously significant parallel finding for Year 2 was inserted into the regression equation, Table 8.2 indicates that the fourth year findings were washed away. Thus, the results about the negative effects of husbands' friends as interferences in the marriage did not constitute

Table 8.2

Summary of Multiple Regression Analyses Predicting Marital Instability from Fourth Year Interferences with Earlier Year Controls (Within White Couples and Black Couples)

Predictor	White Couples (N=132)†		Black Couples (N=91)†		W/B diff.
	B	beta	B	beta	
Wives					
Job	.00	.00	.00	.00	
Family	.02	.02	−.20+	−.18+	*
Friends	.24**	.25**	.16	.15	
(Friends Second Year)	.17*	.19*			
(Friends Third Year)			.04	.11	
Husband					
Job	.02	.04	.08	.11	
Family	.12	.17	.25*	.24*	
Friends	.06	.07	.35**	.38**	**
(Friends Second Year)	.11*	.17*			
(Family Third Year)			.04	.12	
(Friends Third Year)			.00	.01	
Adj. R²	.29***		.34***		

+p<.10
*p<.05
**p<.01
***p<.001

†Reflects the number of couples in which there are no missing data on any of the predictors.

a change from what we discovered before.

For black couples, we find evidence from the Year 4 surveys that interferences from black women's families have positive correlations with marital stability. Involvement with their daughter's marriages on the part of black women's kin may be seen as supportive even if it takes the form of interference. Such involvement may have protective consequences for the couple. One can imagine a family who talks a lot about how the children are being raised, on the one hand, but who agrees to help out during times of stress on the other hand.

The perceived interferences from black husbands' friends are associated with black couples' marital instability. These results are very strong. It could be that these represent the distractions in activities away from home that are disruptive of marital commitment. Both husbands and wives can be very well aware of such disruptions.

SUMMARY

Because in the fourth year we interviewed only those respondents in intact marriages, the information we have about the fourth year can only be used to differentiate the frequency with which couples thought about separating or divorcing during the fourth year. This is a more limited analysis.

Stresses and interferences were examined. The clearest stress affecting marital instability was whether or not from their reports the husband or wife had had an affair. Furthermore, the consequences for instability seem more drastic if the wife had had an affair than if the husband had had an affair. Since Year 4 was the first time we asked about affairs, this result is not necessarily specific to the fourth year.

Another clear stress was husbands' feelings that they lacked privacy. This seems to crop up in the fourth year as a factor contributing to instability. We suggest that it did not appear earlier because the effects of this stress may be cumulative, especially as the relentless demands from parenting gradually become more apparent over the first years of marriage.

Financial stress begins to catch up to white couples in the fourth year, while it had been important earlier for the black couples.

There was a curious pattern of findings with regard to the stress from alcohol abuse in the black couples. Such stress coming from husbands has negative associations with stability, but such stress from wives has positive associations with stability. We speculate that black husbands may become particularly committed to their marriages if their wives are abusing alcohol, since many such husbands probably feel that they brought on that problem with their own drinking.

With regard to interferences, a finding that was true of only black couples

in prior analyses became true for both white and black couples: interferences from husbands' families is associated with thinking about breaking up the marriage. We speculate that it may reflect women's problems with mothers-in-law in both white and black co-cultures.

9

A SUMMING UP: MAJOR FACTORS
AFFECTING INSTABILITY
ACROSS THE
FIRST YEARS OF MARRIAGE

At the start of this research exploration we recognized that we were going to be highly empirical about our overall strategy for uncovering factors affecting instability over the first years of marriage. We have examined a multitude of factors and found many that were significant, many that were individually interesting to learn about, some that made a great deal of sense, some that were puzzling. For all of this we adopted no overarching conceptual model to begin with, nor have we built one as we have gone along. Instead, in the course of our presentation, we offered many, many different ideas that lay behind our construction or consideration of the measures of premarital, personal, and interpersonal factors, stresses and supports, and integrative feelings that may affect the course of a marriage. The preceding chapters have examined these factors across four years. Although we have highlighted a number of these results in integrative comments in each chapter, a task still remains that we had set for ourselves in the very beginning. And that task is to be integratively inductive and ask what it all adds up to. Looking back on the mountain of accumulated findings—indeed two mountains, since the results were so different for the black couples and the white couples—we are well aware that this is a Herculean task. We need some way to sort out the most important findings.

To this end we listed only those significant predictors across all the chapters that were significant at least at the .01 level in both their zero-order and multivariate predictions. In this way we can avoid any variable which in its multivariate treatment becomes highly significant when an arbitrary set of other variables are considered in the regression analysis in which it appears. These are presented in Tables 9.1 and 9.2 separately for white couples and black couples, respectively. We then performed hierarchical regression analyses on each of the two sets, using the following as hierarchical clusters:

premarital; first year; second year; third year; and finally, fourth year predictors. The results of these analyses appear in the last columns of Table 9.1 and Table 9.2. They give us information about how much each of the years of highlighted variables contributes to our understanding of instability. It should be noted that as we add variables from an additional year, we lose those subjects who were divorced or separated before the particular year was added, and hence did not participate in the interview. At each year's addition of variables, therefore, the sample becomes somewhat smaller.

What do the hierarchical regression analyses tell us? First of all, they tell us that the variables from each year that we highlighted significantly add to the overall prediction of stability. We were not merely being redundant as we proceeded through this longitudinal investigation. Of interest was the fact that the most significant leap in our understanding of what goes into instability in marriage occurs at different points for the black couples and the white couples. For the black couples the biggest leaps in adding variables come from the second year experiences and the fourth year experiences, while for the white couples the leaps come from adding variables to premarital variables from Year 1 experiences and from adding variables from the Year 3 experiences.

Why this difference? We realize that the bulk of questions asked in the second and fourth years, because they were based on telephone interviews, were about external situational matters. We refrained from asking many questions about the interactive dynamics of the relationship because we thought these questions were more appropriately asked in face-to-face interviews. Consequently, the strong addition to predictability of instability for blacks may come from our inquiries about the external features of their situation (such as interferences from friends and families, recent stressful events) while the biggest increase in predictability of whites comes from the close-in measures of their relationship. We were picking up this difference in the earlier chapters when we noticed that issues about couple interaction were much more salient in considering the stability of white marriages than they were in considering black marriages.

The factors highlighted in Tables 9.1 and 9.2 clearly give testimony to the major idea that we have been developing in this book, that the parameters and variables that affect the stability of black marriages in modern urban society are not the same as those that affect white marriages. There is an occasional overlap. Four variables noted in Table 9.1 and 9.2 are significantly associated with marital instability in both black and white marriages: in the second year, how much interference the couple sees coming from the wife's friends; the expressed marital unhappiness of women in their second year; frequency of conflict (Year 1 assessments in the case of white couples', Year 3 assessments in the case of black couples) and lastly, from the fourth year assessments, whether the couple reports that the wife had an affair. This is the sum total of the significant predictors that exist for both groups of couples.

Parallel Themes for Blacks and Whites

Nevertheless, in looking over other variables we are also impressed with similar themes that come up in both sets of highlighted findings. And we take that as our first job of inductive integration. What factors do we see in BOTH black and white couples in the results listed in Tables 9.1 and 9.2, even though they are reflected in different specific variables, that help us understand the major contributors to either marital instability or its converse, marital stability? That is to say, even though particular variables may operate differently in black and white marriages, the theme underlying these variables may be the same. We have summarized our conclusions about parallel themes below in a series of thematic integrations about functional and dysfunctional marriages in modern urban society, among both black and white couples. While our conclusions are largely based on Tables 9.1 and 9.2, we include other findings from earlier chapters as they bolster our claims. We have also found it easier to think about these results as factors associated with stability rather than instability. By listing characteristics that contribute to stability, in no way do we wish to imply that these are necessarily features of a full or ideal marriage. Nor are they features that affect all couples. Rather they are characteristics that promote staying the course, hanging in there, in spite of what may be "good for them" in some instances. In discussing each one we will indicate how each plays out differently in black marriages and white marriages.

Thematic Integration 1: Stable Marriages Depend on Women to be Caring, Nurturant, and Responsive Towards Their Husbands

Traditionally women are the kin keepers, which in the case of marriage means that women are delegated the responsibility to see that a couple's or a family's affective life sails on an even keel. To this end, women who are more communal, more open to caring and nurturing will take to the task more easily. Among the white couples, women whose dispositions are judged to be "cooperative" have more stable marriages. So are the white women who indicate that they perceive their husbands' bad feelings when they fight. This kind of caring about their husbands as a positive force for stability can also be seen in the finding that black women who take on a more collaborative style in telling the couple's story are in more stable marriages. And both white and black wives' expressed happiness consistently relates to marital stability, a fact that no doubt reflects wives' willingness to go the extra interpersonal mile if they are content with what is the general tenor of their marriages.

Table 9.1

Highlighted Significant Predictors of Marital Instability Across the First Four Years of Marriage (White Couples)

Stage	Variable	Accumulative R^2
Premarital	Wife's Cooperativeness (−) Husband's Personal Income (−)	.08
First Year	Negative Sexual Interaction Frequency of Conflict Wife's Marital Tension	.34
Second Year	Wife's Marital Happiness (−) Husband's Friends Interfere Wife's Friends Interfere	.41
Third Year	Wife's Understanding of Husband's Negative Reactions to Conflict (−) Husband's Finding It Easier to Talk to Others Couple Spends Leisure Together (−) Husband's Marital Tension Husband's Job Interference Wife's Alcohol Problems	.61
Fourth Year	Wife's Friends Interfere Wife's Affair Husband Feels Lack of Privacy	.69

Table 9.2

Highlighted Significant Predictors of Marital Instability Across the First Four Years of Marriage (Black Couples)

Stage	Variable	Accumulative R^2
Premarital	Number of Years as Couple (–) Husband's Mother's Education (–) Husband's Anxiety	.09
First Year	Husband's Affective Affirmation (–) Wife's Collaborativeness (–) Husband's Marital Happiness (–)	.17
Second Year	Couple Experienced Death of Someone Close (–) Husband's Family Interferes Wife's Friends Interfere Wife's Marital Happiness (–)	.40
Third Year	Incompatibility in Openness to New Things (–) Frequency of Conflict Role Sharing Orientation (–) Wife's Feelings of Control (–)	.52
Fourth Year	Husband's Friends Interfere Wife's Affair Husband's Alcohol Problems	.70

Thematic Integration 2: Stable Marriages Depend on Men Having Clear Evidence That They Are Achievers in the Society

Nothing could be more clear about the importance of a husband's achievement for the stability of a marriage than results showing that white males' personal income prior to marriage is significantly related to marital stability. This measure reflects the potential that the husband has to bring home the bacon and provide for the consumer needs and interests of the couple and the family as it evolves. While not as direct in the correlates of instability among the black couples, the fact that black husbands whose mother's education was high were in more stable marriages, must also reflect the same issue. Men from high social status backgrounds as determined by mother's education are probably able to demonstrate to themselves and their wives that they are achieving people. It was curious in this respect that the men whose fathers were high in educational attainment were in less stable marriages. This result was, however, only apparent in the multivariate treatment of the data.

Further evidence of the importance of husbands' achievement for stable marriages comes in the following: For white couples, the fact that the report that one's job interferes with marriage was a good predictor of instability, when more often than not the interference comes from lack of achievement on the job; for black couples, the fact that husbands' reported anxiety was negatively related to stability, an anxiety that for men comes from failures or anticipated failures in performance, and from the fact that men's alcoholism is negatively related to stability. Although we cannot attribute all alcoholism to lack of achievement, it is highly correlated with it either as a cause or a consequence (McClelland, Davis, Kalin & Wanner, 1972). A major theory of the drinking man is that he uses alcohol as a means to get the temporary illusion of power and effectiveness, when in a number of ways he is not either powerful or effective.

Thematic Integration 3: Stable Marriages Depend on Couples Working Out Compatible Interpersonal and Sexual Interactions, Ones That Minimize Fighting and Tensions About Their Sexuality

It seems a truism to say that stable marriages develop when couples get along with each other, and that conflict is a basis of instability. Both of these findings are clear in our data. What is more important to note, is the type of harmonious interactions that are most salient. On this score the black and white couples differ considerably.

First let us examine the interactive issues for white couples. Sexual interactions seem quite figural. The problems that white couples have in transacting a compatible sexual life seem very important to understanding their

harmony.   So is whether they share leisure activities.   Neither of these compatibilities emerges in analysis of the black couples.   For the white couples, wives' reports of experiences of marital tension are related to instability.   We would suggest that white women who cannot take fighting easily are likely going to further exacerbate tensions in the way couples get along.

Black couples who fight frequently also have difficulty holding on to stable marriages but there is no strong evidence that their sexual interactions play an important part in this picture in addition.   Nor is there any emphasis on shared leisure among black stable marriages.   For black couples, we have the puzzling finding that the <u>more</u> incompatible their openness to experience, the <u>more</u> stable is their marriage.   This suggests that among black couples stability may arise from the development of separate ways of occupying their time.

Thematic Integration 4: Stable Marriages Depend on Husbands and Wives Working Out Harmonious Integrations of Their Respective Social Networks

Interferences felt from friends play an especially important part among factors affecting the stability of urban marriages.   Wives' friends and husbands' friends are noted by unstable couples—both black and white—as being more interfering than they are among spouses in stable marriages.   Clearly the way that a couple feels about their integration in their network of friends makes a difference.

The fact that the same cannot be said about interferences from family is quite surprising.   The family network has had more press as a contributor to well-being in marriage.   But only in the case of black men's family do we find it to be a striking contributor to marital stability.   What form this takes in the life of black couples needs more careful inquiry.

Two other pieces of data that could be used to support the importance of the family network for blacks is the fact that only among blacks is the length of relationship before marriage critical to stability, and only among blacks does the death of someone close to the couple reinforce stability.   While the length of relationship before marriage can mean different things, one possible significance it has is the degree of acquaintance the couple has with their respective networks.   If it is a long relationship, then couples are more likely to have met each other's families and experienced whatever trials come from adopting the new family as part of one's own.   In addition, experiencing death in the family can bind a couple.   Such seems to be the case for the black couples in their early years of marriage.

Thematic Integration 5: Stable Marriages Depend on Men Preserving Some Sense of Independence and Some Control of Their Wives

A man's wife having an affair is a strong correlate of instability in both black and white marriages. While in and of itself it is not surprising, the fact that the comparable question asked about a man's affair did not have such devastating implications for marital stability points to a very strong double standard about sexuality. Either males are clearly more upset than their wives about their partners' extramarital adventures, or more women than men enter such affairs when their marriages are not easily salvageable. At any rate, it is clear in our data that a wife being out of her husband's possessive control in the sexual domain is symbolically more disruptive than a husband's being out of a woman's possessive control.

Among the white couples there is also evidence that husbands like to control their autonomy in general. Husbands who complain of no privacy in their marriage are in more unstable marriages. And it is only among white couples that women's alcohol problems are predictive of marital instability. Having a wife who suffers from alcoholism makes a husband feel more responsible not only to his wife but to the management of the household. The erosion of autonomy could be the reason that marital tensions expressed by white males in the third year are also good prognosticators of marital instability. These tensions may express difficulties white husbands experience in being tied down and having to feel responsible to the household.

Different Themes for Blacks and Whites

Our second task of inductive integration is to bring together results that are different for black marriages and white marriages. As we saw similar themes occurring in Tables 9.1 and 9.2, so we can also see the themes that are different, results that depend on recognition that black marriages occur in a group that has been historically disadvantaged in our society and that white marriages exist in a group that has not experienced this disadvantage.

Thematic Integration 6: Unlike Stable White Marriages, Stable Black Marriages Also Depend on Women Preserving Some Sense of Independence and Control of Their Marriages

Two results found in Table 9.2 are present for black couples and nothing quite parallel to them appears for the white couples. These are: (1) black women who feel they have more control over the well-being of their marriages are in more stable marriages; (2) black couples who have a stronger role

sharing orientation—that is, they think that men and women should be egalitarian in their marital roles and at the same time they are—are more stable than those who have a weaker role sharing orientation.

In both these instances we suggest that what is true for black couples and less clearly true for white couples is the importance of women feeling some autonomy and sense of control in their marriages. Whereas women are supposed to be the kin keepers, as we noted above, it is another thing for them to be autonomous, or get pleasure from being able to be providers. And it is still a much more far reaching thing for women to feel as if they are able to control their marital situation. This force towards autonomy for women seems to be present in the black couples who are in stable marriages.

It also might very well be that our puzzle about why the strong incompatibility in openness to experience was a positive predictor of stability for black couples may rest on this integrative theme. When a black wife and husband find that they are discrepant in the way they orient to experience, it may provide them with a reasonable basis for autonomous activities and fewer shared ventures where their individual needs for autonomy and control may be in conflict.

Thematic Integration 7: Unlike Stable White Marriages, Stable Black Marriages Depend On Husbands Feeling Especially Reassured About Their Acceptance To Their Wives

Two results that are paramount in understanding the stability of the black marriages focus on husbands' concerns about themselves: black husbands who feel affectively affirmed by their partners or think their wives approve of the kind of persons they are, are in stable marriages, compared to black husbands who do not feel this way; and the happier husbands are about their marriage in the first year, the stabler the marriage. No such results emerge for white males. This pattern suggests that black males may be particularly vulnerable to feeling rejected in marriage. This may be from a long history of male underemployment and continued insecurity about adequate and dignified work. In any case, whether it is the man who under these vulnerable conditions becomes less committed to the marriage, or whether it is the woman who may be quick to disrupt the marriage if the financial picture clouds up, is hard to diagnose with our data. In either case the vulnerability of the black marriage is contingent on factors that the more advantaged group does not experience as directly.

As we track these couples beyond these early years of marriage, we suspect that divergences in factors that affect marriages in black and white couples will magnify. And yet we also suspect that parallel themes will continue to exist. All couples, whether black or white, face the ever present

challenge of adapting to each other as they and their children go through new stages in family life. These adaptations are bound to have similar underlying challenges for everyone.

REFERENCES

Acitelli, L.K., Douvan, E., & Veroff, J. (1993). Perceptions of conflict in the first year of marriage: How important are understanding and similarity? *Journal of Social and Personal Relationships, 10*, 5–19.

Acker, M., & Veroff, J. (1991, May). Illusions are not enough: The relationship of accurate perceptions to marital well-being. Symposium talk, American Psychological Society, Washington, DC.

Anderson, C. (1982). The community connection: The impact of social networks on family and individual functioning. In F. Walsh (Ed.), *Normal Family Processes* (pp. 425–445). New York: Guilford.

Antonucci, T. (1990). Social supports and social relationships. In R.H. Binstock & L.K. George (Eds.), *The Handbook of Aging and Social Sciences. 3rd Edition* (pp. 205–226). San Diego, CA: Academic Press.

Bennett, N.G., Blanc, A.K., & Bloom, D.E. (1988). Commitment and the modern union: Assessing the link between premarital cohabitation and subsequent marital stability. *American Sociological Review, 53*, 127–138.

Booth, A., Johnson, D., & Edwards, J. (1983). Measuring marital instability. *Journal of Marriage and the Family, 45*, 387–394.

Bowen, M. (1978). *Family therapy in clinical practice.* New York: Jason Aronson.

Burgess, E.W., & Cottrell, L.S. (1939). *Predicting success and failure in marriage.* New York: Prentice-Hall.

Cleek, M.G., & Pearson, T.A. (1991). Demographic subgroup contributions to divorce cause constellations. *Journal of Divorce and Remarriage, 15*, 33–49.

Cowan, C.P., & Cowan, P.A. (1992). *When partners become parents: The big life change for couples.* New York: Basic.

Crohan, S.E., & Veroff, J. (1989). Dimensions of marital well-being among white and black newlyweds. *Journal of Marriage and the Family, 51,* 373–384.

Cuber, J.F., & Harroff, P.B. (1965). *The significant Americans.* New York: Appleton Century Crofts.

DeMaio, T.J. (1980). Refusals: Who, where and why? *Public Opinion Quarterly, 44,* 223–233.

Eysenck, H.J. (1975). Anxiety and the natural history of neuroses. In C.D. Spielberger & I.G. Sarason (Eds.), *Stress and Anxiety* (Vol. 1, pp. 51–94). New York: Wiley.

Fossett, M.A., & Kiecout, K.J. (1993). Mate availability and family structure among African-Americans in U.S. metropolitan areas. *Journal of Marriage and the Family, 55,* 288–302.

Goffman, E. (1959). *Presentation of self in everyday life.* Garden City, NY: Doubleday.

Goldenberg, I., & Goldenberg, H. (1980). *Family therapy: An overview.* Monterey, CA: Brooks/Cole Publishers.

Gottman, J.M. (1993). The roles of conflict engagement, escalation, and avoidance in marital interaction: A longitudinal view of five types of couples. *Journal of Consulting and Clinical Psychology, 61,* 6–15.

Gurin, G., Veroff, J., & Feld, S. (1960). *Americans view their mental health.* New York: Basic Books.

Hawkins, D.F. (1975). Estimation of non-response bias. *Sociological Methods, 3,* 462–485.

Henderson-King, D.H., & Veroff, J. (1994). Sexual satisfaction and marital well-being in the first years of marriage. *Journal of Social and Personal Relationships, 11,* 509–534.

Huston, T.L., McHale, S.M., & Crouter, A.L. (1985). When the honeymoon is over: Changes in the marriage relationship over the first year. In R. Gilmour, & S. Duck (Eds.), *The emerging science of personal relationships.* Hillsdale, NJ: Erlbaum.

Johnson, D.R., Amoloza, T.O., Booth, A. (1992). Stability and developmental change in marital quality: A three-wave panel analysis. *Journal of Marriage and the Family, 54,* 582–594.

Kanter, R.M. (1977). *Work and family in the United States: A critical review and agenda for research and policy.* New York: Russel-Sage Foundation.

Kelley, H.H. (1983). Love and commitment. In H.H. Kelley, E. Berscheid, A. Christensen, J.H. Harvey, T.L. Huston, E. McClintock, L.A. Peplau, & D. Peterson (Eds.), *Close relationships.* New York: W.H. Freeman & Company.

Kelley, H.H., Berscheid, E., Christensen, A., Harvey, J.H., Huston, T.L., McClintock, E., Peplau, L.A., & Peterson, D. (1983). *Close relationships.*

New York: W.H. Freeman & Company.

Kelly, E.L., & Conley, J.J. (1987). Personality and compatibility: A prospective analysis of marital stability and marital satisfaction. *Journal of Personality and Social Psychology*, *52*, 27–40.

Kochman, T. (1981). *Black and white styles in conflict*. Chicago: University of Chicago Press.

Kurdek, L.A. (1991). Predictors of increases in marital distress in newlywed couples: A 3-year prospective longitudinal study. *Developmental Psychology*, *27*, 627–636.

Kurdek, L.A. (1989). Relationship quality for newly married husbands and wives: Marital history, stepchildren, and individual-difference predictors. *Journal of Marriage and the Family*, *51*, 1053–1064.

Laing, R.D. (1971). *Self and others*. Harmondsworth, England: Penguin Books.

Levinger, G., & Breedlove, J. (1966). Interpersonal attraction and agreement. *Journal of Personality and Social Psychology*, *4*, 367–372.

MacDermid, S.M., Huston, T.L., & McHale, S.M. (1990). Changes in marriage associated with the transition to parenthood: Individual differences as a function of sex-role attitudes and changes in the division of labor. *Journal of Marriage and the Family*, *52*, 475–486.

Martin, T.C., & Bumpass, L.L. (1989). Recent trends in marital disruption. *Demography*, *26*, 37–51.

Massey, D.S., & Denton, N.A. (1993). *American apartheid: Segregation and the making of the underclass*. Cambridge, MA: Harvard University Press.

McClanahan, S., & Booth, K. (1989). Mother-only families: Problems, prospects, and politics. *Journal of Marriage and the Family*, *51*, 557–580.

McClelland, D.C., Davis, W.B., Kalin, R., & Wanner, E. (1972). *The drinking man: Alcohol and human motivation*. New York: Free Press.

McGoldrick, M. (1980). The joining of families through marriage. In E.A. Carter, & M. McGoldrick (Eds.), *The family life cycle* (pp. 93–120). New York: Gardner Press.

Murray, C. (1986). *Losing ground: American social policy*. New York: Basic Books.

Neckerman, K.M., & Kirschenman, J. (1991). Hiring strategies, racial bias, and inner city workers. *Social Problems*, *38*, 433–447.

Oggins, J., Veroff, J., & Leber, D. (1993). Perceptions of marital interaction among black and white newlyweds. *Journal of personality and social psychology*, *65*, 494–511.

Piotrkowski, C.S. (1978). *The work-family system*. New York: The Free Press.

Quinn, R.P., & Shepard, L.J. (1974). *The 1972–1973 Quality of Employment Survey: Demographic statistics with comparison data from the 1969–70 survey of working conditions*. Ann Arbor, MI: Survey Research Center, University of Michigan.

Raush, H., Barry, W., Hertel, R., & Swain, M.A. (1974). *Communication, conflict, and marriage.* San Francisco: Jossey-Bass

Rubin, L. (1976). *World of pain.* New York: Basic Books.

Ruvolo, A.P. (1990). *Interpersonal ideas and personal change in newlyweds: A Longitudinal analysis.* Unpublished doctoral dissertion, University of Michigan, Ann Arbor.

Sillars, A.L. (1985). Interpersonal perception in relationships. In W. Ickes (Ed.), *Compatible and incompatible relationships.* New York: Springer-Verlag.

Slater, P.E. (1963). On social regression. *American Sociological Review, 28,* 339–364.

Smith, C. (1992). *Motivation and personality: Handbook of thematic content analysis.* Cambridge: Cambridge University Press.

Taylor, R.J., & Chatters, L.M. (1991). Religious life. In J. Jackson (Ed.), *Life in black America.* Newbury Park, CA: Sage Publications

Tucker, M.B., & Mitchell-Kernan, C. (in press). Marital behavior and expectations: Attitudinal and structural correlates. In M.B. Tucker, & C. Mitchell-Kernan (Eds), *The decline of marriage among African-Americans: Causes, consequences, and policy implication.* New York: Russell-Sage.

Vannoy-Hiller, D., & Philliber, W.W. (1989). *Equal partners: Successful women in marriage.* Newbury Park, CA: Sage Publications.

Veroff, J., Chadiha, L., Leber, D., & Sutherland, L. (1993). Affects and interactions in newlyweds' narratives: Black and white couples compared. *Journal of Narrative and Life History, 3,* 361–390.

Veroff, J., Douvan, E., & Hatchett, S. (1993). Marital interaction and marital quality in the first year of marriage. In W. Jones, & D. Perlman (Eds.), *Advances in personal relationships* (Vol. 4, pp. 103–137). London: Jessica Kingsley Ltd.

Veroff, J., Douvan, E., & Kulka, R. (1981). *The inner American.* New York: Basic Books.

Veroff, J., Hatchett, S., & Douvan, E. (1992). Consequences of participating in a longitudinal study of marriage. *Public Opinion Quarterly, 56,* 315–327.

Veroff, J., Kulka, R.A., & Douvan, E. (1981). *Mental health in America.* New York: Basic Books.

Veroff, J., Sutherland, L., Chadiha, L., & Ortega, R.M. (1993). Newlyweds tell their stories: A narrative method for assessing marital experiences. *Journal of Social and Personal Relationships, 10,* 437–457.

Voydanoff, P. (1987). *Work and family life.* Newbury Park, CA: Sage Publications.

Voydanoff, P., & Majka, L.C. (1990). *Families and economic distress: Coping strategies and social policy.* Beverly Hills, CA: Sage Publications.

Washington, J.R. (1970). *Marriage in black and white*. Boston: Beacon Press.

White, L.K. (1990). Determinants of divorce: A review of research in the eighties. *Journal of Marriage and the Family, 52*, 904–912.

Wilson, W.J. (1987). *The truly disadvantaged: The inner city, the underclass, and public policy*. Chicago: The University of Chicago Press.

Zung, W.W.K. (1965). A self-rating depression scale. *Archives of General Psychiatry, 12*, 63–70.

Appendices

Alphabetical Listing of Measures Used as Predictors of Marital Instability

Measure	Question(s) Used
Affective Affirmation	"Now let's talk about the special pleasures and good feelings that come from being married. For each one of the feelings on this list, mark an "x" in the box telling how often during the past month or so you have had such feelings—often, sometimes, rarely, or never. During the past month, how often did you: Feel that your (wife/husband) felt especially caring toward you? Feel that your (wife/husband) made your life especially interesting and exciting? Feel that your (wife/husband) made you feel good about having your own ideas and ways of doing things? Feel your (wife/husband) made you feel good about the kind of person you are?" (Index=sum of above items)
Age	"Now we'd like to ask some questions about your background. First, what is the month, day and year of your birth?"
Age Discrepancy	(Differences between wife's age and husband's age)
Alcohol Problems	"In the past month or so: How often has your drinking alcohol or getting high caused problems for family and friends? How often has your (wife's/husband's) drinking alcohol or getting high caused problems for family or friends? (alternatives = all the time, many times, sometimes, hardly ever, or never; index was the product of the husband's perception and the wife's perception)
Ambitiousness	"Here is a list of words that people use to describe themselves. Please use them to describe yourself—the way you really are, not the way you want to be. For each word, circle a number on the scale from one to ten which describes how much you are like that. One means that you are not at all like that; ten means that you are a lot like that. Or, circle any number in between. (1 = not at all; 10 = a lot) Ambitious Next, with the same list, please describe your (wife/husband)—the way (she/he) really is, not the way you want (her/him) to be. Circle the number that shows how much (she/he) is like these words right now. Ambitious" (Index=sum of both own perception and (spouse's) in year 1)

Measure	Question(s) Used
Anxiety	"Here is a list of different troubles and complaints people might have. After each one, please put an "X" in the box indicating the answer which tells how often you have had this trouble or complaint. *all the time/many times/sometimes/hardly ever/never* a. How often have you been bothered by nervousness, feeling fidgety and tense? b. How often have you been troubled by headaches or pains in the head? c. Have you ever felt that you were going to have a nervous breakdown? (Index=sum of 3 items for both year 1 and year 3; all the time = 5; never = 1)
Attractiveness	(Instructions to interviewer: Rate respondent's appearance/attractiveness 1. Very attractive or beautiful 2. Attractive (Above average for age and sex) 3. Average attractiveness for age and sex 4. Unattractive (below average for age and sex) 5. Very unattractive (Index=sum across two independent interviewers)
Attractiveness Discrepancy	(Differences between wife's attractiveness and husband's)
Avoidant Conflict Style	(After discussing last disagreement, sum of own response "I suddenly became quiet and pulled away"; "I went away for awhile to calm down before we talked it out")
Being Catholic	"Is your religious preference: Protestant, Roman Catholic, Jewish, or something else?"

Measure	Question(s) Used
Bossiness	"Here is a list of words that people use to describe themselves. Please use them to describe yourself—the way you really are, not the way you want to be. For each word, circle a number on the scale from one to ten which describes how much you are like that. One means that you are not at all like that; ten means that you are a lot like that. Or, circle any number in between. (1 = not at all; 10 = a lot) Bossy Next, with the same list, please describe your (wife/husband)—the way (she/he) really is, not the way you want (her/him) to be. Circle the number that shows how much (she/he) is like these words right now. Bossy" (Index=sum of both own perception and (spouse's) in year 1)
Broken Home Background	"Did you always live with both of your natural parents up to the time when you were 16 years old? (If no) What happened? (coded for divorce/separation)"
Church Attendance	"Would you say you attend religious services *every week, almost every week, once or twice a month, a few times a year, never?*"
Closeness With Family	"How close do you feel to your family?" very close/fairly close/not too close/not at all close (Index=product of husband's responses and wife's responses)
Cohabitation	"Some couples live together before they get married; others do not. Did the two of you live together for any length of time before you got married? About how long did you live together?"

Measure	Question(s) Used
Collaboration	"Today I'm going to ask you to tell the story of your relationship from the beginning up to now and into the future. We are interested in how married couples' views of their life together either change over time or remain pretty steady. There's no right or wrong way to tell the story. You don't have to remember what you said last time. Just tell it as it naturally comes to both of you right now. So I'll repeat the kind of instruction you were given last time.

I'm talking to both of you together and want the two of you to tell me in your own words the story of your relationship.

I have no set questions to ask you.

I just want you to tell me about your lives together as if it were a story with a beginning, a middle, and how things will look in the future.

There is no right or wrong way to tell your story. Just tell me in any way that is most comfortable.

It's something that couples really enjoy doing.

Each of you can talk, and I hope to hear from both of you. You can agree about the story; you can disagree. Any way that seems comfortable for you.

To help you think of your story, we'll use this guide which describes most people's storyline. You see that a storyline for a marriage usually includes each of these parts:
  How you met
  How you got interested in one another
  Becoming a couple
  Planning to get married
  The wedding itself
  What life was like after the wedding
  Your first couple years of marriage
  What married life is like now
  And what you think married life will be like in the future

As you see, this is a very different way of getting a picture of marriage. Since I did not hear what you said two years ago or in your future this year, you will naturally repeat some of what you said before. That's fine. To tell a complete story you would have to mention many of the matters discussed in the individual interview. |

172

Measure	Question(s) Used
Collaboration/Conflicting	(same narrative instructions under collaboration; Index= Percentage of all changes in speaker from wife to husband and husband to wife coded for whether the person is both collaborating and confirming the person's preceding statement.)
Competence	"Now let's turn to a different subject. In general, how good a (wife/husband) do you think you are—*extremely good, very good, pretty good, or not so good?* When you think about what each of you puts in and gets out of your marriage, how guilty do you feel? Would you say *very guilty, fairly guilty, not too guilty, or not at all guilty?*" (Index=sum of 2-scores of each of the above items.)
Confirming	(same narrative instructions under collaboration; Index=Percentage of all changes in speaker from wife to husband and husband to wife coded for whether the person is confirming the speaker's immediately preceding statement.)
Conflicting	(same narrative instructions under collaboration; Index=Percentage of all changes in speaker from wife to husband and husband to wife coded for whether the person is conflicting with the person's immediately preceding statements.)
Constructive Conflict Style	(After last disagreement, sum of own responses to: "I tried to say nice things"; "I tried hard to find out what my spouse was feeling"; "I listened to my spouse's point of view"; "I tried to make my spouse laugh")
Contact With Family	"These next questions are about your contact with your family and your in-laws. During the past year... a. How often did the two of you together see or have contact with your own family—several times a week, once a week, 2 or 3 times a month, about once a month, a few times a year, or never? b. How often did the two of you together see or have contact with your (wife's/husband's) family?" (Index=product of the sum of husband's responses to the two items and the wife's responses to the two item.)

Measure	Question(s) Used
Control	"Every (wife/husband) experiences times when things between (herself/himself) and (her husband/his wife) are not going as well as (she/he) would like. When such times come up for you, how often do you feel that you can do or say something to make things better—*most of the time, sometimes, or hardly ever?*
	How about when there are no problems? How often do you feel you can do or say something to make things especially pleasant between you and your (wife/husband)—*most of the time, sometimes, or hardly ever?*
	(Index=sum of z-scores of each of the above items.)
Cooperativeness	"Here is a list of words that people use to describe themselves. Please use them to describe yourself—the way you really are, not the way you want to be. For each word, circle a number on the scale from one to ten which describes how much you are like that. One means that you are not at all like that; ten means that you are a lot like that. Or, circle any number in between. (1 = not at all; 10 = a lot)
	Cooperative
	Next, with the same list, please describe your (wife/husband)—the way (she/he) really is, not the way you want (her/him) to be. Circle the number that shows how much (she/he) is like these words right now.
	Cooperative"
	(Index=sum of both own perception and (spouse's) in year 1)
Destructive Conflict Style	(After discussing last disagreement, sum of own responses to: "I yelled and shouted at my spouse"; "I insulted my spouse and called him/her names"; "I had to have the last word"; "I brought up old things")

Measure	Question(s) Used
Difference in Attitude:	
Conflict	"Next, I am going to read you some statements. After each one please tell me if you *strongly agree, somewhat agree, somewhat disagree, or strongly disagree* with that statement.
	a. Disagreements can always be settled if you just talk about them.
	b. Couples should try to avoid disagreements.
	c. Couples should control themselves first before trying to solve a disagreement.
	d. Disagreements in a marriage are healthy.
	e. Disagreements, if not settled, will usually destroy a marriage."
	(Index=sum of Wife's response to each statement—Husband's response to each statement)
Education	(Own Education For Husband—Own Education For Wife)
Importance of Religion	"How important is religion to you personally? Would you say that it is *very important, somewhat important, or not at all important?*"
	(Wife's response to importance—Husband's response)
Openness to Experiences	"Some people are eager to try something new all the time—meet new people, see new places. Others are more interested in doing what they are used to and comfortable with. How about you? Would you say you are *eager to try new things*, or more interested in doing *what you are used to?*"
	(Wife's response—Husband's response)
Preferred Pace of Life	"Some people want life to go more slowly than it is going for them. Others want life to go faster. Generally speaking, would you say that you want life to go *slower*, go *faster*, or is it going *just about right?*"
	(Wife's response—Husband's response)

175

Measure	Question(s) Used
Difference in Attitude: (Continued)	
Rules for Marriage	"Before you begin, I'm going to go over this list of rules with you. 1) If you're fighting, cool off before you say too much. 2) Leisure time should be enjoyed together. 3) Control the way that you show you are angry with each other. 4) Each should have an equal say about all important matters. 5) You have to feel that your partner would never hurt or deceive you. 6) Be ready and willing to compromise when you disagree. 7) Be sure to have some private time away from each other. 8) Marriage partners should keep some of their money separate. 9) Always say what is on your mind, even when you are angry at your spouse. 10) Always settle a fight quickly. 11) Try not to be critical of your spouse. 12) Share equally in household chores. 13) Know the people your spouse spends leisure time with. 14) Listen carefully to one another's point of view. 15) Take time for your own individual friends. 16) Take the time to understand each other's sexual needs." (Index=number of disagreements on whether the rule was "very important".)
Sex Role Attitudes	"Now, I'd like to know whether you strongly agree, somewhat agree, somewhat disagree, or strongly disagree with the following: a. Both men and women should share equally in childcare and housework. b. Both men and women should have jobs to support the family. c. Having a job takes away from a women's relationship with her husband and children. d. The most fulfilling experience a woman can have is becoming a mother and raising a family. e. Having a job takes away from a man's relationship with his wife and children. f. The most fulfilling experience a man can have is becoming a father and raising a family." (Index=sum of Wife's response to each statement—Husband's response)

176

Measure	Question(s) Used
Disclosing Style	"Couples differ in what they talk about with each other. For each subject I read, please tell me how often during the past month you and your (wife/husband) talked about these things—often, sometimes, rarely, or never. During the past month, how often did you: a. Reveal very intimate things about yourself or your personal feelings? c. Talk about the quality of your relationship; for example, how good it is, how satisfying it is, or how to improve it? d. Tell your (wife/husband) what you want or need from the relationship?" (Index=sum of above items)
Easier to Talk to Other	"It is easier to discuss problems with somebody other than my (wife/husband)." *very true, somewhat true, not true at all*
Equity	"All in all, considering how much each of you puts into your marriage, who would you say gets more out of being married—you, your (wife/husband) or both about equal? How do you think your (wife/husband) would answer that? Considering how much each of you puts into your marriage, who would (she/he) say gets more out of being married—you, (her/him) or both of you about equal?" (Index=number of the items where "both about equal" was selected)
Family Density	"Think about the feelings your families might have about each other, now. How close would you say your family feels to your (wife's/husband's) family? Would you say <u>very close, fairly close, not too close</u> or not at all close? How close would you say your (wife's/husband's) family feels to your family? Would you say <u>very close</u>, fairly close, not too close, or not at all close?" (Index=product of the sum of Husband's response and the Wife's response to the above two items)
Family Size Discrepancy	(Number of Husband's siblings—number of Wife's siblings)
Family Support	"As a couple, how many family members and relatives could you call on for advice or help if you needed it? Would you say *many, some, one or two, or none?*" (Index=product of Husband's responses and Wife's responses)

177

Measure	Question(s) Used
Family Interference	"How often did your (wife's/husband's) family or how either of you felt about them interfere —*often, sometimes, or never?* How often did your own family or how either of you felt about them interfere—*often, sometimes, or never?*" (Index=sum of two items)
Father's Education	"What is the highest grade of school or year of college that your father completed?"
Feeling Spouse Doesn't Understand	"Feel your (wife/husband) didn't understand you?" (alternative=often, sometimes, rarely, never)
Feeling Spouse Not Critical	"Now, we would like you to think about what you really do in your marriage. I will read some statements that are similar to the rules you just heard. This time, please indicate how often you actually follow each rule. I will read each statement, and for each one please put an "x" on the box that tells how often you actually follow that rule. The answer choices are: all of the time, most of the time, some of the time, rarely, or never. My spouse tries not to be critical of me."
Feeling Spouse Not Deceive	(Same introduction as Feeling Spouse Not Critical) "I feel sure my spouse would never hurt or deceive me."
Feeling Spouse Understand Sex Needs	(Same introduction as Feeling Spouse Not Critical) "My spouse takes time to understand my sexual needs."
Frequency of Conflicts	"In the past month, about how often have you and your (wife/husband) had a disagreement that upset one or both of you—*almost every day, a few times a week, about once a week, once or twice during the month, or not at all?*"
Friend Density	"Think of all the friends the two of you have, either separately or as a couple. Do most of these people know each other or do most of them not know each other?" (Index=product of husband's and wife's answer)

178

Measure	Question(s) Used
Friend Interference	"How often did things your (wife/husband) did with or for (his/her) friends interfer—*often, sometimes, or never*? How often did things you did with or for your friends interfere—*often, sometimes, or never*?" (Index=sum of two items)
Friend Support	"About how many good friends could you, as a couple, call on for advice or help if you ever needed it? Would you say *many, some, one or two, or none*?" (Index=product of husband's responses and wife's responses)
Had Affair	"Did your wife/husband have an affair?" (Yes/No) Did you have an affair?" (Yes/No) (product of husband's and wife's version of wife affair and husband affair)
Happiness	Items Used to Measure Marital Happiness "1. Taking things altogether, how would you describe your marriage? Would you say your marriage is very happy, a little happier than average, just about average or not too happy? 2. When you think about your marriage—what each of you puts into it, and gets out of it—how happy do you feel? Would you say very happy, fairly happy, or not too happy? 3. All in all, how satisfied are you with your marriage? Would you say you are very satisfied, somewhat satisfied, or not very satisfied? 4. How certain would you say you are that the two of you will be married five years from now? Would you say very certain, fairly certain, not too certain, or not at all certain/ 5. How stable do you feel your marriage is? Would you say very stable, fairly stable, not too stable or not at all stable?" (Index=sum of Z-scores of each of the above items)
Has Older Sibling	"(If one brother)Was he older than you? (If more than one) How many of your brothers were older than you? (If one sister) Was she older than you? (If more than one) How many of you sisters were older than you?"
How Close Family Lives	' How far from you do most of the important members of your own family live? Do they live more than 500 miles away, less than 500 but more than 100 miles, less than 100 miles but not really close by, or close by?" (Index=product of husband's and wife's response to the item)
Husband's Power	"In general, who has more say in your marriage—your (wife/husband) or you?" (coded: 1=Wife; 2=Equal; 3= Husband)

179

Measure	Question(s) Used
Income Adequacy	Ratio of household income to the total needs standard derived from 1) an estimate of the annual food costs determined for each household member from the "economy food plan" used by the Panel Study of Income Dynamics, adjusted for small or large families; 2) adjustments for other needs (transportation, medical care, clothing, housing); 3) an adjustment for inflation.
Jealousy	"Feel worried because of your (wife's/husband's) relationship or attraction to other (men/women) or because of their attraction to (her/him)?" (alternative=often, sometimes, rarely, never)
Job Satisfaction	"In general, how satisfied are you with your job? Would you say you are *very satisfied, somewhat satisfied, somewhat dissatisfied, or very dissatisfied?*"
Length of Time as a Couple	"In what year did you and your spouse really start being involved with each other, that is seeing each other a lot, or just considering yourselves as a couple?"
Marital Tension	"During the past month, how often did you... a. Feel irritated or resentful about things your (wife/husband) did or didn't do—*often, sometimes, rarely, or never?* d. Feel tense from fighting, arguing or disagreeing with your (wife/husband)?" (Index=sum of 2-scores of each item)
Mother's Education	"What is the highest grade of school or year of college that your mother completed?"
Negative Sexual Interaction	"During the past month, how often did you: Feel upset about how you and your (wife/husband) were getting along in the sexual part of your relationship? Feel that your (wife/husband) was upset about how the two of you were getting along in the sexual part of your relationship?" (often, sometimes, rarely, never; sum of two items)
No Privacy	"Feel as if you did not have enough privacy for yourself?" (often, sometimes, rarely, never)

Measure	Question(s) Used
Number of Siblings	"How many brothers did you have when you were growing up? How many sisters did you have when you were growing up?"
Own Education	"What is the highest grade of school or year of college you have completed?"
Parental Status	"How many children have you given birth to/fathered?"
Perceived Similarity in Positive Sexual Interaction	"Now let's talk about the special pleasures and good feelings that come from being married. For each one of the feelings on this list, mark an "x" in the box telling how often during the past month or so you have had such feelings—*often, sometimes, rarely, or never*. During the past month, how often did you: Feel that your sexual life together was joyful and exciting? Feel that your (wife/husband) felt your sexual life together was joyful and exciting?" (Index=amount of agreement between one's own response and perception of spouse's response)
Perceived Similarity in Negative Sexual Interaction	"Now please look at the list on the next page which tells about troubles and complaints some married people have. For each one that I read, mark and "x" indicating how often during the past month you have had this trouble or these complaints—*often, sometimes, rarely, or never*. During the past month, how often did you: b. Feel upset about how you and your (wife/husband) were getting along in the sexual part of your relationship? c. Feel that your (wife/husband) was upset about how the two of you were getting along in the sexual part of your relationship?" (Index=amount of agreement between one's own response and perception of spouse's response)
Perceived Similarity of Positive Conflict Behavior	(Regarding last disagreement number of agreements between husband's and wife's own reactions compared to his/her perceptions of spouse reason with respect to: "Tried to say nice things"; "listened to (other's) point of view"; "tried to find out (other's) feelings"; "tried to make my spouse laugh";)
Perceived Similarity of Negative Conflict Behavior	(Regarding last disagreement number of agreements between husband's and wife's own reactions compared to his/her perceptions of spouse reason with respect to: "yelled or shouted"; "insulted or called names"; "had to have last word")

Measure	Question(s) Used
Personal Income	"Now we are interested in the income that you yourself will receive in 1986, not including any of the income that will be received by your (wife/husband) (and the rest of the family living here). Please look at this page and tell me the letter of the income group that includes the income you yourself will have in 1986 before taxes."
	A. None or Less Than $2,999
	B. $3,000–$4,999
	C. $5,000–$6,999
	D. $7,000–$8,999
	E. $9,000–$9,999
	F. $10,000–$10,999
	G. $11,000–$11,999
	H. $12,000–$12,999
	J. $13,000–$13,999
	K. $14,000–$14,999
	M. $15,000–$16,999
	N. $17,000–$19,999
	P. $20,000–$21,999
	Q. $22,000–$24,999
	R. $25,000–$29,999
	S. $30,000–$34,999
	T. $35,000–$39,999
	U. $40,000–$44,999
	V. $45,000–$49,999
	W. $50,000–$59,999
	X. $60,000–$74,999
	Z. $75,000 And Over
Positive Orientation to Marriage	"Think about a (SAME SEX AS R: woman's/man's) life and how it's changed by being married. For each, tell me whether you strongly agree, somewhat agree, somewhat disagree, or strongly disagree.
	a. (She/He) has many more responsibilities.
	b. (She/He) leads a fuller life."
	(Index=sum of two items)

182

Measure	Question(s) Used
Positive View of Divorce	"Next, I am going to read you some statements about divorce. After each one, please tell me how strongly you agree or disagree with the statement. a. When couples are having marital troubles, divorce may be an acceptable solution to their troubles. b. When a husband and wife divorce, it reflects badly on them as people." (sum of two items in the agreement direction)
Positive Sexual Interaction	"During the past month, how often did you: Feel that your sexual life together was joyful and exciting? Feel that your (wife/husband) felt your sexual life together was joyful and exciting?" (alternatives=often, sometimes, rarely, or never; index=sum of two items)
Race	(By response to voluntary screening questionnaire or by observation at marriage license bureau)
Range of Grounds for Divorce	"Here is a list of reasons people sometimes give for divorcing. For each one that I read, please indicate how good a reason for divorce you think it is. Is it always a good reason, sometimes a good reason, or never a good reason? a. Financial problems b. Lack of Communication c. Religious or value differences d. Conflicts about children e. Not loving each other any more f. Physical abuse of spouse or children g. alcohol or drug problems h. Fighting and arguing j. Extramarital affairs k. Sexual problems l. Mental illness" (for each above 1= never a good reason, 2= sometimes a good reason, 3= always a good reason; score=sum across items)

183

Measure	Question(s) Used
Range of Disagreements	Sum of "yeses" to:
	"Have you and your (wife/husband) ever had any tension or differences about money—that is, how much
	you have, how you spend it, or how much you save?"
	"Have you and your (wife/husband) ever had any tension or differences about whether to have children, when to have them or how many to have?"
	"Have you and your (wife/husband) ever had any tension or differences about relationships with your (wife's/husband's) family?"
	"Have you and your (wife/husband) ever had any tension or differences about relationships with your family?"
	"Have you and your (wife/husband) ever had any tension or differences about how to spend leisure time?"
	"Have you and your (wife/husband) ever had any tension or differences about religious beliefs?"
Relational Affects	[See item for collaboration]
	"Narrative codes for number of affects mentioned by couple in where the couple as unit is both the source and object of the affect; e.g., 'We were in love.'"
Relaxed Time	"During the past month, how often did you enjoy relaxed times just being with each other?"
	(alternatives=often, sometimes, rarely, or never)

184

Measure	Question(s) Used
Rolesharing	"Now let's talk about how you manage household responsibilities. For each of the following tasks or responsibilities, tell me who does it most of the time—is it *you, your (wife/husband), both of you about equally, someone else, or no one at all?* a. Prepare meals b. Does dishes or puts items in dishwasher c. Does food shopping d. Does laundry e. Handles car repairs f. Does yard work g. Does housecleaning h. Writes letters to families i. Pays bills j. (If couple has children) Takes care of children" "Now, I'd like to know whether you *strongly agree, somewhat agree, somewhat disagree, or strongly disagree* with the following: l. Both men and women should share equally in childcare and housework. m. The most fulfilling experience a woman can have is becoming a mother and raising a family." (Index=number both equally in response to: a–j plus degree of disagreement expressed for l and m)
Satisfied with leisure	"In general, how satisfied are you with the amount of time you personally have for leisure? Are you <u>very satisfied, somewhat satisfied, somewhat dissatisfied, or very dissatisfied?</u>"
Satisfied with home	"All in all, how satisfied are you with your home? Would you say you are <u>very satisfied, somewhat satisfied, or very dissatisfied?</u>"
Shared Time	"During the past month, how often was this true: We share interests and hobbies with each other." (alternatives: often, sometimes, rarely, never)
Sibling Older Discrepancy	(Discrepancy of whether husband or wife has older sibling)
Stresses: Had Baby	"Since we last talked a year ago, have you and your (wife/husband) had a baby?"

Measure	Question(s) Used
Stresses (Continued):	
Moved	"Have you moved or changed living arrangements?" (stress coded if either husband or wife said yes)
Someone Died	"Has someone close to either of you died?" (stress coded if either husband or wife said yes)
Someone Seriously Ill	"Did you have a <u>serious</u> illness or health problem?" (stress coded if either husband or wife said yes)"
Someone Unemployed	"Have you been laid off from work or unable to find work for a month or so?" (stress coded if either husband or wife said yes)"
Understanding Negative Conflict Behavior	(Regarding last disagreement, number of agreements between husband's and wife's view of whether the husband (and wife):"yelled or shouted", "insulted or called names", "had to have the last word")
Understanding Negative Sexual Interaction	"Now please look at the list on the next page which tells about troubles and complaints some married people have. For each one that I read, mark and "x" indicating how often during the past month you have had this trouble or these complaints—*often, sometimes, rarely, or never*. During the past month, how often did you: Feel upset about how you and your (wife/husband) were getting along in the sexual part of your relationship? Feel that your (wife/husband) was upset about how the two of you were getting along in the sexual part of your relationship?" (Index=amount of agreement between perception of spouse and spouse's own reactions)
Understanding Positive Conflict Behavior	(Regarding last disagreement number of agreements between husband's and wife's view of whether the husband (and wife's): "tried to say nice things", "listened to (other's) point of view", "tried hard to find out (other's) feelings", "tried to make my spouse laugh")

Measure	Question(s) Used
Understanding Positive Sexual Interaction	"Now let's talk about the special pleasures and good feelings that come from being married. For each one of the feelings on this list, mark an "x" in the box telling how often during the past month or so you have had such feelings—*often, sometimes, rarely, or never.* During the past month, how often did you: Feel that your sexual life together was joyful and exciting? Feel that your (wife/husband) felt your sexual life together was joyful and exciting?" (Index=amount of agreement between perception of spouse and (spouse's own reaction))
Work Interference	"How often do you feel that the demands of your work interfere with your married life? Would you say *often, sometimes, or never?*"
Worry About Money	"Now, we'd like to ask you some questions about your family's financial situation. First, do you ever worry that your total family income will not be enough to meet your family's expenses and bills? a. Would you say you worry *a great deal, a lot, or a little?*"
Zest	"Here are a few statements that people sometimes use to describe themselves. For each one, please tell me how often you feel that way about yourself? a. I feel that I am useful and needed. Would you say you feel this way *always, most of the time, some of the time, or never?* b. What about ... my life is pretty full? c. I feel hopeful about the future? d. My life is interesting?" (Index=sum of 4 items for both year 1 and year 3; always = 4; never = 1)

Respondent Letter from the Survey Research Center

Fall 1986

SURVEY
RESEARCH
CENTER

Dear Respondent:

The University of Michigan's Survey Research Center is conducting an important new study of recently married couples. We are exploring several trends in American marriages and families by learning more about how men and women adapt to their marriages.

Your name was selected from a list of couples who filed for marriage licenses in Wayne County this year. We are interested in talking with both of you about your experiences as a couple. All information you give us will be kept in complete confidence. In appreciation for couples taking time to share their experiences with us, we will be sending each couple a check for $25.

Enclosed is a brochure that will tell you more about surveys and about our study in particular. An interviewer from the Survey Research Center will be contacting you soon to answer any questions you may have and to arrange a convenient time to interview you.

We think you will find the interview interesting and worthwhile. Couples who have already participated tell us they enjoyed the experience. We look forward to your participation in this important study of marriage in these changing times. If you have any questions or want to verify our interviewer's employment with us, please feel free to call us collect at 0-764-8356.

Sincerely yours,

Joseph Veroff, Ph.D.
Project Director
Survey Research Center

INSTITUTE FOR
SOCIAL RESEARCH

THE UNIVERSITY
OF MICHIGAN

ANN ARBOR,
MICHIGAN 48106

P. 462478

INDEX

About the Authors

JOSEPH VEROFF is a Professor of Psychology and research scientist at the Survey Research Center at the University of Michigan.

ELIZABETH DOUVAN is the Catherine Kellogg Professor of Psychology and Women's Studies and a Research Scientist at the Survey Research Center.

Together they have written *The Inner American, Mental Health in America* and other books.

SHIRLEY J. HATCHETT is an Associate Professor of Sociology at the University of Illinois at Urbana-Champaign.

ISBN 0-275-95031-X

90000>

EAN

9 780275 950316

HARDCOVER BAR CODE